Mastering Negotiation

Mastering Negotiation

Michael Ross Fowler

CAROLINA ACADEMIC PRESS
Durham, North Carolina

Library of Congress Cataloging in Publication Data
Names: Fowler, Michael Ross, author.
Title: Mastering negotiation / Michael R. Fowler.
Description: Durham, North Carolina : Carolina Academic Press, 2016. |
    Series: Carolina Academic Press Mastering Series | Includes
    bibliographical references and index.
Identifiers: LCCN 2016036252 | ISBN 9781611630480 (alk. paper)
Subjects: LCSH: Dispute resolution (Law) | Negotiation. | Mediation.
Classification: LCC K2390 .F69 2016 | DDC 347/.09--dc23
LC record available at https://lccn.loc.gov/2016036252

Carolina Academic Press, LLC
700 Kent Street
Durham, NC 27701
Telephone (919) 489-7486
Fax (919) 493-5668
www.cap-press.com

Printed in the United States of America

Dedicated to the Memory of Roger Fisher (1922–2012),
Samuel Williston Professor of Law Emeritus, Harvard Law School
Director, Harvard Negotiation Project

Contents

Series Editor's Foreword

The Carolina Academic Press Mastering Series is designed to provide you with a tool that will enable you to easily and efficiently "master" the substance and content of law school courses. Throughout the series, the focus is on quality writing that makes legal concepts understandable. As a result, the series is designed to be easy to read and is not unduly cluttered with footnotes or cites to secondary sources.

In order to facilitate student mastery of topics, the Mastering Series includes a number of pedagogical features designed to improve learning and retention. At the beginning of each chapter, you will find a "Roadmap" that tells you about the chapter and provides you with a sense of the material that you will cover. A "Checkpoint" at the end of each chapter encourages you to stop and review the key concepts, reiterating what you have learned. Throughout the book, key terms are explained and emphasized. Finally, a "Master Checklist" at the end of each book reinforces what you have learned and helps you identify any areas that need review or further study.

We hope that you will enjoy studying with, and learning from, the Mastering Series.

Russell L. Weaver
Professor of Law & Distinguished University Scholar
University of Louisville, Louis D. Brandeis School of Law

Preface

Mastering Negotiation addresses those who are being taught or already know something about the subject of negotiation, whether through course work, via the counsel of professors or mentors, or through past personal or professional negotiation experiences. It aims to provide these negotiators with keener analysis, better organized approaches, additional insights and ideas, and more sophisticated strategies.

The book looks to synthesize the best current thinking about how to negotiate adeptly. It particularly aims to bring together the most useful ideas advanced by the array of scholars whose writing in one way or another has built on the foundational work, *Getting to Yes*. *Mastering Negotiation* aims to accomplish this in a practical approach that provides the reader with a toolbox of effective concepts — some basic, others intermediate, and still others quite advanced.

In trying to go beyond cataloguing bits and pieces of advice and setting out useful principles, *Mastering Negotiation* proceeds through phases of a typical set of talks from pre-negotiation to the closing of a deal. Thinking about negotiation via stages is a useful organizing concept, but its limitations should also be noted. Communication in an advanced negotiation is often free-flowing. The beginning of one phase and the end of another may not be clear-cut. The sequence of the stages may well be shuffled, and negotiators will sometimes double-back or jump ahead or even skip over something.

Mastering Negotiation also provides counsel on how to overcome various difficulties that commonly arise in negotiation. Particular chapters explore how best to overcome impasses, interpersonal problems, and ethical issues. The book features a chapter on cross-cultural complications and opportunities that speaks to some of the important needs of legal and other professionals operating abroad. Chapter by chapter, *Mastering Negotiation* is designed to help negotiators to plan a strategy that will provide the best chance for them to reach a positive resolution.

"Ours is an age of negotiation," it has been said, with rules, roles, and relations constantly being talked over and talked out.[1] In recent decades individuals, groups, and organizations have shifted the way that they make many decisions. Rather than a society characterized by hierarchy and top-down orders flowing from an authority to subordinates, decision-making in business, politics, and personal life has tended to become more horizontal, a development that has brought negotiation skills to the forefront of many careers.[2]

People in all walks of life negotiate constantly, though often without carefully analyzing just what they are doing. A relative few think critically about how exactly to negotiate effectively. And, while lawyers, executives, diplomats, and various other professionals spend much time negotiating, the negotiation skill set differs in important regards from that of the other daily activities of a litigator, business manager, or foreign policymaker.

Furthermore, while negotiation is regularly done by virtually everyone, it is not easily done, particularly in the advanced negotiations that are our special focus. French statesman François de Callières declared that negotiation "demands all the penetration, all the dexterity, all the suppleness which a man can well possess. It requires widespread understanding and knowledge, and above all a correct and piercing discernment."[3] The chapters that follow aim to help the reader along toward mastering the elements of highly effective negotiation.

Notes

1. I. William Zartman, *Introduction*, in THE 50% SOLUTION 2 (I. William Zartman ed., 1976).

2. William Ury, *An Interview with Roger Fisher and William Ury*, 18 ACAD. OF MGMT. EXEC. 104.

3. FRANÇOIS DE CALLIÈRES, ON THE MANNER OF NEGOTIATING WITH PRINCES, trans. A.F. Whyte 9 (1919).

About the Author

A graduate of Harvard Law School, the University of Virginia, and Dartmouth College and a former practicing attorney at Mintz, Levin, Cohn, Ferris, Glovsky, and Popeo, P.C., in Boston, Michael Fowler is now Professor of Political Science at the University of Louisville. Twice a Fulbright Scholar to Japan and twice a visiting professor for Semester at Sea, Professor Fowler was the founding director of University of Louisville's Muhammad Ali Institute for Peace and Justice and has been awarded the University's Exemplary Multicultural Teaching Award and its Distinguished International Service Award.

A negotiation consultant for clients in the public and private sectors, Michael Fowler has conducted negotiation training courses, seminars, or workshops for lawyers, diplomats, professors, military officers, business executives, and human resources professionals as well as for high school, undergraduate, and graduate students. He has lectured in Argentina, Australia, China, Costa Rica, Ecuador, Italy, Japan, Laos, Mexico, Northern Ireland, Panama, Venezuela, and Vietnam. Among the groups he has worked with are the Louisville Human Relations Commission, the National Forum for Black Public Administrators, and the Guatemalan Electoral Office, as well as the Diplomatic Academy of Vietnam and the Institute of Foreign Affairs in Laos, the training wings of those countries' ministries of foreign affairs.

With *Mastering Negotiation*, Professor Fowler has published seven books as well as articles in such scholarly journals as the *Harvard Negotiation Law Review*, the *Ohio State Journal on Dispute Resolution*, and *Review of International Studies*. Fowler's written work has been assigned in courses at various universities, including Stanford, Columbia, and the Fletcher School of Law and Diplomacy at Tufts.

Michael Fowler's best known works are *Bribes, Bullets, and Intimidation: Drug Trafficking and the Law in Central America* (Pennsylvania State University Press, 2012), *Law, Power, and the Sovereign State: The Evolution and Application of the Concept of Sovereignty* (Penn State Press, 1995), both co-authored with Julie M. Bunck, *Envisioning Reform: Enhancing UN Accountability in the 21st*

Century (United Nations University Press, 2009), co-edited with former U.N. Assistant Secretary-General Sumihiro Kuyama, *With Justice For All?: The Nature of the American Legal System* (Prentice Hall, 1998), and *Thinking About Human Rights: Contending Approaches to Human Rights in U.S. Foreign Policy* (University Press of America, 1987).

William Walker of the University of Toronto termed *Bribes, Bullets, and Intimidation* "an exceptional study," and Peter Andreas of Brown University predicted that it "will instantly become the reference book for understanding the role of Central America in the international drug trade and the profound impact of the trade on the region's countries." Richard Falk of Princeton called *Law, Power, and the Sovereign State* an "invaluable study of sovereignty [that] explores anew one of the most enduring ideas in political theory and illuminates with lucidity the changing nature of the sovereign state." Nobel Peace Prize Laureate Martti Ahtisaari termed *Envisioning Reform* a "timely and valuable contribution" toward the objective of providing "much more serious attention ... [to] global governance wherein the organizations in the UN system are to play a pivotal role." Historian William Manchester of Wesleyan University wrote of *Thinking About Human Rights* that Michael Fowler "provides us with the first lucid, comprehensive analysis of the varied approaches to human rights and achieves the highest goal of a profound writer: he makes us make up our own minds." Kenneth W. Thompson of the University of Virginia observed of this work: "[O]ne of the nation's emerging intellectual leaders... provides a full and illuminating account of recent American thought on human rights and a penetrating analysis of the major issues." Henry Abraham of the University of Virginia called *With Justice For All?* "A welcome, objective, no-nonsense account of the American legal system—where it is and where it ought to be."

Mastering Negotiation

Chapter 1

Choosing the Best Approach for a Negotiation

Roadmap

- **Defining negotiation:** What is a negotiation? How might the term, *negotiation,* best be defined, described, and differentiated from other like terms?

- **Detailing the positional-bargaining approach:** What is positional bargaining, why is it a familiar approach to negotiation, and what marks the process of positional bargaining?

- **Identifying a positional bargainer's tactics:** How do positional bargainers use starting and fallback positions, and haggle, dicker, and bluff?

- **Appraising the positional approach:** What advantages and disadvantages are associated with positional bargaining?

- **Detailing the interest-based negotiation approach:** What is interest-based negotiation, what is its logic, and what are its pros and cons?

- **Selecting an approach:** What factors might a negotiator bear in mind in choosing between positional and interest-based approaches?

"Those who are possessed of a definite body of doctrine and of deeply rooted convictions upon it will be in a much better position to deal with the shifts and surprises of daily affairs."

—Winston Churchill[1]

Circumstances matter greatly in negotiation. Resolving a dispute, whether legal, commercial, political, or diplomatic, may differ in important respects from structuring the terms of a transaction, whether a contract, merger, or purchase and sale. One would not expect to negotiate a landlord-tenant dispute just as one does a mutual-defense treaty, nor a joint venture in the exact manner of a collective-bargaining agreement. Consequently, as negotiators grapple with any particular problem or opportunity, they will draw on some but not others of the ideas presented in the pages that follow.

Nevertheless, many concepts are relevant across different types of negotiating problems. The thinking that leads to a successful resolution in one context may well apply to another. And, some negotiations flow across categories. One scholar noted "[N]egotiations that begin as deals can, and do, deteriorate into disputes," while highly skilled negotiators "try to convert a dispute into a deal and to prevent a deal from becoming a dispute."[2]

Mastering Negotiation is especially concerned with negotiation by lawyers and others who work on behalf of clients or organizations and have to grapple with complicated scenarios. *Complex negotiations*[3] are particularly challenging since they include at least one and often more of the following factors: numerous parties, multiple involved issues, a legal context, an international setting, scientific or technical intricacies, significant cross-cultural differences, or tangled, long-lived, or baggage-laden conflicts or disputes, whether personal, group, national, or international.

Among the particular transactions that might qualify as complex negotiations are joint ventures, employment contracts, mergers and acquisitions, real estate transactions, intellectual property licensing, and long-term supply contracts between manufacturers and distributors.[4] Many political or diplomatic problems would fit into this category as well. Ethnic conflict, public policy issues, and crises of various kinds tend to bring on complex negotiations, as do trade disputes and arms control negotiations.

Effective complex negotiation involves a negotiator's experience and such intangible senses as tact, savvy, and intuition. But, it also draws on what has been called "a systematic body of propositions, knowledge, and teachable skills."[5] This is important since the level of negotiation skills and expertise applied to a given problem can bring the parties to very different outcomes, some markedly better than others.

A. What Is a Negotiation?

So, what exactly qualifies as a *negotiation*? The term certainly can be used with distinct ideas in mind, and it may connote somewhat different things to different people and within different cultures.

1. A Definition and Description of Negotiation

Negotiations are best thought of as discussions between different parties that aim to adjust differences, conclude a transaction, take advantage of an opportunity, or manage or resolve a dispute or conflict. Ordinarily, the parties are interdependent in the sense that each is looking to gain something and each has something to give that the other wants. The hope is to craft a mutually beneficial outcome that both sides believe to be better than their alternatives.

Beyond these fundamental points, negotiations share the following basic characteristics. The parties identify one or more problems or opportunities and initiate communication about them in hopes that they will be better off with a jointly created agreement of some kind than without one. An exchange of views then occurs in which questions are posed, information set out, answers considered, and points made about the parties' interests and perspectives on the situation. The hope is that this process of discussion will lead to a mutual agreement about future conduct.

This interactive discussion need not take any particular form. It can be covered in a single exchange or stretched over multiple sessions. It can be conducted face-to-face or at a distance, by oral means or via the written word. Often, the actions of the parties as they negotiate can play into the discussions, certainly true of strikes, walk-outs, and lockouts in labor disputes, to take one prominent example.[6] Then, quite frequently, one or the other or both negotiators are serving as agents, negotiating on behalf of someone else, whether an individual, a group, or an organization. Indeed, a corporation or a government is unable to negotiate for itself; rather, it always uses an agent of some kind.

Although compelled negotiations occasionally occur, ordinarily, the parties voluntarily enter the talks in order to see if it might be possible to reach a negotiated resolution. This mutual desire to negotiate typically provides initial momentum and can sometimes help to overcome difficulties that may arise.

Each side normally enters a negotiation with particular goals or objectives in mind. Each tends to negotiate having already put some thought into the resolution it would like to see occur. However, good negotiating is also creative in that the process frequently stimulates new ideas. In a successful negotiation an outcome is created that the parties support since it goes beyond the prior state of affairs, when they were not yet acting in concert.

The ultimate aim of a negotiation, then, is to formulate a resolution to which the parties will agree since it somehow benefits them. At a minimum each will see agreement as better than their alternatives. The process of negotiation leads one side or the other or both to create one or a number of proposals for dealing with the circumstances before them. Possible resolutions are then appraised and may be amended, countered by an offer from the other side, or, at times, taken back and reformulated. Eventually, the parties decide whether to move toward a formal agreement, reject the negotiation effort and end the talks, or continue negotiating in hopes of finding a more beneficial outcome than has hitherto been suggested. If the counterparts do find common ground, they then work out details of a resolution which can be oral but is often laid out in written form.

Note that, while a debate can sometimes sound like a negotiation for a period, debaters are not, ordinarily, aiming to resolve their differences. Rather, they are engaged in a verbal competition, each trying to score points against the other. A dictated outcome is also not a negotiation since a more powerful party simply forces a weaker one to do what it wants. There may be no need to formulate a resolution at all beneficial to the other side.

In contrast, a negotiation implies a tradeoff: each party gives up something in order to get something else that it especially values. It also often involves the invention or discovery of something new, something that goes beyond the choice as previously seen.

2. The Negotiation Dynamic

Consider, then, the negotiation dynamic. A range of different approaches exists to dealing with the many issues that arise in daily life. One might simply choose to do nothing, let matters rest and hope that the problem improves or evaporates over time. Various factors might cause the other party to change its actions or orientation. An individual deeply involved in the situation might move away, change jobs, retire or die. Conceivably, a legislature might take up a relevant question, perhaps passing a law that speaks to the situation.

At the other end of the spectrum of possible reactions, if one litigates or arbitrates a dispute, the aim is to get a court or an arbitrator to order the other side to do what one wants. Here, one would put an argument to a third party and would have to abide by his or her decision. This certainly has its advantages. One side might determine that creating a binding legal precedent through a court case is more attractive than negotiating an agreement.

Yet another way to approach a problem is to employ self-help, that is, boldly take an available action without bothering to negotiate. Striking a course unilaterally can be attractive since bringing another party in on a decision tends to require compromises. Thus, an unhappy spouse might file for divorce. A business might terminate certain employees and replace them with an automated service. A government might go war, seeking to coerce a favorable outcome by force of arms.

In particular circumstances compelling reasons might favor each of these alternatives to negotiation, and yet each is also associated with significant problems. Doing nothing may bring about no forward progress at all, at least for a long period. Positions can harden, and frustration set in. Taking a dispute to court usually triggers a lengthy and costly undertaking. Adjudication may be uncomfortable for parties, as they are compelled to testify about different matters. Once the court case begins, parties may feel that they have lost control of the process. Expenses will mount, often precipitously so, and may never be fully recovered.

Moreover, a court will typically decide in favor of one party and against the other, making much litigation into an all-or-nothing proposition. This can be a sobering prospect for parties who might prefer a compromise in which each gains something. It can also be difficult to predict accurately the results of a court case. Before trial each litigant usually focuses considerably more attention on their own arguments than on their opponent's. This may lead each side to over-estimate its chances of winning. And, litigation may so sour relations between the different sides as to eliminate the possibility of a future productive relationship.

Negotiation is a subtler method of attending to complex problems. A negotiator is trying to work with the other party to find an outcome to which both sides are agreeable. The question becomes—how can the negotiators use their intellects to construct a mutually satisfactory agreement, something better than any option that either party sees away from the negotiating table? But, as the saying goes, "it takes two to tango." If one side feels that a negotiation is futile or that it is already progressing toward its goals without negotiating, the effort on the part of the other party to negotiate will likely fail.

When two or more parties are willing to negotiate, they engage in a particular form of communication, one that often involves ready interaction. In such circumstances long-winded speeches, no matter how artfully composed, often fall flat. Instead, the most effective negotiators tend to be comfortable with a series of ad hoc exchanges with their counterparts.

In a courtroom presentation a litigator tries to bring the judge or jury around to his or her perspective on the legal issue at hand. In contrast, negotiators look to influence their fellow negotiators. This can be quite challenging since many people are conditioned to resist persuasion by one they take to be an adversary. They thus create counter-arguments, and the communication soon reverts to a debate. An essential part of the art of negotiation is to move beyond arguments to create agreement. Future chapters will lay out an array of paths to do just that.

3. Group Negotiations

The more complex the problem, the more likely it is to be, or become, a group negotiation. Sometimes the group consists of two teams, one from each side. At other times, multiple negotiators assemble—sometimes representing parties singly and sometimes with teammates—in order to consider together a problem or opportunity. Yet another variety of group negotiation involves a large conference aimed at working out some issue or problem that the parties face.

In each of these scenarios multiple people will be interacting with one another. This creates a different dynamic than found in one-on-one talks, and it brings new issues and problems into play for the negotiators. Moving even from two to three parties brings about "surprisingly rich" complexities.[7] Consider the following strategic issues. In a *triangular negotiation*, that is, one among three parties, whom do you approach first, and do you compromise with them before approaching the third party? What if two other parties have a previous understanding and are acting in concert coming to you? When do you try to woo away another member of the triangle, and how do you go about doing so?

All of these issues are then writ larger still when three parties turns to six, nine, twelve, or dozens. Think, for instance, of the complexities inherent in closing a deal when different parties are promoting an array of package resolutions. Howard Raiffa observed: "If there are fifteen parties, there may on the table initially be six packages, which may fuse to four and then to three. Packages change continually: some fuse; others fractionate and come together with shifting coalitions."[8] And, the possibility always exists that a portion of the total group will come to a deal in lieu of or in addition to an agreement by the whole.

B. Detailing the Positional-Bargaining Approach

People tend to negotiate via two basic methods: a *positional bargaining* approach or a method variously termed *principled, problem-solving, interest-based*, or *mutual gains negotiation*.

1. Identifying Positional Bargaining

Positional bargaining is a conventional mode of negotiating that centers on each side assuming a particular posture and then making demands of the other.[9] The word *bargaining* implies that the negotiator's aim is to gain a bargain, that is, a singularly attractive outcome, achieved via "an adversarial process of give and take."[10]

This method centers on each negotiator staking out *positions*. That is, each articulates his or her stance or demand on key issues, in that way laying out their side's view of what it would take to reach an agreement. A position is an articulation of the negotiator's preferred solution to the problem or opportunity before them. Although the hope is that a strongly asserted position will cause the other side to accept those terms, one's counterparts are free to declare their own, contrasting, position. In that case at key moments in the negotiation what one side wants is juxtaposed with what the other side wants.

When significant differences exist between the respective positions announced by each side, as is often the case, the parties see if it is possible to narrow that gap. Typically, each demands more than it actually expects to receive, and often through a series of small compromises, each shifts its position, usually slowly or haltingly, in the direction of the other. Either their revised positions ultimately overlap, in which case a deal is likely to result, or one or the other or both parties give up, ending the negotiation.

2. The Familiarity of Bargaining

Early in life, most of us experience positional bargaining. As a child, we might negotiate this way with a sibling, friend, or parent. As we get older, we might visit a yard sale or flea market. We might watch people bargain by adopting contrasting positions on television or in movies. One might be introduced to positional negotiation in the purchase of a used car.

In fact, people often "wheel and deal" in selling used items—bikes, canoes, lawn mowers—and, whenever prices are not fixed ahead of time, positional bargaining might occur to determine a price. One might see people negotiate over the terms of a deal to provide yard services. Or, one might watch bargaining over the cost of parking in a private lot near a stadium. In the country a farmer and landowner might come to an agreement over the price of a horse or of bales of hay.

Tourists often practice positional bargaining while abroad. In Mexico or another Latin American country, one might hear a vendor call out to a passing potential customer, "Fifteen pesos for these bananas." The customer might take a look and reply, "They look small and green; a couple have bruises on them. I won't pay more than five." The vendor might open a banana and offer a bite, while suggesting a compromise on a "final" price. The key point here is that the very "essence of much bargaining involves changing another's perceptions of where in fact one would settle."[11]

3. The Process and Tactics of Positional Bargaining

In positional bargaining "you ask for more than you expect to get, you offer less than you expect to give, you compete as to who can be more stubborn and who can better threaten to walk away from a deal."[12] A positional bargainer typically magnifies ("talks up") what he or she has offered to give up and diminishes ("talks down") what the counterpart has offered to contribute. The process of assuming positions, arguing about their appropriateness, and then reformulating them often takes considerable time, since each negotiator wants to be sure the other will not yield readily to it. The central idea is that, if you are able to persuade the other side via debate, you may not need to make a concession at all. Hence, a seasoned positional bargainer tries out arguments to see if they will work before moving to meet the other side in a compromise.

Harvard economist John Kenneth Galbraith once quipped, "Faced with the choice between changing one's mind and proving that there is no need to do so, almost everyone gets busy on the proof."[13] As a negotiator explicates, clarifies, and defends a position, he or she may become more committed to it and less inclined to compromise much, if at all. Positional bargainers thus often argue, feign disbelief, and drag their feet before moving, grudgingly, in the direction of the other side. Since neither negotiator knows where the other will agree, each side looks to make the smallest possible steps toward the other's position, hoping in that way to arrive at the most advantageous resolution.

Parties adhering to positional bargaining often think in terms of a *starting point*, a series of possible *fallback positions*, and an ultimate fallback stance sometimes termed a *bottom line*. Fallback positions thus reflect movement away from a negotiator's starting point and toward the counterpart's position. A bottom line would be the minimal resolution needed in order to reach an agreement.

Early in the talks a positional bargainer might try to *anchor* the negotiation in a place that is favorable to them. That is, he or she would try to make a strong argument in favor of a particular number or other point in hopes that this opening position will influence the remainder of the discussions. That first proposal might serve to stake out a particular zone of possible resolutions, and the outcome might be in the neighborhood of that initial position.

For example, on a used car lot your opening bid might be "I'll pay $5,000 for that old Chevy Camaro. It badly needs a paint job, the interior is worn, and the tires need replacing." Privately, you might acknowledge to your buddy that you would really be willing to pay ten thousand dollars. Five thousand would be your starting point; you might be fully prepared to fall back, if need be, to $6,500, or, if that did not secure a deal, to $8,000. Ten thousand would stand as your bottom line. Your negotiation *strategy* would involve presenting arguments to the sales person about the proper price of the car or how much you could pay. And, your ultimate aim would be to try to get a resolution as close to your starting point as possible.

In positional bargaining each side tries to alter the expectations of the other, while wearing down resistance to its position. The hope is that in that way the negotiator will gain an agreement on something close to its terms. Consequently, much of the process of negotiation involves each negotiator trying to pull the other toward a previously announced viewpoint: an intellectual tug of war.

a. Leaving Bargaining Room

In offering up a position, each side looks to leave some *bargaining room*, or *room to negotiate*, that is, some ability to move away from their position and toward the other side's position while still ending up with an attractive deal. For example, a banking executive proposes buying a small local bank for $10 million, knowing full well that the board of directors is prepared to pay $12 million, but leaving some room to negotiate with the sellers.

In simple positional bargaining the course of the negotiation can amount to little more than a series of compromises between the different starting points, as both sides feel one another out for movement, while trying to reach the most advantageous resolution for themselves. Movement toward each other's positions will ordinarily be small so long as each believes that shaving a bit off its position might just result in a deal. In this style of negotiation the participants whittle away at their differences.

This is a common method of negotiation around the world. In all likelihood the price the carpet seller calls out, as a potential buyer walks through a Middle Eastern bazaar or a North African souk, is a substantially inflated number. The seller might very much hope that the buyer simply *caves in*, and under the pressure of having to answer on the spot or under some duress accepts the outstanding proposal in full without requesting any changes. But, he or she might well be surprised at such naïveté, since the offer made is not what the seller truly expects to receive. Similarly, the amount that an interested buyer responds with is, likewise, a deflated figure.

Positional bargainers routinely pad their demands for several reasons. Padding provides room to retreat. The other side may be more willing to agree once it has received a concession. And, if a deal does materialize, the returns are likely to be greater than if no padding had occurred.[14] However, typically, each side is well aware of what the other is up to. An extraordinarily high offer often triggers a similarly outrageous counter-offer: one cancels out the other, and no one is especially advantaged by the tactic or is inclined to yield quickly thereafter.

b. Haggling, Dickering, and Bluffing

The effort by each side to dislodge the other from its position and get it to adopt a new position nearer its own usually involves considerable discussion back and forth, referred to as *haggling* or *dickering*. As they bargain, positional negotiators often verbally spar with each other since they tend to put great stock in who has the upper hand and who appears to be in charge of the negotiation, steering it in an advantageous direction.

In this approach to negotiation, bargainers try to screen off many of their true feelings from their counterparts. As is said of poker players, they "play their cards close to the vest." For instance, positional bargainers might purport a lack of interest in something in which they are actually extremely interested. The assumption is that an opposing negotiator will be in a prime position to extract more value for an item that is clearly desired.

As a consequence, positional bargainers not only frequently misrepresent their real feelings but pride themselves on their ability to do so convincingly. To a positional negotiator, *bluffing* is simply an integral part of the game of negotiation. By bluffing I mean that a negotiator pretends something to be the case when it is not in order to see if the other side is foolish, inexperienced, or concerned enough to accept the bluff at face value.

Although bluffing about the price at which one would buy or sell is quite common, a negotiator might bluff about any number of things. For instance, he or she might claim to have an attractive alternative, when none actually exists. Another bluff might involve making references to an outside constraint, such as when a negotiator justifies rejecting a proposal by referring to a "company policy" which, in fact, does not exist. Or, a negotiator might advance an extreme, one-sided proposal, threatening to end the negotiation if matters are not settled on those terms, when no real intention of walking away exists.

In one way or another a bluffing negotiator works to deceive the other side into giving a better deal that it really needs to. Two scholars suggested, "[T]he more a negotiator wants to bluff, the more he needs to appear trustworthy in order to carry off his deception when the moment comes."[15] Of course, since a negotiator who bluffs about too many things soon loses credibility, bluffing does have some practical limits. And, a real loss of credibility occurs when a negotiator's bluff is called and he or she is exposed as having misrepresented something. Note, too, that as one experienced negotiator put it, "[T]here's only one thing worse than to be caught bluffing. It is *not* to be bluffing, but to have the other side *think* you are."[16]

One extreme variety of a bluff is *brinkmanship,* in which one side or the other or both bring the parties to the edge of disaster—perhaps once and for all terminating the negotiation—in hopes that the other side will back down. In this regard one sometimes see references to the *game of chicken*, associated with the James Dean movie *Rebel Without a Cause*, in which teenaged drivers hurtled at one another in cars, trying not to be the one who swerved to avoid a collision. Whoever changed direction was then scorned as a coward; the one who kept going was considered a hero. A negotiator playing this game uses some impending disaster and the bluff that he or she will not stop it to try to compel the other side to yield and accept a demand.

c. Making Concessions

A *concession* is something the other side wants provided to it in a spirit of compromise. Negotiators often expect concessions to be reciprocal: I make a concession to you, and I expect you, then, to make a concession to me. In a *quid pro quo* exchange a negotiator refuses to give up something without gaining something else in return. Positional bargainers thus regularly pace their concessions by linking them to those being made by their counterpart. Moreover, concessions usually become successively smaller the longer the process of bargaining occurs. The intent is to signal that the negotiator's ability or willingness to concede items is drawing to a close.

For these reasons positional bargainers often carefully compare the concessions that each side has made. That is, in demanding additional movement from a counterpart, a negotiator will point out how much has already been conceded from his or her original position. In making such arguments, each side is inclined to exaggerate the worth of what it has offered up to date, while denigrating the other side's concessions as negligible, not nearly an equal exchange.

The process of moving toward one another's position, via these concessions, is obscured by the fact that each side is trying to deceive the other as to what exactly it will settle for. Each negotiator tries to persuade the other that he or she simply cannot concede anything else. Uncertainty as to whether or when to make a concession permeates, and often slows, the positional-bargaining process: "Making a concession when the other side won't simply rewards their bad behavior. Yet not making one can precipitate a contest as to who can be more stubborn."[17]

Indeed, just what a concession that is made signifies may be quite unclear. A concession might demonstrate goodwill, inviting reciprocal behavior from your fellow negotiator, but it might also reveal weakness, leading your counterpart to be obdurate, holding out for an upcoming collapse.

Complicating all this further is the fact that not only do parties successively adopt different positions, but they also constantly adjust their goals, as each tries to reach the most advantageous outcome possible. One source observed: "Although in theory it is easy to imagine the position descending until it reaches the other party's fixed threshold of acceptability, in reality the threshold is not fixed at all. When the other party see the opponent readily making concessions, it raises its threshold of acceptability to wring the largest concessions out of the opponent."[18]

d. The Course of Positional Bargaining

Positional-bargaining strategies differ on whether to begin with an extreme position, one that maximizes your ability to make later concessions, or start from a more reasonable stance and remain more firm as the haggling starts. Making a significant move toward your counterpart's position could signal that you are serious about coming to an agreement. Furthermore, former U.S. Secretary of State Henry Kissinger reasoned: "The more outrageous the initial proposition, the better is the prospect that what one 'really' wants will be considered a compromise."[19]

However, inflating your demands too much at the outset can also be risky. The opposing negotiator might at any time conclude that you are an unreasonable person or have so thoroughly mis-assessed the situation that further negotiations are senseless. The two sides may seem so far apart that agreement is highly unlikely. Alternatively, a negotiator may simply lose credibility as he or she slides away from initial high demands. "Once we begin to retreat from a padded position," it has been observed, "we begin to acquire a reputation for retreating. An adversary might reasonably conclude that if we came down once, we will come down again. Then many may not believe us when we say that we have come to the end of the padding."[20]

A contrasting positional-bargaining approach, then, is to formulate an opening offer which attracts the other side. This more modest offer must be carefully calibrated: what you ask for must please you, but also entice the other side, and still provide room to maneuver in the ensuing dickering.

In any event, opening demands by opposing negotiators engaged in positional bargaining are usually exchanged rather early in the negotiation process, with each then critically scrutinized and assessed by the other. The details of and rationales for the opening stances may be elucidated, and potential problems associated with turning down the respective offers may be aired. Then, typically, each side will request concessions from their counterpart, often paired with a rationale as to why this would be reasonable or proper. While some movement toward one another's positions is likely to occur, compromises tend to be modest, as each negotiator tries not to move too far from the original position declared.

Throughout the process of positional bargaining a savvy negotiator tries to conceal from the other side anything that would give that counterpart an advantage or *leverage*, for instance, information on how badly something is wanted or needed or what one would settle for. Amidst all the evasion and, perhaps, deception, how, then, does one convey the message at the end of the negotiation that the talks really will be over if something very close to the current terms is not accepted? This is a repeated problem for positional bargain-ers, and they often use *body language*, tone of voice, or urgency of commu-nication to try to get this message across.

Sometimes, to signal that this "dance of negotiation" is ending, a positional negotiator will simply declare an *ultimatum*: "That's the best I can do. Do you want a deal on those terms or not?" Think of a *take-it-or-leave-it offer*, then, as a final proposal whose terms suggest that no more compromises are possi-ble and a rejection will cause the negotiation to end. (Of course, it is always possible to respond to a take-it-or-leave-it ultimatum with a counter-offer. This may or may not be considered, but will "call" the bluff of the other side, if it is indeed a bluff.)

4. The Nature of Positional Bargaining

Since the essence of positional bargaining involves doing the minimum pos-sible to accommodate the other side and still gain an agreement with them, the process of grudging accommodation often provides an adversarial, com-bative, or competitive feel. The different sides may become intent on "win-ning": making out better than the opposing negotiator.

Some positional negotiations turn into power plays with each side flexing its muscles then pitting the strength of its arguments, threats, and leverage against its adversary's. Others might best be characterized as contests of will-power with each side trying to persuade the other that it is not going to give in. Egos can easily become involved as the parties openly conflict, taking issue with each other's reasoning and vying with one another to control what is hap-pening at the bargaining table.

a. A Distributional Focus

As the negotiators contend with each other, no one wants *to leave money on the table*, that is, conclude the negotiation for less money or other assets than the counterpart would actually have been willing to pay or transfer. Often, the overriding focus of positional bargaining is on how the benefits, money, or goods ought to be divided between the different sides. Here, one more for me is one less for you. And, the central focus of many positional bargainers is to gain more than one's opponent of whatever is at stake in the negotiation.

If you initiate a negotiation with a focus on the proper distribution of com-modities, the parties may perceive the talks as a *zero-sum game*, a phrase bor-rowed from game theory to identify a situation in which whatever one gains the other loses. Each side then advances arguments aimed at gaining the other side's agreement to a deal that reflects their position or something close to it. A canny positional bargainer will work on persuading the other side that it should actually be perfectly content with something less than it had wanted at the outset of the talks.

b. Compromises

For all of the jockeying between the parties, usually positional bargaining ultimately depends on compromise for agreements to occur. The negotiators make certain concessions, if pressed and if they appear necessary to reach a deal. However, determining whether and to what extent to compromise can be a time-consuming process: "The standard minuet ... requires a large number of individual decisions as each negotiator decides what to offer, what to reject, and how much of a concession to make."[21] Once both parties believe no better proposal is likely, or, when they get worn down, they may make a final compromise, and then, so long as both have gained enough of what they were looking for, they agree.

c. Positional Tactics and Emotional Responses

Since persuading the other side that one cannot move far in their direction is a vital part of the positional-bargaining approach, a negotiator may designate various matters as *non-negotiable* that is, beyond the scope of negotiation. The implication is that discussing a non-negotiable subject is futile since no compromise is possible.

A related positional-bargaining tactic is to *stonewall*, that is, adamantly refuse to budge from a position or completely evade discussions about something. The hope may be that the party that wants to talk about it will give up or drop the subject. Alternatively, the stonewalling party may aim to gain some substantive concession in exchange for agreeing to discuss the topic.

A positional bargainer will use a range of arguments, supplemented by appropriate body language, to persuade the other side that further movement will not happen. The effort is to justify to the counterpart why a negotiator is locked into a previously announced position and why it would be unwise or illogical for it to move toward the opposition's stance. The threat, implicit or explicit, is that the negotiation will end if the other side refuses to agree to the positional bargainer's terms.

The maneuvers associated with different positional tactics can raise the emotional ante as frustration sets in. Disputes may arise over who is being obstinate and unyielding and who is ready to compromise. One or the other or both parties may begin to threaten, browbeat one another, try to demonstrate their willpower, or enumerate past grievances to stimulate feelings of guilt. All of these pressure tactics are aimed at trying to move the other side toward agreeing to a particular position.

C. Appraising the Positional Approach

1. Some Advantages of Positional Bargaining

a. Familiarity and Tradition

Humans sometimes seem to negotiate instinctually by adopting positions. Certainly, the basic ideas of the positional-bargaining approach have the advantage of being easy to observe, learn, and understand. Positional bargaining is so ingrained in the negotiation practices of many cultures that in much of the world this is the typical way that negotiations have been conducted since time immemorial.

One reason is that the process of adopting extreme positions and then moving slowly toward one another often does succeed in bringing about an agreement. Both sides haggle with each other until they reach the conclusion that the deal on the table is about the best they can do. If positional bargaining failed to produce so many agreements, it would not be relied upon so often. One scholar put it like this: "The typical 'dance of concessions,' in which the parties pretend to be ready to walk out while assessing the possibility that the other is telling the truth, may be frustrating and inelegant, but it tends to work well in practice."[22]

Furthermore, sometimes "customs and expectations may be so fixed that any benefit that might occur from negotiating in a different way would be outweighed by the transaction costs of trying to do so."[23] Thus, when governments negotiate with one another after a long and arduous internal process of reaching a consensus among different departments and individuals, elements of positional bargaining are very likely to be seen, at least as the negotiation gets under way. In hostage negotiations an exchange of opening positions is all but inevitable since the constituencies of both sides find it vitally important to lay out the deadly consequences of failing to yield.

The negotiation of contracts for professional athletes typically proceeds along a positional-bargaining path.[24] Here, the key term tends to be financial, overwhelming quality of life and other such *ancillary issues*. In these dollar-driven negotiations most sports agents and many team executives relish reputations for tough *distributional bargaining*, where a dollar for the team means one less for the player or vice versa.

Indeed, positional bargaining characterizes many varieties of labor negotiations. Sometimes parties are legally mandated to exchange opening proposals. Something absent from that original position, in theory, need not be discussed at all, and, in practice, will often make its way back into the negotiation only at the price of a concession elsewhere. Moreover, the rank-and-file members of the union may believe that only tough positional bargaining will bring about the best possible agreement. Furthermore, a union might rely "on positional consensus for its internal unity."[25]

b. Useful in Particular Circumstances

Even one who would be reluctant to bargain by positions in a weighty dispute might find it to be an efficient and appropriate method when dealing with a problem where the stakes are small, or one in which no continuing relationship is likely. Imagine, for instance, traveling far from where you live and purchasing a used jeep from a dealer there or buying an item when visiting a distant farmer's market. Alternatively, if the parties perceive no way to "expand the pie," they may be inclined to maximize their own slice of it and opt for positional bargaining.

Furthermore, the *process* of positional bargaining has some strategic points to recommend it. A negotiator might hope to anchor the discussions within a zone relatively near an opening position. In addition, positions have the advantage of often being quite easy to grasp: "A position is likely to be concrete and explicit; the interests underlying it may well be unexpressed, intangible, and perhaps inconsistent."[26]

Moreover, taking an extreme position and making grudging concessions from it may leave a positional bargainer feeling certain that he or she has not given away too much too quickly. No negotiator wants to be left with the sinking feeling of having badly underestimated how much the other side might have settled for. In this regard one scholar pointed out that positional bargaining: "allows each negotiator to explore various possible agreements before settling, to obtain as much information as possible about the other negotiator and his or her preferences, before closing off the discussion." He added: "It allows each party to give its respective constituency some sense of the degree to which the other side has already been 'moved,' thereby maintaining constituency support for the positions taken in the negotiation."[27]

2. Some Disadvantages of Positional Bargaining

Although any of the above reasons might incline negotiators toward positional bargaining, this method has some real disadvantages, too. A negotiator's position on an issue might be influenced by anger, fear, or pride. It might reflect short-sighted or stunted thinking. Any of these could not only obstruct agreement but cause negotiators to short-circuit an otherwise promising negotiation process.

a. Tactics Invite Reciprocal Treatment

Another drawback to relying on a negotiation method that involves staking out a personally advantageous position, revealing one's true views on many points reluctantly if at all, and looking to bluff to gain advantage whenever possible is that one's counterpart often sees or senses these tactics and reciprocates with more of the same. When one side starts from an extreme stance or embarks on a contest of willpower, this may induce the other to do likewise. When one negotiator presents a stubborn and unyielding front, the other tends to follow suit. And so, deadlocks commonly occur in positional bargaining.

It is true that savvy negotiators can use positional-bargaining techniques and still figure out ways to overcome difficult impasses. But, positional negotiations, especially those undertaken by less sure-footed negotiators, risk degenerating into unproductive debates. Clashing positions frequently turn negotiations into arguments over why one starting point or fallback position was valid and the other was not.

Positional bargainers might also debate who is more justified in feeling aggrieved. In some circumstances they might be inclined to argue about how a court might rule should a legal case be pursued. Or, the parties might find themselves arguing over who is most at fault for the fact that an agreement has not yet emerged or does not seem to be coming together smoothly. But, when we voice our thoughts, most of us most of the time sound perfectly reasonable to ourselves. And, only very rarely does one debater publicly concede that the other has the better argument. Hence, for negotiators, such debates may not be a productive, or the most productive, use of their time.

Then, when the two sides have a continuing relationship, what happens in one negotiation can spill over and affect the next. A party that feels compelled to accept a take-it-or-leave-it offer in one situation may relish the thought of turning the tables the next time the two sides negotiate.[28] A continuing series of positional negotiations can thus become ever more difficult over time.

b. Parties Can Overlook Potential Deals

Another cardinal problem with this method of negotiation is that sometimes the positions taken are so far from each other that there appears to be no *zone of possible agreement*. That is, what each side wants, the other side does not seem able to provide. Or, each party may be so convincing in its arguments in favor of its own position that the negotiation appears to be hopelessly stalemated.

These common scenarios can cause the parties to give up and walk away from the bargaining table, even in situations in which a neutral observer, fully aware of all of the facts and actual views of each party, might concoct a mutually beneficial negotiated resolution. As Ben Franklin once observed: "The worst outcome is when, by overreaching greed, no bargain is struck, and a trade that could have been advantageous to both parties does not come off at all."[29]

c. Creativity Can Be Stifled

Although creative positional bargainers certainly do exist, the process of negotiating by juxtaposing contrasting positions often stifles creativity. The concept of a bottom line tends to focus attention on a single dimension, such as the price being negotiated.[30] Moreover, formulating new and imaginative options that might create real value for the parties is best undertaken in an atmosphere of good will, where the parties are working together toward the common goal of finding a mutually acceptable resolution.

But, much positional bargaining reflects little effort to truly understand the problem from one another's perspectives, much less to build the trust between the parties that may assist them in finding creative options that satisfy key interests. That the parties can be boxed in by prior arguments supporting their positions further hampers creativity.

d. Claiming Value versus Creating Value

People adopt a positional-bargaining approach in hopes that it will help them in distributional bargaining, that is, it will enable them to get the biggest possible share of the pie that may be divided between the parties. One of the key functions of negotiation involves what negotiation theorists call *claiming value*, that is, where resources are in limited supply and must be allocated between the parties, grasping as many of the assets at issue as possible. By starting with extreme demands and making concessions only grudgingly, positional bargaining is aimed at doing just that.

Another function of negotiation, however, involves what is termed *creating value*, that is, figuring out ways to bring new benefits to each side, to expand the pie that is to be divided, and, ultimately, to make each side better off with the deal created. An example may help to clarify.

Consider a contract between a professional athlete and a sports agent and the issue of a percentage fee in compensation for arranging endorsements. If the provision is conceived of in terms of claiming value, the athlete will want the smallest percentage to go to the agent: every dollar that goes into the agent's pocket is one less dollar in the athlete's bank account. If it is conceived in terms of creating value, however, the athlete will want the agent to have a healthy incentive to go out and find advertising deals and then to press to make the financial returns as large as possible. Hence, reducing the percentage fee to a bare minimum would appear quite short-sighted.

As a negotiating method to create value, positional bargaining often falls short. Positions, by their very nature, focus the attention of the parties on one specific answer to the problem or opportunity they face.[31] Positional bargainers thus spend much energy trying to create arguments that would justify their continuing to adhere to their current positions. They also frequently bluff one another. Even when positional bargainers are receiving exactly what they want, they try to make it appear that they are compromising in hopes of extracting something else from the other side. The process of hiding their true interests, goals, and motivations frequently causes shared interests and objectives to be overlooked.

e. Other Problematic Circumstances

If some circumstances seem reasonably appropriate for a positional approach, in others relying on this method of negotiation might cause real problems. Think, for instance, of very sophisticated problems divided into numerous issues. Turning each into a positional wrestling match may court disaster. Or, consider negotiations in a moment of crisis, when the parties really need to move efficiently toward an agreement, rather than consume precious time bluffing and haggling.

Alternatively, think of negotiations with many parties. In the field of environmental policy one might imagine a *negotiated rulemaking* in which industry representatives, public interest groups, and government officials attempt to work together to fashion an environmental regulation. Or, think in foreign affairs of the large gatherings of diplomats and legal advisers as dozens of governments join to try to negotiate new understandings of the content of international law in some field.

Consider negotiations that are a part of extremely important long-term relations between the different sides: legal issues between family members, labor issues between a management and a union, or regulatory issues between a corporation and a government agency. Perhaps business managers think a potential employee will provide them with valuable work for years if an agreement can just be reached. In each of these cases the same counterparts may well be there next month or next year or even into the more distant future, and how one behaves today will likely influence relations and negotiations in days ahead.

Yet another scenario in which positional bargaining might not function well would be a negotiation in which emotions are running high. Digging into contrasting positions and then calling for concessions may bring both parties to end up walking away from the talks. When each has a short fuse, positional-bargaining tactics might exacerbate their underlying frustrations.

Another situation in which positional bargaining might undercut the chances for a negotiated resolution would be when two businesses face an exciting common opportunity to join forces somehow. Think, for instance, of a joint venture in which the companies involved are trying to capitalize on synergies while minimizing redundancies. Their aim is to work in tandem over an extended period, and the negotiation often focuses on which side has what competitive advantages to contribute and how matters might best be merged in the new combined entity.

Furthermore, should deception play a role in a negotiator's strategy, the potential costs of misleading a fellow negotiator ought to be taken into account. With time, the deception may not remain hidden, and omissions or false statements might return to haunt one who used them in an effort to maximize gains. Many negotiators, whether they are operating in a personal or a professional capacity, will not want lying or shading the truth to be the kind of behavior that others come to associate with them. And, deception that later comes to light may end up undermining long-term interests. This could destroy a positive *working relationship* and make future negotiations much harder to conclude.

Finally, the more complex the negotiating problem, the more difficult it can be to assess the relative power of each side. These uncertainties can bring the parties to shy away from the test of strength and the opportunistic behavior that is often associated with positional bargaining. Rather, finding a fair way to resolve distributive problems, while cooperating to formulate creative options, might be a more attractive way to proceed.

In all these cases, negotiators might feel ill-served by the basic tenets of positional bargaining.

D. Introducing the Interest-Based Negotiation Approach

On account of the drawbacks of positional bargaining an alternative method of negotiating may sometimes be thought advisable, particularly for more complex and weighty problems. But, how exactly should the human tendency to bargain by positions be altered? What would be a different approach to negotiation better suited for circumstances deemed inappropriate for positional bargaining? That theoretical puzzle led various scholars, many of them associated with the multi-university consortium in the Greater Boston area known as the Harvard Program on Negotiation, toward creating a different model of negotiation. This came to be called interest-based or principled negotiation, or sometimes problem-solving or mutual gains negotiation.

I prefer the phrase interest-based negotiation since the term *principled* has a potentially confusing double meaning. Some take it to imply that the approach is a more morally virtuous mode of negotiating. Others focus on principles in the sense of fundamental precepts that its proponents feel ought to inform and undergird negotiation strategies. Much of the remainder of this book explores different dimensions of interest-based negotiation. This chapter simply lays out the essence of the approach, while contrasting it with positional bargaining.

The interest-based negotiation approach was first laid out, in it most fundamental form, in the popular text *Getting to Yes: Negotiating Agreement Without Giving In*, by Roger Fisher, William Ury, and Bruce Patton. It focuses attention on seven key elements of negotiation—relationship, communication, interests, options, legitimacy, alternatives, and commitments—with maxims and supporting points about each designed to help negotiators to attain positive outcomes in a wide range of situations.

1. Emphasizing Interests Over Positions

At the very heart of interest-based negotiation is the view that negotiators should emphasize interests over positions. Complex negotiations pose special challenges since they may have many issues to resolve, multiple parties involved, sophisticated objectives to try to attain, or a multitude of operative facts and perspectives. Here, it can be especially important to try to get beyond opening positions and delve into the underlying concerns that are truly motivating the parties.

One goal of interest-based negotiation is to have the parties come to feel joint ownership of the problem or opportunity. Two authorities cautioned, however, "The people you negotiate with seldom experience an epiphany and suddenly own a problem with you. It takes work to bring them along with you ... A sense of interdependence ... must emerge from a deeper understanding that you are both implicated in the problem and must work on its solution together."[32]

Furthermore, in positional bargaining, by definition, the parties spend much time and energy in carefully articulating their positions. Since an interest-based negotiator anticipates the need to dislodge a positional counterpart from the positions adopted, he or she does not encourage the process of defining those positions in ever more detailed fashion. Rather, the effort is to focus the attention of both parties on the underlying interests. Then, the task of the negotiator is to try to align those interests in a settlement acceptable to both sides.

2. The Logic of Interest-Based Negotiation

The interest-based negotiator counsels that, as one negotiates, he or she should be alert for, and spend some time probing for, the interests of the other side. An important portion of a negotiation conducted via this collaborative problem-solving approach ought to involve trying to better understand how the other party views the situation. This highlights the following questions.

- What is really driving my counterpart?
- What does the other side feel that it wants or needs?
- What concerns or motivates it?
- What is seen as quite problematic, and what, as an enticing opportunity?

3. Some Advantages of Interest-Based Negotiation

Interest-based negotiators see a number of marked advantages to adopting their approach.

a. Overcoming a Reluctance to Negotiate

Potential negotiators confronting extreme opening positions could dismiss too precipitately the chances for reaching a negotiated agreement. The negotiator may have taken a position at the onset of negotiations simply to see if any possibility exists of coming to a resolution on extremely favorable terms. Alternatively, a party may feel an urgent need to go "on record" with a tough opening statement, and this might well be phrased in positional terms. A position could thus reflect internal dynamics, that is, such a statement might be made primarily to please or pacify some important constituents.

Sometimes a potential party is reluctant to negotiate, perhaps dismissing it as probably a waste of time. Here, by appealing to the possibility that some of their key interests will be served, an initially skeptical fellow negotiator can sometimes be drawn into serious talks. Consequently, one who might be turned off if confronted by an initial position, could have their eyes opened to the chance to negotiate a mutually beneficial outcome through an interest-based approach.

b. Fostering a Productive Working Relationship

Its proponents feel that the case for using the interest-based method becomes quite strong when negotiators must tackle complex disputes. To reach an agreement and certainly to find an optimal one, the parties will likely have to work collaboratively. Interest-based negotiation is more conducive to the task of fostering a cooperative and productive working relationship than is positional bargaining.

Consider also negotiations involving long-term relationships. Think, for instance, of a professional athlete negotiating a possible agreement with a sports agent. If the deal occurs, there will be an important continuing relationship. While the two individuals might be envisioned as sitting on opposite sides of the bargaining table as they consider a contract, they would be working in tandem, negotiating with different sports teams and others, once the deal is consummated. Establishing good working relations is critically important to signing the best possible playing contracts as well as perhaps landing lucrative endorsement agreements. In such circumstances interest-based negotiation would have much to recommend it.

c. Increasing the Number of Possible Resolutions

Another reason to favor interest-based over positional bargaining is that, typically, positions can be satisfied in a limited number of ways, perhaps in only a single way. An example may illuminate this. Imagine a city positioned along a large river and in a location where major highways form a crossroads. As the city grows and traffic increases, people consider whether to build another bridge across the river that runs through the downtown area. Someone expressing their views on the proposed bridge as a position might say, "That bridge ought to be built ten miles east of the city so that a bypass can divert through traffic to the west." Another might respond, "That bridge idea should be scrapped immediately. It's a boondoggle that will haunt this community for years to come." In declaring their views in terms like those, people would be staking out positions. Each of their positions would feature one possible resolution to the public policy issue at hand.

A different approach would be to try to determine the interests of the various parties involved, highlighting underlying concerns in an effort to find a way to resolve them in some mutually agreeable way. In this approach, rather than focusing upon the opening stances of the parties, one would aim to explore the motives of those speaking out on the bridge project. Why exactly do some see a new bridge as desirable, and why might it prove problematic?

Couching the discussion in these terms might lead to an examination of other possible resolutions that could speak to the concerns laid out. For instance, a negotiator might say, "Our first priority must be to cut the congestion downtown where these different highways merge." Or, another might suggest, "In an era of tight state and local finances we ought to avoid undertaking public works that impose an undue burden on the taxpayer." Still another might argue,

"Since the wetlands along the river east of the city help to support aquatic life and wildlife key to the surrounding ecosystem, the environmental impact of a bridge project should be important to all living in or around the city."

Each of the latter statements is worded, not simply as a stance or demand, but as an expression of concerns. It sheds light on what motivates the individual. Reducing traffic downtown, avoiding costly public projects, and minimizing threats to the environment are points that go beyond positional stances and begin to elucidate the interests of the respective parties. If negotiators think in terms of interests, they may significantly expand the range of possible resolutions to the problem or issue they are considering.

For instance, if a key concern is reducing traffic jams downtown, that problem might, in fact, by alleviated by a new bridge with a bypass connected to the highway headed west. But, that same concern might also be addressed by other options. Different forms of improved public transportation might solve the problem: larger buses or more of them, a new train route, a subway or monorail. Alternatively, more roads, larger highways, or a road system laid out differently, such as with a beltway or with car pool lanes or additional entry and exit points, might serve the purpose. And, the negotiator whose chief interest is to cut back on downtown traffic might end up being satisfied with a range of possible resolutions.

4. Possible Disadvantages to Interest-Based Negotiation

To focus negotiations on the interests of the parties does often take considerable time. If the negotiators are operating under very tight deadlines, it may sometimes be thought preferable to adopt a positional approach and immediately exchange ideas about possible settlement points.

Furthermore, an enormous number of simple transactions are successfully concluded while completely avoiding the drawn-out processes of interest-based bargaining. Think, for instance, of all the commercial activity reflected in a stock exchanges as shares of stock are bought and sold with no one considering the interests and alternatives of the other party.[33]

Some have argued that, while interest-based negotiation occurs in many cultures, it especially suits the cultural values of the United States and other Anglo cultures that elevate "individualism, egalitarianism, and direct communication."[34] In some cultures the expression of interests contrary to those of another party might be frowned upon, and the interests of all the parties might not be viewed as equally legitimate.

It is sometimes further contended that interest-based negotiation is inappropriate when collective interests are favored over individual ones. In fact, however, collective interests are rightly viewed simply as another category of interests, one featured in the goals and negotiation discourse of particular negotiators, such as those from societies that espouse community values. In some circumstances differences in perspective between those with individualistic and collective orientations might open the door to useful trade-offs.

E. Selecting an Approach

Some negotiators are inclined to use interest-based negotiation when relations with a counterpart are likely to be continuing and positive and to opt for a positional approach when relations are likely to be strained. For example, if I am negotiating something like a joint venture agreement with a fellow negotiator and we are both enthused about future prospects, then I choose an interest-based model. But, if I am negotiating to try to reach an out-of-court divorce settlement or partnership dissolution, then I opt for a positional approach. The rationale seems to be that, when confronted with positions, the other side will be less likely to take advantage of the situation to reach a favorable deal for themselves. Hence, some reason that the more tense, bitter, or adversarial the context, the stronger is the case for adopting a positional-bargaining approach.

The flaw in this reasoning is that a negotiator who opts for positional bargaining because of strained or otherwise problematic relations going into the negotiation may well end up with no deal, but instead a stalemate of contrasting positions. Indeed, the more difficult are relations, the better off you may be with interest-based negotiation. If you choose positional bargaining, you may be far more likely to walk away without a negotiated agreement, even when particular potential deals might well be in both of your interests.

Bear in mind, too, that, while interest-based negotiation is often viewed as diametrically opposed to positional negotiation, another approach would be to see the two negotiation styles as opposing poles on a spectrum but one in which negotiators might sometimes draw on one and sometimes on the other model. Indeed, any particular negotiation might contain positional and interest-based elements.

Finally, recognize that an exchange of opening positions typically puts the negotiators on a path toward positional bargaining throughout the talks. However, this is by no means a necessary result of positional openings. Simply because positions have been laid out early on does not necessarily mean that either party is committed to pursuing positional-bargaining strategies for the remainder of the negotiation. Thus, if positional bargaining seems unlikely to be fruitful, a skillful negotiator is often able to move the talks from the positional method to an interest-based, problem-solving approach. As we will see, an important first step in this direction is to begin to ask questions that uncover the interests underlying the declared positions.

In any event, whichever approach to negotiation you prefer to adopt, understanding the differences in the two approaches ought to help negotiators to choose elements to fit their strategy and otherwise to negotiate effectively with their counterpart.

Notes

1. WINSTON CHURCHILL, THE SECOND WORLD WAR: THE GATHERING STORM, vol. 1, 210.
2. HOWARD RAIFFA, NEGOTIATION ANALYSIS 86, 191 (2002).
3. The words that are placed in bold italicized type on their first use in the text correspond to entries in the glossary.
4. ROBERT H. MNOOKIN, SCOTT R. PEPPET, & ANDREW S. TULUMELLO, BEYOND WINNING 128, 254 (2000).
5. I. WILLIAM ZARTMAN & MAUREEN BERMAN, THE PRACTICAL NEGOTIATOR ix (1982).
6. BRIGID STARKEY, MARK A. BOYER, & JONATHAN WILKENFELD, INTERNATIONAL NEGOTIATION IN A COMPLEX WORLD, 4th ed. 2 (2015).
7. HOWARD RAIFFA, THE ART AND SCIENCE OF NEGOTIATION 252 (1982).
8. Id. at 253.
9. ROGER FISHER, WILLIAM URY, & BRUCE PATTON, GETTING TO YES 4 et seq. (2d ed. 1991).
10. ROGER FISHER & DANIEL SHAPIRO, BEYOND REASON 68 (2005).
11. David A. Lax & James K. Sebenius, *Three Ethical Issues in Negotiation*, 2 NEGOTIATION J. 364 (1986).
12. Roger Fisher, *An Interview with Roger Fisher and William Ury*, 18 ACAD. OF MGMT. EXEC. 104 (2004).
13. JOHN KENNETH GALBRAITH, ECONOMICS, PEACE, AND LAUGHTER 50 (1971).
14. ROGER FISHER, INTERNATIONAL CONFLICT FOR BEGINNERS 95–97 (1969).
15. ZARTMAN & BERMAN, supra note 5, at 28.
16. JAMES C. FREUND, SMART NEGOTIATING 69 (1992).
17. ROGER FISHER & DANNY ERTEL, GETTING READY TO NEGOTIATE 5 (1995).
18. ZARTMAN & BERMAN, supra note 5, at 173.
19. HENRY KISSINGER, THE NECESSITY FOR CHOICE 205 (1961).
20. FISHER, supra note 12, at 99.
21. FISHER, URY, & PATTON, supra note 9, at 6.
22. RAIFFA, supra note 2, at 108.
23. Roger Fisher, *A Code of Negotiation Practices for Lawyers*, 1 NEGOTIATION J. 108 (1985).
24. Brian S. Mandell, *Unnecessary Toughness*, in NEGOTIATING ON BEHALF OF OTHERS 263–72 (Robert H. Mnookin & Lawrence E. Susskind eds., 1999).
25. Chris Provis, *Interests vs. Positions*, 12 NEGOTIATION J. 306 (1996).
26. FISHER, URY, & PATTON, supra note 9, at 44.
27. Jeffrey Z. Rubin, *Some Wise and Mistaken Assumptions About Negotiation*, 45 J. OF SOCIAL ISSUES 206 (1989).

28. ROGER FISHER & SCOTT BROWN, GETTING TOGETHER 142 (1988).

29. RAIFFA, supra note 7, at 33.

30. Roger Fisher and Wayne Davis, *Authority of an Agent*, in NEGOTIATING ON BEHALF OF OTHERS 74 (Lawrence E. Susskind & Robert H. Mnookin eds., 1999).

31. FISHER & BROWN, supra note 28, at 143.

32. DEBORAH M. KOLB & JUDITH WILLIAMS, THE SHADOW NEGOTIATION 208 (2000).

33. Roger Fisher, *Beyond YES*, 1 NEGOTIATION J. 68 (1985).

34. Catherine H. Tinsley, *Culture and Conflict*, in THE HANDBOOK OF NEGOTIATION AND CULTURE 197 (Michele J. Gelfand & Jeanne M. Brett eds., 2004).

Checkpoints

• In positional bargaining, after both sides make contrasting declarations of what it will take to reach an agreement, they look to narrow the gap through a series of compromises, as each negotiator tries to gain concessions from the other.

• In trying to pull the other side toward one's position, a positional negotiator wants to make the smallest possible concessions to the other side so as to arrive, ultimately, at the most advantageous resolution.

• In positional bargaining each negotiator is inclined to exaggerate the worth of what he or she has given up, while down-playing the concessions received, while each tries to deceive the other as to what it will actually settle for.

• The chief aim of the negotiators throughout this process is to stick as closely as possible to their opening stance and to move to their fallback positions reluctantly.

• Positional bargaining is a familiar approach that is perhaps best suited for dealing with a simple problem, one where the stakes are small, or one in which there is not likely to be any continuing relationship.

• Positional-bargaining tactics have the disadvantages of inviting reciprocal treatment and stifling creativity.

• Positional bargaining might be a problematic approach for negotiations divided into numerous issues, those with many parties, those in which long-term relations are quite important, or those where emotions are running high.

• Interest-based negotiation focuses on using interests — defined as what the negotiators want and need, what concerns and motivates them — as the building blocks toward a mutually beneficial agreement.

• Typically, positions can be satisfied in a limited number of ways, perhaps a single way; shifting to a focus on interests can significantly expand the number of resolutions that the parties might find beneficial.

Chapter 2

Pre-Negotiation: Arranging and Preparing for a Negotiation

Roadmap

- **Choosing to negotiate:** Are there good reasons to negotiate, do the advantages outweigh the disadvantages, and is a dispute or conflict ripe to be resolved?

- **Agreeing to negotiate:** What subjects will the parties negotiate, by what medium, and over what time period?

- **Negotiating on behalf of another:** Why do agents so often negotiate for principals, and what issues regarding parameters, instructions, and authority are likely to arise?

- **Preparing to negotiate well:** How does a negotiator best prepare before a negotiation?

- **Working with your own side:** Why does an organization confronting a complex negotiation so often assemble a negotiating team? What are the special challenges associated with team negotiations, and how should a team be selected and prepared?

- **Differentiating between internal and external negotiations:** What distinguishes an internal from an external negotiation, and what are the special difficulties associated with internal negotiations?

- **Organizing your preparation:** How does a negotiator organize pre-negotiation preparation to uncover useful facts, analyze the problem or opportunity, plan how to make points effectively, and think through the difficult issues of creating values and dividing items?

- **Identifying appropriate goals:** How should a negotiator set explicit goals and aim for good yet realistic outcomes, while avoiding common errors and accounting for such complexities as multiple goals and the need to prioritize among them?

The pre-negotiation phase starts when one or more parties consider negotiation as a possible option. It ends when formal negotiations begin or when the idea of negotiations is abandoned, at least for the moment. Though an exploratory prelude to the talks, pre-negotiation can be a highly significant part of many advanced negotiations.

A complex negotiation not only takes time, effort, and resources, it often involves accepting certain risks as well. Should the parties fail to reach agreement, they and their constituents may be disappointed or frustrated. Blame may be assessed. Opportunities may pass by. Conflicts and problems may be exacerbated. Pre-negotiation enables the different sides to identify any reservations they may have about negotiating and assess the chances for reaching a successful resolution. They can thus determine whether it is worthwhile to assume the risks and move forward with a negotiation.

If the parties do decide to negotiate, they must diagnose the situation and identify the matters to be negotiated. They also need to consider such logistical items as the place and time for the negotiation, and, perhaps, how expenses ought to be divided between the parties. During these initial interactions, relations between the negotiators or the parties may be initiated or renewed. A new relationship can be forged or a pre-existing one modified.

Some aspects of pre-negotiation involve the different sides starting to work with one another: deciding to negotiate and agreeing on various preliminary matters. Others involve each party getting itself ready to negotiate: learning about the situation, gaining some understanding of its counterpart, analyzing the substance of the problems and opportunities at hand, setting explicit and realistic goals, fashioning a strategy to try to reach them, and drawing up a preparation memorandum to assist in interactions at the table. All of these matters can affect the negotiating of substantive matters that follows.

A. Choosing to Negotiate

A first step is that the parties learn of one another's existence or consider some prior contact they have had. As they feel one another out about possible negotiations, thoughts begin to be traded about the particular set of circumstances the parties face.

Although either or both sides may be concerned about raising expectations too high, one or the other may allude to the possible benefits of a negotiation. When one party does not immediately see a real need to negotiate, the other might look for ways to demonstrate that the status quo is unappealing or problematic. Or, incentives might be introduced that would change the balance sheet in favor of negotiating. Indeed, parties occasionally find ways to raise the costs of standing pat.[1]

In short, whether the situation appears to be painful or hopeful, the parties need to become convinced that matters might improve if they negotiate or deteriorate if they fail to do so. An essential first step is get the different sides talking to one another. In this regard civil rights advocate Bernard LaFayette suggested approaching a reluctant potential counterpart and saying, "I know you don't want to negotiate or communicate, but if you were, what would you want to discuss?"[2]

American diplomat Harold Saunders once observed that pre-negotiation is all about "getting one's mind around the problem."[3] The essence of what is happening in these early informal exchanges is that the parties are creating and selecting among different ways to view the situation before them. In this regard note the possibility of doubling back: the parties might "get to the table, encounter serious obstacles, suspend negotiation, and return to pre-negotiation to consider other negotiating formats and options."[4]

Once each side recognizes that a useful negotiated agreement is possible, the next task is to *frame* the negotiation, that is, to determine what delineates this negotiation by identifying who the necessary parties and issues are.[5] What exactly ought to be negotiated, and what should be set aside to be dealt with later, if at all?

As the negotiators exchange thoughts on this, they may discuss what should be on the *agenda* for the substantive talks. Some issues are singled out to come center-stage under a spotlight of attention. Others might be bundled together or subordinated, and still others could be put off for another day. (The topic of agendas is explored in more detail in Chapter 3.)

As the parties begin to gather information and make sense of it, negotiators often think of things and uncover information that later proves to be quite significant when the negotiation proper begins. At the same time, within each side negotiators may be interacting with clients, team members, constituents, and stakeholders, gaining assent, overcoming possible obstacles, and working out *instructions* and strategy. For all of this activity, however, the costs of pre-negotiation tend to be relatively low, with parties free to withdraw if moving to formal negotiations comes to appear inauspicious.

1. The Concept of Ripeness

Particularly in dispute or conflict situations, negotiation theorists sometimes refer to issues of *ripeness*, that is, whether the moment has arrived when parties are really ready to try to seriously negotiate the issues before them toward some resolution. Ripeness connotes a certain urgency the parties feel to get a deal done. Note, however, that negotiations that occur undertaken at an earlier period may also be valuable in that they "may prevent a conflict from escalating and positions from hardening."[6]

Nevertheless, the analogy of fruit ripening on a tree until it is ready to be picked is often heard. On occasion, reference to it helps to generate momentum toward serious negotiations. The image is not perfect, however, since one or the other of the parties, or outside interested actors, can help to bring about a ripe moment. Indeed, the relationship between the parties can be what ripens as much as the issues themselves.[7]

If the circumstances do not seem ripe, then the parties may decide simply to manage the problem, perhaps awaiting a change in perspectives. Lines of communication can be kept open so that the parties are prepared to spring into action when the timing appears to be more auspicious.[8] Or, someone might work to bring about a ripe moment.

I. William Zartman analyzed ripeness by focusing attention on what he termed a *hurting stalemate*: that is, a conflict in which neither side is able to achieve its goals at acceptable levels of costs. Such a stalemate "can be a very fleeting opportunity, a moment to be seized lest it pass, or it can be of long duration, waiting to be noticed and acted upon ...."[9] In some cases an impending catastrophe could threaten to impose truly substantial costs, thus serving a purpose similar to a deadline.

Bear in mind, though, that not all ripe situations lead to negotiation.[10] Not infrequently, people respond to increasing pain or the threat of it by staying the course or, perhaps, redoubling their resistance to change.[11] In a conflict situation the different sides might consider carefully the consequences of failing to negotiate. One scholar envisioned the two parties walking to the edge of a "Lover's Leap," staring together into the abyss below, considering what might happen if no resolution were to emerge, and therefore resolving to negotiate to try to avoid impending disaster.[12]

A fresh look at the balance sheet of pros and cons might also bring on a ripe moment. One side may have been long content with the status quo or discouraged about the chances of altering it. However, if the parties perceive new opportunities, hitherto unexplored ways in which *interests* and objectives might be satisfied, or if one side or a third party persuades the other of such things, they may both conclude that more is to be gained than lost by negotiating.

B. Agreeing to Negotiate

Once the parties have decided to negotiate, *preliminary negotiations* focus on the logistics that must be worked out before the talks on substantive issues begin. What will the negotiation be about? How do the different sides frame the issues? When exactly do the parties plan to negotiate, and using what form—face-to-face talks, or by letter, fax, e-mail, or telephone? The issues to be negotiated, any time constraints, and the personalities involved might play into decisions about meeting in person versus conducting negotiations in phone calls or otherwise. The parties may raise these issues within each side and then with each other.

1. Where, When, and How?

People naturally want to arrange a negotiation so as to be reasonably comfortable during it. One threshold issue is who should host the negotiations? And, essentially, you can meet at your place, at the other side's location, or at some other site, a convenient place or a neutral one in some regard. Many complex negotiations will require more than one session, offering the opportunity of alternating locations.

Apart from saving the time and costs of traveling somewhere, negotiating in your own office might enable you to draw on particular resources such as your files or library or your secretary or assistant. On occasion, technical or technological requirements may be significant. A room of some particular dimensions might be advantageous, as might a private place nearby for a *caucus*. In a group negotiation one might anticipate needing a number of conference rooms for break-out sessions. These might be more readily available at one site than another.

In trying to maximize the chances for a successful outcome, a negotiator might thus see a particular venue as conducive to a negotiated resolution or he or she might want to avoid a place seen as inauspicious. For seasoned negotiators a cardinal factor is how best to promote the comfort of all in attendance. The effort is often aimed at minimizing tension and awkwardness, while treating people well and operating in an above-board, straightforward way.

One source further counseled: "Contrary to the accepted wisdom, it is sometimes advantageous to accept an offer to meet on the other side's turf. It may put them at ease, making them more open to your suggestions." The authors also noted another added benefit to being the visitors and not the hosts: "If necessary, it will be easier for you to walk out."[13]

Issues about when to negotiate also often arise in this preliminary stage. How long will it take the sides to prepare? Do the parties anticipate a single session or multiple negotiating rounds? Are there potential conflicts associated with this date or that one? Furthermore, one side might wish to begin the process of establishing productive working relations before the date of the substantive negotiation. Should opportunities be carved out ahead of time for the counterparts to talk or meet?

The organizers of one Cold War meeting between U.S. and Soviet officials chose to preface the talks with a New England lobster dinner: "We figured no one wearing a bib around the neck and trying to crack open lobster legs could remain aloof for long. Our hunch turned out to be correct — laughter and good natured humanity broke through."[14]

2. Avoiding a Fixation on Logistics

Highly successful negotiations can be carried out when held in quite different places and organized in quite different ways. Thus one does not want to get too bogged down in these issues. Certainly, one does not want to make the substantive problems more difficult to resolve by unnecessary initial conflict over logistics. Parties that argue too vigorously over preliminary matters are sometimes said to be fussing over "the shape of the table."

It is true that the way that seating is arranged might factor into a negotiator's strategy, bringing on a more collaborative or more adversarial feel. And, in diplomatic and some other discussions the configuration of the table could be tied to which parties are the principal negotiators and which are excluded or marginalized. Nevertheless, under most circumstances, it is best to move forward toward the substantive talks expeditiously, even if they are not being arranged exactly as you might wish.

However, should you yield to the other side on preliminary matters, you might remind your fellow negotiators that "in the interest of reaching an agreement" you have agreed to meet at the site or the time or in the way that they preferred.[15]

3. With Whom?

The nature of the issues at hand is one important factor in determining who should try to negotiate it. Who would do the most effective job of negotiating, and why? This is clearly a pre-negotiation question of paramount importance within each side, where the decision is normally settled. Occasionally, however, it may be possible to influence the other side's decision of whom they send to negotiate.

Those in the negotiation from the outset should also consider whether other parties ought to be invited to join in their talks as well. Will the right parties have their representatives at the table? Do others have key information or necessary expertise? "The greater the number of parties to a negotiation," it has been observed, "the more difficult it will be to reach any agreement at all. But only if the relevant parties and interests are included in the negotiations is the agreement reached likely to 'stick.' "[16]

Would including more parties be a positive step, enhancing the chance that a negotiated resolution will be reached that satisfies key interests, or might it prove to be a mistake, complicating or obstructing agreement? Since each additional negotiator "imposes costs: communication gets more difficult, and the task of managing the process gets harder," one authority suggests the rule of thumb: "invite the people you need and no more."[17] Note, too, that it may make sense to change the composition of the group after the negotiation commences and it becomes clear that particular parties are absent and needed or present and superfluous.[18]

C. Negotiating on Behalf of Another

Sometimes negotiations occur between the very individuals whose interests are at stake. A landlord negotiates with a tenant, a professor with a dean, one spouse with another. In these cases, the negotiators "speak for themselves and are free to make offers and reach agreements as they see fit."[19] In the advanced negotiations that are our special focus, however, the more common situation is that one person negotiates for another or for an organization—for instance, a business, government, or union.

Thus, when negotiations of any degree of complexity occur, *agents* are likely to be negotiating on behalf of *principals.* In the negotiation context an agent may be defined as a deputy authorized by a principal to act on his or her behalf by representing the principal's interests in negotiations with another. The principal in a negotiation is often thought of as the client. More specifically, the principal is the party who has directed and authorized the agent to act subject to his or her ultimate control and direction.

Here, you might think of an accountant (one type of agent) representing a taxpayer (a principal) before the government, or a workplace representative (an agent) trying to negotiate an agreement for a union (a principal) with an outside counsel (an agent) hired by the board of directors of a corporation (a principal). Two attorneys would be acting as agents as they negotiated a divorce settlement between a husband and wife, as would a prosecutor working out a plea-bargain agreement with the defense lawyer for an imprisoned drug trafficker, or an entertainment agent negotiating a contract for an actress.

1. Why Hire a Negotiator?

These days, in many walks of life, people routinely call on the services of others. They make use of expertise in hopes of gaining a better outcome more efficiently, while reducing the time and stress they have to personally devote to something. These relationships certainly permeate complex negotiations.

Here, a principal—occasionally an individual but more commonly a company, a government agency, a labor union, or some other entity—selects an agent to negotiate on its behalf. When the principal is an organization of some kind, those officials or employees concerned with the subject of the negotiation must work out various matters in *internal negotiations* before the agent can negotiate effectively for them. What are the organization's objectives and interests in the negotiation? These may be viewed differently by different individuals, departments, divisions, or authorities.

One negotiating for another often has the advantage of having a certain distance or detachment from the problem. A client may be so caught up in the details of the problem or the history of relations with the other side that it is much more difficult to see the situation from their counterpart's perspective, to work with them productively, and to reach sensible compromises.

You might hire an agent fearing your own emotional involvement might lead talks to turn testy or belligerent. Or, principles who want to remain on good terms with one another might let their agents wrangle over something like the provisions of a contract.

When the external negotiations commence, the principal looks to capitalize on the agent's knowledge, negotiation experience, and reputation. In various ways the agent's professional skills can help to achieve a strong negotiated resolution. Literary or sports agents, for instance, might draw on their own contacts among publishers or teams. An investment banker would bring special expertise to bear in negotiating an acquisition on behalf of a corporate client. A lawyer representing one party ought to have specialized knowledge as well as ready access to the attorney for the other side.

Years ago, one authority identified true legal craftsmanship in "practical, effective, persuasive, inventive skills for getting things done, any kind of thing in any field; in wisdom and judgment in selecting the things to get done; in skills for moving [people] into desired action ...; and then in skills for *regularizing* the results."[20]

2. Constraints on Agents

When an agent negotiates on behalf of a principal, two sets of discussions take place. Apart from the negotiation with the other side, the client and the negotiator should have an ongoing internal dialogue about what is happening and should happen in the negotiation. These are sometimes referred to as *back table negotiations.*

a. Negotiating Parameters

Someone negotiating on behalf of another will often have to work within particular *parameters*, that is, specified limits, constraints, or directions. These are often set by the principal or client, but they are sometimes related to the context of the negotiation, including the laws, rules, and policies within which it occurs. For instance, a collective-bargaining agreement within a particular industry might establish parameters for a labor negotiation.

One significant set of parameters involves the constituencies and stakeholders that a negotiator is trying to please. The perspectives of those people must often be taken into account as the negotiation progresses. Imagine, for example, two lawyers negotiating a labor dispute. One might have a union constituency to please, while the other would have to report to the company's top executives and its board of directors.

b. Negotiating Instructions

Specific "marching orders" issued to a negotiator are labeled *instructions*, and a set of instructions serves both to provide guidance and to restrict freedom of action. Negotiators frequently feel that they can best serve their client if they are given considerable latitude to work out an agreement and not be handcuffed by overly rigid instructions. A leading American diplomat counseled: "It is difficult for a negotiator to say specific sentences or words. I find it far better in negotiations to have a very clear outline of where we want to go and a very clear understanding of the issues."[21]

More general instructions are also sometimes taken as evidence of the principal's confidence, a tangible demonstration of the principal's trust in the agent. What can be of great importance to an agent and to his or her counterpart is how much "clout" the negotiator has with the client. This does not necessarily mean the authority to make binding commitments, but instead "the ability of negotiators to persuade their principals — their bureaucracies, governments, or corporate organizations — to accept deals made at the negotiating table."[22]

A recurring problem is that instructions tend to focus in single-minded fashion on the commitments that might be made at the end of the negotiation. Instructions oriented toward positional bargaining often lay out what a negotiator's initial demand should be, what concessions might then be made, and what sets of resolutions the negotiator could ultimately accept. Instructions for one using an interest-based negotiation approach, however, ought to focus instead on matters like interests, including their priority and possible trade-offs, criteria of fairness, alternatives to a negotiated agreement, and creative options. A detailed discussion of what commitments ought to be made should really be the final step in the negotiating process, not the initial one.[23]

c. Negotiating Authority

One central question in creating negotiating instructions involves the negotiator's *authority*, and here three core issues often come to the fore.[24] First, what is the negotiation about? A negotiator may be authorized to discuss certain subjects and not others. Second, how freely can the negotiator pursue different aspects of the negotiation? What matters are open to discussion with the other side, and what matters are to be kept on a confidential basis between the party and its agent? The third matter of authority involves the issue of to what the negotiator is empowered to agree for his or her principal. Can the negotiator commit on behalf of the principal or must all substantive resolutions be taken back to the principal for final approval?

d. Restrictions versus Flexibility

The overarching issue regarding instructions and authority involves how much flexibility the principal wants to permit the negotiator. When might it be best to tightly restrict one's agent, and when more appropriate to give plenty of room to work creatively with the other side?

The type of problem or opportunity to be negotiated ought to be carefully considered as well. On the one hand, a principal might grant an agent broad authority when a crisis makes time of the essence or when the stakes being negotiated are not extraordinarily high. If the principal and agent are very familiar with each other or the agent is both an expert negotiator and very knowledgeable about the subject-matter, some principals would incline toward granting extensive authority.

On the other hand, if the negotiator has not worked extensively with the client or is inexperienced — either a professional at the outset of his or her career or one whose knowledge of the particular subjects of the negotiation is limited — the principal might want to restrict the agent's authority. Would any negotiated resolution be likely to be a one-time affair or might it set a lasting precedent? Moreover, if the agent has interests different from the principal's, or if the negotiator does not have clear incentives to ensure that the principal's interests will be optimally served, less authority might be called for.

If providing too much leeway troubles the client, he or she might be able to attend the negotiation and, hence, be present to add thoughts on the spot. Or, the negotiator could simply be instructed to bring back any potential agreement for consultations before finalizing it. The agent might work with the other side to create a package that both could recommend to their clients.

Note, in complex negotiations, even when a negotiator has the authority to close a deal, it will often be more sensible not to do so. Certain terms in the agreement might give the negotiator pause, particularly when the deal involves a potential resolution that is creative, or unusual, in some respect. He or she might be well-advised to return to the client for final input before any binding decision is made.

3. Advising a Client on Negotiation Matters

On occasion, a principal simply dictates negotiating parameters to an agent. For instance, a senior partner or a government department might provide a lawyer or official with a set of instructions, detailed orders laying out objectives and strategy. A seasoned negotiator bears in mind, however, that instructions can often be revised. Indeed, one British ambassador quipped that his job was all about "helping my opposite number get new instructions."[25]

a. An Interactive Process

Advising a client is best conceived as an interactive process. And, frequently, a good deal of give-and-take occurs between the principal and agent over instructions, authority, and parameters. Ideally, the client solicits the negotiator's counsel. The two then think together through the most important dimensions of the negotiating problem and discuss how best to proceed. And, if the client overlooks the agent's assistance here, the negotiator ought to suggest having such a discussion.

For the interactions to produce sound counsel, however, the negotiator must know and understand the client—its perspectives, interests, and decision-making processes, and any relevant history concerning the problem or opportunity at hand.[26]

Although the principal should be the one who ultimately decides on the proper course of action, that decision might well hinge on joint analysis. The negotiator should try to ensure that the client is making an informed choice and understands the likely risks, benefits, and other consequences of different possible negotiating approaches.

Note, however, that the counseling process might proceed rather differently in one scenario than another. An attorney expert in family law, advising a client undergoing a first divorce, would have a different challenge than a labor attorney, trying to inject his or her own expertise while formulating a consensus among different coalitions within a union that regularly participates in the collective-bargaining process. Whatever the topic, however, before the negotiation the client and negotiator should analyze matters together.

b. What Is the Question at Issue?

Attorney James Freund suggested that an agent should become involved in a principal's decision making in different ways with respect to three categories of items. First, some matters fall right within the agent's expertise. For example, a sports agent ought to be expert in performance incentive bonuses. Here, he or she should be assertive in offering advice. Second, other matters fall within the principal's expertise, for instance, a business judgment as to what price ought to be paid in acquiring a smaller company. Here, the negotiator should defer to the client or to experts such as investment bankers or management consultants. Finally, with respect to many issues both principal and agent will have significant knowledge. And, here, the principal, who ought to make the final decisions, can determine how much to encourage or elicit the agent's counsel.[27]

c. The Interests/Positions Distinction

It is often particularly useful, as instructions are drawn up, to bear in mind the distinction between *positions* and *interests* elucidated further in Chapter 4. A principal may be inclined to formulate a position: "a statement of what the negotiator will demand or the minimum that he or she has authority to accept."[28] "Focusing on interests," it has been observed, "requires richer discussions between principals and agents than commonly occur."[29]

A question such as "What exactly do you see as in your best interests?" invites principal and agent to discuss how best to understand the principal's interests. One of the most important functions of an agent may thus involve thinking through the problem with the representatives of the principal, raising questions, offering opinions, and, perhaps, helping the representatives to re-calibrate their understanding of their interests.

4. Midstream Reporting

At times, principals are present while an agent negotiates. More frequently, however, the negotiators simply report back to their clients, to keep them apprised of what has occurred or to try to gain their assent to an agreement. In order to make informed ultimate decisions about taking a deal or rejecting it, principals ought to be kept abreast of the progress of negotiations.

Principals may not understand how important this midstream reporting can be, or they may be distracted by other matters. However, savvy clients require that their negotiating agents report back to them regularly and in detail.[30] The negotiator should review what has been learned of the other side's interests and its **walk-away alternatives,** as well as any **creative options** or possible **neutral standards** or **objective criteria** that have been raised. (These concepts are explored in detail in chapters 5 and 6.) If a template for an agreement has been created, this should certainly be reviewed. And, a thorough midstream report should include the agent's expectations regarding the path toward completing the negotiation. (A number of interesting ethical issues can arise in the agent-principal relationship, and Chapter 10 considers these further.)

D. Preparing to Negotiate Well

In his memoirs noted American lawyer and statesman James Baker related his father's advice concerning what he called "the 5 Ps": "Prior preparation prevents poor performance."[31] The unfortunate truth is that too many negotiators are too persuaded of their own negotiation skills and too ready to "wing it" in talks with the other side without adequate preparation.

Many people do not spend nearly enough time or put nearly enough thought into getting themselves ready to negotiate well. They neglect to learn key facts, and they fail to think clearly about their goals and strategy. Far too often, their thinking about fundamental aspects of an upcoming negotiation has been rushed or scattered or altogether absent.

Some neglect to alter their preparation to take into account the characteristics of their fellow negotiators or even the particular circumstances before them. Others have no systematic method of negotiation preparation. They might simply think over a situation quickly and launch in by picking up the telephone, sending an e-mail, or walking into a meeting. They may never have given much thought to distinguishing strong from weak preparation.

Unprepared negotiators fail to resolve many issues that might be brought to a positive conclusion. One scholar observed that when preparation is shorted: "[N]egotiations often collapse, drag on interminably, or leave unclaimed potential gains on the table ..."[32]

To negotiate as effectively as possible, one must get ready carefully and thoughtfully. "Purposeful preparation," has been called, "a launching pad for successful negotiation."[33] Good preparation maximizes one's effectiveness and minimizes the chances of being caught unawares. It puts a negotiator in a position to think clearly and creatively about the problems or opportunities posed so as to negotiate the optimal agreement.

1. A Preparation Period

Preparing well is a deliberate process. However, some very good and quite highly compensated attorneys do not spend even a modest fraction of the hours that they would prepare for a court appearance, preparing to negotiate. After noting, "[w]hen it comes to preparation, many people throw up their hands and say, 'But I can't afford the *time* to prepare,'" William Ury countered, "The truth is that you can't afford *not* to prepare. Take the time even if means taking time out of the actual negotiation itself. Negotiations would be a lot more effective if people spent more of their limited time preparing and less in actual meetings."[34]

One difficulty associated with becoming well-informed about the subject of an upcoming negotiation is that you usually have to uncover "a great deal of unnecessary information about the subject ... in order to gather a few highly relevant facts. The more one knows about the history, geography, economics, and scientific background of a problem, as well as its legal, social, and political implications, the more likely it is that one can invent creative solutions."[35]

Some of the information dug out in pre-negotiation preparation may be faulty, and it is virtually always incomplete. Consequently, a significant part of most complex negotiations will involve negotiators testing the facts with which they came to the table while trying to ferret out more of the information that is missing.

2. Benefits of Assembling a Negotiating Team

An organization confronting an important negotiation often decides to assemble a negotiating team to work together on its behalf. Although it costs time and money to involve multiple negotiators, it may be thought necessary to draw on different fields of expertise. In particular, having technical expertise that is immediately available may be quite useful. Here, for instance, you might tell the other side: "We'll bring along one of our engineers." Your counterparts will likely reciprocate, bringing along their own technical expertise, and you both may be in much better shape to handle certain issues.

A complex negotiation is likely to encompass a wealth of distinct issues, and particular team members may be more comfortable or more effective negotiating one aspect of the problem than another. Colleagues from within an organization may be able to provide each other with support and analysis from different perspectives. Consequently, the teammates selected ought not be too similar. Instead of a team of clones, a diversity of perspectives is usually preferable.[36] One negotiator may have a relevant specialized background; another may be adept at working with financial matters. One may have relevant cultural knowledge; another may have the interpersonal skills needed to set a positive tone and develop a strong working relationship.

But, you also want to steer clear of internal gridlock, where the differences among the teammates cannot be reconciled. An effective negotiating team presents a united front and communicates well together. One partner can support the other when he or she falters, overlooks something, misstates a point, or loses the thread of the discussions. While one person talks, a teammate can think creatively, record what is going on, check the agenda and plan what ought to happen next, or analyze some aspect of the way the negotiation has been proceeding.

Having two or more minds at work on a negotiating problem may be advisable for other reasons as well. A group of negotiators might do a better job of *brainstorming*, generating creative options, or locating appropriate standards or criteria. It may be considerably more difficult to overwhelm a team with data, or stress or intimidate its members, than might be the case with a single negotiator. And, teammates with diverse backgrounds and perspectives are likely to focus on distinct aspects of the negotiation. How precisely they recall particular points will vary, something that may be important when proposals are being formulated in the closing stage of a deal.

Alternatively, different constituencies within an organization may be especially concerned with the results of the negotiation. Hence, including their representatives may be necessary to gain an agreement. One might think, for instance, of an inter-agency group including representatives from the White House, the Department of State, the Justice Department, Treasury, and so on. Or, consider a labor union that selects representatives from different of its groups in order to increase the likelihood that the membership as a whole will ratify any agreement that emerges from the negotiations.[37]

3. Preparing the Team

Good preparation is especially important when negotiating with teammates. Particularly in a complex or fast-paced negotiation, the members of your team ought to strive to think in unison about the substance of what is happening at the negotiating table.

Some team members may be concerned with how to restrain a hardliner on their side who might say things that ruin the chance for any agreement.

Others might be worried about how to stiffen someone who might yield more in distributive bargaining than is necessary to reach a deal. Depending on the composition of the team and the hierarchy of its members, one might want to agree on internal ground rules, "such as 'no offers will be accepted at the table' or 'every member has veto power.'"[38]

Preparing a team is a task that is often rushed, but should not be. It takes time to talk through key aspects of the problem together, identify and, if possible, hammer out differences of opinion, and compare one another's estimates of the other side's goals, interests, and walk-away alternatives. How does each person view the problem or opportunity and what are their thoughts on the best strategy to use?

Negotiating partners should certainly enter the talks having already jointly considered purposes, goals, and strategy. Box 2.1, laying out team preparation questions, suggests that considerable preparation time will be needed to consider how best to negotiate effectively as a team.

Box 2.1 — Team Preparation Questions

The following questions are well worth careful consideration.

- How are you are going to organize yourselves to be as productive and efficient as possible?

- Is there a logical division of tasks?

- Is one of the negotiating partners expert about certain matters, and might it be best to have that person take special responsibility for taking the lead when that subject-matter arises?

- How can the teammates present a united front, and what specific steps might be taken to support one another?

- Are there topics to be avoided or circumvented, and how might that best be accomplished?

- In short, how can the team increase the chances that its members supplement and complement each other rather than work at cross-purposes?

- How might partners signal back and forth about when to caucus and confer privately with one another?

- What other matters might be important as you try to coordinate your efforts and build an effective team?

Another point worthy of particular discussion involves what issues or subjects your side might want to bypass. If prior to the external negotiation you have not thought this through together, one team member may be carefully circumventing a topic, while the other stumbles into a discussion that his or her partner wanted avoided altogether. Identify those topics or points your side would prefer not to speak about, or dwell on, and figure out effective ways to skirt them as gracefully as possible. Then, if it turns out that you must deal with those issues to some extent, figure out ahead of time, with joint thought and discussion, which negotiator is going to take the lead in dealing with them and how he or she plans to do so.

4. Difficulties of Team Negotiations

Although assembling a group to work together on one side of a negotiation may be quite advantageous, team dynamics raise real challenges as well. Talks are often slowed since many of those at the negotiating table may feel the need to speak up, offer their views, and make their presences felt. Active participation makes them feel comfortable and justifies their presence, but it may very well elongate the negotiating process.

Multiple people are also very likely to bring along different perspectives and even diverse goals. Their strategic views as to how best to proceed may vary as well. This is especially the case since the members of a negotiating team are typically drawn from different parts of an organization so as to draw on their special expertise or elicit input from particular divisions. They may even be operating under distinct sets of instructions from their superiors or colleagues.

To function effectively vis-à-vis the other side, the various teammates need to coordinate their efforts and, wherever possible, present a unified front. Sometimes, however, this can bring on an intolerance for dissenters or those with perspectives not shared by the majority of the group.[39] Hence, teams face real challenges in capitalizing on their strengths and minimizing their weaknesses.

5. Differentiating Between Internal and External Negotiations

In many scenarios, then, before businesses, governments, unions, or other organizations undertake *external negotiations* with outside counterparts, people first negotiate within their own side. These *internal negotiations* aim to coordinate the team, especially to hash out the differing perceptions of interests, objectives, and strategies that the different team members bring to the negotiation. They start prior to the external negotiation and continue during it.

Although often vitally needed, these internal negotiations can also complicate matters. Indeed, typical group negotiations have been said to "require three agreements—one across the table and one on each side of the table."[40]

Internal and external negotiations are best thought of as separate spheres of negotiation with somewhat different sets of aims and concerns. The challenge of conducting effective internal negotiations with your colleagues differs in important respects from the challenge of negotiating externally, with your counterparts. Negotiations with insiders and with outsiders should be closely linked, each interacting with the other. For example, matters learned in the external negotiation ought to be brought back into internal discussions to enlighten those making decisions within the organization.

6. Common Problems of Internal Negotiations

The fact that the negotiators all belong to one organization suggests that they may be more animated by a spirit of compromise. Moreover, a hierarchy within the organization may ultimately be able to determine disputes among them. However, internal perspectives can differ markedly. People or factions within an organization often have conflicting visions, and with their distinct organizational responsibilities, they may perceive quite different interests.

Beyond this, both individuals and divisions or departments may feel intra-organizational competition and be inclined to jealously guard their turf. Indeed, those within an organization, busily pursuing the development of their own careers, may be especially inclined to exaggerate or misrepresent their interests for strategic purposes related to internal power struggles.

Arriving at a consensus on complex negotiation issues, one acceptable to multiple factions and useful to the negotiator, seldom occurs without real time, thought, and effort devoted to it. Among the common problems, although the organization's external negotiator should be included in and participate in the internal negotiations, he or she may not, in point of fact, be sufficiently involved. Indeed, internal negotiations can sometimes be even more bitterly divisive than external ones. Consensus, if possible at all, may depend on internal deals, and *side payments* of various sorts may have to be made to bring along those who would otherwise be disgruntled.

A different issue arises when many people are consulted within a sizeable entity—a branch of a government or a large corporation perhaps. When a number of them add to the directions to be given to an external negotiator, their input can lack coherence. Particular directives might work at cross-purposes. A key challenge here is to gain the benefits that could accrue when many people join to think through how a negotiation might best proceed but do so in a way that is strategically sensible and does not impose rigidity and unduly curtail a negotiator's flexibility.

In particular, one does not want the negotiator to be bound by so many and so strict instructions that it is difficult to work creatively and flexibly with the other side. A dilemma that sometimes arises in these internal negotiations might be phrased as follows: "If a representative does not push for internal consensus, she will have more flexibility in negotiations but more internal disagreement around a proposed settlement. If the representative pushes for strong internal consensus, she will have less flexibility in bargaining but more internal agreement about a proposed settlement."[41]

Eventually, negotiating counterparts from the other side may look to take advantage of divisions or conflicting views. A negotiator might want to caucus with, or simply direct comments and arguments toward, the fellow negotiator who appears most sympathetic to the views about to be expressed. And, if the differences between the members of a negotiating team are never reconciled in an internal negotiation, then that party may be vulnerable to divide-and-conquer tactics during the external negotiation.

E. Organizing Your Preparation

Effective negotiators who put time and thought into getting ready to negotiate may well differ on the exact steps that they take. However, certain fundamental matters ought to be a part of everyone's preparation for an important negotiation.

1. Uncovering Useful Information

Judge Learned Hand once referred to a good litigator as a lawyer with a "bathtub mind." By that he meant that a skillful lawyer preparing to go to trial would fill up his or her mind with all of the relevant facts and law regarding the case, only later to drain and refill it with the facts and law regarding the next case.[42]

Similarly, before an important negotiation begins, a seasoned negotiator tries to grasp all he or she can regarding the situation to be negotiated. Negotiators should be asking themselves: "What key points, what missing information, what particular details ought I to try to learn about, anticipating that they might come in handy during the upcoming talks?" Internet searches, library research, public records, and conversations with knowledgeable individuals can all reveal valuable information about what is really driving other parties: what they have done in the past, what they hope to do in the future, what they seem most concerned about.

a. Data on Opposing Party

Effective negotiation preparation involves trying to gain a thorough understanding of the circumstances surrounding the subject of the talks. The negotiator, the client, or an outside consulting firm could look to uncover data that might illuminate some aspect of an upcoming negotiation.

To take one example, imagine a senior professor considering a lateral employment move from one university to another. Public institutions such as universities that receive state funding periodically publish the salary figures of their faculty. Discovering what other professors in the university are earning would be one example of useful empirical data to collect during pre-negotiation preparation.

A publicly traded company will have available annual reports with considerable information that can reveal details of what the business has been doing. One might find hints as to what the company might be looking for in a future agreement and why. In addition, records issued by local, state, and federal agencies might help a negotiator to discover a wealth of information relevant to different negotiations. For example, in an upcoming real estate negotiation critically important data might include the sale of comparable houses, or farmland, or industrial sites. Just as a potential car buyer is interested in gaining accurate data on what an automobile dealer paid for a particular vehicle model, so negotiators in other contexts should be alert to the information provided by consumer organizations and other repositories of relevant information.

b. Characteristics of Negotiating Counterpart

Another dimension of preparing to negotiate effectively involves learning something about one's counterparts at the table: their mind sets and personalities, their favored strategies, and the cultural influences that might affect their behavior. Here, it is well worth keeping in mind William Ury's assertion that "The single most important skill in negotiation is the ability to put yourself in the other side's shoes. If you are trying to change their thinking, you need to begin by understanding what their thinking is."[43]

A negotiator might see if it is possible to find someone acquainted with the other side, perhaps even one who has negotiated with the same counterparts in the past. This can prove to be enlightening and well worth time in preparation. For instance, where people from different cultures negotiate, considering whether and how cross-cultural sensitivities or influences might come into play can be a critically important part of pre-negotiation preparation. Should you find someone who knows your likely counterpart, you might pose some open-ended questions, such as: "If you had to negotiate with that person again, what would you do differently? What is your best advice for me?"

Box 2.2 lays out other, more specific questions to bear in mind regarding one's counterpart.

Box 2.2 — Relevant Questions about One's Counterpart

The following questions, to be taken up in pre-negotiation preparation, may help a negotiator to gain a better sense for the mind set, personality, and likely strategy of a counterpart.

- Why do your counterparts want to negotiate with you, and what seems likely to most concern or motivate them?

- How might your counterpart's personality best be characterized? How might he or she be most readily persuaded?

- What key features of their background are worth noting — education, professional experience, etc.? What is their position, and how does it relate to the upcoming negotiation?

- How might one build rapport and a positive working relationship with them? Are there particular topics or points that it might be tactful to skirt or avoid in negotiating with them?

- What is their reputation as a negotiator — deceptive or a straight shooter? Would a well-prepared negotiator be alert for any particular moves?

- How is your counterpart likely to see the substance of the negotiation? If you were confronting the situation as they are, how would you view the issues to be negotiated?

- What intangible factors may be driving your fellow negotiator or the party he or she represents? For instance, what does the other side consider its turf? What might appeal to their egos? What might enhance their reputations?

- What methods of negotiation, strategies, and tactics has the other side favored in prior negotiations?

- After past negotiations has this negotiator worked faithfully to follow through on commitments?

2. Analyzing the Problem or Opportunity

If you dedicate one part of pre-negotiation preparation to gathering relevant facts about the other side, you also need to spend some time analyzing the contours of the negotiation problem before you. You might start with a brief factual summary. If someone who knew nothing of what was going on needed to be brought up to speed in short order, what points would you particularly emphasize? Just as a litigator might prepare a statement of facts for a judge or jury, so a negotiator might marshal key points as well.

From that foundation a skillful negotiator might move on to analyze in detail the negotiating problem or opportunity confronting the parties.

- What is likely to be the most problematic aspect of this negotiation?
- What appear to be the most difficult issues to resolve?
- Do you anticipate inter-personal conflicts?
- How about issues involving the process of negotiating, such as contending with multiple parties at the table or with complications of a technical, financial, or scientific variety?

Then, to help to bring together the analysis, a negotiator could aim to encapsulate in a single sentence or a paragraph or so, the key negotiating challenge or challenges faced in these particular circumstances.

3. Planning to Make Points Effectively

Another significant aspect of pre-negotiation preparation brings a negotiator to consider how best to advance the most important points that he or she would like to make. The issues to be laid out, the arguments one wants to make, the efforts to influence the other side and affect its thinking in positive ways, all of these can be approached more or less effectively, and they can have a real impact on the negotiation.

Consider an example involving diplomacy. During World War II, when the Manhattan Project concluded with the test explosion of an atomic bomb, President Harry Truman believed that he now had considerable leverage over America's Soviet ally. Truman figured he could now get perhaps 85 percent of what he wanted from Soviet leader Josef Stalin.[44] Truman's diplomatic approach, however, was simply to find a moment at the Potsdam Conference to mention casually to Stalin that the United States now had a very big bomb. The Soviet leader, whose intelligence service was already keeping him apprised of the project's progress, acted unimpressed, and this first effort at nuclear diplomacy ended up producing few tangible effects. In his memoirs Truman nowhere mentions any thought about how to approach Stalin most effectively and put the new information he had gained to best advantage.

In a complex negotiation advance planning may be essential to present one's points most effectively. Would charts, graphs, or other visual aids help to clarify a particular point? Sometimes, exhibits or diagrams will help the parties to visualize some aspect of a problem. A short PowerPoint presentation clarifying some aspect of the situation might be in order.

The items one might need or want during the negotiation merit some thought as well, and pre-negotiation preparation is the time to get oneself organized to negotiate well. There may be papers or documents that ought to be brought along. Or, perhaps, the negotiator will simply need to remember such prosaic, though perhaps quite essential, items as a watch, calculator, yellow pad, or flip chart.

a. Thinking through Distribution Issues

Less experienced negotiators are often especially poorly prepared to talk about money and other items that will need to be divided, allotted, or allocated between the parties. Frequently, negotiators whose preparation is lacking prefer to work on building productive relations and talking about other matters that they perceive to be less contentious. Hence, they put off or dance around those key issues regarding numbers. In doing so, however, they frequently are—and appear to their fellow negotiators to be—nervous, apprehensive, and ill-at-ease about a central matter to be negotiated. They did not arrive at the negotiating table ready, at the appropriate moment, to present their views convincingly as to how items ought to be distributed among the parties.

Sometimes, neither party wants to "walk through the door" here; each is, in effect, saying "After you, after you." The justification that negotiators often point to in such circumstances is that they really wanted the other party to move first so that they could counter the initial proposal. After all, they reason, "what if the other side's proposal would have been even better than what I had in mind?" Under particular circumstances, this certainly might be a sound tactic, an important part of a thoughtful strategy, but negotiators should make a conscious decision to take that approach, and not slump to it because they are really not very well-prepared.

Thus, in pre-negotiation preparation, if one important issue involves the distribution of items between the sides, one might think about what would be a fair and compelling approach to making such a division? (In Chapter 5 we will consider the use of objective criteria to assist negotiators in resolving such distributive matters.) What proposals spring to mind that both sides might support? Is there some neutral standard that might narrow the field of possibilities and perhaps lead on to a resolution?

b. Considering the Creation of Value

Alongside a focus on distribution issues, pre-negotiation preparation is also a time to consider how "the pie might be expanded." That is, how might the parties draw on their different talents and resources to come up with something new, to create value that might make the ultimate negotiated resolution much more beneficial to them? This is a topic that we will also explore in Chapter 5. For now, realize that pre-negotiation preparation ought also include some time to think creatively about the situation and what interesting or innovative options might be invented. Roger Fisher used to speak of the importance of an "elegant option" to bring the parties in a complex negotiation to an agreement. Although these ideas sometimes spring from brainstorming and other dynamic interactions of negotiators during the talks, the seeds of creative thinking are often laid during careful preliminary preparation.

F. Identifying Appropriate Goals

In the pre-negotiation phase each side ought to think carefully about just what it wants—its substantive *goals*—and why exactly it hopes to achieve them. A key aspect of setting goals involves imagining a better future. Forcing oneself to set out objectives brings a negotiator to think carefully about the possibilities for cooperation, about what is and is not realistic, and about how the parties might work together in innovative or imaginative ways to benefit each other.

1. Why Set Explicit Goals?

Having laid out ambitious yet realistic goals is enormously helpful. Articulating objectives serves to motivate, to center one's thinking and concentrate one's energy. In particular, thoughtfully setting goals is the first step toward creating a strategy, a comprehensive plan to try to achieve those objectives, one that might call on an array of ideas from the various chapters in this book.

British diplomat Lord Caradon was once asked what was the most valuable lesson he had learned in his years in public service. Caradon recounted that early in his career, while working in the Middle East, he and his superior had to visit numerous communities to contend with an array of requests and disputes. They got in the habit of pulling their jeep over to the side of the road before entering any village so that they could get out and discuss what the two wanted to accomplish before they left. Then, afterwards, they would again stop the jeep by the roadside to think through whether they had achieved what they had set out to do.[45]

Certainly, one requirement for acting effectively in a negotiation is to have clear and specific purposes in mind. Identifying explicit objectives should be at the top of every negotiator's pre-negotiation planning list. Skillful negotiators think precisely about their aspirations. Concentrated thought about goals organizes a negotiator's thinking and is a natural starting place for moving on to assemble an effective strategy.

This is important to grasp since a common error for negotiators is to pass too lightly over the issue of what exactly they are trying to accomplish. Too often, they intend, simply, to communicate about a subject to see what can be agreed to. And yet, meeting with the other side with the idea of achieving any sensible available agreement is too vague and indefinite an objective to offer much guidance. If we have not specified what we might like the other side to do, the job of persuading or influencing them will lack focus.

As part of their pre-negotiation deliberations about goals, experienced negotiators give some thought to the form of the agreement they are envisioning, given the circumstances that they face. At one end of the spectrum the parties might be looking to resolve all of the outstanding issues that they confront in a binding legal document such as a contract or treaty. At the other pole, they might simply be interested in hearing what each other has to say and agreeing to meet again, if warranted.

In between those poles lie a variety of other possible outcomes, characterized by different scopes and different forms. One might fashion a more limited written agreement whose terms covered only particular matters. Or, the parties might reach a handshake deal, draft a letter of intent or memorandum of understanding (MOU), or fashion a joint recommendation to take back to their principals. The cardinal point here is that alongside substantive goals regarding the issues, negotiators should also think about the form or type of outcome being pursued.

2. What Goals Should Be Set?

Good pre-negotiation preparation should involve challenging and thought-provoking questions about objectives.

- Under these circumstances, what exactly would constitute a good and realistic outcome?

- What is the best you could hope to achieve with a real possibility of getting it?
- What is nothing but wishful thinking?

Still, it is important to aim high. You are unlikely to gain more in a negotiation than you entered it trying to obtain. Multiple studies have demonstrated that negotiators who aspire to challenging goals tend to reach better results.[46] Your task as a negotiator is thus to set objectives that will make you happy if you fulfill them but that are possible to attain. If you cannot reach or nearly reach your goals, your job is to try to negotiate an agreement that exceeds your best walk-away alternative so that your side can at least leave the negotiation in better shape than before.

Occasionally, when facing a bleak situation, the only realistic goals may be rather modest ones. But, ordinarily, a party that meets its objectives should be quite satisfied. Furthermore, while stretching to attain goals, a negotiator should aim to reach the best deal possible under the circumstances. The key error to avoid — one that formulating challenging goals nicely counteracts — is to settle for a quick compromise on terms that both negotiators can countenance but about which your side, at least, remains unenthusiastic.

3. Complexities in Setting Goals

Various factors can complicate the effort to set ambitious yet realistic objectives. Let us consider some of them.

a. Goals That Set Precedents

In thinking about their goals, negotiators ought to consider whether the results of the negotiation might set a *precedent*. If so, what precedent does the negotiator want to set, and why? By precedent I mean that the outcome has follow-up repercussions since people may view it as an example of how something ought to be done or as a justification for future actions. For example, the way that an agreement between a union and a company deals with particular issues might then set a precedent that extends beyond a single factory or plant, perhaps even affecting the industry as a whole.

b. Converging and Conflicting Goals

Realize, too, that one's goals may converge with those of one's fellow negotiator, or conflict with them, or some may conflict and others converge. Should common objectives become apparent, this is well worth emphasizing to one another since working on those goals is likely to help the parties to build momentum toward a mutually beneficial resolution. Indeed, whenever one feels a need to regain forward progress, it may be useful to return to matters on which the different sides see eye to eye. Your common ground can be the base from which you march off to traverse more divisive terrain.

Still, at times, a party has a goal that involves preventing its counterpart from obtaining something. Consider a simple example. A parent might negotiate with a teenager over upcoming summer activities, looking to gain an agreement that he or she will not be attending a concert that has in the past been rowdy. This variety of objective is sometimes referred to as an *interdiction goal*, that is, one party's objective of having its counterpart *not* gain or do something.

c. Multiple Goals

Skillful negotiators in a complex negotiation ordinarily set multiple goals. In this regard goals that at first glance might seem self-evident may appear simplistic or short-sighted with additional thought and discussion. Where a party once perceived a single goal, with additional thought other important objectives become apparent.

For example, on one level a lawyer negotiating a settlement with another will want to gain the largest sum or give up the least amount of money for the client. Similarly, a business ordinarily engages in a deal with another to maximize its profits by selling high or buying low. However, over the long term restoring or establishing a positive working relationship could dwarf the importance of the exact dollar figure agreed on.

In addition, buyers need to focus not only on how much they are spending, but on what exactly they are getting for their money. One's delight in gaining a good price will quickly sour if the quality of the items gained is shoddy. But, satisfaction over a decent price for items of fair quality might turn into real enthusiasm for the deal if the agreement also included a strong warranty or free or discounted service for a period of years.

Sellers must consider not only the magnitude of immediate profits, but how the agreement positions them for future earnings. Profits can be assessed in the short term or over many years, and while certain dealings might bring in considerable income at once, a different agreement might lead to a relationship that would maximize profits in years ahead. Indeed, a single-minded focus on gaining the most profits possible immediately might actually jeopardize opportunities for gain over the long term. Hence, one dimension of setting goals involves striking a sensible balance between current and future aspirations.

Or, imagine discussions over a possible services contract, perhaps a consulting business expert in crisis management negotiating with a large company facing a potential public relations disaster. Securing the contract would be one goal. Receiving the highest possible compensation for the work to be done would be another. Having the opportunity to perform well for a major corporation, enhancing opportunities for return business, would amount to a third. Developing one's reputation within the business community might stand as another. Gaining market share relative to competitors would be quite attractive, too.

d. Prioritizing Among and Assessing Goals

What further complicates the process of thinking about goals is that in a negotiation of some sophistication not only will the parties be likely to have identified multiple objectives, but some will be more and others less significant. The negotiation might be a success if some goals were attained, even if others were not.

Some negotiators prepare by listing their goals in a rank order. Others assign numerical values to help them to quantify what is most and least important. Still others cluster their objectives in terms of low, medium, and high importance. Decisions that may eventually have to be made about tradeoffs are far easier if one has carefully prioritized. In closing a deal, a negotiator will appreciate having thought through in advance whether trading off satisfying a high-priority goal for several modest ones would be worthwhile or not.

Note, however, that determining which goals are most and least important may depend in part on where, in a range of possible outcomes, that particular issue would be resolved. One scholar illustrated that point by observing of negotiating an employment contract: "If we are talking about a range of possible salaries that is very small and a range of vacation days that is very large, then the issue of vacation days may be more important than the issue of salary."[47] In any event, thinking through the priority of one's goals and how they might relate to one another leaves negotiators better situated to negotiate effectively.

Box 2.3 — Thinking about Goals

The following list of questions is designed to help negotiators to organize their thinking about their objectives.

- What is the panoply of possible goals, and how might they best be prioritized?
- What is our leading goal, and why?
- How do we balance short-term impulses with long-range ambitions?

> - As we contemplate the upcoming negotiation, what outcomes would be ideal, good, and satisfactory? Which would be inadequate?
> - Where many objectives have been set, would, for instance, a potential resolution that met goals two, five, and six be worth signing, even if the leading goal were only partially satisfied and goals three and four had to be scrapped altogether?

4. Common Errors to Avoid in Setting Goals

a. The Problems of Undershooting and Overreaching

In trying to be sure to gain a resolution, a negotiator might set out goals that are insufficiently challenging—too cautious or conservative and not ambitious enough. Sometimes, consciously or subconsciously, we place the bar low because that makes it easier to clear. We set our very modest goals, shying away from possible disappointment and making our negotiating abilities look wonderful at a superficial glance. But, even should we obtain them, these goals do not really make our side of the negotiation very happy.

Negotiators who are undershooting may not grasp how much a fellow negotiator wants or needs what they can deliver. Consequently, they sell themselves short, setting out only a single goal or some ordinary objective. Sometimes, in the course of discussions a negotiator may come to see possible windfalls or new opportunities completely overlooked during pre-negotiation preparation.

The opposite error is to "over-stretch," to aim for objectives that are never likely to be achieved. In considering their own interests and imagining an ideal scenario from their own perspective, negotiators end up laying out goals that are not feasible or realistic. At times, the dimensions of what might be a perfect resolution crowd out of one's thinking the need to find something mutually beneficial to which both sides might really agree. Real world constraints should not be ignored. "A wish," it has been noted, "is a fantasy, a hope that something might happen; a goal is a specific, focused, realistic target that one can specifically plan to achieve."[48]

b. The Problem of Cramped Thinking

Yet another difficulty arises when negotiators become too wedded to the specific goals laid out in prior preparation. Since the course that the discussion will take is often unpredictable, a skilled negotiator must be prepared to revise and reassess goals during the negotiation. Negotiators may occasionally need to acknowledge to themselves that certain of the objectives set beforehand were unrealistic and should be discarded. And, a good negotiator is alert to possible resolutions that might serve his or her interests well even if they do not speak to a goal identified before the talks began.

Confusing issues by the constant reshuffling of goals is likely self-defeating. However, as you communicate with your counterpart and think more deeply about the problem or opportunity that you share, new objectives or amended ones may suggest themselves. A party should avoid having its pre-negotiation thinking about its objectives confine and cramp thought processes during the talks. Do not allow prior thought about goals to reduce the flexibility and creativity needed to arrive at an optimal agreement. Reexamine and reformulate goals when necessary.

c. The Problem of Becoming Distracted

While each of these potential problems with goals is significant, perhaps the chief error to avoid is becoming so distracted by other matters that you lose your focus on reaching your goals. Too many negotiators are too readily diverted from the pursuit of even their most important objectives. Your counterpart may annoy or frustrate you. You may become embroiled in debates or arguments. One way or another, the process of interacting with the other side may become so absorbing that what you entered the negotiation trying to accomplish recedes from your thought processes.

An experienced federal mediator once noted that his role enabled him to "peek at both sides' cards" and "see from the end result whether each side maximized ... its gain in the negotiation." He argued: "[S]ome of the highest-paid professional negotiators make the same mistakes day in and day out.... [T]ime and again it was all too easy for them to become wrapped up in ancillary issues like ego and saving face. In the process they lost sight of the ultimate goal."[49]

If you sense that a renewed focus on your goals and how to reach them may be in order, take a short *recess* to review your objectives, the rationales for setting those goals, and the priority you place on them. Assess where exactly you are in terms of achieving what you originally set out to do.

G. Final Preparation

1. Drawing Up a Preparation Memorandum

For most negotiators trying to arrive at a mutually beneficial agreement in a complex scenario, the act of writing things down is immensely helpful. For example, when people write out their goals, they tend to become more committed to achieving them and more focused on finding an effective strategy to do so. Negotiators should thus create a preparation memorandum, that is, a brief document covering points and ideas likely to be useful in an upcoming negotiation.

The memo should have an extensive section on interests, a special focus of Chapter 4. What are your interests, and what is your best estimate of your fellow negotiator's interests? Try to arrive at appropriate and logical ways to organize, prioritize, and make sense of the interests on each side.

Next, consider what you do not know—missing facts and information—and formulate a list of questions that you may want to pose to the other side. These would be questions that you would like your counterpart to answer and that you would be looking for an opportunity to ask. Inevitably, some pre-arranged questions will be discarded, since they will be shown to be irrelevant, already addressed, or, perhaps, counter-productive. However, the negotiator ought to try to ask many of the questions thought up during preparation.

Another portion of the memo should involve goals. What are your aspirations for the negotiation, and what do you think the other side hopes to gain from negotiating with you? Are you looking for a very specific and detailed agreement, or something much more general, like an exchange of views. Can you make a firm commitment? Do you want to do so, or would you prefer to take a tentative deal back to a client or superior?

Yet another matter to be considered involves walk-away alternatives, and, in particular, the *Best Alternative to a Negotiated Agreement (BATNA)*. In Chapter 5 we will explore this concept in detail. For now, note that a thorough preparation memo would include thoughts on BATNAs. What is your BATNA? What do you suppose theirs might be? This will help to determine which deals should be accepted and which rejected.

Your preparation memo should also consider the standards of legitimacy taken up in Chapter 6. What are possible objective criteria, precedents, or norms that might narrow disagreements over distributional matters? I would also include a short section on options. How might value be created, with benefits to one, or the other, or both sides?

And, finally, I would conclude my preparation memo with a comprehensive statement of strategy. What plan do I aim to follow to try to reach my goals in this negotiation? What is the road map that I have in mind for the negotiation? Can I also spell out the essence of an alternative approach should the strategy need to be abandoned?

Interests, missing information, goals, BATNAs, standards, options, and strategy, a memo covering those points ought to help to get you ready to negotiate as efficiently and skillfully as possible.

2. Practicing for an Important Negotiation

Lawyers preparing to argue a very important case frequently rehearse. They might have colleagues serve as jurors and listen to the arguments they plan to make or sit in on their presentation of an appellate case and act as judges in oral argument, peppering them with relevant questions. Finding time for preparation of this kind clearly makes sense: imagine "a tennis player who played only in tournaments and never practiced, or a musician who put on only concerts or recitals but never rehearsed."[50]

Unfortunately, practicing for an upcoming negotiation occurs much less often. It can, however, be enormously helpful, making a negotiator much more comfortable at the negotiating table, ready to work effectively toward an optimal agreement. One simply needs to recruit a negotiating partner and then have someone familiar with the circumstances write out one or more sets of mock instructions for that person. Then, dedicate some time to simulating the upcoming actual negotiation, perhaps with experienced onlookers sitting in to critique what occurs.

Such simulated negotiations can be especially beneficial if a number of versions of the basic instructions are generated. This enables a negotiator to work with a counterpart who is pursuing different sets of objectives and with somewhat different understandings of the facts and, perhaps, distinct strategies. Furthermore, it provides the possibility of switching roles, so that a negotiator steps into the shoes of his or her counterpart and sees just how the problem might feel from that perspective.

If you cannot prepare a full-scale dress rehearsal for your negotiation, it may be useful to undertake *role reversal*. That is, to gain a better understanding of the other side's perspective, one takes on the role of the other party, explains the perspectives of the other side, and in that way explores in detail their view of the situation. One source concluded: "Often clients have known the other party in a dispute or deal for a very long time—especially in the case of marriage or business partners—and they understand much more about the other party's concerns than they may be willing to admit. Role reversal helps clients to express this buried knowledge."[51]

An effective role-reversal technique is to have the negotiator or the client move to a different chair and ask that they now "become" the other party, putting themselves so thoroughly in the role of their counterpart that they use the word "I" as they answer questions from the other side's perspective. The person leading the role-reversal effort then starts with some easy questions to assist the person in adopting their new role and speaking as if he or she were the other party. Then, increasingly pointed questions are formulated about the other side's vision of the case as well as their goals and strategy.

"One element of being well-prepared," it has been suggested, "is to be able to present the other side's point of view more persuasively than they can — and to explain convincingly why you still differ."[52] In short, excellent preparation pays real dividends, and expert negotiators spend considerable time getting ready to negotiate before substantive talks begin.

Notes

1. Deborah M. Kolb, *Strategic Moves and Turns*, in THE NEGOTIATOR'S FIELDBOOK 402 (Andrea Kupfer Schneider & Christopher Honeyman eds., 2006).
2. Amy C. Finnegan & Susan G. Hackley, *Negotiation and Nonviolent Action: Interacting in the World of Conflict*, Program on Negotiation, Harvard Law School, January 25, 2008, http://www.pon.harvard.edu/events/negotiation-and-nonviolent-action-interacting-in-a-world-of-conflict/.
3. I. William Zartman, *Pre-negotiation*, in GETTING TO THE TABLE 5 (Janice Gross Stein ed., 1989).
4. Janice Gross Stein, *Preface and Acknowledgments*, in GETTING TO THE TABLE x (Janice Gross Stein ed., 1989).
5. Marcia Caton Campbell & Jayne Seminare Docherty, *What's in a Frame?*, in THE NEGOTIATOR'S FIELDBOOK 37 (Andrea Kupfer Schneider & Christopher Honeyman eds., 2006).
6. HOWARD RAIFFA, NEGOTIATION ANALYSIS 376 (2002).
7. I. WILLIAM ZARTMAN & MAUREEN BERMAN, THE PRACTICAL NEGOTIATOR 59 (1982).
8. DEBORAH M. KOLB & JUDITH WILLIAMS, THE SHADOW NEGOTIATION 202 (2000).
9. I. William Zartman, *Timing and Ripeness*, in THE NEGOTIATOR'S FIELDBOOK 146 (Andrea Kupfer Schneider & Christopher Honeyman eds., 2006).
10. *Id.* at 148.
11. RAIFFA, supra note 6, at 148.
12. Jeffrey Z. Rubin, *Some Wise and Mistaken Assumptions About Negotiation*, 45 J. OF SOCIAL ISSUES 205 (1989).
13. ROGER FISHER, WILLIAM URY, & BRUCE PATTON, GETTING TO YES 135 (2d ed. 1991).
14. WILLIAM L. URY, THE THIRD SIDE 163 (2000).
15. PATRICK J. CLEARY, THE NEGOTIATION HANDBOOK 87 (2001).
16. Rubin, supra note 12, at 202.
17. RAIFFA, supra note 6, at 393.
18. *Id.* at 395.
19. Jeffrey Z. Rubin, *The Actors in Negotiation*, in INTERNATIONAL NEGOTIATION 93 (Victor A. Kremenyuk ed., 1991).
20. Karl Llewellyn, *The Crafts of Law Re-Valued*, 38 ABA JOURNAL 801 (1942).
21. W. Averell Harriman, *Observations on Negotiating*, 9 J. OF INT'L AFF. 5 (1975).
22. Jeswald W. Salacuse, *Law and Power in Agency Relationships*, in NEGOTIATING ON BEHALF OF OTHERS 172 (Robert H. Mnookin & Lawrence E. Susskind eds.,1999).
23. Roger Fisher, *Negotiating Inside Out*, 5 NEGOTIATION J. 35–36 (1989).
24. Roger Fisher, *A Code of Negotiation Practices for Lawyers*, 1 NEGOTIATION J. 108 (1985).
25. FISHER, URY, & PATTON, supra note 13, at 77.

26. Jeswald W. Salacuse, *The Art of Advising Negotiators*, 11 Negotiation J. 391–401 (1995).

27. James C. Freund, Smart Negotiating 178–80 (1992).

28. Fisher, supra note 23, at 34.

29. Robert H. Mnookin & Lawrence E. Susskind, *Introduction*, in Negotiating on Behalf of Others 4 (Robert H. Mnookin & Lawrence E. Susskind eds., 1999).

30. Roger Fisher & Wayne Davis, *Authority of an Agent*, in Negotiating on Behalf of Others 71 (Robert H. Mnookin & Lawrence E. Susskind eds., 1999).

31. James Baker, The Politics of Diplomacy 134 (1995).

32. I. William Zartman, *Processes and Stages*, in The Negotiator's Fieldbook 96 (Andrea Kupfer Schneider & Christopher Honeyman eds., 2006).

33. Raiffa, supra note 6, at 195.

34. William Ury, Getting Past No 16 (1993).

35. Roger Fisher, *Negotiating Power*, 27 Am. Behavioral Scientist 154 (1983).

36. Thomas R. Colosi, On and Off the Record 40 (1993).

37. David M. Sally & Kathleen M. O'Connor, *Negotiating in Teams*, in The Negotiator's Fieldbook 548 (Andrea Kupfer Schneider & Christopher Honeyman eds., 2006).

38. *Id.* at 551.

39. *Id.* at 548–49.

40. Howard Raiffa, The Art and Science of Negotiation 166 (1982).

41. Joel Cutcher-Gershenfeld & Michael Watkins, *Toward a Theory of Representation in Negotiation*, in Negotiating on Behalf of Others 38 (Robert H. Mnookin & Lawrence E. Susskind eds., 1999).

42. Sol M. Linowitz, The Betrayed Profession 94 (1994).

43. Ury, supra note 34, at 19.

44. Walter LaFeber, The American Age 426 (1989).

45. Ury, supra note 34, at 15.

46. Andrea Kupfer Schneider, *Aspirations*, in The Negotiator's Fieldbook 272 (Andrea Kupfer Schneider & Christopher Honeyman eds., 2006).

47. Raiffa, supra note 6, at 214.

48. Roy J. Lewicki, David M. Saunders, & John W. Minton, Essentials of Negotiation 32 (2d ed. 2001).

49. Cleary, supra note 15, at 3.

50. Roger Fisher & Danny Ertel, Getting Ready to Negotiate 113 (1996).

51. Robert H. Mnookin, Scott R. Peppet, & Andrew S. Tulumello, Beyond Winning 183 (2000).

52. Fisher, supra note 24, at 108.

Checkpoints

- In pre-negotiation the parties determine if they want to negotiate with each other. If so, they begin to prepare, working out some logistical matters together, while readying themselves to negotiate.

- The different sides appraise the pros and cons of undertaking negotiations, while analyzing, in conflict situations, whether the situation is ripe to negotiate. They think through who would participate in a possible negotiation, what the talks should cover, and what matters might best be excluded.

- When an agent negotiates on behalf of a principal, he or she faces the constraints of negotiating parameters, instructions, and authority. The key issue is how much flexibility the principal will permit the negotiator; in some circumstances tight restrictions make sense, while in others permitting the negotiator leeway will help the parties to arrive at an optimal agreement.

- In advising a client on negotiating matters, the negotiator might press the client not to lay out a position to try to achieve, but instead to focus on the range of interests that might be satisfied. A negotiator will have more flexibility to work with the other side creatively if the aim is to have the ultimate agreement serve the client's underlying interests, rather than meet a detailed position.

- In complex negotiations, even where a principal has granted an agent broad authority, the negotiator will often want to obtain the client's approval before finalizing the deal.

- One assembles a negotiating team, rather than sending a single negotiator, when the different team members bring with them distinct expertise, backgrounds, viewpoints, constituencies, or interpersonal skills.

- Common problems associated with team negotiations include difficulties of coordinating the team into a reasonably united front as well as the slower pace of the talks, as more voices are raised and as the people bring different perspectives and diverse goals and strategies.

- As opposed to the external negotiations that occur between different parties, internal negotiations take place within an organization, prior to and often during the external negotiation, with the aim of coordinating the team, including ironing out different perceptions of interests, objectives, and strategy.

- A leading problem in internal negotiations is that people or factions within an organization may have quite different understandings of the organization's interests or goals, and when numerous people are consulted for their views regarding an external negotiation they typically assemble a position, which can then be difficult for the negotiator to work with.

- Rather than passing lightly over their goals, negotiators should set out objectives that, if achieved, will satisfy their key interests and please their constituencies. They should bear in mind, however, that over-stretching and reaching for unrealistic goals might increase the chances that no negotiated resolution occurs.

- Negotiators should be sure not to lose sight of the objectives they were pursuing as they entered the negotiation, while remaining open-minded about adding new goals or redefining them in light of their interactions with the other side.

Chapter 3

Initiating Talks:
Launching a Negotiation
Productively

Roadmap

- **Building productive relations:** Why spend time cultivating a strong working relationship? What type of working relationship might a negotiator hope to have with the other side, and what could be done to foster such relations?

- **Being trustworthy:** Why exactly is trust an asset for a negotiator, and distrust a problem? How might a negotiator demonstrate trustworthiness and guard against being distrusted? How might a negotiator avoid misplacing trust, and how and why might it be advisable to try to proceed independent of trust?

- **Setting a tone:** What tones might a negotiator look to promote, how might a negotiator try to set a particular tone, and how might this help to bring about a productive opening?

- **Creating an agenda:** How and why might negotiators choose to create an agenda listing the issues to be discussed in the order that they will be raised?

- **The importance of asking questions:** Why is posing intelligent questions an important part of initiating substantive communication with your counterpart, and to what ends do negotiators use questions?

- **The importance of listening:** How and why do skillful negotiators listen effectively, and what exactly is meant by active listening?

- **Using and reading body language:** How do people communicate through their expressions and actions, and how might one be alert to body language?

Since initial impressions can have lasting consequences, many negotiators are intent on opening a negotiation in a positive way. Yet, they are often uncertain as to how exactly to proceed. Even experienced negotiators sometimes feel awkward, clumsy, or uncomfortable as a negotiation commences. Some fear appearing in a negative light, perhaps uncertain, insincere, or manipulative.

Hence, they rush into the substance of the talks, rather than planning an opening that is an integral part of their strategy. This chapter explores what an opening might set out to achieve, and how a negotiator might best start to interact with a counterpart.

The constructive working relations that negotiators try to establish, the tones that they look to set, the questions they pose, their efforts to listen actively and effectively, and the body language they watch for, all of these are related to the effort to get information and weigh its credibility.

Information has been called "the life force of negotiation."[1] Only through the exchange of information can the parties come to understand one another's perspectives and interests. And yet, seasoned negotiators want to provide some information but withhold other items, points that might undercut their bargaining position. Part of the art of effective negotiation involves making good choices about what to tell the other side, when to say it, and what not to disclose.

Gathering and appraising information is not only a highly significant part of negotiation but often a lengthy one since the parties usually have different perceptions and perspectives and are trying to press forward their own interests and goals. This process starts in the opening phase of a negotiation. And, rather than hurrying through it, an experienced negotiator works patiently to promote productive relations, set a tone congruent with his or her strategy, and begin to interact substantively with intelligent questions and sound active listening.

A. Building Productive Relations

At the outset of many complex negotiations the parties try to foster an environment in which to negotiate well. Although this is especially true of those pursuing interest-based strategies, it can apply to positional bargainers as well. With strong working relations the parties ought to make more rapid and efficient progress. The ability to draw on productive working relations may be especially important should the talks turn difficult. (Chapter 6 explores how negotiators might think creatively in order to overcome impasses.)

A strong negotiating relationship can have lasting consequences. If an agreement is struck, the parties may need to work closely with one another to implement it. Consider, for instance, a divorce case in which a child lives with one parent, but visits the other on particular weekends. Almost inevitably, unforeseen contingencies will arise. The agreement's provisions may not clearly cover them, or they may interfere even with schedules drawn up with great care. Something unexpected arises, whether a problem or an opportunity, and the parties must adjust.[2] Under these and a host of analogous circumstances, constructive working relations can be of real value long after the original negotiation is concluded.

Indeed, having cultivated a good working relationship occasionally turns out to be even more important than the transaction at hand, when the relationship leads to future deals. Even if no agreement is reached under the present circumstances, the counterparts may find themselves negotiating other matters in the future, drawing on the productive relations established earlier.

By contrast, poor relations tend to slow and complicate negotiations. A strained relationship typically makes negotiators less likely to cooperate with each other, brainstorm options together, or compromise to close a deal. Personal tension or hostility can make an already challenging set of circumstances even more difficult to work with effectively.

Absent strong working relations, even if a deal is struck, a party may be more inclined, eventually, to renege on commitments. When relations are sour, implementation of the agreement may be hampered by foot-dragging, or some problematic provision could be overlooked, misinterpreted, or "misunderstood."[3] Trying to enforce such an agreement in court could be expensive, time-consuming, and perhaps fruitless. Hence, the time and effort dedicated to establishing a strong working relationship has real potential to minimize future problems.

Since many good reasons exist to establish positive working relations, negotiators are often quite interested in doing so. However, in all aspects of negotiation, including this one, circumstances can matter greatly. One may want to go about developing a working relationship differently, for instance, in a situation marked by bitter historical animosity or substantial cultural differences than one in which the negotiators, while unknown to each other, share similar backgrounds and perspectives. Let us start, however, with ideas that can be applied to many different situations, expecting to use common sense and strategic thinking to tailor them to suit diverse scenarios.

1. The Content of a Positive Working Relationship

In a good working relationship negotiators are comfortable with one another and prepared to engage easily and readily so as to make practical progress on the problems or issues before them. Although a deal may or may not emerge, negotiators interacting positively should be able to work productively on the issues. They are sometimes said to have "good chemistry" with one another.

Useful working relations do not depend on one negotiator accepting another's arguments. One might fully expect some strategic posturing. One's fellow negotiator is likely to be quite self-interested, as opposed to altruistic. He or she may well be looking to claim quite favorable, or even more-than-favorable, terms. Beyond this, one side may not approve of the way the other has been acting with respect to various matters. None of these traits must necessarily fracture or destroy positive working relations during the negotiation.

Instead, the essence of a good relationship is that the negotiators are able to communicate effectively about the situation that they face. In fact, constructive working relations come into their own when the negotiators are called on to deal with significant differences in interests, perceptions, and principles.[4]

Negotiation is sometimes concerned with resolving differences and sometimes with capitalizing on shared opportunities. In either case negotiators working well together can shift from what are sometimes characterized as *face-to-face* over to *side-by-side negotiating*, when the circumstances so warrant, such as when they are looking to find potential joint gains or create promising options together.[5]

Constructive working relations also differ from the personal relations of close friends or dating or married couples. A sound relationship between negotiators emphasizes intellectual exchanges conducted in a professional manner. Indeed, research suggests that those in a personal relationship tend to be uncomfortable bargaining with one another. Too often, both individuals seize on quick compromises, looking to end the negotiation with something each can live with. They often devote minimal time to exchanging information and creating joint gains, rather than engaging in the more involved problem-solving aimed at fashioning an optimal agreement.[6]

Although the effort in complex negotiations is to develop professional relations rather than bonds of deep, lasting friendship or romantic interest, developing a relationship of any kind takes time and patience. Good relations do not materialize at once; rather, they grow and strengthen over time. One real test of a good relationship is whether you look forward to working with that person again, should a new issue to be negotiated arise in the future.

2. Developing Good Working Relations

"How you treat people at the beginning of a negotiation," it has been observed, "often determines how willing they are to work with you."[7] Apart from acting graciously, with appropriate opening pleasantries, how does one set about building a positive working relationship early in the proceedings?

First and foremost, working relations should be tailored to the people involved, fitting the characteristics of those individuals and the situation they face. It is usually a good idea not to wait for the other side to initiate the type of relationship you want, but to be proactive. If it is possible to begin to develop rapport with one's fellow negotiators before substantive negotiations begin, so much the better. Informal meetings, whether over a meal or in another comfortable setting, may enable negotiators to get to know one another, relax, and share some experiences. Seasoned negotiators gain rapport with the other side in many different ways. One of Ben Franklin's techniques was to borrow a book or ask for some other minor favor from his fellow negotiator. He was then, in a small but significant way, both connected to and indebted to his counterpart. This personal interaction provided a foundation from which to build positive working relations.[8]

It is worth bearing in mind, however, that one side alone cannot develop a strong working relationship. Both negotiators must want to have positive relations and be willing to try to foster them. Occasionally, one negotiator will be indifferent or hostile to this process. Perhaps he or she has no interest in rising above past clashes. Or, the negotiator may want to project a tough, contentious image or emphasize formal or arm's-length relations.

In such circumstances the best policy for the other side is to continue to work toward developing positive relations whenever possible, but to refrain from an overbearing effort to engender them in the face of opposition. This is likely to be fruitless, and the effort, counter-productive. Nevertheless, bear in mind that quite strong working relationships sometimes emerge after long incubation periods.

a. Drawing on the Similarity Principle

One possible step in trying to strike up a positive relationship is to see if you have common threads in your backgrounds. Your personal lives, professional careers, or networks of acquaintances may somehow be intertwined. Perhaps at some point you have lived in the same place or attended schools, colleges, or universities that share something.

The process of finding such points of connection takes advantage of the "similarity principle": "[W]e tend to trust people who appear more ... familiar to us—people who like us, share our general interests and experiences, and identify with the same groups."[9] Even under circumstances that are potentially quite contentious, emphasizing some similarities can help to dissipate tension. For instance, officials from a corporation negotiating with environmental activists might find some common ground by focusing upon shared concerns. Maybe they live near one another, or their children play outdoors, hike in the same parks, or fish in the same lakes and streams.[10]

b. Demonstrating Respect for the Other Side

While emphasizing similarities may help to set matters off on an auspicious footing, only with substantive negotiation does a strong working relationship truly develop. As you begin to negotiate, project respect for your fellow negotiator, for who they are, for the difficulties with which they are contending, and for their efforts to help to find a mutually agreeable resolution. A simple but effective way to demonstrate your regard is to inquire as to their thoughts and perspectives. Giving the other side the time and space to express its concerns fully and, perhaps, to vent about problems may be very useful, as is listening carefully to their answers.

To build the relationship, you try not to undercut, interrupt, or embarrass the other negotiator, and you show sensitivity toward your counterpart's need to save face on occasion. Also important, where you are able to do so without harming your own bargaining position, you answer questions in a direct, truthful manner. Since it is important to every negotiator that his or her good points register with the other side, acknowledging persuasive ideas made by one's counterpart can be a very important step toward gaining a positive relationship.[11]

When the other side is trying hard to find a mutually beneficial resolution, look for opportunities to show that you appreciate their efforts to cooperate. And, when your fellow negotiator persuades you of a point, acknowledge it. Not only does this buttress good working relations, but it may pay dividends in the future should the other side reciprocate. By telling the opposing negotiator when persuaded of something, you hope that "he will recognize that the rule of reason is alive and well in these negotiations. Then when *I* make a persuasive argument on a different point later on, he should treat it with the same respect that I just gave his."[12]

The broader point is that open and honest, sincere and straightforward communications tend to strengthen relations, while lies, evasion, double-talk, and broken promises undercut them. After noting "A little bit of dishonesty can create a lot of distrust," Roger Fisher and Scott Brown pointed out how problematic it can be to say things that appear to be inconsistent: "what I say today should agree with what I said yesterday and what I will say tomorrow. What you heard me telling someone else should fit in with what I told you."[13]

c. Showing One's Reliability

Arriving at a negotiation well-prepared can be a vital step toward establishing a productive working relationship. Then, demonstrating that you are reliable on minor matters can work to build confidence that the same will be true of larger ones.[14] "When Robert McNamara was secretary of defense," two scholars recalled, "he made it a point to arrive on time for all meetings. His reputation for reliability on small things that people could see spilled over to enhance his credibility with respect to commitments that were not so easily verifiable."[15]

To show that you are reliable, you avoid making promises that you may not be able to keep. You demonstrate that the other side can rely on your word. When you create expectations, you then do your very best to meet them.[16] If the other side is persuaded that you are a reliable counterpart, you have usually made real strides toward establishing a sound working relationship.

d. Avoiding Imposing Conditions

A negotiator will sometimes be tempted to make positive relations contingent on initial substantive concessions. The message sent will be, once you have proven that you are ready to do something for me, thus showing that you are serious about negotiating in good faith, then we can see about developing constructive relations. An even more manipulative tactic is to develop a positive working relationship, but then pretend to take umbrage at something, eventually offering forgiveness but only in exchange for concessions.[17]

In either case imposing such conditions tends to be counter-productive. One is unlikely to build a strong relationship with the attitude: "Make me a substantive concession. Give me something. Demonstrate that it's worth my time to work with you. Then, we can have a good relationship." Adopting such a stance comes off as arrogant and illegitimate.

Similarly, you ought not leave the impression that you and your fellow negotiator must see eye to eye or you cannot work constructively together. Instead, having sound working relations to draw on is especially important when disagreements arise. Although the hope is that a good working relationship will help the parties to find common ground, agreeing with each other should not be the *sine qua non* of a constructive working relationship.[18]

B. Gaining Your Counterpart's Trust

Perhaps the ultimate goal in developing positive relations is for the negotiators to come to trust one another. Although a constructive working relationship takes time to develop, a trusting one requires deeper bonds and thus takes considerably longer to nurture. In this regard it may be useful to conceive of trust in separable, divisible terms, rather than as a unitary, all-or-nothing matter. That is, rather than wholeheartedly trusting a negotiating counterpart, the wiser course may be "to trust someone in some contexts, but not in others, and similarly distrust them in some contexts but not in others."[19]

Sometimes one side tries to engender trust by a tactic such as purposefully divulging a fact contrary to their own interests.[20] Although such a step could conceivably help, one usually weaves together a trusting relationship only over considerable periods of interaction. Hence, while one can do particular things to help to develop a trusting relationship, it may not be possible to reap its rewards for quite some time.

1. How Trust Can Be Beneficial

Still, gaining mutual trust is potentially a great benefit in negotiating complex agreements. One scholar argued, "With trust, deals get done. Without it, deals are harder to negotiate, more difficult to implement, and vulnerable to changing incentives and circumstances."[21] Former U.S. Treasury Secretary and Secretary of State James Baker likewise recalled, "If honesty and trust developed, even the most contentious talks could be brought to a successful conclusion."[22]

It has been suggested that one side is likely to trust the other when it believes that the other side is positively concerned with its interests as well as with their own.[23] However that may be, acting in a trustworthy manner—one that your fellow negotiator finds fair, honest, sincere, and reliable—can increase your influence substantially.[24]

Although the nature of negotiation is such that complete candor is rare, negotiators who trust one another will be more likely to bring each other into their confidence on certain matters. More information can be shared without fear that it will be misused. Consequently, problems can often be resolved and deadlocks overcome more readily. Indeed, a party might purposefully highlight trust issues, while testing to see if that trust might be misplaced, by engineering "minor occasions where it is at the mercy of the other."[25]

In addition, one key aspect of negotiation involves assessing whether promises and commitments are, in fact, likely to be carried out. Negotiators must concern themselves with whether their counterparts will abide by their word or not. In this regard, the credibility of an offer may be directly linked to the reputation of a negotiator or a party.[26] Trust can thus bring proposals to be taken seriously.

Then, once a deal is concluded and the parties turn to carrying out its terms, trust comes to the fore again. "[G]ood faith implementation," one authority declared, "depends on the trust and confidence that exists between the parties to a negotiation."[27] Negotiators who have taken the time and effort to develop a trusting relationship will be well-positioned to deal effectively with each other and help the parties to work through future problems.

2. Sources and Signs of Distrust

Let us move next to distrust. Unfounded suspicions can poison the atmosphere of a negotiation. Biases and stereotypes can bring one to vilify another unfairly. If you do not trust someone, you guard what you say to them, constricting communication. You are even more cautious about what you will commit to and what risks you will accept.

Trust can evaporate almost instantaneously. It is, of course, possible to rebuild broken trust. One might apologize, offer reparations, and quickly provide a sincere explanation of what occurred.[28] Still, it is likely to take a long time to repair the damage to the relationship, if that is indeed possible. Hence, try not to hurry to find a fellow negotiator untrustworthy without good evidence.

Among the things that most often cause distrust in negotiation are dishonesty, back-stabbing, unreliability, erratic or unpredictable behavior, and careless commitments made too casually. If you lose faith in your counterpart, you may choose to walk away from a potentially beneficial deal, reasoning that "working out my problems on my own is safer than reaching agreement with you."[29] Or, as Secretary Baker recalled: "[I]f the relationship ... became infected with distrust and discord — then it mattered little how far apart the parties actually were. The perception of mistrust overwhelmed any objective reality."[30]

An underhanded or unscrupulous counterpart can readily take advantage of a negotiator who is too trusting. To consider one of many possible examples, one negotiator might try to foster trust in a counterpart in hopes of interjecting last-minute claims that might be granted because of the bond developed between the two sides. Thus, negotiators ought to be open to building trusting relations but prudent about taking risks until they are confident that their trust will not be misplaced.

A negotiator might distrust another, with good reason, on account of his or her reputation or past personal experiences. And, since no one wants to be naive or to get exploited, be alert to the following warning signs that a negotiator may be looking to manipulate, or otherwise profit by, feelings of trust.

- Requests designed to make you feel guilty if you turn them down.
- Requests to gain information that might normally be considered confidential.
- Requests that money or other items of value change hands up front before the deal is consummated.
- Requests that you place yourself in a position that is quite risky for you but not for others.[31]

When substantial distrust does arise, you need not necessarily break off negotiations, but you should bear the trust issues in mind, avoid disclosing matters that could leave you in a precarious position, and find safeguards to protect your side of the negotiation whenever possible.

3. Proceeding Independent of Trust

Limiting one's trust in another can reduce one's vulnerability and guard against exploitation. Since even an alert, realistic, and skeptical negotiator can find, on occasion, that he or she has trusted unwisely, it is good practice to try to draft an agreement such that carrying out its terms does not hinge on one party's trust in the good faith and honest dealings of the other. This is what Roger Fisher had in mind when he argued, "[T]he less an agreement depends on trust, the more likely it is to be implemented."[32] Later, he and Scott Brown expanded on that point, pointing out that this is why landlords ask tenants for security deposits and banks do not loan significant sums, even to creditworthy homeowners, without gaining a mortgage on the property. "Such security arrangements," they concluded, "limit the damage if a promise is broken. Often more important, they reduce the likelihood that it will be."[33]

To manage potential problems of trust, specify what each party is committed to do and look for opportunities to build into the agreement consequences such that something significant is lost if a party does not carry through as promised.[34] Some deals can be structured so that both sides must perform their undertakings simultaneously. There may also be ways to monitor implementation, creating opportunities to inspect and verify compliance with the terms of the agreement.

C. Setting a Tone

A negotiation can be launched in any number of possible directions, and part of preparing an effective strategy involves considering issues regarding the tenor, demeanor, or ambiance of the upcoming talks. The trajectory of a negotiation can be very much influenced in positive or negative ways. Indeed, when asked just after a negotiation to analyze what occurred, people often put great stock in the tone that was struck early in the proceedings. This highlights another important question in launching a negotiation productively: given one's strategy, what is the best tone to try to set in the opening phase?

The tone that one negotiator wants to establish can be reciprocated by another, or the tones of each negotiator can contrast or clash. A tone may catch on and dramatically affect a negotiation, or it can prove to be difficult or impossible to maintain. The salient point here is that a careful negotiator should consider what tone he or she would like to promote and that tone should be tailored to fit the strategy being pursued. It should be congruent with the other elements of an overall negotiating plan.

1. The Range of Possible Tones

In most complex negotiations a party will want to act in the manner of a calm, confident professional. This implies extending basic courtesies to one's fellow negotiators and, after a cordial opening, moving expeditiously to the business at hand. Unprofessional conduct might include acting rudely or in boorish, boisterous, or vulgar ways. Beyond these self-evident points, however, what other aspects of tone might usefully be kept in mind?

Although many advanced negotiation skills take considerable practice, negotiators often find that projecting a particular tone comes naturally. Throughout much of our lives we hear different tones and, on occasion, practice setting them. For example, consider the question, "Is this what you really want?" Think of how that question might be said with very different intonations and emphases. If the words are said "abruptly and abrasively" a mood would be set that would differ markedly from the impression left if it were said quietly and with concern.[35]

Just as a parent can sit down for a discussion with a child and, depending on the occasion, adopt one of a multitude of tones, so a negotiator can look to establish different tones depending on the particular circumstances and on their personalities and negotiation strategies. A harmonious, conciliatory, or cooperative tone contrasts with an adversarial or combative one. In a negotiation one can imagine striking a serious or a light-hearted tone; one that is formal and proper, dignified and polite, or genial, laid-back, colloquial. If actions during an extended negotiation are a significant part of one's strategy, it is important that the tone struck be congruent with the actions taken.

A tone appropriate to one context may be out of place in another. A negotiator trying to entice a well-known musician to sign a contract with a symphony will adopt a very different tone than one looking to conclude an agreement with an imprisoned drug kingpin to provide information to police. Two experienced attorneys negotiating the provisions of a merger or purchase-and-sale agreement are likely to have a different tone than the members of an extended family trying to work out an agreement to look after a jointly owned summer home.

In the course of a lengthy negotiation multiple tones are often evident. Indeed, tones can swing very suddenly as the moods of the participants shift or as someone's negotiating strategy calls for a change, perhaps to emphasize a particular point. Hence, a savvy negotiator bears in mind the question: "What does the tone that my counterpart is trying to set reveal about his or her strategy?"

2. Establishing a Constructive Tone

Those grappling with a complex problem through interest-based negotiation will ordinarily try to set a tone that is, among other things, broadly cooperative. In this approach to negotiation, although each side looks, first and foremost, to serve its own interests, each hopes to do so by working with the other to construct an agreement that is mutually beneficial. Relaxed and comfortable negotiators, at ease cooperating with one another, are more likely to solve problems together creatively and effectively than those who feel tense and uptight.

One way to encourage a productive tone of this sort is to select language that suggests that the negotiators are working side-by-side on the issues before them. A negotiator could speak of the problems or opportunities the parties confront as if the two sides were colleagues looking to put their heads together to invent a resolution that serves key interests for both.

A negotiator might talk to a counterpart about what "we" are going to do or the challenges "we" face: "we're in this together," "we'll have to work this out." One federal mediator observed that some of the best negotiators he had worked with used "we" constantly: "we have a problem," "we have some difficult issues to solve," and so on. He wrote, "[T]his tactic ... is very useful, calming, and sincere. In many ... negotiations, you are tied together with your counterpart at some level and you—collectively—*do* have a problem to solve."[36]

Since people tend to be more comfortable when others are acting in the same way that they are, a negotiator can look for ways to parallel their counterpart's behavior. How might this be done? How can I negotiate in sync with my fellow negotiator? "I can adopt a manner that is harmonious with yours," it has been suggested, "in terms of pace, volume and tone of voice, formality or informality, degree of relaxation, and so forth."[37]

Establishing a productive tone early on can be important in helping the parties over whatever difficulties lie ahead. There may well be clashes of interests to contend with. In the rapid give-and-take of a fast-paced negotiation certain thoughts may not be tactfully phrased, and some statements by each side could be taken personally or otherwise received quite negatively. But, once a reservoir of positive feelings has been established, such comments are often passed over lightly, as each side opts not to take offense at misstatements or poor phrasing.

3. Changing a Negative Tone

If at some point a negotiator feels relations have soured or the talks have started to spiral off in the wrong direction, it may be time to try to change the tone. Perhaps one or more negotiators have become pessimistic or complacent. Tensions or frustrations may have developed. The psychological challenge, when participants start to feel hopeless, dejected, or antagonistic, is to find a way to change the mood at the table.

In this regard Patrick Cleary recounted an example of the power of changing a negative tone that occurred in the midst of a dispute between the owner of a car dealership and a young woman who had bought a car there that turned out to be a lemon. After the two had made conflicting presentations before an arbitrator—the woman arguing that the dealership should buy back her car and the dealer asserting that he had completely fulfilled his obligations to her—the woman turned to the dealer and looked him directly in the eye. "'I want to ask you a few questions, but before I do,' she said, 'I just want to commend you for your honesty.'" She continued, speaking sincerely: "'You and I have different views of what your obligations to me are, I know, but you could have cut the facts differently, could have tried to spin them more in your favor, but you didn't…. You're an honest man,' she concluded, 'and I thank you for that.'" The arbitration soon turned into a successful negotiation as the dealer then offered to trade her a different model car.[38]

Skillful negotiators are alert for opportunities to change an unproductive tone. Further, some prior thought during preparation about how a negative tone might best be changed may pay real dividends. The circumstances of the negotiation will often suggest how best to change a particular tone. However, note that taking a recess or caucus provides the opportunity to come back after the break with a fresh demeanor. A marked shift in body language can also work to change a negative tone: getting up, moving around, altering the seating arrangement. Or, one might take another look at the agenda and opt to return to a particular topic or introduce a new one. Seasoned negotiators use such devices to try to regain a positive dynamic.

a. Using Humor

One way to set a positive tone, or recover one, is to use humor. In negotiations the best humor tends to be spontaneous and light-hearted, as opposed to a planned joke or bitter, biting, ironic, or sarcastic wit. At an opportune moment, something understated, a clever point administered with a light touch, might very well be a safe and effective variety of humor.

When used appropriately, humor can disarm, defuse tension, or smooth over an otherwise awkward moment. Self-deprecating humor can make a negotiator look human in their counterpart's eyes. As negotiators build working relations, they can use humor to connect with each other, develop camaraderie, or warm up a cold, formal, or strained atmosphere. Then, when negotiators tire, humor can help them to regain perspective by changing the subject for a moment and lightening the mood.[39] Since people enjoying something tend to perform better at it, humor may well encourage joint problem-solving.[40]

However, trying to inject humor into a negotiation can be risky, too. What one person finds amusing or light-hearted might not be received well by another. Humor that appears to another as making light of serious matters is obviously problematic. An off-the-cuff comment that one's counterpart finds biased or tasteless or that embarrasses another might cause real offense with serious repercussions for the effort to work together. In a group negotiation an inside joke that appeals to one negotiator might leave another feeling excluded or belittled.

Negotiators should thus be quite sensitive to timing as well as to the different varieties of humor they might draw upon. They should look for an appropriate moment and for a type of humor likely to gain a positive response. For example, when someone has just made an earnest proposal, responding with a joke would be out of place. Poking fun at a fellow negotiator's name, culture, ethnicity, or personality is counterproductive.

"It is always a good idea," one authority advised, "to try to imagine how we look in the eyes of our counterparts."[41] That counsel applies well to efforts to inject humor into a negotiation. Sensitivity to how you might appear to others helps negotiators to determine what would be a judicious use of humor and when it might be best to refrain from trying to use it.

When an awkward or offensive attempt at humor goes awry, the challenge to the other parties may be to overcome something that has now become an obstacle to working together harmoniously. One might think of ways to register disapproval, but without causing a negative impact on the course of the negotiations. For example, one analyst of humor in negotiation has suggested: "One experienced mediator I know has been known to cry 'Foul!' in a jocular tone when humor has gotten out of hand."[42]

D. Creating an Agenda

Another early step in a negotiation involves setting an agenda, that is, an overview of the upcoming talks. It is certainly possible for parties to negotiate without taking the time to create an agenda to which both agree. Each might simply have in mind their own lists of what needs to be discussed. One might favor a free-flowing discussion over a more tightly organized one. Or, the issues might be very clear and not in need of being explicitly identified. Sometimes, a negotiator views trying to negotiate the agenda as one more potential difficulty, and one that could be sidestepped. In many negotiations, however, establishing an agenda has much to recommend it.

1. Why Have an Agenda?

Ordinarily, the agenda identifies the issues to be negotiated, listing the items that will be discussed in the order that the parties plan to raise them. Not only can issues be presented or defined in different ways, but the manner in which they are posed can have significant repercussions. Negotiators should thus think carefully about how exactly to describe the matters to be negotiated and in what sequence they want to tackle them.

On occasion, an agenda might also set forth the different stages that the parties anticipate. For instance, negotiators might agree, "Let's first review our understanding of the circumstances, then follow that with a phase in which we explore interests, move to one devoted to brainstorming and generating options, and conclude by thinking through what commitments we can make."

One reason to set an agenda is that negotiators can lose focus, particularly when multiple issues and high stakes cloud their thinking. They can overlook matters or spend too much time trying to solve the wrong problem. In a negotiation of some complexity establishing an agenda can provide structure, while enabling the negotiators to visualize the order and the flow of the talks. Since the agenda items are, in a sense, mileposts on the journey toward a resolution, they can help to keep the negotiators on track, while imparting a sense of progress as different items are discussed and the shape of an eventual agreement begins to emerge.

Where a negotiation session is proceeding under time constraints, negotiators occasionally include in the agenda estimates of how much time should be allotted to at least the initial discussion of each item. And, plainly, not all issues need to be considered in equal depth. Even if no such guidelines are included, the agenda's very existence can serve to remind the negotiators of how much ground needs to be covered. Its presence can prompt the parties not to spend too much time on any one agenda item.

2. Negotiating the Agenda

Since different parties are likely to have distinct goals, interests, and strategies, their preferred agendas may conflict. Occasionally, a negotiator is as concerned with issues kept off an agenda as those placed on it, and views may differ as to what the parties should exclude from the negotiation. All this suggests that the different sides may need to negotiate the agenda before they move to substantive points. Some parties consider agenda issues in preliminary negotiations; others use the opening phase of the substantive negotiation to work out this type of framework for the talks.

a. Strategic Implications of Agendas

In a negotiation of any complexity virtually any agenda has some strategic implications. The order in which the parties approach the different issues to be negotiated can make a negotiator's strategy easier or more difficult to put into effect. Hence, a negotiator should think carefully about the best way to frame the issues and the sequence that he or she favors in dealing with them.

To illustrate, consider the hypothesis that in a negotiation "moves to claim value ... frequently drive out moves to create more of it ..."[43] Consequently, a negotiator might choose to order agenda items so that value-creating tasks come before distributional ones.

Or, consider a situation in which the parties must cooperate to succeed and yet their relationship has soured. Over the course of a lengthy and complex history significant differences have arisen, exacerbated perhaps by misunderstandings and misinformation. Although people often take a sour relationship as a given and assume that relations will never improve, this can be a problematic approach. One might instead conclude that the relationship issues ought to be confronted before the two sides attempt to hammer out something like a contract or a business plan.

Although one should not minimize the difficulties inherent in improving poor relations, one also does not want to work to "stitch up a wound while leaving a bad infection inside." If the parties jump into the substance of contractual provisions, they might very well start the negotiation irritated with each other and continue upset throughout. If significant relationship issues are never addressed, the enterprise could rapidly become dysfunctional despite sensible, creative agreements concerning substantive issues. And yet, if it proves possible to effectively manage the core interpersonal problems, the parties ought to be much better positioned to focus productively on the details of who will commit to do what, under what circumstances, and for what compensation.

Certainly, when the state of relations between the parties is a key agenda item, an important strategic issue is whether and when to speak to those issues in the negotiation. If it is possible to explain particular past misunderstandings, to express a wish for better future relations, or even to apologize for whatever role one played in the prior deterioration of the relationship, this may enable the parties to move toward working together more expeditiously and effectively.

b. Amending Agendas

That said, while the content of an agenda has real strategic significance, most parties most of the time will be disinclined to press their counterparts too vigorously over the agenda. Since both sides are often intent on establishing a positive, productive working relationship, negotiators tend to be open-minded, ready to compromise, and eager to move quickly through discussions of the agenda.

Furthermore, in a negotiation an agenda need not be considered "fixed in stone." In a legislature or a like meeting proceeding under parliamentary rules, control of the agenda can dictate what issues get discussed. By contrast, ordinarily a negotiating agenda simply acts as a road map; it is "seldom a once-and-for-all agreement that precludes later additions and amendments ..."[44]

As the parties come to see more clearly the contours of the problem or opportunity facing them, items may need to be added to the agenda. And, particularly when a negotiation carries on over time, events may occur that cause the negotiators to want to adjust their agenda, adding or subtracting items. If an item is inadvertently left off the agenda, parties will rarely balk at adding it at a later point during the talks. Similarly, if a party advances a good reason to rearrange the topics on an existing agenda, the other negotiators will often acquiesce.

Finally, note that, on occasion, for strategic purposes a negotiator might not want to identify in a straightforward way all the items to be addressed in an upcoming negotiation. People sometimes refer to *hidden agendas*, that is, important matters that are purposefully kept off the sequential list of items to which the parties have agreed, but that a negotiator expects to introduce at some moment that he or she finds especially auspicious.

3. Resolving or Tabling Agenda Items

Another implication of agendas merits a word of caution. The very presence of an agenda may lead negotiators to talk through their interests concerning a particular matter and move directly into possible resolutions to that issue. An alternative order, however, would involve, first, clarifying interests regarding the different issues, *tabling* each agenda item after that initial discussion. (By tabling an issue, a negotiator means to set it aside—to hold that matter in solution, one might say—with the intent of returning to it at a more propitious moment.)

Then, once the parties' underlying concerns have been fully discussed with respect to all of the agenda items, the idea would be to move on to brainstorming options, and eventually packaging different resolutions. The formula of discussing, understanding, tabling, moving on, and then returning has the advantage of enabling a negotiator to link issues and create a package resolution. (The difference between a *checklist* and a *packaging negotiation* is taken up further in Chapter 11 on strategy.)

E. The Importance of Posing Questions

Negotiation has been called "a process of discovery" in which the parties learn about "the possibilities and impossibilities of their common situation" by exchanging perspectives and information about it.[45]

The process can be creative and adaptive in that skilled negotiators invent and innovate as well as adjust and reorganize their thinking en route to trying to create a resolution to which both sides can agree. But, the negotiation process is also ambiguous and uncertain. Negotiators frequently have different visions and perspectives. They typically withhold some facts and viewpoints from their fellow negotiators. To deal with fragmentary information, negotiators must make estimates, proceed on the basis of their assumptions, and exercise good judgment.[46]

All relevant facts known to one side are not likely to be known by the other. A negotiator may be completely in the dark about certain points, may have skeletal information about others, and no direct knowledge, only hearsay, speculation, or vague assumptions, about still other matters.

As one starts to negotiate, remember that, in the words of I. William Zartman and Maureen Berman, "All perceptions are selective." They went on: "No one perceives everything that there is about a situation or a relationship. Even those elements that each side may describe as 'facts' can be perceived in quite different ways; the salience or meaning of the facts may be different to different parties ..."[47] Deborah Kolb and Judith Williams likewise observed, "How people see a problem depends on their experience. A dancer knows her world in a different way than the research physicist. A marketing specialist's slant on a new [research and development] ... initiative might diverge dramatically from that of the project's engineer. These differences in perception matter when you negotiate."[48]

Many people carry an image in their minds of an expert negotiator as a quick-talking individual, adept at creating and advancing offers, demands, warnings, and threats. The public may imagine that the negotiation of a complex problem quickly devolves into either a seductive encounter, with each negotiator trying to entice the other into agreement, or a no-holds-barred wrestling match, with the two sides trying to manipulate, threaten and coerce one another. Those images, however, miss the essence of much skillful negotiation.

In fact, effective negotiation of complicated problems must first involve intelligent communication about the situation that the parties confront. Seasoned negotiators grappling with a challenging situation put many questions to their counterparts in hopes of filling in some of this missing information.

- What are the exact dimensions of the problem or opportunity?
- What is each side most concerned about, how does each view the situation, and what exactly does each want?
- What interests might be served by coming to an agreement?
- What shape might a deal eventually take?

1. Using Questions to Advance Understanding

From early on in a negotiation, you formulate questions in order to uncover matters, to find out and check out what has been going on, to sharpen your understanding of a situation, and to clarify and test prior assumptions and estimates. You pose questions to better understand the circumstances — the underlying facts, the interests, goals, and visions of the other side, the needs and attitudes of those with whom you are negotiating as well as the constraints under which they may be operating.

The central purpose of asking questions is to gain information potentially useful in coming to an agreement. However, another notable purpose is to demonstrate to the other side that one genuinely wants to understand their perspective on matters so as to work effectively together toward fashioning a mutually beneficial outcome. Thus, opening the substantive portion of a negotiation with questions may be congruent with the other aspects of a strong opening phase, including setting a positive tone and fostering a constructive working relationship. (Yet another cardinal reason to ask questions is to counter deception, a topic explored in Chapter 10 on Ethical Negotiation.)

The cardinal point here is that the give-and-take of questions and answers forms an inherent part of skillful negotiation in complex circumstances. American businessman Henry Ford once observed, "If there is any one secret of success, it lies in the ability to get the other person's point of view and see things from that person's angle as well as from your own."[49] U.S. diplomat Averill Harriman likewise suggested that it is of transcendent importance in a negotiation "to look at the other fellow's point of view. We need to recognize what is useful in what he says and work from there."[50] Similarly, James Baker, reflecting on negotiations in private practice, observed: "I learned that if I could put myself in the position of the other lawyer and his or her client, understand how they saw the issues, and appreciate the constraints they faced, then I had a better chance of working through the issues and reaching an agreement."[51]

The anticipating and estimating of pre-negotiation preparation can be quite useful, but it usually pales in significance in comparison to the progress made as the parties interact at the table, learning more about facts and perceptions, and considering, probing, and giving feedback on the different issues. This is what really helps the negotiators to craft a mutually agreeable resolution to a complex situation.

2. Varieties of Questions to Ask

Questions pertaining to a particular negotiation may be broad and open-ended or quite specific. They may be tangible and concrete or abstract or hypothetical.

a. Generic Questions

Some questions are generic in the sense that they apply to numerous negotiations. If you are approaching a negotiation as a joint problem-solving endeavor, you might start with an open-ended question such as "What are your initial thoughts on how we might respond to the situation that we face?" On the one hand, perhaps your thoughts and your counterpart's dovetail in some significant ways. In that case you may be able to seize on the commonalities in your thinking and begin to work together on certain matters right away. On the other hand, if the other side has a completely different approach, you can hear them out and respond with your own ideas.

One generic issue, of interest in many contexts, is what authority the opposing negotiator has. To what extent can he or she make commitments or float proposals? Are particular matters going to be advanced "provisionally" (that is, for instance, "... provided that our Board of Directors agrees ...")? Most important, can your counterpart come to a final agreement? Must he or she take a potential deal back to the client to be approved or rejected? Or, are there particular aspects of the problem or opportunity about which the negotiator has been granted full authority and other aspects in which it has been limited? A negotiator might want to pose questions to determine the "lay of the land" in this regard.

In various situations one might also be interested in determining what the other side expects the negotiating session to produce. For example, if one side is expecting the meeting to produce a skeletal agreement in bullet points and the other is looking for a legally binding contract with a complete set of carefully drafted provisions, these differing expectations ought to be sorted out early in the talks. All of these might be characterized as generic questions, applicable to many different negotiations.

b. Specific Questions

As you get deeper into a negotiation, generic questions will naturally give way to more targeted and focused ones, and these will usually be most helpful in progressing toward an agreement.[52] The vast majority of questions posed in a negotiation will thus depend upon the particular circumstances being faced. And here, negotiators need to consider carefully what might be termed "the unknowns," that is, those matters about which they lack information, but that might very well make them a better informed, more knowledgeable, or perhaps more creative negotiator if they did know them.

For example, one negotiating an employment contract might want to be as sure as possible that the potential employee has the particular traits that are most important to carrying out the job successfully. For instance, how extensive is the person's experience in computers? What courses has the faculty candidate taught? How has the injured knee of the rugby player responded to treatment?

Or, to fashion a mutually profitable joint venture, a negotiator might need to gain a firm grasp of the history, the finances, or the corporate culture of a particular company. Even more specifically, one might want to understand the most likely risks of a proposed transaction. What trends characterize the business climate of late? What data might be projected to estimate future opportunities or issues?

c. Hypothetical Questions

Yet another category might be termed "what if ..." questions. Here, the aim is to glean useful information by posing different possibilities to your counterpart. One authority offered the following example: "If someone gives you an estimate on home improvement, but says they can't start for six months, ask 'what if' you paid a premium of 30 percent or 50 percent, could he start earlier? If he says no, then he really is constrained ... If he says yes, then it's a matter of money and priorities."[53]

3. Techniques of Asking Questions

a. Formulating Questions

From pre-negotiation preparation forward, negotiators formulate questions to put to the other side. Before the negotiation begins, one ought to consider carefully the following.

- What important information do I lack?
- Might we agree on certain facts, thus staking out some common ground?
- What facts that I don't know would make me a more capable negotiator if I knew them, that is, more able to come to a resolution that I like and that the other side will also accept?
- What questions might best elicit that information?

Good negotiators pose many questions and start asking them early in the negotiation. Not only is there much to try to understand more clearly, but one's fellow negotiator is unlikely to respond to every inquiry and certainly not answer each one as fully and clearly as possible. Fortunately, a complete satisfactory answer to any one question is rarely of decisive importance. Rather, the information and impressions gleaned from responses to a host of questions is significant. So, one inquires about a great variety of things and works further with the answers that seem notably revealing or insightful.

In this process a negotiator tries to be patient and respectful but persistent, all while engaging well with the other side. Here, one's attitude in asking a question can be of great importance. Rather than cross-examining a counterpart, a skillful negotiator converses with them, calling on interpersonal skills whenever possible. Often, the good cheer and humor one injects in the dialogue, and the light touch one exhibits in trying to extract information, go far toward determining the quality and usefulness of the answers being elicited.

b. Discarding Counter-Productive Questions

Realize, too, that it might be wiser not to ask some questions. A series of detailed questions about the other side's position might move the negotiation toward positional bargaining and encourage your counterpart to dig into an opening stance. And, no one wants to waste time answering questions that are superfluous in light of the prior discussions. Furthermore, a question that is likely to be answered in a rote or automatic way is usually not going to advance the discussion very far. If you expect the other side to have a completely predictable or stock answer, you might choose to inquire about other matters instead.

All of this underscores that, in trying to gain useful answers, it pays to consider carefully what to ask, what not to ask, and how best to frame what you do want to ask. Posing questions in the style of a prosecuting attorney is off-putting. Probing too extensively or in too pointed a manner can raise a counterpart's defenses.[54] Part of the art of negotiation is to adroitly incorporate the key questions you hope to have answered into the intelligent conversation about the situation that you are having with the other side.

c. The Timing of Questions

Every bit as important as coming up with insightful questions is the moment and order in which you choose to put them to your fellow negotiator. A good question asked at the right juncture might get a very useful answer, but it might be ignored, or might even lead the negotiation in negative directions, if asked at the wrong time. Determining when is the most opportune moment to pose a particular question is another aspect of negotiation that is a matter of strategy, informed by a negotiator's senses of tact and psychology. One point to note, however, is that, to get information, we must often, in turn, divulge information. One might, therefore, ask a particularly important question after having just answered one posed by the other side.

F. The Importance of Listening

The next points are simple but vitally important. It is not enough merely to ask questions. A skillful negotiator must also fully absorb the responses. This means that one's counterpart needs to be given ample time, space, and attention to answer questions completely. Should the other side be sidestepping a question or struggling to formulate a response to it, do not rush to fill in the silence and move the conversation along. Rather, wait expectantly for their answer.

Good negotiators think on their feet, that is, they have honed the ability to respond, often flexibly and creatively, to new information that they receive. To do this, one must really listen to and understand the other side. Frustration quickly sets in when someone with whom we are conversing seems to hear our words but fails to truly understand what we are saying.

"Every negotiator," it has been said, "faces two realities about what they hear: people don't always mean what they say; people don't always say what they mean."[55] Excellent communication often hinges upon the negotiators forcing themselves, or each other, to think clearly and precisely and then concentrating so as to transfer exact thoughts from one mind to another without ambiguities or misunderstandings intervening. Since this type of communication is often essential to solving challenging problems, one must bear down to articulate points accurately and thoroughly and one must often work to draw out one's counterpart.

A key part of effective listening involves the negotiator projecting genuine interest and really engaging in what the other side is saying. "The effort," two scholars advised, "begins with an open mind—thinking of the person you are negotiating with not as an opponent or as a means to serve your own ends but as someone who can illuminate the situation and has insights that might differ radically from yours."[56]

Emphasizing that you are very interested in their perspective not only makes your counterparts feel appreciated, which might very well contribute to positive working relations, but it might cause them to think more clearly and express their thoughts more carefully than they otherwise would.

One must thus make a concerted effort to concentrate when listening, trying to comprehend fully what one's fellow negotiator actually thinks. A skillful negotiator attends not simply to words, but aims "to gather the ambience that surrounds them, to listen for the mood, character, atmosphere, and emotional tone that put the words into a context."[57] An experienced negotiator also attends to what the other side is not talking about: what topics are being avoided, consciously or subconsciously?

When paired with learning to ask good questions, developing excellent listening skills can pay real dividends. A skillful negotiator can learn much about interests, perspectives, and goals, while filling gaps in knowledge and correcting prior misconceptions. Not only can all this help to take some of the guesswork out of negotiation, but it can reveal paths to creative negotiated resolutions.

1. The Concept of Active Listening

A negotiator practicing *active listening* frequently poses open-ended inquiries, and asks clarifying, follow-up questions. He or she periodically shows the other side that its points are, in fact, registering by paraphrasing what has just been said. That is, the active listener repeats the point just made, but puts the thought in different words and then looks for a reaction: "Do I have it right?," "Is that the essence of your point?"

When a negotiator rephrases something found to be significant, complex, or surprising, and the counterpart amends or corrects the paraphrasing, so much the better. If need be, you can then state your new understanding of the point to make sure that you now fully comprehend what your fellow negotiator has said. Revisions are to be welcomed, not resented, since they are a key part of the process of clear and precise exchanges.

Centuries ago, University of Paris theologians laid down the following rule: "One can speak only *after* one has repeated what the other side has said to that person's satisfaction."[58] Although the virtues of active listening have been extolled in fields like counseling and psychotherapy since at least the early 1960s, negotiation theorists have come to grasp their value more recently. Active listening can ensure that the other side knows that you are attending to their perspective and have fully gathered in what has just been said.

The trickiest aspect of active listening is to convey the message that you are hearing your fellow negotiator's key points without also leaving the impression that you necessarily agree with those points. Perhaps you fully agree; perhaps you are in partial accord; perhaps you completely or partly disagree. Phrases such as the following enable a negotiator to head off misunderstandings.

- "We'll have to think about the extent to which we agree with you, but we definitely see what you're saying."
- "Of course, *our* perspective on what you're saying may differ a bit from *yours*, but I do think I now understand your key concern here."
- "Give us some time to consider these points you've made, but we certainly can see now how things look from your side of the table."

(Appendix 1 on linguistics and negotiation reviews a host of like phrases, put to good advantage by skillful negotiators.)

For several reasons active listening is especially important to interest-based negotiation. First, it fosters joint problem-solving. One negotiator is making an evident effort to try to understand the other's goals, problems, or thinking about the situation they confront. Furthermore, if your counterparts are not convinced that you are hearing and understanding them, they are much less likely to focus on grasping your points. For what you say to resonate with them, they will often need plain and unmistakable reassurance that the thoughts they have advanced have fully registered with you.

A counterpart unsure whether his or her points have really been taken in often redoubles efforts to have you listen to them. Hence, people repeat themselves. When the other side articulates and re-articulates the same thoughts, the natural tendency is to get angry or frustrated and to respond by repeating your own points. The negotiation then stalls. The active listener, instead, paraphrases what their fellow negotiator has just said or asks a clarifying question. This signals that, while you may or may not *agree* with what the other side has said, you have definitely heard and understood the point they have just made.

These active-listening skills can have an even greater impact if later in the negotiation you can recall statements that the other side made earlier and work them into the discussion. Show your fellow negotiator that what they have said has made it from your short-term into your long-term memory, that their points have had an impact, and that you are committed to seeing if it is possible to work with them, attending to their perspectives and interests as well as your own.

Although taking extensive notes may interrupt the flow of a negotiation, jotting down some key thoughts may help you to recall and put them to use even after a good deal of time has passed by. In addition, in trying to absorb another's points, some people find it helpful to take periodic breaks. Asking questions, listening to answers, paraphrasing, and asking follow-up questions is mentally taxing. Stopping for refreshments or simply to step outside momentarily can help negotiators to commit points to memory.

G. Using and Reading Body Language

Part of the art of effective negotiation involves reading people. Whenever a negotiator is meeting a fellow negotiator in person, rather than speaking on the telephone or sending an e-mail, he or she should bear in mind that messages are often conveyed by body language, that is, communications delivered via posture, gestures, or facial expressions.

Those non-verbal messages may be conscious or subconscious, positive or negative, crystal-clear signs or simply vague indications. Understanding how to use and read body language is an aspect of negotiation that ought not be overlooked. The principal goal is to draw some conclusions, if only tentative or speculative ones, of the attitudes and reactions of one's counterpart.

1. Communicating through Expressions and Actions

Attending carefully to a fellow negotiator's body language can reveal something of their innermost thoughts. For hundreds of thousands of years human beings have been interpreting body language to help to understand one another.[59] We will see in Chapter 9, body language messages can vary from one culture to another, sometimes quite dramatically. But, just as people intuitively know something of negotiation, having done it from an early age, so some basic body language ideas ought to be quite familiar.

A furrowed brow typically expresses puzzlement; a man stroking his beard might indicate he is evaluating the situation; a woman grasping both hands of another is likely to be expressing sympathy. Sitting with hands clenched and ankles locked around each other often indicates tension. As we deal with others in an array of different circumstances, we pick up on many of these signs instinctually and, at times, subconsciously.

Perhaps most obviously, people communicate every day by facial expressions. We speak of "poker faces" and "come hither looks." You show someone that you are paying attention by looking them in the eye. You encourage a fellow negotiator to keep talking by nodding, while a grimace, a frown, a tight-lipped face, or a wrinkled brow indicates a negative reaction. The very same words project quite different messages if said with a smile while looking directly at someone or in an expressionless monotone while staring away.

Note, too, that emotions can plainly affect our bodies. We blush and feel heat in our ears or cheeks; perspiration trickles down our sides; we have the sensation of butterflies dancing around in our stomachs. Two scholars wrote, "Fear gets our body and mind ready to run. Anger gets us ready to fight. We may not follow through with the tendency, but our body and mind prepare us to do so. Thus, an emotion affects us whether we like it or not."[60]

Certain of the physiological reactions to different emotions can be masked or perhaps even suppressed; others are not so easily controlled. William Ury noted, "Whereas liars can manipulate words, they cannot easily control the anxiety that raises their voice pitch. Nor can they control the symmetry of their facial expressions; a liar's smile, for instance, may become crooked."[61] One source noted, "A liar might have difficulty coordinating her behavior—saying no while nodding yes, for example. Liars also sometimes forget to add the gestures, pitch variations, raised eyebrows, and widened eyes that we make naturally when telling the truth."[62] By attending to such matters and pressing another with follow-up questions when suspicions are aroused, you may be able to gain a better sense for when your counterpart is being deceptive and when matters are being circumvented or spun out in a questionable way.

An individual's posture, whether sitting or standing, could also be telling. People slouching in their seats project less interest than those sitting forward, who appear intent on what is going on. Brisk or sluggish movements around the room in which the negotiation is occurring might convey a message. The constant twitching of a knee could signal impatience. Patting a counterpart, grasping their arm, or embracing them signal underlying thoughts. One might draw a conclusion even from an individual's breathing. Quick, rapid, and shallow breaths might suggest that someone is nervous or unsure of themselves.

The looks that people give each other, the way they touch one another, the distance they assume in speaking, all of these may very well contain signals of what they are thinking. A head cocked slightly to the side might indicate real interest in what is being said. So too might sitting up and leaning slightly forward so as to face a fellow negotiator more directly. A hand covering one's mouth might indicate uncertainty in what is being communicated, and the folding of arms across the chest could underscore defensiveness or a negotiator's disapproval of what is being said.

2. Being Alert to Body Language

Since much can be read into body language, negotiators should be conscious of the messages they might be sending. "We are often unaware of our feelings," two authorities suggested. "Insecurity, frustration, fear, or anger can take hold and begin to affect our actions without our realizing what is happening. Someone else may notice that my neck muscles have tightened, my face has begun to flush, or an edge has crept into my voice long before I recognize anger in myself."[63]

Nevertheless, one ought not be overly confident of one's ability to read body language: many of these signals are ambiguous and easily misread. Moreover, a counterpart may be using body language tactically, in an attempt to mislead. Recall Shakespeare's line in Hamlet: "One may smile, and smile, and be a villain." Some non-verbal movement may be meaningless: downcast eyes could simply reflect a shy disposition; a hitching shoulder might just be an idiosyncratic mannerism.

Certainly, a skillful negotiator would not act prematurely on the basis of half-formed impressions about something as inherently ambiguous as body language. However, although it would be unwise to read too much into any single expression, gesture, or posture, a series of different body language signals might very well reveal something noteworthy.

Especially worth attending to are *gesture-clusters*, groups of related non-verbal body movements that together are likely to communicate some attitude. A series of actions might all suggest something. For instance, a negotiator who looks down at the table, pinches the bridge of her nose, frowns, furrows her brow, then wags her head slowly from side to side is making multiple gestures of disapproval at what has been happening.

Since negotiators must sometimes make educated guesses as to what their counterparts are actually thinking, body language is a fascinating part of the art of negotiation. Two authorities wrote: "We can learn whether what we are saying is being received in a positive manner or a negative one, whether the audience is open or defensive, self-controlled or bored…. Nonverbal feedback can warn you that you must change, withdraw, or do something different in order to bring about the result that you desire."[64]

Negotiators should also be aware of their own non-verbal communication. They guard against sending false or negative signals, including conveying boredom or hopelessness or lack of interest. Savvy negotiators intent on eliciting cooperation might align their voices and their posture, gestures, and other body language with those of their fellow negotiators. One source noted, "Mimicry seems to make us feel comfortable with others and encourage us to trust them."[65]

When meeting people in his office as Secretary of State, Dean Acheson would get up from behind his desk and take a chair alongside his guest.[66] Similarly, to encourage joint problem-solving, a negotiator might stand up, walk around, sit down next to a counterpart rather than across the table. He or she might write on a flip-chart or blackboard while turning to field suggestions from others, all to underscore the message that they really need to work on the problem side-by-side.

Certainly, non-verbal communication is quite relevant to many of the points made in this chapter. In the opening phase consider the messages sent by the way in which counterparts are greeted, eye contact and posture, even perhaps the pressure of handshakes as the parties meet each other. A negotiator might try to set a positive tone conducive to joint problem-solving through the use of particular facial expressions at the outset of the talks. He or she might arrange seats at the negotiating table in a particular way. An astute active listener would make a point to maintain good eye contact and a posture suggesting real interest in what is being communicated.

A key characteristic of complex negotiations is that they are characterized by the communication of considerable information. Although some points are stated quite explicitly, many are not. Some things may be hinted at or alluded to indirectly. Other matters are not stated clearly enough for another negotiator to grasp the precise meaning. Negotiators try to hide or circumvent still other items, something that leaves their counterparts estimating the truth of the matter.

From the moment a negotiation is initiated, a skillful negotiator should be alert, actively trying to make sense of the other side's statements, gestures, silences, and omissions, looking for opportunities to use their own body language tactically as a part of their overall strategies. All this is yet another integral part of launching an advanced negotiation in a productive fashion.

Notes

1. ROY J. LEWICKI, DAVID M. SAUNDERS, & JOHN W. MINTON, ESSENTIALS OF NEGOTIATION 60 (2001).
2. John H. Wade & Christopher Honeyman, *A Lasting Agreement*, in THE NEGOTIATOR'S HANDBOOK 488 (Andrea Kupfer Schneider & Christopher Honeyman eds., 2006).
3. THOMAS R. COLOSI, ON AND OFF THE RECORD xiv (1993).
4. ROGER FISHER & SCOTT BROWN, GETTING TOGETHER xiii, 8, 21, 154 (1988).
5. HOWARD RAIFFA, THE ART AND SCIENCE OF NEGOTIATION 132 (1982).
6. William R. Fry, Ira J. Firestone, & David L. Williams, *Negotiation Process and Outcome of Stranger Dyads and Dating Couples*, 4 BASIC & APPLIED SOCIAL PSYCHOLOGY 15 (1983).
7. DEBORAH KOLB & JUDITH WILLIAMS, THE SHADOW NEGOTIATION 164 (2000).
8. ROGER FISHER & DANIEL SHAPIRO, BEYOND REASON 58 (2005).
9. G. RICHARD SHELL, BARGAINING FOR ADVANTAGE 68 (1999).
10. PATRICK J. CLEARY, THE NEGOTIATION HANDBOOK 41 (2001).
11. Roger Fisher, *A Code of Negotiation Practices for Lawyers*, 1 NEGOTIATION J. 110 (1985).
12. JAMES C. FREUND, SMART NEGOTIATING 134 (1992).
13. FISHER & BROWN, supra note 4, at 111.
14. COLOSI, supra note 3, at 8.

15. Fisher & Brown, supra note 4, at 113.

16. Roy J. Lewicki, *Trust and Distrust*, in The Negotiator's Fieldbook 199 (Andrea Kupfer Schneider & Christopher Honeyman eds., 2006).

17. David A. Lax & James K. Sebenius, The Manager as Negotiator 237 (1986).

18. Fisher & Brown, supra note 4, at 19.

19. Lewicki, supra note 16, at 192–93.

20. Donald C. Langevoort, *Half-Truths*, in What's Fair 400 (Carrie Menkel-Meadow & Michael Wheeler eds., 2004).

21. Shell, supra note 9, at 59.

22. James Baker, The Politics of Diplomacy 134–35 (1995).

23. Dean G. Pruitt & Sung Hee Kim, Social Conflict 25 (2004).

24. Roger Fisher, *Beyond YES*, 1 Negotiation J. 68 (1985).

25. Fisher & Brown, supra note 4, at 35.

26. Roger Fisher, International Conflict for Beginners 122 (1969).

27. Colosi, supra note 3, at 59.

28. Lewicki, supra note 19, at 201.

29. Fisher & Brown, supra note 4, at 107.

30. Baker, supra note 22, at 135.

31. Fisher & Brown, supra note 4, at 72.

32. Fisher, supra note 24, at 68.

33. Fisher & Brown, supra note 4, at 120.

34. Shell, supra note 9, at 240.

35. Jim Camp, Start With No 117 (2002).

36. Cleary, supra note 10, at 38.

37. Fisher & Brown, supra note 4, at 96–97.

38. Cleary, supra note 10, at 40.

39. Ansgar Wimmer, *The Jolly Mediator*, 10 Negotiation J. 194–95 (1994).

40. Karen King, *But I'm Not a Funny Person ...*, 4 Negotiation J. 119–23 (1988).

41. Alexander G. Nikolaev, International Negotiation 280 (2007).

42. King, supra note 40, at 122.

43. Lax & Sebenius, supra note 17, at 246.

44. Philip H. Gulliver, Disputes and Negotiations 127 (1979).

45. Id. at 70.

46. Freund, supra note 12, at 37.

47. I. William Zartman & Maureen Berman, The Practical Negotiator 95 (1982).

48. Kolb & Williams, supra note 7, at 161.

49. Dale Carnegie, How to Win Friends and Influence People 37 (2d ed. 1981).

50. W. Averell Harriman, *Observations on Negotiating*, 9 J. of Int'l Affs 1 (1975).

51. Baker, supra note 22, at 134.

52. Kolb & Williams, supra note 7, at 220.

53. Cleary, supra note 10, at 40.

54. Kolb & Williams, supra note 7, at 162.

55. Howard Gadlin, Andrea Kupfer Schneider, & Christopher Honeyman, *The Road to Hell is Paved with Metaphors*, in The Negotiator's Handbook 30 (Andrea Kupfer Schneider & Christopher Honeyman eds., 2006).

56. Kolb & Williams, supra note 7, at 140.

57. Fisher & Shapiro, supra note 8, at 28.

58. William Ury, The Third Side 148 (2000).

59. Gerard I. Nierenberg & Henry H. Calero, How to Read a Person Like a Book 4 (1971).

60. Fisher & Shapiro, supra note 8, at 216.

61. William Ury, Getting Past No 42 (2d ed. 1993).

62. *Body Language in Negotiation Process and Beyond*, Program on Negotiation, Harvard Law School, April 14, 2016, http://www.pon.harvard.edu/daily/negotiation-skills-daily/negotiation-techniques-and-body-language-body-language-negotiation-examples-in-real-life.

63. Fisher & Brown, supra note 4, at 48.

64. Nierenberg & Calero, supra note 59, at 14.

65. *Body Language*, supra note 62.

66. Fisher & Shapiro, supra note 8, at 61.

Checkpoints

- A constructive professional relationship with their counterpart helps a negotiator to work efficiently and effectively and to overcome obstacles and challenges, while creating a reservoir of good will that may help the agreement to be implemented and bring the negotiators to work together again in the future.

- A positive working relationship does not require a negotiator to accept a counterpart's values or arguments or approve of how the other side has been acting; instead, it connotes the ability to communicate well about the circumstances the negotiators confront, including especially the differences the parties must contend with.

- To develop good relations, a negotiator is proactive in trying to develop rapport by methods such as drawing on the similarity principle, demonstrating respect for the other side, and showing reliability, while avoiding imposing preconditions such as the need to first make substantive concessions in order to have good relations.

- A negotiator considered trustworthy by the other side has an asset of real value to draw on, while distrust can be a formidable problem, increasing the odds against a successful resolution and, should a deal occur, requiring special arrangements to try to ensure that the agreement is properly implemented.

- A negotiator can try to set any of a number of different tones in his or her opening, and a productive tone can help the parties over later "rough sledding," as potentially problematic statements are passed over lightly and do not become major obstacles.

- Skillful negotiators can use humor — ideally spontaneous and light-hearted in nature — to set a positive environment, recover one that has turned negative, or smooth over an awkward moment; however, attempts to inject humor are also inherently risky, and it is important to be sensitive to how the humor might appear to others.

- Many negotiators find it useful to determine, early on, whether the problem or opportunity that the parties face might be divided into discrete issues to be addressed in a particular sequence, that is, they look to establish an agenda.

- In framing the issues in diverse ways and in a particular order, an agenda can be advantageous or disadvantageous to a particular party. Every agenda has strategic implications.

- Rather than jumping into efforts to entice or manipulate the other side, negotiators confronting complex problems are well-advised to start to interact with their counterparts by establishing an intelligent conversation about the problem or opportunity before them.

- From the opening phase of a negotiation forward, seasoned negotiators use questions to learn about facts, understand the perceptions of the other side, and gain feedback on key issues, while countering possible deception.

- Considerable thought should be put into formulating different varieties of questions, discarding potentially counter-productive ones, and determining the most appropriate timing for posing particular questions.

- Experienced negotiators tend to have excellent listening skills: they give the other side the time, space, and attention needed to answer questions fully, they draw out their fellow negotiators, and really listen to them so as to gain true understanding.

- Active listening entails posing open-ended questions, clarifying answers with follow-up inquiries, and paraphrasing the other side's points to demonstrate that they have been fully absorbed.

- From the opening phase of a negotiation on, negotiators should attend to their own and their counterpart's body language so as to avoid sending false signals or overlook clues as to how the talks are progressing.

Chapter 4

Getting Down to Substance: Working with Interests

Roadmap

- **Moving beyond positions into interests:** Why should negotiators look to move past the initial positions declared by the parties to explore their underlying interests, and what is the significance of objective and subjective interests?

- **Prioritizing, analyzing, and working with interests:** How does a negotiator go about understanding and then engaging with the interests of both sides? What is the spectrum of interests that negotiators may hold in relation to one another, and how might these be worked with to bring about an agreement?

- **Discussing interests productively:** How should a negotiator discuss interests constructively with a counterpart? Why is it so important to gain a close understanding of interests and to probe to better grasp interests?

- **Creating an interest-based resolution:** Why exactly does a negotiator look to serve the interests of his or her counterpart, and how can interests be assembled in an agreement?

- **Sharing information:** How much and which information should a negotiator share with the other side? Why does a negotiator reveal some and withhold other information? What is the sugarcoating problem? Why might a negotiator misrepresent some of his or her concerns?

Chapter 1 led the reader through some important considerations in choosing an approach for a complex negotiation, while sketching out the difference between bargaining by positions and negotiating by aligning the interests of the parties. We will next explore how to engage further with the substance of the problem or opportunity, focusing on the concept of interests and the process of working with interests to resolve differences and reach a potential agreement.

101

A. Moving Beyond Positions into Interests

The best negotiators, it has been said, have "a relentless curiosity about what is really motivating the other side."[1] The interest-based approach starts from the premise that the problems or opportunities that confront the negotiators will be dealt with more skillfully if the discussions can move beyond a focus on the positions that one or both sides have taken, that is, their initial stances or declarations of what they would like to have or, even more specifically, of what it will take to reach an agreement. The analysis of interests aims to shift attention instead to the underlying motivations that are actually driving the parties.

By interests, then, is meant the true concerns of those who are negotiating: what they need, what they want to happen, what will make them secure, what they fear or worry about. The fundamental idea of interest-based negotiation is that, when confronted with a complex problem, negotiators can work with the distinct interests of the parties—some of them possibly shared, overlapping, or dovetailing, others of which could be different, contrasting, or conflicting—to arrive at an agreeable settlement of the issues being negotiated.

Some people assume that interests necessarily reflect values that are individualistic, and perhaps selfish or self-centered. In fact, this need not be the case at all. If one's underlying concerns involve altruistic concerns, community matters, or relationships within a society, these, too, qualify as interests. Interests are "*whatever* each party cares about that might be affected by a negotiation. These range from basic human needs to reputation to self-image to relationships to legitimacy to the financial terms in the contract."[2]

1. Different Uses of the Term *Interest*

One difficulty that sometimes arises in grasping and then implementing an interest-based approach to negotiation is that people commonly use the terms *interest* and *interests* in a number of different ways. If someone says, *"She is a fascinating woman because of the breadth of her interests,"* the reference is to those matters that hold someone's attention, about which they are curious, amused, or fascinated. One often gains some knowledge or cultivates some expertise about one's interests, used in this sense of the term. By contrast, if someone says *"His hopes for great wealth stem from the interests he has inherited in oil wells,"* the word refers to something quite different—a matter of ownership, the title held in oil-producing property.

a. Stakes versus Preferences

When negotiators refer to interests, they usually have in mind two additional uses of the term. Sometimes they are referring to something in which a party has a clear stake, that is, something that logically affects that side of the negotiation. For example, the mayor of a city negotiating with city council members might declare, *"Our community has an interest in minimizing drunk driving."* Since intoxicated drivers impose an array of costs on a municipality, the city has an evident stake—free from the personal feelings or viewpoints of this or that city representative—in minimizing drunk driving to the extent possible. In this sense such an interest is objectively present.

At other times, however, negotiators use the term *interest* to refer to something that might or might not be important to a party. For example, the owner of a lawn service might ask a homeowner, *"Do your neighbors have any interest in whether we prune the row of ornamental cherry trees along your property line?"* Here, some neighboring homeowners could care less, while others might be quite concerned since the decision could affect their view or the shade cast on their property, and neglecting the job might bring on fallen limbs or a split trunk that could kill a tree. Hence, such an interest might or might not be important to the property owners next door.

b. Objective versus Subjective Interests

This brings us to the distinction between objective and subjective interests. An *objective interest* is one that really does, in fact, promote the welfare of that side of the negotiation. For instance, imagine the sale of a large piece of machinery. Any purchaser would be concerned that, once bought and installed, the machinery would function properly. A favorable service agreement might speak to that objective interest.

In an objective approach the circumstances at hand determine the interests. In foreign affairs this was what Lord Palmerston had in mind when he declared of Great Britain: "We have no eternal allies, and we have no perpetual enemies. Our interests are eternal and perpetual, and those interests it is our duty to follow."[3]

In contrast, a *subjective interest* can be thought of as a personal preference or an individual concern. Whether or not fulfilling that interest, in fact, serves a party's well-being could be debated. A subjective interest could be a matter of taste or judgment. It could be motivated by some positive or negative emotion. It could be so focused on short-term considerations as to overlook a long-term dimension or vice-versa. It could be something entirely idiosyncratic or something that many people in that situation would be concerned about. Nonetheless, the party identifies it as something important to them.

Although people sometimes characterize the interests in a negotiation as either objective or subjective, negotiations often involve both varieties of interests. Imagine, for example, a salary negotiation for a new job. Virtually any potential employee would have an objective interest in maximizing the salary term, while any employer would prefer to pay a relatively lower salary. Here, the financial stakes of the parties determine their respective objective interests. The potential employee, however, might or might not also be concerned with a variety of other issues: her job title, perhaps; the extent of travel she would have to do; or whether she could add her "personal days" to her vacation time for the year. Each of these interests would be subjective in the sense that they would be preferences, important to some job candidates but not to others.

This objective-subjective distinction is worth bearing in mind at different points in the negotiation process. One would be when a negotiator meets with a client to discuss important aspects of an upcoming negotiation, and the two share perceptions of interests. Perhaps the negotiator sees the client's formulation of interests as misguided or mistaken. Often, in reasoning with one another, they shape a vision, or revise an existing vision, of their side's objective and subjective interests.

Consider, for instance, an attorney and client meeting to discuss an upcoming negotiation in a divorce case. The lawyer might focus "the attention of her client on the consequences of a protracted battle for the well-being of children. If the client had previously defined the case around retribution, this would involve significant reshaping of the client's perception of his interests."[4]

Note, too, that individuals or factions within an organization often view the entity's interests in quite distinct lights. Departments within a corporation or a government bureaucracy might present differing views of interests. Even in a small organization, perhaps a non-profit or a family business, individuals might perceive diverse interests at stake in an upcoming negotiation.

This is very much in keeping with the concept of subjective interests. Think of these as perceptions of interests created during pre-negotiation preparation and, not infrequently, during the negotiation itself, as each party thinks through the issues and begins to work with the other side. Social scientists might term this a constructivist perspective on interests. People construct their interests by reflecting, discussing, and thinking about different relevant factors.

From the planning stage forward, those pursuing an interest-based approach will want to be thinking about the stakes and concerns at issue in the negotiation. They will want to be alert to all of the interests of the parties, objective and subjective, their own and those of their fellow negotiators.

B. Prioritizing, Analyzing, and Working with Interests

Taking an interest-based approach to a complex negotiation calls on negotiators to go beyond simply listing the interests of the different sides and give real thought to their priority. Interest-oriented negotiators look to gain a close understanding of what is most important to each side, what is only moderately so, and what are interests, but of marginal concern.

It is important to see that negotiators, even sometimes those on the same side of the negotiation, may very well not think exactly alike regarding the priority of interests. People will draw on their own values, attitudes, and cultures as they assess what is most and least important to them. Intelligent, well-prepared negotiators will often come to quite different conclusions about their own and their counterpart's interests.

Differing conceptions of interests may be reflected, then, in varying goals and strategies. Proposed options and ultimate resolutions may be rooted in divergent assessments of interests. Nonetheless, skillful negotiators should strive toward a careful, logical view of what their side's interests are and in what order, while also gaining an understanding of what the other side's interests look like and what its priorities appear to be.

Prioritizing interests can help negotiators to envision a possible agreement. I want to know what is most important to you, and vice versa, so that we can create an agreement that we both like. A deal needs to serve at least some of the primary interests on both sides or one party or the other is likely to balk at accepting it. Note, too, that the nature of negotiation is such that rarely does a negotiator obtain everything that he or she wants. Consequently, understanding the priority of interests on both sides helps negotiators to see what trade-offs might be made to reach a deal.

1. Categorizing Interests

To prioritize interests, negotiators need to analyze them. A useful first step is to categorize. Some interests might be short-term in orientation; others, long-term. Then, one might ask, which is more important? Does one side need some early return on the agreement, or can the parties think primarily in terms of benefits over the long haul?

Some interests are common to many negotiations, such as the desire to set a positive precedent or avoid a problematic one. Other interests are completely fact-specific, that is, they are a concern in one particular context but may not arise at all in another. Certain interests involve matters that will definitely happen; others involve aspirations—a party's hopes, plans, visions, or dreams. Again, which of these are most significant? By categorizing interests, one can begin to assess what is most and least important to the parties.

2. Appraising the Spectrum of Interests

In fact, a range of different interests could markedly affect any particular negotiation. To take one example, a pair of negotiators might assemble a contract with dollar provisions that both sides see as quite satisfactory; however, if the discussions ignore another important interest, such as establishing and maintaining a positive work environment over time, then the deal might still fall apart. If one or both sides become unhappy—perhaps feel ill-used, or treated disrespectfully, or called upon to do more than their fair share in certain circumstances—the arrangement might disintegrate despite advantageous financial terms.

Let us consider next, then, the spectrum of interests that negotiators on different sides of a problem or opportunity might find within a given negotiation.

a. Separate Interests

With *separate interests* one negotiator has an underlying concern or motivation that does not impinge in any way on a different underlying concern or motivation of another. For example, a young couple buys farmland intending to grow organic crops. A first concern is with soil erosion since much of the acreage they want to plant has never been properly contoured. Access to one field, however, is too narrow for a bulldozer to enter without the costly dynamiting of large rocks. The property just down the road is owned by independently wealthy absentee landowners who are retaining ownership of their land in order to provide equal shares of real estate to their children upon their death. When the farmers inquire of the absentee landowners as to whether they might gain permission to bring a bulldozer across their property, their principal underlying interests are separate and distinct. The central concerns of one do not encroach or interfere with those of the other. This may open the door to a negotiated agreement.

b. Shared Interests

In contrast, with *shared interests* both sides in a negotiation have a common underlying motivation or concern. Identifying what might be termed a "coincidence of interests" often brings momentum to a negotiation. Brothers and sisters, for instance, might share an interest in arriving at an equitable procedure to divide up the personal effects of a deceased parent. Two governments might share an interest in blocking the plans of another that both see as an ideological rival. At the most fundamental level, parties have common interests in negotiating to see if each can do better than its walk-away option, or they may share interests "in profiting as much as we can from this deal."[5]

Even in the most bitter disputes, certain shared interests can be evident. Think, for instance, of labor-management differences. A corporation and a union may have had a difficult history. They may sharply disagree on many points and have to contend with a host of conflicting interests. Nevertheless, both share a fundamental interest in the company's continuing as a viable business, serving satisfied customers, and gaining market share over time. That shared interest may help the negotiators to bridge their differences.

Or, consider an example from international politics. When the M-19 terrorist group took over the Embassy of the Dominican Republic in Bogotá, Colombia in 1980, holding scores of diplomats hostage, neither negotiators for the Colombian government nor for the hostage-takers wanted to trigger a political crisis that would bring the Colombian army to overthrow the country's democratic government. Although their visions of Colombia's ideal political regime frontally conflicted, the two sides shared the interest of wanting to avoid a military coup.

Starting from that common ground, the negotiators worked out a resolution that freed the hostages while respecting certain core government principles. And, in the aftermath of the resolution of the Dominican Embassy hostage crisis, the M-19 chose to enter the formal democratic process in Colombia as its own political party.[6]

Parallel interests of this sort may be found even more frequently in friendlier contexts. A corporation negotiating an employment contract with a business executive shares the interest that both would like to see the value of the company's stock rise over time. Sports or literary agents negotiating a contract to represent a prospective client share the desire to maximize the financial return in the client's contract with a team or publisher. Or, imagine an expansion team in a new summer football league that is looking to contract with a recognized but retired sportscaster to encourage fan interest in local broadcasts. Both sides share interests in the team and league thriving over the term of their agreement.

When interests are shared, negotiators can work with each other to see what each might do, separately or jointly, to fulfill those overlapping interests. They may be able to find creative options that make the deal attractive because it speaks to their common concerns. Consequently, shared interests, like separate interests, might help to bring about a negotiated resolution.

c. Dovetailing Interests

Still other interests might be characterized as *dovetailing*. Here, the interests of one negotiator differ from those of the other but the two mesh nicely. The same resolution serves the different interests of the two sides. Imagine, for example, a divorce in which one spouse very much wants custody of the children and other very much does not.

An oft-cited example is that of two children who both want an orange, but one is looking to squeeze out the juice for a fruit punch while the other wants to use the peel for candy.[7] Both children benefit if they divide the parts of the orange intelligently. When negotiators discover such dovetailing interests, these can form the foundation for an agreement. And, articulating just where interests dovetail can make conflicting views, goals, or aspirations seem manageable and enhance prospects for a negotiated resolution.

Imagine here three neighboring businesses in an industrial park where the one in the middle has put up for sale a sizeable tract of its land. Past relations have been strained as employees have clashed over a series of minor disputes. With respect to the real estate up for sale, however, the trucking company to the north could use a portion of the property for expansion and, if it acquired the land, would pave an acre for a parking lot. The neighbor to the south is a bus company, which might install a series of underground storage tanks on the land, a convenient and cost-effective way to fuel its fleet of buses.

Whether the two potential buyers end up purchasing the land together and subdividing the parcel, or one buys it and leases a portion to the other, they capitalize on their dovetailing interests. And, the interests that mesh may help to bring the parties to see their other differences as eminently manageable, providing momentum for other agreements leading to a more cooperative or prosperous future.

d. Tangible and Intangible Interests

Most complex deals involve some *divisible commodities*, such as money, crops, or stocks and bonds, and these often form the heart of the agreement. But intangible matters may be quite important, too. Enhancing one's reputation would be one example, as would saving face in a difficult situation (a topic taken up in more depth in Chapter 9 on culture). One party may care about issues of status, clout, or identity. Another may have charitable or altruistic motivations, while a third is concerned with prestige, goodwill, or self-esteem. Still another may be swayed by an agreement's effect on recognition, credibility, or honor. All of these are intangible interests.

Rather than being absorbed solely with the interests that have financial implications, negotiators should consider as well those that are psychological and linked to emotional well-being. A sports star might want to keep playing alongside current teammates. A supervisor might want to be viewed in a positive light—as fair, honest, and upright by the company's employees. In settling outstanding issues related to an estate, a negotiator might want to ensure satisfaction all around the family: that all the siblings feel reasonably content with their inheritance. Someone who has been libeled or defamed may be much more concerned with repairing his or her reputation or receiving a sincere apology than in counting how many dollars might be received as a result of the incident.

Intangible interests could involve feeling understood, appreciated, respected, fairly treated, or left alone. "[A] bitter divorcing couple," it has been observed, "may actually prefer a financial outcome that requires absolutely no future contact between them over another that is better for both in tax terms, say, but requires them to deal with each other in the future."[8]

Since human nature is complex, whether a dispute is resolved or an opportunity capitalized upon may not always depend on how much money passes from one side to another. Individuals may be motivated by pride. They may be looking for acknowledgment of their efforts by others. They may want to feel stable, secure, or comfortable.

Whether the context is something being sold, or a divorce settlement, or a partnership being dissolved, or items in an estate being divided for distribution, the parties may have grown quite attached to something—whether a house or a horse, a car or a violin, an heirloom—and want to possess it for emotional reasons or find a buyer who will take good care of it.

In short, financial considerations, while often the centerpiece of a negotiation, are rarely the only consideration, even in quite complex scenarios. Imagine, for instance, a university hiring a highly regarded scientist to start a cutting-edge research program in its medical school. Salary is bound to be quite important, but the new professor may also be intent on assessing laboratory facilities, research assistants, vacation time, office space, teaching obligations, and relations with the central administration.

Negotiators should certainly bear in mind intangible motivations and look for ways to speak to and satisfy them, if they can. But, assessing just how important an intangible interest is can be challenging. How does one prioritize, or put a value on, an interest like avoiding the stress and anxiety of going to trial? Here, careful, analytical thought may help a party to arrive at some useful conclusions. For instance, David Lax and James Sebenius suggest that someone trying to appraise the value of avoiding anxiety during a trial imagine that a pharmacist had a product that would completely eliminate such a feeling.

How much would the person be willing to pay for it? They concluded: "To assess tradeoffs among intangible interests, it is sometimes helpful to imagine services one could buy ... to satisfy the same interests."[9]

e. Conflicting and Inconsistent Interests

A hard fact that negotiators must contend with is that some interests clash. With *conflicting interests* one of my underlying concerns or motivations is at odds with one of yours. A neighborhood committee is vitally interested in the peace and quiet of its community and the security of its children. A developer's prime interest is to profit from installing a shopping center on the edge of this neighborhood. But, building stores and operating them may draw in traffic that conflicts with the neighborhood's existing image as a safe and tranquil sanctuary. The neighbors may first try to stop the development project altogether through litigation, but if that effort fails then the challenge is to work out present and future problems. The negotiators must see if they can find practical, innovative, fair ways to deal with the key issues and differences likely to arise.

With *inconsistent interests* pursuing or fulfilling one interest may make achieving another more difficult to carry out, even perhaps impossible to achieve. As one source put it, "You want the rent to be lower; the landlord wants it to be higher. You want the goods to be delivered tomorrow; the supplier would rather deliver them next week. You definitely prefer the large office with the view; so does your partner."[10] The negotiation over such matters may appear to be a zero-sum competitive contest, in which each is trying to get more and give up less of a fixed amount. Here, hard choices, sacrifices, and compromises may ultimately have to be made, and these are the stuff of complex negotiations as well.

Where interests clash, one issue before negotiators involves whether they can be reconciled. Is there a creative way to meet these interests that are at odds with each other such that each party might still be motivated to come to a negotiated resolution? Perhaps there is a trade-off to be made. Might the sting of a higher rent be compensated for by improvements to the apartment? Could the partner who gets the smaller office be otherwise compensated? What would be a fair outcome to a problem of clashing interests?

Note, too, that, on occasion, an agreement is possible even when the interests of the different sides conflict. A group seizes hostages to gain publicity to attract funding and recruits; a government wants to free the hostages but also to choke off support for the extremists. The terrorists believe that the government permitting a taped message to air on national television will result in favorable publicity and advance its cause. Government officials might view the same message as one that the public will find repellent or unintelligible. Thus, the West German government resolved one hostage crisis via the broadcast of what it saw as the "hysterical and incoherent demands of the Baader-Meinhof Gang."[11] Despite interests that could hardly clash more frontally, a negotiated resolution still proved to be possible.

Or, consider a much more common scenario: a possible stock deal within a small business in which the major shareholders have diametrically opposed views concerning future profits. One very much wants to enlarge the business, perhaps using a public offering to finance nationwide expansion. A significant minority shareholder emphatically disagrees with that possible course of action, believing that various economic factors make it far too risky a gamble. He would prefer to sell out if expansion is to occur, cashing in his financial stake in the company since he believes its value may drop precipitously.

The potential buyer analyzes the situation completely differently. She believes the business to be on the cusp of real success, particularly if the business model is brought onto a national stage. She very much wants to increase her holdings so as to capitalize on what she sees as an exciting business opportunity. An agreement for the sale of the stock becomes possible precisely because of the conflicting views.

f. Needs and Values

Some people conceive of a party's needs or its values as being one variety of interests — particularly fundamental or deep interests.[12] Others see them as a different category altogether. After identifying interests as things a party wants that usually take the form of a currency one negotiator can trade with another, Deborah Kolb and Judith Williams wrote: "Values, on the other hand, cannot be traded or compromised, and yet they often define what a negotiator holds most dear. When we discover something about the other person's value system, we open a window on what drives his or her decisions." They concluded: "Differences in interest we can bargain over; differences in values require another order of understanding before we can work through them."[13]

In this same vein Rob Ricigliano pointed out that negotiators often conceive of interests as matters that an agreement can "satisfy" and, hence, that can be resolved at a particular moment in time. Needs and values differ in that they often stand as continuing challenges over time. Ricigliano noted that "my need for security does not go away if I am secure today," and "satisfying one's sense of justice in one case does not mean that justice is no longer an important concern."[14] With respect to needs and values, the parties are likely to have to take a long-term perspective. Perhaps they fashion a deal in which the need is met or the value respected over a lengthy period.

C. Discussing Interests Productively

In going to work on the substance of any complex problem or opportunity set before them, interest-based negotiators should try to understand the separate, shared, dovetailing, tangible and intangible, and conflicting or inconsistent interests as well as the needs or values that may be motivating the parties. Engaging with the underlying interests is exceedingly important since interests can be the core building blocks that negotiators use in constructing a resolution they both favor.

Part of the art of negotiation involves having your antennae out to pick up important signals about the other side's perspective. Seasoned interest-based negotiators will constantly be asking themselves such questions as:

- "Did I correctly assess my counterpart's true motivations?"
- "Which concerns did I not understand so well when I was preparing for the negotiation?"
- "What interests am I hearing about for the first time today?"

What points, then, should negotiating counterparts bear in mind as they turn to discussing interests? First, not all negotiators will be equally comfortable in openly discussing their interests. Some will be pursuing a positional approach. Others may feel that one is inquiring into interests to gain *leverage* over them. And, still others may doubt whether negotiators can cooperate very readily when conflicting interests and differing objectives are evident.

Sometimes a negotiator's attitude can help to overcome a reluctance to discuss interests. Setting a constructive tone, encouraging a problem-solving climate, and establishing strong working relations might bring about a productive discussion of interests. Still, as two scholars wrote: "Even when we are genuinely interested in the other person's thinking and feelings, he or she might question our sincerity. Negotiators don't automatically assume that [an] expressed concern … is real. It takes some convincing, some active demonstration that goes beyond the perfunctory or the expedient, to override these doubts."[15]

Let us look next at how that might be done.

1. Aim for a Close Understanding of Interests

As inexperienced negotiators begin to talk about interests, they sometimes lapse into a pattern of simply repeating a thought or two about the other side's interests. One ought to go a good deal further than this. Experienced negotiators often speak of "getting into the shoes" of their counterpart or "seeing the problem through their eyes." The goal here is not necessarily to *sympathize* with the other side's viewpoint, that is, to feel real compassion for the other person's circumstances. It does, however, often help to be able to *empathize* with the other side's perspective. This entails trying to grasp what it feels like to see the situation—the facts, goals, choices, possibilities—the way that the other negotiator does.[16]

The salient point is that you are not just *uncovering* interests at arms length in a dry, intellectual exercise, but instead are trying to gain a real understanding of what exactly is driving the other side. What does your fellow negotiator need from this negotiation, and why? What type of resolution would he or she prefer? How might your counterpart's interests fit with your own, and what might that mean for the shape of the ultimate negotiated resolution? A discussion in which you really engage with the other side's interests often goes far toward persuading a counterpart that he or she will be able to work, think, and invent with you, as the negotiation proceeds.

2. Probe to Better Grasp Their Interests

One simple but useful way to probe basic statements about interests is to ask "Why?," "For what purpose?," or "What exactly do you mean by that?" Even when the expected answer might seem obvious, a negotiator can often learn quite a bit by attending carefully to how the other side answers these questions.

For instance, a potential employee assumes that the company she is negotiating with wants her to start working January 1st, the date set in the draft contract. She would actually much prefer to take a vacation first and begin her new job a month later. She inquires about their interest—"Why January 1st? What if I were to start working on February 1st?"—and learns that her new employer actually has an interest in "waiting for an office to open or wants to keep its payroll down for the next quarter" and is not so opposed to having the employee start later.[17]

Asking "what if" and "why not" questions can also be quite useful in determining the motivations and priorities of one's counterpart. For example, in a contract negotiation one might inquire: "What if we lowered the base salary but increased incentives? Would you welcome that, or not?" In negotiations over a real estate transaction one might ask: "So, why not divide the property into parcels? You could then sell the house and surrounding lawn to a third party, but sell me the rest of the land so that I gain the acreage I need to graze my llamas. We might both end up better off." Even if the hypothetical suggestions prove to be dead-ends, by posing the questions and hearing the answers, you are encouraging your counterparts to delineate their interests more clearly.

In trying to understand just where their counterpart is coming from, a negotiator might also consider carefully all the constituents to whom the other side answers. What are the interests of the organization or client that the negotiator represents and other *stakeholders* that the party might need to please or satisfy? Think carefully as well about those outsiders who have an interest in the matter since an agreement might help or harm them. If they are also pleased by the terms of an agreement, this may help to ensure that the provisions are carried out as the negotiators contemplated, without future interference, thereby avoiding extra costs and uncertainties. Finally, it may also be useful to keep in mind that a negotiator working on behalf of another may still have his or her own interests to serve. A negotiator might want to be rehired or to move expeditiously toward a resolution. He or she might feel a need to appear competent or creative, tough or practical, to others at or away from the table.

In a negotiation of some complexity the interests of each side are seldom completely self-evident. Discerning what they are requires thoughtful interaction, good judgment, and persistence and insight in posing questions. A complex interest-based negotiation is often marked by revelations, a fresh understanding of some aspect of the situation that brings issues to be seen in a fresh light.

Hence, one has to be alert to new information, then be flexible to work what you have discovered into an innovative deal that both sides find to be attractive. In this process, gaining an informal understanding of how the circumstances at issue appear *from your counterpart's perspective* is vitally important. The more keenly you grasp their objective and subjective interests, the sharper is your vision of what might be offered up to satisfy them as well as what might be gained for yourself in a deal to which they will agree. (The latter, of course, is the point that will ultimately be of transcendent importance from your own perspective.)

3. Cab Driver Example

Let us consider next an example of how interests might be worked with creatively in circumstances to which it is easy to relate. In teaching negotiation to students traveling to multiple destinations on the Semester-at-Sea program, I have seen them struggle, at first, in bargaining with taxi drivers in foreign countries. Their initial inclination is to view the cab driver as largely controlling the negotiation. The driver knows the distance to popular destinations and the structure of cab fares. Taxis can be scarce in large cities, and ports can be located in unsavory areas. The students at first see their negotiation with a cab driver in classic distributional terms. Every unit of currency that goes to the driver comes out of the student's pocket. They view communications with drivers as one-time negotiations, and their goal is simply not to be taken too outrageously.

With experience, however, the students come to see that the drivers actually have multiple interests that might be served by a fair negotiated resolution. For the taxi driver, making a short-term profit on a single cab ride is definitely an important interest, but gaining a satisfied customer who might call for that particular cabbie for a return fare could be a factor as well.

Profits over a bit longer term, say the entire period the ship will be in the port, could motivate a cabbie too. The recommendation of one satisfied student to his or her friends, who might then call the same cab company and request that particular driver, could be of some weight. This is particularly the case since taking a group of students on a day-long or overnight drive might far eclipse the profits that the taxi driver could expect from trolling around the city, competing with dozens or hundreds of other cabs to take people on short fares. Hence, a cab driver might very well be motivated to get to know some of the students, develop positive working relations with them, and provide a fair price and prompt service with safe driving.

Then, students might well have hard currencies—euros, U.S. dollars, Japanese yen, and so on—that a cab driver might prefer to the local currency as compensation. And, items the students have brought along—hats, clothing, watches, high-technology gadgets, and alike—may be unavailable or far more expensive in that country. The cabbie might want such items or know someone to whom they could be sold at a handsome profit. Then, those traveling through multiple countries are in and out of an array of markets and may have regular access to duty-free shops in ports and airports where various goods are sold at discounted prices to foreigners. Hence, students may have already bought some items on their travels that they would be willing to part with in the right deal. For all of these reasons, *barter transactions*, in which commodities are exchanged rather than money, might enable students to save cash, while leaving the cab driver feeling satisfied, well-compensated, and eager to please.

When two dozen students began to think creatively with multiple cab drivers in a slew of foreign countries, the number of innovative deals they reached was astonishing. To see and capitalize on these possibilities, however, you must enter such a negotiation with an open and creative mind, ready to engage with another as a negotiator who also has a range of interests to try to satisfy. You must be willing to communicate intelligently with that person, put yourself in your counterpart's shoes and start an intelligent conversation with them about how each could help the other toward its goals.

The broader lesson here is that, as a negotiator, you are well-advised to work with your counterparts, try to see life from their perspectives, and inquire closely into their interests and goals. Profits can often be envisioned in the short-term or the medium- or long-term with different repercussions for agreements. Often, sellers are centrally concerned with price, but they may also be very interested in retaining good customers and increasing market share. A buyer might compensate a seller with straight cash or with some other compensation. In short, creative agreements are the fruits of productive discussion of interests.

4. Discussing Your Own Interests

To arrive at an agreement that meets as many of your interests as possible as completely as possible, you will usually need to ensure that the other side understands your most important concerns. The art of interest-based negotiation involves bringing one's counterpart around to become engaged in helping you to satisfy your interests. But, for the other side to do that, you will need to understand and work with their interests, too.

It is also important to bear in mind that, if you are engaged in a collaborative problem-solving effort to find a mutually beneficial outcome, you not get so wrapped up in identifying the other side's interests that you end up shorting the discussion of your own interests. What particular concerns do you want your fellow negotiators to focus on, as you work together to create an outcome that you both support?

In a complex negotiation there may also be certain interests that you prefer to keep private, at least for the moment and perhaps throughout the negotiation. For example, one might fear that the urgency of one's need for something might provide leverage to the other side. Or, one might not want to spotlight a particular interest for fear it would bring about a strong adverse reaction from a counterpart. In such situations the savvy negotiator might pursue those sensitive interests more subtly, perhaps waiting for an opportune moment to suggest a tradeoff that in the overall context of the negotiation might well be attractive to both sides.

Another approach to discussion of interests would withhold discussion of some of them for a time since the negotiator prefers to encourage a process in which both sides go back and forth in progressively disclosing information on interests. This tactic responds to the concern that one side would provide much more information on its interests than the other would. Hence, Howard Raiffa proposed what he termed a "graded approach": "some of A's interests can be openly shared with B; some A may choose not to divulge; and some might be disclosed in an adaptive manner depending on how forthcoming the other ... turns out to be."[18]

When you do choose to articulate your important interests, the challenge is to do so in a way that really registers with, and perhaps even appeals to, your counterpart. You want to make your own perspective on what is really driving you come alive for those listening. A skillful negotiator thus devotes some time in pre-negotiation preparation to determining the most effective and engaging way to explain his or her interests to the other side.

In preparing and undertaking a strategy that draws on the interest-based approach, negotiators are well-advised to ask "why," "what if," and "why not" questions of themselves or their own side. By continually asking these questions, negotiators move toward discovering deeper motivations and not simply relying upon the surface declarations, the initial stances, of the parties. They thereby develop a precise understanding of their own interests that they can articulate well to their fellow negotiators.

Then, presentation of interests is important as well. Clear and open discussion of interests can work to promote joint problem-solving. But, stating things simply, directly, and vividly often requires real concentration and, sometimes, forethought. It is all too easy in a negotiation of any complexity for your points to get tangled up and ultimately lost in long confusing sentences and paragraphs.

Note, too, that a good sense of pace or timing is often important since points may be overlooked or forgotten if a slew of interests is blurted out one after another in disorganized fashion. Instead, a skilled negotiator presents interests in a thoughtful manner, giving his or her counterparts sufficient time so that they can absorb the key points and ask clarifying questions, if necessary.

D. Sharing Information: Pros and Cons

The effort to learn about interests and their priority brings us to the perennial issue of how much and what information to reveal to the other side. If the process of working cooperatively with one another is to result in a mutually beneficial negotiated resolution, the two sides must share a good deal of information. At the same time, each is likely to designate certain matters as confidential. Negotiators often see pros and cons to revealing things to the other side that it does not already know. Let us think about some of them.

1. Why You Reveal Information

By opening a window to the other side on what concerns you, you give them the opportunity to help you to find a possible solution that you both like. The reciprocal sharing of information can generate momentum toward an agreement, while withholding many views, facts, and goals can stunt the problem-solving process. If the negotiators are trying to resolve a difficulty or capitalize on an opportunity together, they need to understand a good deal of each other's visions, interests, and perspectives. If you keep your counterpart in the dark about your actual motivations and objectives, then you may be dramatically limiting the ability to work together constructively. You may have to come up with the possible solutions—solutions that you like and that you hope they will also agree to—all by yourself.

But, if you discover what is really driving the other side, what its needs and concerns truly are, and if you reveal something of your own core interests, then you are in a position to work together with your fellow negotiators to invent ways to reach your respective goals. For this reason, rather than relying on what the other side thinks that we want—which may be wholly or partially erroneous or quite incomplete—we describe for them what we really are looking for.

In the best of circumstances people in a complex negotiation are often in the dark about many things or confused by them. Withholding considerable information can exacerbate this lack of understanding. It can also lead a counterpart toward false assumptions, perhaps assumptions that are more problematic than disclosing the information would have been. If the negotiators never really understand one another's interests, they may be hard-pressed to figure out what a proposal would need to contain in order to gain an agreement.

Providing the other side with information may also work toward enhancing the other negotiator's confidence or trust. Being frank and up-front with them underscores that you are genuinely trying to work together to come to an agreement that you both can support. A negotiator may be legally obligated to reveal certain information, such as known property defects in a home sale, or he or she may feel that honesty or upright ethical behavior requires disclosure of some fact.[19] And, with respect to some potentially problematic information, one's counterpart may already know something about it or be likely to discover it in due course. Revealing such information might be a strategically sound decision.

When one side shares its views, it tends to encourage a dynamic in which the other side does so as well. An important part of human nature involves the reciprocal sharing of information. In many different circumstances we tend to be much more inclined to tell someone something if they have told us about something else. You reveal some little known fact to me; I respond by sharing something similar with you. When we want to establish a relationship or maintain one, we bring someone into our confidence, and then we expect them to do likewise.

Although some might take this to be naive behavior, in fact, as Howard Raiffa, an eminent scholar in the field, noted, "Negotiations characterized by truthful exchange of information and interests are surprisingly common."[20]

The fact is having revealed information to one another can be extremely useful when the negotiators turn toward generating creative options, overcoming impasses, and, eventually, closing a deal. Hence, as an interest-based negotiator tries to work cooperatively with the other side, sharing thoughts about goals, positions, and interests, he or she looks to project being an honorable and genuine counterpart, diplomatic, tactful, and straightforward.

2. Why You Withhold Some Information

And yet, this issue has another dimension, too, that ought not be overlooked. "All too often," it has been observed, "bluffing, threats, trickery, exaggeration, concealment, half-truths, and outright lies come to mind when we think of negotiations." Here, Raiffa noted: "Dialogue may not be reciprocated on equal terms. Unscrupulous parties may exploit strategically sensitive information to boost their own payoff. Negotiators may engage in strategic misrepresentation of their own interests in the hope of tricking the other party into making concessions."[21]

Moreover, negotiators, especially those who are poorly prepared, sometimes provide information to the other side that they later regret. Sharing an unusual amount of information might lead your counterpart to assume that you are desperate to reach a deal.[22] Even more important, disclosing certain things could hurt a negotiator's bargaining position by divulging real weaknesses of one sort or another. If you are completely candid with the other side, you might show your counterpart the urgency of your needs. Being too revealing of your interests might indicate where you would settle, thus revealing the minimum the counterpart needs to do to secure your agreement.

An experienced negotiator will consider: "Might this particular fact or point of view, once shared with the other side, later put me in an uncomfortable position or somehow be used against the interests of my side of the negotiation?" For example, while a negotiator may be inclined to share considerable information about interests, he or she might withhold full information about the intensity of those interests.[23]

A negotiator might also choose not to share inner thoughts about what trade-offs would be acceptable and unacceptable. And, he or she might resist disclosing too explicitly the priority of interests. Here, the fear would be that one's counterpart might lose motivation to work very hard to satisfy interests that have already been identified as less important. Once the interest is seen as well down the list of priorities, then the other side might be inclined to ignore it.

Still other items might be shared or not depending on the state of the relationship, for instance, the degree of trust that has developed between the negotiators. Certainly, it would be wholly legitimate not to discuss matters told to you in confidence, or financial information considered private, or proprietary processes and other manufacturing or industrial secrets. But, a negotiator might also choose to keep confidential his or her ambitions, the state of relations with others, or other personally sensitive topics.

On occasion, a negotiator might be instructed to keep the identity of his or her principal confidential. If it were known, the other side might try to take advantage. For instance, a wealthy individual or entity might fear that a seller would demand a higher price than otherwise believing that the buyer could afford it. A developer trying to assemble a parcel from adjacent lots might be concerned that holdout tactics would raise costs and might fear having to pay more than market value if neighbors realized who was behind the offer.

In determining what to divulge and what to withhold, less-experienced negotiators should bear in mind that sharing all of their thoughts with their fellow negotiators is not necessary in order to have a productive, respectful working relationship or to instill a positive, cooperative tone. Seasoned negotiators understand that certain matters may be freely shared; others are innately confidential. Part of the art of negotiation and a significant component of negotiating strategy involves determining into which category particular pieces of information ought to fall.

3. The Dangers of Sugarcoating Matters

Another aspect of sharing information involves the accuracy of what is said. Here, it can be critically important not to *sugarcoat* matters. Too often, inexperienced negotiators are so intent on nurturing their positive working relationship with their counterpart that they transmit false or misleading signals, or circumvent or dance about what they truly think. They spin points toward what the other side might like to hear at that moment, obscuring what they truly think.

Sugarcoating creates false expectations. It can raise hopes that will never be fulfilled. Often, this eventually leads to frustration. Sugarcoating can also greatly elongate the negotiation process and obscure whether a negotiated resolution is, in fact, possible. By contrast, being straightforward—directly confronting difficulties and being up front about your differences with the other side—can markedly assist communication.

If you have grave problems with something said, it is incumbent on you, as a skillful negotiator, to express them. You might, for instance, change your style or the tone of the negotiation temporarily: lower your voice, speak more seriously and deliberately, and get the message across. This approach is more likely than sugarcoating to help to propel matters toward a constructive conclusion. Here, one might recall the declaration by Mahatma Ghandi: "A 'No' uttered from the deepest conviction is better and greater than a 'Yes' merely uttered to please, or what is worse, to avoid trouble."[24]

4. Thinking Ahead about Information Sharing

You should aim to be able to defend, with a logical, sensible, reasonable argument, why you chose to reveal, or not to reveal, particular matters during the negotiation. A skillful negotiator thinks ahead of time about what items he or she wants to share with the other side, and why, and which he or she would prefer not to reveal, or not to reveal at once, and why that is the case.

The critically important factor here is often timing: when exactly to reveal information? Is there an optimal moment to divulge certain matters to the other side? And, how exactly does one plan to fend off inquiries into matters better kept private, at least for the moment?

Intelligent and effective negotiators may differ considerably on how much information to impart to the other side in different circumstances. Beginning negotiators often act cautiously and defensively and are strongly inclined not to share much information at all. This inclination is often linked to a negotiator's desire to minimize potential damage. I fear that my counterpart might find a way to use a certain piece of information against me, and so I try to keep it to myself.

More experienced negotiators realize that the tendency to withhold too much information may greatly curtail a developing agreement: its scope, its creativity, its ability to serve key interests in an optimal way. As Howard Raiffa concluded: "Open disclosure of strategically sensitive information can be a powerful influence in a negotiation. The more one side judiciously shows its hand, the more the other side will disclose. The better the relationship, the more the two sides trust each other, the more open they can afford to be, and the more valuable the agreement they are likely to reach."[25]

5. Learning about What Concerns the Other Side

Let us think next about the situation where you would like to learn more about the other side's concerns. What ought a negotiator bear in mind here?

a. Frank Disclosure of Concerns

As the two sides probe for information, each being presented with a sequence of choices about what to reveal and what to remain guarded about, a negotiator will sometimes come right out and disclose interests. A negotiator looking to cooperate with another may not want to hide interests from the other side. To the contrary, negotiators often want their interests to spring to life for their counterparts, so their chief concerns take a position at the head of the list of matters that need to be dealt with.

For example, imagine that I am negotiating with a farmer. He will cut and bale the hay on my farm and take it to feed his cattle in exchange for an annual payment to me. Assume that one of my underlying concerns is to receive the compensation for my hay in time to pay my property tax bill. As we negotiate, I may very well want the farmer to understand and focus on that interest, rather than hide it.

That dynamic is true of many interests in many different sets of circumstances. If the other side does not know what I really care about, how will they work with me to fashion an agreement with provisions that we both accept and approve of? It is quite true that a careful, thoughtful negotiator will not want to highlight, raise, or divulge various matters to an opposing negotiator. But, keeping the other side in the dark about central concerns may not be a part of a negotiator's strategy at all.

b. Strategic Misrepresentation about Concerns

Nevertheless, in some contexts a negotiator might look to skirt any detailed discussion of particular interests. With respect to my wanting compensation for my hay in time for my taxes, I could fear the farmer might react by saying, "Sure. I'll meet your interest there, but realize in that case I can't pay you as much."

In fact, a negotiator might mislead the other side about key interests as part of strategic misrepresentation of any number of matters: the party's priorities or its objectives, for instance. The general manager of a sports team, engaged in trade discussions with another, might not immediately reveal the team's interest in a particular player, just as a tourist might walk through a Middle Eastern bazaar and feign indifference to something she very much wants. Indeed, in various circumstances a negotiator might see a strategic advantage to downplaying or appearing neutral about something he or she really wants to gain, while pretending to be attached to something that he or she is actually quite prepared to give up.

Or, a negotiator might purposefully overstate an interest in something with the idea of conceding that point later in exchange for something else. Frankly disclosing one's interests, or even revealing one's interests more thoroughly than the other side does, could very well eliminate the possibility of using such tactics. This could have significant consequences in a complex negotiation.

Furthermore, on occasion, a party may have what is sometimes termed a *vested interest*, that is, a personal stake or special attachment of some kind to an existing arrangement or institution. And, this might be seen as embarrassing to reveal. Whether a third party must be satisfied, or a political debt paid off, or budget constraints respected, significant interests, as a negotiation begins, may be obscured.[26]

c. Trying to Determine Hidden Concerns

Given these various reasons not to fully disclose all of one's interests, a negotiator may suspect, as a negotiation progresses, that he or she has not yet fully appreciated the interests of the other side or, perhaps, has completely misconstrued certain of them. Since some negotiators are not inclined to discuss their interests freely, sometimes the process of discovering and analyzing interests is more subtle than simply accurately assessing interests ahead of time or directly asking the other side and discovering or confirming what concerns them. Only through holding an intelligent conversation, asking questions, listening carefully, and perhaps judiciously estimating motivations can a party gain real insight into what is actually driving key aspects of the negotiation.

One might gather valuable information about the undisclosed interests of another party or their priority from noting which topics they want to talk about and which they prefer to avoid. Clues could lie in their body language or their tone of voice as different matters are raised. Yet another approach would be to advance possible resolutions with different features—package A, package B, and package C—and carefully absorb how the other side responds to the differences in the proposals.[27]

Ultimately, you may have to make an informed guess as to what the other side really thinks. And, under such circumstances even seasoned negotiators sometimes misconstrue what is actually in their counterpart's mind.

d. Thinking through Certain Concerns Together

Sometimes, the problem is not so much uncovering matters the other side has screened from view. Rather, your counterpart may not have thought clearly and comprehensively about their interests. Perhaps one's negotiating partner is unprepared. Or, the circumstances may be quite complex. Or, missing information might muddle the other side's conception of its interests.

In a complex negotiation it is not uncommon to have to think through with one's fellow negotiators just what their interests might be: "For many, only by talking through their needs and interests in a supportive context do they come to know what those interests really are."[28]

One should be careful here, though. Clearly, it would be counterproductive to lecture at a counterpart as to how they should view their own interests. A negotiator who, in a condescending or paternalistic manner, tells the other side what they really should think and what they ought to want is a frustrating and ineffective partner.[29] Negotiators should certainly resist the inclination to try to solve another party's problems, while ignoring their counterpart's perception of the problem and perhaps working against their will.

Nonetheless, a skillful negotiator will sometimes dissect the situation that confronts both parties, trying to draw the other side into the conversation. In this intelligent discussion of a shared problem or opportunity, each negotiator helps the other to focus on and consider important points in a new light, something that might cause them to re-organize or re-orient their thinking.

E. Creating an Interest-Based Resolution

So, why exactly is it so important to work with interests extensively in a negotiation? Your aim is to arrive at an agreement that satisfies your own interests quite well, but it is also to satisfy the other side's interests sufficiently that your counterpart will voluntarily join in the deal.

I serve your interests; you serve mine—that is the essence of the bargain that underlies interest-based negotiation. Reasoning of just this sort led Adam Smith to write, "It is not from the benevolence of the butcher, the brewer or the baker that we expect our dinner, but from their regard to their own interests."[30] Furthermore, a negotiator looking ahead might hope to have his or her counterpart's interests met to such an extent that the other side is motivated to come back and negotiate again in the future.

In a very real sense, then, your job as a negotiator is not simply to attend to your own concerns, as exceedingly important as that goal obviously is. Rather, it is also to satisfy your fellow negotiator's interests, where you can or must do so. You want to meet their interests sufficiently that they are motivated to agree as well. One negotiation authority put it like this: "I do not need to like or trust you in order to negotiate wisely with you.... All that is necessary is for me to find some way of getting what I want ... by leaving the door open for you too to do well."[31]

As a matter of negotiation theory, then, the chief reason you look for ways to serve the other side's interests is not to get your counterpart to like you. It is not to show that you are broad-minded and flexible. You may want to help solve their problems for them or you may not care deeply about that. In any case this is not your leading concern. The central purpose of looking to serve the other side's interests is not even to help the cause of being a good person responsive to the needs of others. Instead, the principle reason is to give your counterpart sound, sensible reasons to serve your interests in turn.

Toward these ends, a thorough exploration of each other's interests often goes far toward turning a negotiation into a joint problem-solving exercise, rather than an adversarial or competitive contest. There is no gainsaying the fact that working with the interests of both sides takes time. One should acknowledge as well, however, that turning a complex negotiation into a positional contest is very likely to occupy a lot of time too, perhaps even more time than pursuing an interest-based resolution would take.

It should also be pointed out that a quick negotiation is often assumed to be an efficient one. Certainly, a negotiation that feels stalled or overly repetitive turns frustrating, a state of mind that benefits no one. However, a skillful negotiator is not simply aiming to find a speedy solution that both sides can live with. To negotiate well, it is not enough to get a deal, any deal, that offers you some benefits and to which your counterpart will also acquiesce. Instead, you want to press for the best outcome that can possibly be achieved under the existing circumstances.

In short, an expert negotiator aims to satisfy his or her own interests as completely and well as possible. While this counsel may sound self-evident, many fail to heed it. Rather, they find some common ground with their counterpart and settle too quickly for a deal that both can tolerate. By contrast, the most effective negotiators will not finally resolve a problem on any particular set of terms until they have satisfied themselves that no better resolution is available.

Here, merely discussing interests in a passing or superficial way is likely to be insufficient. Pushing forward too rapidly bypasses the deliberation needed to come to an optimal negotiated resolution. An impatient negotiator who presses on toward creating options and closing a deal immediately after a cursory examination of interests undercuts the process of working together effectively and thoroughly to create the best possible agreement.

Really digging into the interests, laying out concerns of your own, and inquiring as the other side's with intelligent questions and follow-ups shows your fellow negotiators that you understand their perspectives and are looking to satisfy their interests, where you can. That interest-based dialogue often persuades a counterpart that you can work together in a way that could very well lead to an outcome both sides like.

As negotiators cooperate in this way, they gain a stake in trying to create a negotiated resolution that suits each side well enough to agree. With time, then, the discussion shifts from identifying interests to working with them to fashion a possible resolution. Here, an interest-based negotiator might benefit from having the questions laid out in Box 4.1 in mind.

Box 4.1 — Formulating an Interest-Based Resolution

When the discussion shifts from identifying interests to working with them to fashion a possible resolution, a negotiator should have a number of questions in mind.

- What have been areas of common ground where we seem to think alike?
- What could be some key pieces of a mutually beneficial agreement?
- What could the other side do that would serve my interests?
- What could I do that would meet some of the other side's interests?
- What shared interests might we capitalize on to assemble a deal attractive to both parties?
- How about interests that are separate and distinct, but that do not conflict? How might satisfying those interests form a part of the negotiated resolution?

And, then, of course, real thought and discussion ought to be put into conflicting interests.

- Where do our interests, in fact, conflict?
- How might we be able to bridge our differences?
- Are there ways to circumvent conflicting interests or arrange them in a resolution that both sides support?
- If not, how might these be managed in an evenhanded way that both sides see as legitimate and fair?

The overall question might be put as follows.

- Can each side's interests be satisfied sufficiently and fairly so that both are enthusiastic about a mutual agreement or at least find a negotiated resolution preferable to walking away?

---

1. Moving on From an Interests Discussion

Sometimes, the different sides in a negotiation launch in eagerly, exchanging ideas about interests, but eventually the discussion stalls. The negotiators seem to be repeating each other, and frustration or weariness sets in. To forestall or overcome this, negotiators need to develop a good sense for when to wind up their discussion of interests and begin to create options, solve problems, and ultimately assemble a possible deal.

The overarching aim of one negotiating by the interest-based method is to discuss interests until you feel fairly confident that you have articulated your own interests as fully as seems necessary and that you understand much of what comprise your counterpart's core concerns. When the different sides are confident that they see the actual matters at stake, not just the proxies or the initial positions, they are ready to progress from talking about interests to creating options.

Recall, too, that one can always double back, clarifying or digging further into interests in the midst of the future phases of the negotiation. So, aim for a discussion of interests that is crisp as well as thorough. To keep momentum going, avoid redundancy, and be ready to move on when matters get repetitive.

Once the negotiators feel that they have a good grasp of the interests of the different sides, the time has come to consider again the negotiating issues, perhaps re-articulating the problems or opportunities you face. Then, interest-based negotiators look to build on one another's thinking in an effort to resolve all of the issues that ought to be dealt with in order to reach a negotiated resolution. Upcoming chapters explore different ideas of how to do this as efficiently and effectively as possible.

Notes

1. G. Richard Shell, Bargaining for Advantage 87 (1999).
2. James K. Sebenius, *What Roger Fisher Got Profoundly Right*, 29 Negotiation J. 162 (2013) (italics in original).
3. Lord Palmerston, Speech in the House of Commons (Aug. 7, 1844).
4. Joel Cutcher-Gershenfeld & Michael Watkins, *Toward a Theory of Representation in Negotiation*, in Negotiating on Behalf of Others 31 (Robert H. Mnookin & Lawrence E. Susskind eds., 1999).
5. David A. Lax & James K. Sebenius, The Manager as Negotiator 106 (1985).
6. Michael R. Fowler, *The Relevance of Principled Negotiation to Hostage Crises*, 12 Harv. Neg. L. Rev. 287–89 (2007).
7. Roger Fisher, William Ury, & Bruce Patton, Getting to Yes 56–57 (2d ed. 1991).
8. Lax & Sebenius, supra note 5, at 73.
9. *Id.* at 75, 86.
10. Roger Fisher, William Ury, & Bruce Patton, Getting to Yes 81 (2d ed. 1991).
11. James Bennett & Thomas Saaty, *Terrorism: Patterns for Negotiation*, in Terrorism 281 (Robert Kupperman & Darrell Trent eds., 1979).
12. Dean Pruitt & Sung Hee Kim, Social Conflict 15 (3d ed. 2004).
13. Deborah Kolb & Judith Williams, The Shadow Negotiation 194 (2000).

14. Rob Ricigliano, *A Three-Dimensional Analysis of Negotiation*, in THE NEGOTIATOR'S FIELDBOOK 58 (Andrea Kupfer Schneider & Christopher Honeyman eds., 2006).

15. KOLB & WILLIAMS, supra note 13, at 156.

16. Robert Mnookin, Scott Peppet, & Andrew Tulumello, *The Tension Between Empathy and Assertiveness*, 12 NEGOTIATION J. 217 (1996).

17. SHELL, supra note 1, at 84.

18. HOWARD RAIFFA, NEGOTIATION ANALYSIS 199 (2002).

19. *An Example of the Anchoring Effect—What to Share in Negotiation*, Program on Negotiation, Harvard Law School, March 22, 2016, http://www.pon.harvard.edu/daily/negotiation-skills-daily/what-to-share-in-negotiation/?m.

20. RAIFFA, supra note 18, at 83.

21. *Id.*

22. *An Example of the Anchoring Effect—What to Share in Negotiation*, Program on Negotiation, Harvard Law School, March 22, 2016, http://www.pon.harvard.edu/daily/negotiation-skills-daily/what-to-share-in-negotiation/?m.

23. Roger Fisher & Wayne Davis, *Authority of an Agent*, in NEGOTIATING ON BEHALF OF OTHERS 75–76 (Robert H. Mnookin & Lawrence E. Susskind eds., 1999).

24. WILLIAM URY, THE POWER OF A POSITIVE No 7 (2007).

25. RAIFFA, supra note 18, at 199.

26. GLEN FISHER, MINDSETS 82 (2d ed. 1998).

27. Lee Ross, *Reactive Devaluation in Negotiation and Conflict Resolution*, in BARRIERS TO CONFLICT RESOLUTION 39 (Kenneth J. Arrow et al. eds., 1995).

28. KOLB & WILLIAMS, supra note 13, at 224.

29. ROGER FISHER & SCOTT BROWN, GETTING TOGETHER 140 (1988).

30. ADAM SMITH, AN INQUIRY INTO THE NATURE AND CAUSE OF THE WEALTH OF NATIONS 22 (1993).

31. Jeffrey Z. Rubin, *Some Wise and Mistaken Assumptions About Negotiation*, 45 J. OF SOCIAL ISSUES 198 (1989).

Checkpoints

- Where the term "positions" signifies what the parties initially pronounce as their stance, desired resolution, or declaration of what it will take to reach an agreement, the term "interests" refers to the underlying concerns of the parties: what they need, what they want to happen, what will make them secure, and what they fear or worry about.

- An objective interest is something that, in fact, promotes the welfare of that side of the negotiation. In contrast, a subjective interest is a personal preference or concern.

- In appraising the interests of the different parties, negotiators should bear in mind that interests can be separate or shared, and tangible or intangible; they can dovetail with one another or conflict. Interests can also reflect the needs and values of the parties.

- In learning about or estimating the interests of the other side, negotiators should not just list the interests at issue, but try to gain a sense for how their counterparts prioritize their interests. What seems to be most and least important?

- Although an opposing negotiator may not enter a negotiation wholly comfortable with discussing interests, one's opening can help to overcome this reluctance by setting a constructive tone, encouraging a problem-solving climate, and establishing strong working relations.

- Negotiators should aim for a close understanding of the other side's interests and should be prepared to probe to better grasp them, using such techniques as "why," "for what purpose," "what if," and "why not" questions.

- The better your grasp of their interests, the more keen is your vision of what you can offer up to satisfy them and what you can gain for yourself.

- Do not get so caught up in working with the other side's interests that you end up giving short shrift to your own interests. Instead, identify the most important concerns that you want your counterpart to understand and focus on as you work with them to create a mutually beneficial outcome, and figure out how to make those interests of yours come alive for your counterpart.

- Put some thought as well into which of your interests you prefer to keep to yourself at least for the moment. Why are these private concerns, and under what circumstances, if any, might you opt to reveal them?

- To avoid frustration and redundancy, be prepared to move on from your discussion of interests once you feel that you grasp the actual matters at stake — the underlying needs, concerns, and motivations.

Chapter 5

Analyzing Walk-Away Alternatives, Leverage, and Power

Roadmap

- **Assessing walk-away alternatives:** What are the concepts of a Best Alternative to a Negotiated Agreement (BATNA) and a reservation value? Why are they so integral to interest-based negotiation?

- **BATNA analysis:** How does analyzing the parties' BATNAs assist in determining when to accept or reject a particular proposal? What are the implications of underestimating and overestimating a BATNA? How might BATNA analysis affect negotiation strategy?

- **Determining leverage:** What is the concept of leverage? How does a negotiator appraise the leverage of different parties? How might leverage be used and countered?

- **Negotiating power:** What are the fundamental elements of negotiating power? How does authority affect a negotiator's power? What are some of the means by which one obtains influence over others? Why are considerations of power specific to the task at hand? How does one's negotiating capabilities affect one's power? What complexities make appraising negotiating power challenging?

As negotiators engage with each other, exploring one another's interests and starting the process of constructing proposals that speak to and satisfy various of those interests, their thinking is often influenced by considerations of walk-away alternatives, leverage, and power. This chapter explores how to think through alternatives to a negotiated agreement and how, if they are attractive, to capitalize on them in your negotiation. We will also consider how to contend with the leverage that your counterpart might have, and we will examine the factors that might bring a sense of power to one side or the other. All of these points, when applied to the specific circumstances of a complex negotiation, might contribute in important ways to a negotiator's overall strategy.

A. Assessing Walk-Away Alternatives

In thinking carefully about negotiation, one should distinguish between *alternatives* and *options*.[1] Alternatives are things a party can do should a negotiated resolution not come to pass, that is, the different routes that might be pursued if the negotiation does not produce an agreement. Options are things the parties could agree to do, singly or together, as part of a negotiated resolution. Let us turn next to assessing walk-away alternatives.

1. The BATNA Concept

From pre-negotiation preparation forward, negotiators should focus attention on each side's BATNA, an acronym that stands for Best Alternative to a Negotiated Agreement.[2] Initially devised and popularized by interest-based negotiators, the BATNA idea has become an integral part of negotiation theory, commonly used by negotiators pursuing various different strategies. It stands as one of the most important contributions that the interest-based school has made to the theory and practice of negotiation.

Put simply, a party's BATNA is its preferred walk-away alternative. It is the most promising course of action for a negotiator to follow, if he or she cannot reach an agreement with the other side. Should the chance for a negotiated agreement fall through, a party's BATNA is the choice that is most likely to meet its interests. If it has no promising alternatives, a party's BATNA could be the default outcome that will occur if no agreement is reached with the other side.

The cardinal lesson is that negotiators should always bear in mind what exactly they will do if no agreement is reached with the other party or parties at the bargaining table. Ask: what is your best alternative to arriving at an agreement with your counterpart? What can you do without the other side's assent? Then, also ask: what is the best alternative that the other side can choose to take without you? Each party has its own *best* alternative to a negotiated agreement: you should know your own BATNA and try to find out, or at least estimate, the other party's BATNA.

In this regard it is important to realize that life sometimes imposes either-or choices on us. A driver must take one route instead of another. A hiker cannot walk up and down a hillside simultaneously. So it is with BATNAs. In fact, a negotiator can choose only a single alternative, not a whole host of them. As the authors of *Getting to Yes* observed, "You may be telling yourself that if you do not reach agreement on a salary for this job you could go to California, or go South, or go back to school, or write, or work on a farm, or live in Paris, or do something else. In your mind you are likely to find the sum of these alternatives more attractive than working for a specific salary in a particular job."[3] Unfortunately, however, you cannot pursue all of your alternatives at once. Instead, you have to select what appears to be the most attractive of them.

A particular alternative could be judged to be the most attractive one for any of a range of reasons. It might cost the least, or offer the most profits. It might be the most efficient or have the best chance of success. It might set the best precedent or provide the most subsidiary benefits.[4]

Your Best Alternative to a Negotiated Agreement with the party in front of you might well be a deal with someone else. If this customer is unwilling to pay your price, you might wait for the next. If this business balks at signing a contract with necessary protections for your side, you look for another more reasonable partner. Or, a BATNA might involve taking some step yourself, embarking on unilateral action rather than trying to coordinate with another. For example, if I cannot negotiate a reasonable deal with a computer systems consultant to reconfigure the network in my corporation and its subsidiaries, we will assemble our own information technology experts and do the job in-house.

Another possibility is that one's BATNA to what is currently being offered could be simply to continue to try to work things out with one's counterpart. One approach might be to suggest mediation or arbitration. Or, one might prefer to keep on negotiating: "in arms control, organizational deliberations, or minor marital disputes, failure to agree may involve worse relations, foregone benefit, and altered settlement possibilities, but in any case the necessity may remain of continued dealings among the same parties."[5]

In some circumstances your BATNA might be to do nothing and wait to see what happens next. For example, the BATNA of a professional athlete engaged in a salary negotiation could involve holding out, that is, choosing not to play as the season starts, foregoing compensation for the moment but also causing the team to lose his or her services.[6] There, the hope would be that the team would re-consider and return to present a better offer.

In short then, depending on the circumstances, a BATNA could be any of a wide array of possibilities: "going to court, going out on or taking a strike, buying something else or doing without, making the item internally, finding a different supplier or buyer, crafting an alternative alliance, or even mounting an invasion."[7]

2. A Reservation Price or Value

Another concept, often paired with a BATNA in the deliberations of experienced negotiators, is called a *reservation price* or *reservation value*. This refers to the least-attractive proposal for which a negotiator would still decide to come to an agreement, a point just past the one at which a negotiator really does not care whether he or she accepts the offered agreement or opts to pursue his or her BATNA.[8]

A reservation value is not necessarily identical to a BATNA, since a negotiator weighing whether to accept a proposal might take into account an array of other factors. There might be significant transaction costs involved in walking away to one's BATNA as opposed to accepting a particular deal. Accepting the deal as offered might just be quite convenient, and this might bring a party to agree, even if his or her BATNA was comparably attractive. A seasoned negotiator would incorporate such considerations into his or her reservation price.

In legal negotiations the analogous phrase *settlement price* is sometimes employed to designate the point at which a party will decide to settle a legal claim rather than pursue the case in court. In analyzing the attractiveness of the BATNA of adjudicating the dispute, a party ought to consider carefully court and litigation costs, the likely magnitude of the damages award, and the chances that the court would ultimately decide in favor of the other party.

The overarching point here is that, although a BATNA might show real promise of bringing a good outcome, it is rarely entirely certain that the hoped-for result would really come to pass. And, biases might distort one's calculations that the BATNA's benefits would, in fact, occur. One study, for instance, found that "Each party tended to view its own chances in court as better than the other side viewed them."[9] An intelligent negotiator would certainly have to factor into the equation the chance that the BATNA would ultimately fail to deliver the planned benefits. For this reason, parties averse to risk might want to take an offered deal, even if the walk-away alternative promised a result somewhat more attractive in other regards.

Under normal circumstances, a negotiator will not reveal his or her thinking about reservation values for fear that the counterpart will then move to or very near the reservation value with an offer or proposal.[10] This is sometimes termed a *low-ball offer or proposal*, that is, one that is aimed at being barely sufficient to gain an agreement.

Since many negotiators are reluctant even to discuss BATNAs, opposing negotiators may be able to do no more than estimate their counterpart's reservation value. One way to do this is to attend carefully to the pattern of offers and counter-offers that are being made in the course of the negotiation. "By seeing how people respond to counter-offers," one authority advises, "you can make a reasonable judgment about what their reservation price really is."[11]

3. The Purposes of BATNA Analysis

a. Accepting or Rejecting Offers

A first reason to analyze so carefully your best alternative to a negotiated agreement and your reservation value is to help you to decide when to take a proposal and when to turn it down. One scholar noted that, whether you have a delicious or a dreadful BATNA, it can serve as a standard that helps you to determine whether you ought to approve or refuse a particular proposal.[12]

When an interest-based negotiator believes that he or she has reached the best potential resolution that the other side will also agree to, the automatic next question is "would an agreement along these lines exceed my BATNA and reservation price?" Negotiators sometimes fall head-over-heels in love with a potential deal they have been trying hard to create. It is better to appraise a possible agreement rationally, and reject it if the chances of eliciting a more attractive offer from another party are strong. If the proposal is significantly better than one's BATNA and reservation price, however, then the negotiator will ordinarily want to move forward toward accepting the deal.

I say "ordinarily" since occasionally a party confronts a situation in which one's counterpart makes a final offer that is indeed better than one's walk-away alternatives, but that still seems quite unfair. A negotiator in that position might bridle at accepting a very lopsided proposal. Under those circumstances he or she might feel taken and opt for a BATNA instead.[13]

In this regard note that, although in many circumstances accepting or rejecting an agreement is primarily a matter of cost-benefit analysis, on occasion, that very decision can affect one's values. One authority observed, "Some values are trivial, some can be traded, and some we use to identify who we are in the world—and compromising those may be, in some cases, literally more than our life is worth." He went on, "asking someone to make a commitment to a settlement that is perceived as unfair or unjust is likely to tap into our core philosophical approach as to who we are and how we relate to others."[14]

b. Implications of Weak and Strong BATNAs

A negotiator who sees the BATNA of his or her side as less-than-ideal may be able to find or create a better BATNA during pre-negotiation or even in between negotiation sessions during the course of extended talks. To take one of many possible examples, in the early 1970s the government of Malta renegotiated a military base agreement with Great Britain. By developing alternatives with Libya and the Soviet Union in the course of negotiations with the British, Maltese Prime Minister Dom Mintoff was able, eventually, to secure a very favorable deal.[15]

A particularly difficult situation arises when negotiators find that they have high aspirations in a negotiation, but are saddled with a poor BATNA and reservation value. If their aspirations prove to be unattainable, can they lower their sights? Can they become reconciled to accepting a somewhat disappointing resolution but one that remains better than no deal at all? Or, do their aspirations distort their judgment so that they walk away from a potential deal that would leave them better off if they accepted it?

When the parties in a given negotiation come to see that all sides have a weak BATNA, they ought to re-double their efforts to work creatively with each other. The realization that their BATNAs are not promising should lead both to be as flexible and adaptable to the other side's interests as they can, looking to compromise and find reasonable common ground if at all possible. Under these circumstances, as William Ury pointed out, intelligent negotiators bear down, saying: "'You know what? There's got to be a deal here."[16]

If your BATNA is quite strong, that, too, is something well worth bearing in mind. If you have a very good BATNA, you will need an even better deal from your negotiating counterpart or you will simply opt for the alternative that you have in mind. Furthermore, if you are at an impasse with the other side but you have an excellent BATNA, it may not be a wise use of your time and resources to devote an enormous amount of energy to overcoming the deadlock. Instead, opt for your strong BATNA.

c. When a BATNA Is Underestimated

A negotiator needs to try to make a logical, clear-eyed assessment of what is their best alternative at that moment in time. Some negotiators are inclined to underestimate their BATNA—they overlook the fact that they have a strong alternative and focus in single-minded fashion on their ability to come to a negotiated resolution with their current counterpart.

Then, sometimes a negotiator with a quite good BATNA finds that his or her counterpart seems to be underestimating it. If my own BATNA is, in fact, considerably better than my counterpart seems to think it is, I will usually want to reveal and discuss it.

Let us say I am a young attorney, with expertise in criminal law, and I would like to relocate to Omaha, Nebraska to be near my spouse's family. Ideally, I would work for a particularly well-respected law firm in the city, but I could go to work as a prosecutor there, and, in fact, I already have an offer from the district attorney's office. In an interview at the law firm I have targeted, I ought to let the hiring committee know that I already have an offer in hand to serve as one of Omaha's prosecutors. The firm needs to see that it must put together a particularly attractive offer to ensure that I come to work for them, rather than for the D.A.

By, in fact, having a fairly good BATNA and by informing my negotiating counterpart about it, I demonstrate that my bargaining position is better than if I had no contending job offers at all.

d. When a BATNA Is Overestimated

Another common trap that can snare a negotiator is to assume that your counterpart has a much better BATNA than is, in fact, the case. One who focuses on the evident flaws in his or her own BATNA may be inclined to make ungrounded assumptions about the strength of the other side's walk-away alternatives. Inexperienced negotiators, in particular, have a marked tendency to overestimate their counterpart's BATNA, especially when their own BATNA leaves much to be desired. They make unwarranted assumptions, often on very thin evidence, and they then sometimes settle on quite disadvantageous terms. It is thus important to critically analyze the assumptions you may be making about your counterpart's alternatives.

Other negotiators tend to overestimate their own best alternative: they fail to assess accurately the benefits versus the drawbacks of their walk-away plan or how readily it can actually be achieved. People often see what they want to see. In analyzing BATNAs, a well-prepared negotiator can perceive his or her own walk-away alternative quite clearly, but may be able only to guess at the other side's BATNA. Since people tend to under-value things that they do not know much about, psychologists report that asymmetric information of this kind commonly leads to *optimistic overconfidence*, a distorting of judgment in favor of your own side and against your counterpart's.[17]

One instance in which this often comes up is when an attorney paints a rosy picture for a business executive or other client of winning a case in court, a picture that passes lightly over all the costs associated with litigation. To determine if adjudication, in fact, qualifies as one's best alternative and to appraise just how good an alternative it is, one needs to give serious thought not only to the likelihood of winning, but to the length of time it will take to reach a final verdict and the financial costs that are likely to accumulate in the interim. Human costs might also be associated with litigation, including the time and stress involved as well as the possible damage to relationships.

Of course, if the other side has apparently overestimated my BATNA, or if I have a terrible BATNA and my counterpart does not know it, I will much prefer to steer the negotiation in directions other than BATNA discussions. Let us say that I am a recently graduated student just finishing an internship in

London. I would very much like to find a job there for another year or two, but I must now earn some decent compensation or I will not be able to afford the cost of living. However, the organization with which I interned has no openings. I have no offers in hand, am woefully short of money, and have a ticket to fly home at week's end. If I do gain a last-minute interview, I may not want to describe my problematic circumstances since this might tempt the company to make a very low offer, knowing how desperate I am.

In Chapter 11 we will consider various issues of negotiating ethics. For now realize that a negotiator has no recognized ethical responsibility to reveal to a negotiating counterpart his or her lack of strong alternatives.

4. Potential BATNA Complexities

In sum, then, useful BATNA analysis hinges on properly appraising one's own walk-away alternatives and discovering or judiciously estimating those of one's counterpart. If the other side is unwilling to reveal its BATNA, as will often be the case, one should try to make an educated guess about what they will be likely to do if no agreement materializes. Then, to help to determine what needs to be done to reach an agreement, one ought to weigh the two BATNAs to see which is stronger, relative to the other.

A skillful negotiator uses rational dispassionate analysis to try to guard against either overestimating or underestimating the strength of the walk-away alternatives on both sides. And yet, often, neither side will open up to the other concerning its BATNA. The reason is that, if I know your alternatives, I will have a good idea of the minimum you will accept. Consequently, I am unlikely to offer much more than that minimum, even if I could very well do so.

Although BATNA analysis is sometimes straightforward, it can be challenging. The stronger the field of alternatives, the better will be the one designated as the best. However, neither determining a robust range of possible alternatives nor selecting the most attractive one are obvious or necessarily self-evident tasks. You may have to inquire of yourself: "What else might I do?," and think carefully and creatively about the answer. And, you may need to review your goals, envision a future state of affairs you would like to attain, and then ask, "How might this be achieved?"[18]

Similarly, when a negotiator goes to work for a client, one of the most important tasks of pre-negotiation preparation involves working through BATNA analysis together. How well do the available alternatives to a negotiated agreement meet the client's interests, and which exactly would be the best alternative?

Further complications arise since BATNAs are not static. During protracted negotiations a walk-away alternative that once looked promising can sour or entirely disappear. And, in the midst of the talks one's counterpart may gain a much more attractive BATNA. All of a sudden one may need to do considerably more to reach an agreement that the other side will accept.

Yet another key dimension of BATNA analysis involves assessing, and perhaps referring to, your counterpart's best walk-away alternative. If you can spotlight a weakness in the other side's BATNA, this may move them toward an agreement as effectively as highlighting the strength of your walk-away alternative.

In some situations it may also be possible for one side in a negotiation to worsen the other side's BATNA. Imagine, for instance, a basketball team negotiating with its coach on a new contract. If no agreement materializes, the general manager has one other top coaching candidate in mind and the team's BATNA is to pursue that other candidate. However, the two coaches know and like one another, and the current coach persuades his friend to tell the media in no uncertain terms that he has no interest in the team in question. Suddenly, the general manager must find a different, and perhaps lesser, walk-away alternative.

It is important to realize, however, that risks are often associated with working to worsen the other side's BATNA in the midst of a negotiation. Depending on the circumstances, such a move may cause real tension, even escalating hostility. It may damage the working relationship or invite tit-for-tat tactics in which the other side looks to worsen your BATNA, in turn. Whether or not to take a such a step can thus be a difficult question of negotiation strategy.

5. BATNAs and Negotiation Strategies

One additional point about BATNAs is worth emphasizing. A negotiator saddled with a weak BATNA ought to be prepared, ultimately, to settle for a less advantageous deal than if he or she had a much stronger walk-away alternative. But, how much should a poor BATNA affect a negotiator's goals? Here, the answer should vary from negotiator to negotiator and from one set of circumstances to another. This is another important matter of negotiation strategy.

A negotiator saddled with a problematic BATNA will often choose to aim for less-ambitious goals. However, this may not always be the wisest course of action. First, weighing the BATNAs of each party may be revealing. If the other side also has a very unattractive BATNA, their negotiator may be quite motivated to assist in serving your interests. If they perceive their BATNA to be even worse than yours, you may be in a better bargaining position than you at first anticipated.

Alternatively, if you believe that you can conceal your flawed BATNA and if, in the circumstances you face, you are not especially risk averse, you might want to aim for goals every bit as attractive as if your BATNA was actually much better. For example, a job candidate with an impressive resume but with only an unattractive alternative job position in hand and no immediate prospects of another job offer might still request a relatively high salary, trusting that his or her potential employer might assume an array of alternative job possibilities that, in fact, do not at present exist.

B. Referring to BATNAs

As negotiators move from the opening phase into the substance of the negotiation and on into the creation of options, the talks may touch on the best alternative to a negotiated agreement that one or the other or both parties have. A negotiator who knows, or can accurately estimate, the other side's BATNA has some idea of how enticing a potential negotiated resolution must be in order to gain his or her counterpart's assent. I say "some idea" since it is usually not entirely clear how a fellow negotiator values his or her BATNA as opposed to different potential negotiated resolutions.

In any event, when one's BATNA is not so strong, revealing it could be problematic. Consequently, a well-prepared negotiator must have devoted some thought to whether and when to engage in a BATNA discussion with the other side. The following important questions ought, then, to be considered carefully in pre-negotiation preparation.

- If I have a weak BATNA, what might I not want to reveal about it, and how am I going to keep that information from the other side without harming the positive relationship I have been trying to develop in the course of my talks with them?
- Assuming I would very much like to discover whether my estimate of the other side's BATNA is on or off target, how might I do that without causing offense or injecting awkwardness into the negotiation?

1. Sensitivities Concerning BATNA Discussions

Inquiring of a counterpart as to what he or she might do if no agreement is reached can be a sensitive matter. To gain an agreement, it may be necessary to concentrate the attention of a party on the weakness of one or both BATNAs. In some circumstances, however, it might be taken as prying into private affairs. Should a sports team inquire of a potential free agent they would like to sign, "So, what other teams are bidding for your services right now?," the player's agent might very well want to keep that information confidential.

Of course, if one has a particularly strong BATNA, a negotiator might welcome discussing it, since the other side will have to exceed that walk-away alternative to gain agreement. But, a negotiator with a weak best alternative to a negotiated agreement may have to settle, ultimately, for a less-advantageous deal than if his or her BATNA was much stronger. This creates a real incentive to deceive the other side as to one's BATNA. A negotiator may thus want to regard his or her alternatives as a private matter beyond the scope of information readily shared with their counterpart.

Nevertheless, knowing the other side's BATNA can be quite useful. On the one hand, a negotiator who has put time, effort, and thought into developing positive relations with a counterpart may not want to jeopardize them with offensive questions. On the other hand, should the answer to such a question be valuable, a negotiator might consider when would be an opportune moment and what might be the best possible phrasing to elicit an honest response.

In general, I believe that negotiators tend to ask too few sensitive questions, not too many. If you pose a question and then the other side refuses to answer it, a solid working relationship will usually enable you to move on without significant repercussions. And, you may very well have learned something from the fact that the other side dodged your question.[19]

2. When BATNA Discussions Are Useful

Furthermore, should it be obvious that neither side's BATNA is auspicious, discussion of that fact could be a useful reminder that compromise might be in order so as to attain a negotiated resolution and avoid the less-than-ideal walk-away alternatives. One scenario in which this can arise is when the parties confront the possible choice of going to court to resolve a dispute, but a legal case would be costly and time-consuming. Opting to go to court might also be unattractive for both parties since they might very well be reluctant to cooperate or work together in the future after undergoing an adversarial legal proceeding. Moreover, the judge or jury's decision would be all-or-nothing in the sense that one side or the other would prevail. For various reasons, then, both parties might very well prefer a negotiated compromise resolution in which each met certain of its interests.

C. Factoring Leverage Into the Negotiation

1. The Concept of Leverage

Leverage refers to a negotiator's ability to move the other side toward doing what he or she wants, ultimately increasing the negotiator's chances of attaining his or her goals. The reference, of course, is to the action of a lever. That is, a strong bar, placed in the correct position, then pressed, can shift or move a large weight, even one that might at first appear difficult or impossible to dislodge.

Boston lawyer Bob Woolf, one of the most famous sports and entertainment agents of the twentieth century, once noted, "Every reason that the other side wants or needs an agreement is my leverage—provided that I know those reasons."[20] After noting "[l]everage is based on the other party's *perception* of the situation," one scholar concluded, "[Y]ou have the leverage the other side thinks you have. If the other party thinks you are in a strong position, you are—at least for the moment."[21]

When one side believes that it has leverage over its counterpart, a key strategic issue involves how best to apply that leverage. How does one ensure that the leverage you enjoy is put to best advantage? Does one quietly allow leverage to go to work, or is there an opportune moment to raise something that provides leverage? How might it best be done in a smooth, not awkward, and telling, not ineffective, way?

Then, when a negotiator feels that the other side has leverage, the issue becomes how to cope with it, how to keep the counterpart's leverage from bringing on a poor result. Here, note that some negotiators tend to give leverage considerations undue weight. One experienced lawyer counseled, "Don't become obsessed with some positive factor that's working in your counterpart's favor, or paralyzed by a disturbing negative that's undermining your interests. Rather, keep your eyes open for overlooked countervailing factors to mitigate the leverage. Better yet, sprinkle some helpful new ingredients into the pot."[22]

To grasp the effect of leverage on a negotiation consider the following illustration. A young couple is interested in buying one of three quite similar farms, each of which is priced higher than the couple can easily afford. The first property is owned by a widow who has lived there for some decades and whose adult children are pressing her to move to a retirement home at some point in the coming years. The second features a horse barn and already has had visits from several potentially interested buyers. The third is owned by two people who have just concluded an expensive divorce and have each moved to cities hundreds of miles distant.

The presence of multiple potential buyers for the second property provides leverage to the seller there. "Competition puts pressure on a buyer to pay top dollar," it has been observed, "while stiffening the seller's resolve to hold out for it."[23] The personal circumstances confronting the divorced couple—reasons that they would feel compelled to sell as soon as possible—provide the buyer with considerable leverage that would be less telling in negotiations to reduce the purchase price set by the widow, whose projected move is not immediately necessary. Hence, so long as the couple thinks of the three farms as roughly equal in value to them, the best bet for reducing the purchase price would be the third property, owned by the recently divorced couple.

2. Appraising the Leverage of the Parties

a. The Strength of Wants and Needs

In determining overall leverage in a negotiation, one must acknowledge that, just as A may have leverage with respect to B on account of certain factors, so, too, B may enjoy leverage over A with respect to other matters. We must, therefore, be careful to look at both sides of the equation so as not to skew the results. Does Party A have its own needs and fears, and can Party B resolve them through something it could agree to do? Often, what is most key is the balance of leverage between the parties.

Assessing the leverage of the parties to a negotiation requires appraising which side of the scales is more weighed down? Is A's leverage over B the weightier, or would B's over A take precedence? Who has the advantage in a particular situation? "Who," as Richard Shell observed, "has the most to lose from a failure to agree?" He went on to ask: "What do I control that the other side wants, what do they control that I want, and who stands to lose the most if no deal gets done?"[24]

The balance of leverage involves the comparative advantages and disadvantages of the different sides. To assess it, consider first what the parties want or need. Any negotiator who has or controls something that is worth a lot to the other side can be expected to press the advantage and try to extract quite a bit in exchange for the item.

Plainly, in many scenarios quite a few different factors will influence leverage. Sometimes leverage is balanced between the parties, and other times it piles up on one side much more than the other. One lawyer, experienced in negotiating complex deals, noted that sometimes leverage-creating factors "operate in tandem, multiplying each other's effects. At other moments they work at cross purposes, vying for predominance and neutralizing the overall impact."[25]

Concerns over leverage are one important reason that negotiators do not reveal all of their inner-most thoughts to one another. A negotiator might reason, if I have a particularly intense weakness—something I particularly need or fear—I do not want the other side to focus on it. By the same token, if my counterpart feels especially vulnerable, I may not want to disclose that the situation is actually better than he or she thinks. Because each side may want to keep certain matters involving leverage to itself, negotiators often have to make educated guesses as to what is really going on.

In estimating the other party's needs, a negotiator should consider carefully that party's BATNA. Comparing the BATNAs of the different sides shines a spotlight on an important aspect of their relative leverage. The side with the more favorable BATNA has leverage since he or she does not lose as much should the negotiations fail to produce an agreement. Consequently, as one scholar put it, the side that "has particularly attractive alternatives ... can legitimately seek a larger share of the jointly created pie."[26]

Furthermore, indicating that one might walk away from the deal is a more telling move for the party with more leverage. One with a stronger BATNA will not feel as compelled to reach an agreement, but having a poor BATNA will make a party less comfortable and more in need of a deal. Who has the most to lose if an agreement fails to materialize?

If you can improve your BATNA, you therefore lessen the leverage the other party has over you and enhance your own leverage. For example, imagine a faculty member interviewing for a chaired position at another university. If the professor takes the new offer to the home university's administration, the provost or dean might well offer a large salary increase. And, this might then cause the other university to sweeten its offer. The faculty member has in a sense created an impromptu auction between contending universities and can be expected to benefit from it.

b. Urgency: The Pinch of Time

As you appraise leverage, it is important to focus not simply on the magnitude of the needs and fears at issue but also on their urgency. Occasionally, both sides feel the pinch of the passage of time equally, but more often than not the timing of a potential deal squeezes one side more than the other. For example, one business wants to acquire another and has an attractive target in its sights, but first needs to sell off one of its own divisions. It wants to move quickly to conclude that sale.

A party could have notable wishes and concerns, and see them as a crisis requiring immediate action. Alternatively, it could feel no great need to resolve them immediately. Or, its fears and desires could fall somewhere in between those poles. The more imperative is your need, and the fewer alternatives you have to meet it, the more leverage is held by one who can satisfy that need. So, the experienced negotiator keeps assessing, just how urgent are an opposing party's concerns and desires, and how urgent are those motivating my side?

Note that this is another matter in which one side may not want to be entirely candid and up front with its counterpart. Since seasoned negotiators will be alert to signs of intense need, appearances matter. One scholar observed, "[W]e can surmise that the bargainer who is willing to wait longer, to probe more patiently, to appear less eager for a settlement will be more successful."[27]

c. The Ability to Take Away Something of Value

Since leverage is closely linked to vulnerability, if one side is able to take away something of real value from the other, it has leverage over it. For instance, when parties that are engaged in litigation are negotiating a possible settlement, one side may be better able to handle the costs of the pretrial discovery process than the other.[28] By threatening or beginning to engage in extensive discovery—sending interrogatories, scheduling depositions, and so on—one side demonstrates that if a settlement does not occur, the other side will have to spend considerable resources in the trial process. Often, both parties in such a situation jockey with one another, each trying to show that it is not to be easily swayed by such pressure. Behind such posturing, however, skillful negotiators take stock of which side is actually more vulnerable.

"To gain real leverage," Richard Shell argued, "you must eventually persuade the other party that he or she has something concrete to lose in the transaction if the deal falls through."[29] Imagine, for instance, a family business in which certain of the members are setting the direction of its activities. Others, however, are upset with how the business is being run and might even welcome a sale. In a negotiation over what will happen in the future, the unhappy members—even if in the minority—will have some leverage if those running the business see their ability to bring on a sale as viable.

Note that leverage of this sort can serve as a leveling factor in the hands of the weak. Thomas Schelling, a seminal thinker in the field of bargaining and negotiation, wrote of "coercive deficiency," which has been described as "a persuasive tactic of the weak, who cry for help lest they do something that everyone will regret."[30]

d. Normative Leverage

The term *normative leverage* refers to a party's desire to act in accordance with its own norms, beliefs, and principles. A negotiator might frame an argument in terms of the other's values, gaining some leverage that way.[31]

To illustrate, consider hostage negotiations and other communications with extremists. Radical groups often have strong normative beliefs about how people should act. A negotiator can appeal to the other side's deep-seated desire to remain true to their own system of values and morality. For instance, during the 1979–80 hostage crisis in Iran, German Ambassador Gerhardt Ritzel held a series of discussions with leading clerics. He reasoned with them not in terms of international law or the norms of modern international relations but focused instead on statements in the Koran, including some concerning the gentle treatment of foreign envoys. This argument was taken directly to the Ayatollah Khomeini and may have provided a normative rationale for the eventual release of the American hostages.[32]

3. Using and Countering Leverage

As parties negotiate, they may feel the leverage of one side or the other. When that feeling is strongest, a party is in the best position to ask for things that it wants. That is, it can capitalize on the perception its counterpart has of its leverage. However, where one party seems to have greater leverage than the other, it is worth bearing in mind that pressing that advantage too far might have the potential to jeopardize the deal.

Should your counterpart seem to be enjoying more leverage, it may be worth looking for ways to counter that advantage. One way to do that is for a negotiator to work to generate a better BATNA, thus reducing its need to do the deal. Or, where one side has leverage because the other must meet a deadline, the disadvantaged party might try to manufacture its own deadline for its counterpart. For example, it might assemble an attractive package but require a response to it within a designated period of time.[33]

Since a negotiator with leverage has something of real value in the effort to reach a favorable agreement, negotiators look to avoid allowing their leverage to dissipate. This sometimes arises in the context of relationship-building. Negotiators intent on developing a strong relationship sometimes choose to set their counterpart's minds at ease about some matter, perhaps not reflecting that they are sacrificing leverage in doing so. Whether to take this step or not is a strategic decision, one which may be worthwhile in particular circumstances. In general, however, a seasoned negotiator looks for other ways to build a positive relationship and conserves the leverage enjoyed over the other side.

Finally, note that leverage is often a shifting, not a constant, factor. As the negotiators are working with each other, outside developments may occur that change a party's view of what it wants or how necessary it is to move forward. Hence, bearing in mind that circumstances can change, you may be well-advised to push on to close a favorable deal when you feel that you have nicely capitalized on your leverage and both sides are ready to commit to a favorable deal.

a. Working with Coalitions

In a multi-party negotiation some of the negotiators may come together in a *coalition* that joins forces to work as a unit to try to achieve some objective. Most basically, a negotiator wants to form or to join a coalition that would advance his or her interests. This may be thought of as another way to use leverage or counter the leverage of others.

i. Creating a Coalition

Although sometimes a coalition emerges in pre-negotiation or right at the table as parties discuss the situation confronting them, coalitions often form during a caucus. Certainly, the members of a coalition often feel the need for additional consultations in the midst of a negotiation. As circumstances change, new facts come to light, or opportunities develop, the group needs to meet for discussions. Some coalition members may want to remain on the prior course. Others may look to change the goals or strategy of the coalition, consolidate the group or disband it altogether.

ii. The Benefits of Coalitions

Parties formulate coalitions to take advantage of the strength that comes with numbers. The hope is that the group will turn out to be composed of like-minded allies who will help it to serve its key interests. A coalition is particularly attractive to a party that feels as though, individually, it has a strictly limited ability to influence others at the negotiating table. In such a situation the fear is that the group as a whole will not end up supporting its objectives.

However, when a number of parties combine their strength and act in unison, they can become a much more formidable presence at the table. In general, the larger the coalition, the more difficult it is for the rest of the group to ignore the points made by the coalition members. If a coalition agrees that, unless all of its members are satisfied, it will not sign a deal, then the coalition may be able to block a developing agreement.

iii. Difficulties Associated with Coalitions

Often, however, while certain matters unite a coalition, others pull it apart. The members tend to have somewhat different sets of goals, interests, and strategies. The ability to build an effective coalition depends on finding a way to bind the coalition together and perhaps expand its membership over time. Those leading a coalition thus face the following challenge: at a table crowded with parties, none of whom see the situation just as you do, can you form common approaches that will advance some of your vital interests, even when your coalition partners may not be with you on other matters?

In fact, the members of a coalition do sometimes shift. Experienced negotiators do not feel locked into any particular coalition, and may retire from a coalition or move to another grouping if a more advantageous possibility comes along. Should the rest of the coalition come to favor taking a course that one party judges to be adverse to its interests or strategy, a negotiator who once joined a coalition may need to move on. Certainly, when a coalition wants to close a deal on terms that would be worse than the BATNA of a coalition member, that member should leave the coalition and start to work against it. This is sometimes done by forming a counter-coalition, often called a *blocking coalition.*

Another difficulty involves those who resist joining a coalition for cultural reasons. In distinguishing between what he called Machiavellian and principled cultures, one authority noted, "In multilateral negotiations, culture may have a say when building coalitions. Some actors will agree to join forces with people who have common interests regardless of who they are; other actors will cooperate only with people who share the same values."[34]

iv. Cross-Over Players

In some sizeable groups two or more coalitions develop and contend with one another, sometimes with members shifting sides as the talks progress. Where a negotiation is marked by contending coalitions, a negotiator who might become a member of more than one coalition is sometimes referred to as a *cross-over player.* Members of the different coalitions might then approach the cross-over player in hopes of enticing that person to join them.

Since distinct coalitions would each like to have the cross-over player as a member, he or she has leverage that others lack. The cross-over player might use different tactics to capitalize on that leverage and move the other coalition members closer toward his or her preferred course of action. For instance, the cross-over player might raise doubts about his or her continued membership, perhaps meeting with members of the opposing coalition.

b. The Pros and Cons of Coalitions

The tactic of forming coalitions is often looked upon favorably as a positive step that groups take toward coming to an agreement. The power of strong parties can be balanced, to some degree, by weaker parties who ally, and the assumption is that this will result in a resolution that is more just and fair.

However, although strong parties sometimes abuse their strength, weak ones, on occasion, act irresponsibly. A coalition may have the ability to block an agreement or to stonewall on certain issues. It could stifle creativity and kill the spirit of joint problem-solving that is often needed to resolve complex problems. So, coalition-building can be productive, but it does not automatically assist parties in creating a negotiated resolution.

Box 5.1 — Leverage Questions

- Can Party A provide what Party B is looking for?
- Is there another party that can also provide it? Would the terms likely be comparable, better, or worse?
- How significant are B's needs or desires?
- How about A's wishes, needs, and desires? Can B meet them, and how significant and urgent are they?
- What is Party A most concerned about, and can Party B help?
- If so, just how worrisome is the concern?
- Alternatively, might Party B be very worried about something that Party A might do? Of course, B might also have leverage over A.
- Which party is more in need of moving quickly to reach a deal (or, at least, moving quickly to determine whether a deal can be reached)?
- Can one side take away something worthwhile that the other possesses?
- Since sunk costs sometimes provide leverage, which side has already invested more time, energy, and costs in coming to a deal?
- In comparing the BATNA of one side with the other, who has the better one? Who loses what if the deal falls through? Who will lose more?
- Does a party to the negotiation feel a real need to act in accordance with its own norms, beliefs, or principles?

D. What Brings Power to a Negotiator?

The concept of leverage involves the extent to which a party is in a better or worse bargaining position. The concept of negotiating power is closely related but broader in scope. The question it speaks to: "How does a negotiator use the resources at his or her disposal to bring about a preferred or beneficial outcome?"[35]

In all human affairs the extent of one's power depends upon the particular circumstances being faced. The schoolyard bully is powerful because of size, weight, and attitude in comparison with those of the other children. When armies are equipped with the same weapons, have similar leaders and employ identical tactics, the ultimate test of power may be numerical superiority. The power of navy vessels may be connected not only to weaponry but to speed and maneuverability, the skill of the captain and training and esprit de corps of the crew.

In Chapter 1 we saw how negotiators try to use their intelligence to resolve problems or opportunities before them. What brings power in these particular circumstances? In the negotiating context the concept of power may be analyzed by thinking of the respective authority, means, and capabilities of the parties. These are the fundamental elements of negotiating power.

1. Authority and Negotiating Power

A first element of negotiating power involves authority. Modern societies are organized via hierarchies of authority established within governments, businesses, religions, institutions, and other organizations. A person's position within that hierarchy may carry with it both the legitimacy and the legal or institutional competence to make certain decisions. And yet, people, confronting that hierarchy, still often negotiate with the authority figure. Here, negotiating power as authority may come into play.

For example, a student may go to a professor to request taking the final exam in a class on an alternative date. The student might have an interest in going out of town to attend a wedding, which conflicts with the exam date. The professor needs to get the final grades to the registrar on time. He or she also aims to treat all students evenhandedly and to try to give them the grade for the course that they deserve, not providing any one of them with an advantage in testing or saddling any one with a disadvantage. A negotiation ensues to see if a mutually agreeable alternative exam date can be found. However, within the university hierarchy the professor has the authority to determine whether an exam will be taken on the regular date or some other one. His or her authority thus provides negotiating power.

The title, duties, and responsibilities of a particular job may be an important element of negotiating power. "There are times when people respond to directions from another, even directions they do not like," it has been noted, "because they feel it is proper (legitimate) for the other to direct them and proper (obligatory) for them to obey. This is the effect of legitimate power."[36]

Thus, one source of negotiating power is authority. A person's position may provide him or her with the ability to make certain decisions. Within that society these will often be clothed with a certain legitimacy. In this sense power is connected to social organization.

2. Means and Negotiating Power

A second dimension of power in the context of negotiation involves the means to obtain influence over others in order to reach particular goals. This includes not just the legitimacy of authority, but any means that contributes to one side's influence on the other.

For instance, a party with a very good BATNA has negotiating power. The more you can do for yourself, if you walk away from a negotiation, the more powerful a negotiator you are. As one scholar put it, "[T]he better my best walk-away (BATNA) and the more credible my willingness to walk, the more power I have in the negotiation."[37]

Box 5.2 — Sources of Power for Organizations

There follows a list of resources that could be a source of power for an organization involved in a negotiation. Under particular circumstances each might provide the means to influence another toward accepting a proposed negotiated resolution.

1. Money, in its various forms: cash, grants, bonuses, salary, budget allocations, financial reserves, and discretionary dollars.

2. Supplies: raw materials, components, pieces, and parts.

3. Labor: available supply, human capital, capable administration, staff that can be allocated to a problem or task.

4. Time: free time, the ability to meet a deadline or control its timing; if time pressure is present, the ability to help someone to meet or move a deadline.

5. Equipment: tools, vehicles, machines, technology, computer terminals and software.

6. Critical services: repair, maintenance, upkeep, installation and delivery, technical support, transportation.

7. Interpersonal communication: verbal praise, encouragement, and support for good performance or criticism for poor performance that brings someone to account.

8. Reputation: for integrity, resolve, determination, or other qualities that might affect a negotiation.

Points 1–7 are adapted from ROY J. LEWICKI, DAVID M. SAUNDERS, & JOHN W. MINTON, ESSENTIALS OF NEGOTIATION 137 (2d ed. 2001).

Bear in mind here that certain resources or instruments of power can be effective only for certain specific uses. The power to achieve one goal may not translate into the power to achieve another. As Karl Deutsch put it, "The power to knock down a person does not give us the power to teach that person to play the piano or to do calculus or figure skating. The power to bomb and burn a village cannot be completely or easily transformed into the power to win the sympathies of its inhabitants, or to govern it with their consent, ... [or] to produce ... the skills, values, and ... loyalties ... essential for democratic governance."[38]

Furthermore, the greater the power, the more unwieldy it may be with respect to particular tasks. Here, Deutsch pointed out: "A charging elephant can smash down a large obstacle, but he cannot thread a needle. Indeed, he cannot make a right-angle turn within a three-foot radius. The greater the brute power, mass, speed, and momentum of the elephant, the harder it is for him to control his own motions, and the less precise his control becomes."[39]

The resources or instruments of power then have to be orchestrated so that they, in fact, influence the behavior of one's counterpart. Does one party want something of which the other has a supply? Here, the issues of leverage noted above come into play. How urgent is the party's need, and are there other possible suppliers?

Perceptions can also be quite significant in this regard: what my counterpart thinks about my strength may well outweigh what strength I actually have. "The other side may be as much influenced by a row of cardboard tanks as by a battalion of real tanks," Roger Fisher pointed out. However, he continued, "A general who commands a real tank battalion ... is in a far stronger position that one in charge of a row of cardboard tanks. A false impression of power is extremely vulnerable, capable of being destroyed by a word."[40]

3. Capabilities and Negotiating Power

Another dimension of power involves not authority or substantive resources, but negotiating capabilities. Power is frequently thought of in terms of whether one has the ability to get one's way, to prevail in achieving a goal while overcoming possible obstacles. In this tradition negotiating power has been defined in terms of the ability to influence the decisions of others.

In many negotiations this variety of negotiating power comes in the first instance from skill, knowledge, and expertise.[41] A powerful negotiator is more resourceful, has better ideas, a superior strategy, or more experience concerning how to prepare and how to proceed in the talks. In this tradition one scholar noted, "Good working relationships based on some combination of respect, admiration, perceived need, obligation, and friendship are a critical source of power in helping to get things done."[42]

Advanced skills in finding relevant information, and then assembling, organizing, and presenting it, are other capabilities that may influence a counterpart.[43] Power in negotiation also comes from good ideas about how to marshal facts and ask questions; how to communicate (to listen and to advocate), and how to generate creative options and find promising packages likely to gain agreement.

Expertise in the particular subject-matter of the negotiation is a like form of power. An expert has mastered some skill or body of knowledge. Their arguments have credibility and experts "are accorded respect, deference, and credibility based on their experience, study, or accomplishments."[44] Hence, one's skills, expertise, and ability are yet another aspect of negotiating power.

4. Assessing Negotiating Power

In plotting strategy and interacting at the bargaining table, savvy negotiators assess the negotiating power that they and their counterpart wield. They may also work to alter the existing distribution of power, such as by improving their walk-away alternative. In this regard the authors of *Getting to Yes* observed, "Developing your BATNA is perhaps the most effective course of action you can take in dealing with a seemingly more powerful negotiators."[45] In any event power is one variable that enters their thinking about what goals are realistic and what resolutions to a negotiating problem or opportunity ought to be embraced.

In a scenario of any complexity, however, appraising who has how much negotiating power can be challenging, and caution is often in order. "Total negotiating power," as Roger Fisher observed, "depends upon many factors...."

Exercising negotiating power effectively means orchestrating them in a way that maximizes their cumulative impact."[46] Whether a party is going to be able to do that under the circumstances of any particular negotiation is an open question.

In fact, negotiating power is a sufficiently complicated concept that it may be quite difficult to assess. Power is inherently relative and changeable, not absolute and constant. What makes a negotiator powerful can differ from one set of circumstances to another. Power is also relative to the task at hand. You cannot rationally decide if you have sufficient power unless you know just what you aim to accomplish with that power.

Moreover, the power of one party is relative to the power of others. That is, the extent of one's power depends in part on the needs, resources, and vulnerabilities of one's counterpart. And, power is relative to whatever constraints might exist on using that power. For instance, on one level the governments in charge of states that possess nuclear weapons have elite power. However, since significant limitations have developed since World War II regarding the use, or even the threatened use, of nuclear weapons, having a nuclear stockpile may not be a decisive factor vis-à-vis many international issues.

Less-powerful parties are often inclined to *under*estimate what power they do have and to *over*estimate what power is ranged against them. The stronger party often acutely feels constraints that may prevent it from exercising its power. But, the weaker side frequently overlooks or fails to grasp these limiting factors.

The authors of *Getting to Yes* noted the risks of trying to determine which side is more powerful and then basing your negotiation behavior on that assessment: "If you conclude that you are more powerful, you may relax and not prepare as well as you should. On the other hand, if you conclude that you are weaker than the other side, there is a risk that you will be discouraged and again not devote sufficient attention to how you might persuade them."[47] Instead, they suggest preparing carefully, searching for allies and resources, and thinking positively—setting challenging goals and aspiring to reach them.

5. Power and the "Shadow Negotiation"

Power is sometimes applied as people negotiate over the substantive issues before them. But, it is also sometimes employed in what Deborah Kolb and Judith Williams have termed the *shadow negotiation*.[48] This involves "whose interests and needs will hold sway, whose opinions will matter, and how cooperatively [the parties] ... are going to work together."[49]

The shadow negotiation is about impressions, credibility, legitimacy, and influence as the parties position themselves vis-à-vis one another. Negotiators engaged in the shadow negotiation assert their power through strategic moves, often designed to put other negotiators on the defensive by undermining their confidence or competence. They might challenge another negotiator's expertise, belittle another's ideas, or criticize his or her style. Alternatively, a strategic move might flatter another or make an appeal for sympathy.

The negotiator targeted by the strategic move might respond with silence, with a defensive counter-move, or with what Kolb and Williams call a "turn": that is, resisting the strategic move, shifting the dynamic, and reframing the point being discussed. For instance, a negotiator might interrupt the talks with a recess or show that he or she recognizes the move by questioning, correcting, or diverting it.

Deborah Kolb drew on international trade negotiations to relate an example of a strategic move and a resulting turn. U.S. Trade Representative Charlene Barshevsky was negotiating an intellectual property issue with a Chinese counterpart, who suddenly leaned forward in a menacing fashion and declared, "It's take it or leave it." Kolb wrote, "Barshevsky, taken aback by the harsh tone, surprised her counterpart by sitting quietly. She waited 30–40 seconds—an eternity given the intensity of the negotiation—and came back with a measured reply: 'If the choice is take or leave it, of course I'll leave it. But I can't imagine that's what you meant. I think what you mean is that you'd like me to think over your last offer and that we can continue tomorrow.'"[50]

Barshevsky turned the strategic move by interrupting the flow of the negotiation with silence, demonstrated that she was not taken in by the move and that it would not work and then diverted attention back to the problem, while suggesting the other side reconsider its position and reconvene the negotiations later. In fact, the Chinese negotiator came back with a compromise the next morning.

E. Conclusion

A party's walk-away alternatives, including most prominently its Best Alternative to a Negotiated Agreement, its leverage and the negotiating power at its disposal provide an important part of the larger context within which a negotiation occurs. By bearing in mind the BATNAs of the parties, maximizing the influence of the leverage they have and minimizing that of the other side, while capitalizing on the power they can bring to bear, negotiators can advance toward finding favorable common ground. By that I mean a resolution that serves the interests of a negotiator quite well, while still being agreeable to both sides since it is mutually beneficial and better than either can do away from the table.

Notes

1. Amy C. Finnegan & Susan G. Hackley, *Negotiation and Nonviolent Action: Interacting in the World of Conflict*, Program on Negotiation, Harvard Law School, Jan. 25, 2008, http://www.pon.harvard.edu/events/negotiation-and-nonviolent-action-interacting-in-a-world-of-conflict/.

2. Roger Fisher, William Ury, & Bruce Patton, Getting to Yes 97–106 (2d ed. 1991).

3. *Id.* at 101.

4. David A. Lax & James K. Sebenius, The manager as Negotiator 244 (1986).

5. *Id.* at 50.

6. Michael Wheeler, *First, Let's Kill All the Agents!*, in Negotiating on Behalf of Others 238, 240 (Robert H. Mnookin & Lawrence E. Susskind eds., 1999).

7. James K. Sebenius, *What Roger Fisher Got Profoundly Right*, 29 Negotiation J. 163 (2013).

8. Howard Raiffa, The Art and Science of Negotiation 126 (1982).

9. *Id.* at 75.

10. Robert H. Mnookin, Scott R. Peppet, & Andrew S. Tulumello, Beyond Winning 22 (2000).

11. Alan Strudler, *On the Ethics of Deception in Negotiation*, in What's Fair 151 (Carrie Menkel-Meadow & Michael Wheeler eds., 2004).

12. Wheeler, supra note 6, at 244.

13. Mnookin, Peppet, & Tulumello, supra note 10, at 22.

14. Kevin Gibson, *Ethics and Morality in Negotiation*, in The Negotiator's Field book 180 (Andrea Kupfer Schneider & Christopher Honeyman eds., 2006).

15. W. Howard Wriggins, *Up for Auction: Malta Bargains with Great Britain, 1971*, in The 50% Solution 208–233 (I. William Zartman ed., 1987).

16. William Ury, *An Interview with Roger Fisher and William Ury*, 18 Acad. of Mgmt. Exec. 107 (2004).

17. Daniel Kahneman & Amos Tversky, *Conflict Resolution*, in Barriers to Conflict Resolution 46 (Kenneth J. Arrow et al. eds., 1995).

18. Howard Raiffa, Negotiation Analysis 18, 200 (2002).

19. James C. Freund, Smart Negotiating 66 (1992).

20. Bob Woolf, Friendly Persuasion 129 (1990).

21. G. Richard Shell, Bargaining for Advantage 111 (1999).

22. Freund, supra note 19, at 50.

23. *Id.* at 44.

24. Shell, supra note 21, at 110.

25. Freund, supra note 19, at 93.

26. Raiffa, supra note 18, at 200.

27. Raiffa, supra note 8, at 78.

28. Robert H. Mnookin & Lee Ross, *Introduction*, in Barriers to Conflict Resolution 10 (Kenneth J. Arrow et al. eds., 1995).

29. SHELL, supra note 21, at 99.

30. I. WILLIAM ZARTMAN & MAUREEN R. BERMAN, THE PRACTICAL NEGOTIATOR 205 (1982).

31. RAIFFA, supra note 8, at 104–5.

32. Michael R. Fowler, *The Relevance of Principled Negotiation to Hostage Crises*, 12 HARV. NEG. L. REV. 292–94 (2007).

33. ROY J. LEWICKI, ALEXANDER HIAM, & KAREN WISE OLANDER, THINK BEFORE YOU SPEAK 41 (1996).

34. Guy Olivier Faure, *International Negotiation*, in INTERNATIONAL NEGOTIATION 405 (Victor A. Kremenyuk ed., 2002).

35. WILLIAM M. HABEEB, POWER AND TACTICS IN INTERNATIONAL NEGOTIATION 15 (1988).

36. ROY J. LEWICKI, DAVID M. SAUNDERS, & JOHN W. MINTON, ESSENTIALS OF NEGOTIATION 135 (2d ed. 2001).

37. Sebenius, supra note 7, at 164.

38. KARL W. DEUTSCH, ANALYSIS OF INTERNATIONAL RELATIONS 31 (1978).

39. *Id.* at 31–32.

40. Roger Fisher, *Negotiating Power*, 27 AM. BEHAVIORAL SCIENTIST 150 (1983).

41. *Id.* at 153–55.

42. JOHN KOTTER, POWER AND INFLUENCE 40 (1985).

43. LEWICKI, SAUNDERS, & MINTON, supra note 36, at 135.

44. *Id.* at 136–37.

45. FISHER, URY, & PATTON, supra note 2, at 106.

46. Fisher, supra note 40, at 152.

47. FISHER, URY, & PATTON, supra note 2, at 178–79.

48. DEBORAH KOLB & JUDITH WILLIAMS, THE SHADOW NEGOTIATION (2000).

49. Deborah Kolb, *Strategic Moves and Turns*, in THE NEGOTIATOR'S FIELDBOOK 401 (Andrea Kupfer Schneider & Christopher Honeyman eds., 2006).

50. *Id.* at 405, citing James K. Sebenius & Rebecca Hulse, *Harvard Business School Case: Charlene Barshevsky (B)* (2001).

Checkpoints

- The acronym BATNA stands for Best Alternative to a Negotiated Agreement. It is the most promising course of action for a negotiator, if he or she cannot reach agreement with the other side.

- A reservation value is the least-attractive proposal for which a negotiator would still decide to come to an agreement, a point just past the one at which a negotiator really does not care whether he or she accepts the offered agreement or opts to pursue his or her BATNA.

- Negotiators ordinarily keep their reservation value confidential to guard against their counterpart creating a low-ball proposal, one barely sufficient to gain an agreement.

- If one side's BATNA is, in fact, considerably stronger than the other side seems to think it is, the negotiator with the attractive BATNA will normally want to reveal and discuss it.

- If the other side seems to have over-estimated my BATNA, or if I have a very weak BATNA and my counterpart does not know it, I will try to avoid a BATNA discussion.

- A negotiator saddled with a weak BATNA should be prepared, if need be, to settle for a less-advantageous deal than if he or she had a much stronger walk-away alternative.

- The extent to which a poor BATNA ought to affect a negotiator's goals is a matter of negotiation strategy that hinges, in part, on whether one's counterpart is likely to know, or find out, how deficient the BATNA really is.

- Leverage refers to a negotiator's ability to move the other side toward doing what he or she wants, ultimately increasing the negotiator's chances of attaining his or her goals.

- The extent of a negotiator's leverage is usually a function of how strongly or urgently his or her counterpart wants or needs something and how vulnerable each party is.

- The balance of leverage between the parties is often a key variable in a negotiation. There is the leverage that A may have with respect to B, but also B's leverage with respect to A. Who in the end has more leverage?

- When your counterpart seems to have more leverage, an experienced negotiator looks for ways to counter it; for instance, if you improve your BATNA, you undercut your evident need to come to an agreement with this party.

- One source of negotiating power is authority: a person's position may provide him or her with the ability to make certain decisions, and these will be viewed within that society as legitimate.

- Apart from authority, one side may have the means to influence another in a negotiation through other factors. However, considerations of power tend to be specific to the task at hand. That is, the power to gain one result may not translate to the power to gain another.

- Finally, negotiating power also hinges on the skill, knowledge, and expertise of the negotiator. A powerful negotiator has better ideas or more experience concerning how to prepare and proceed effectively.

Chapter 6

Problem-Solving: Putting Objective Criteria and Creative Options to Work and Dealing Effectively with Impasses

---

Roadmap

- **Distributional bargaining:** Why is dividing up, or allotting, items of value among the parties a notable challenge in many negotiations?

- **Neutral standards/objective criteria:** What are examples of neutral standards or objective criteria, and how can these help to resolve distributional problems? How might the negotiators determine which one to use, and what problems might arise in this regard?

- **Creative options:** Why can thinking creatively be so critically important in a complex negotiation? Why is it also particularly challenging, and what can negotiators do to stimulate the creative process?

- **Brainstorming:** What do negotiators mean by the term *brainstorming*? How is it done most effectively, and why is it sometimes resisted? Why is it so significant to alert the other side that you are now brainstorming?

- **Impasses:** What different negotiation dynamics tend to bring on impasses? What are effective techniques for overcoming stalemates?

As negotiators explore their goals, positions, and interests, they also begin to envision what a possible negotiated agreement might look like. Too often, however, negotiators become fixated on the first resolution discussed that both sides could accept. Rather than settling for a mediocre deal, negotiators should aim to reach an optimal agreement. To do this, a more measured process is needed in which multiple options concerning a complex negotiation are created and thoughtfully considered. Different elements of possible resolutions are mixed and matched, some points dropping out while others are added, with the ultimate aim being a very good resolution, to which both sides will agree.

Hard bargainers are inclined to short-change the process of generating options. Instead, each side is focused on its favored resolution, and each typically tries to persuade the other of the flaws in their proposals and the advantages in the formulation it is pressing. The approach in interest-based negotiation is to have two sides work together to try to construct an outcome that serves enough key interests of the parties that each will be motivated to sign on. The negotiating process involves thinking up multiple options, sifting through them to find the most promising, aligning options to serve interests, and then developing creative ideas in a mutually beneficial outcome.

A. Dealing with Issues of Distributional Bargaining

Negotiations sometimes go awry since it is often quite difficult or distasteful for one side to yield to what the other demands of it. This is especially the case in distributional bargaining, that is, problems that require allotting dollars or other items of value among the parties: profits to be split, land to be parceled out, goods to be allocated, … generally, … [anything] that one party can consume, use, or enjoy while excluding others from the benefits."[1] Here, every item that goes to one, making it better off, does not go to the other, leaving it worse off than it might be.

Dividing up items of value is but one aspect of negotiation. Alternatively, a negotiation may be driven by "[i]ssues of recognition, of dignity, of acceptance, or rights and justice."[2] Or, a negotiation may hinge on figuring out how to create more of something both sides like. In fact, negotiators often feel some tension between working creatively together to create a larger pie, presumably beneficial for both, and gaining a larger slice of whatever pie is in existence.[3]

"If two negotiators both want something," it has been advised, "the first question that comes to mind should not be 'how can I get the bigger share?' but 'How might we make more?'"[4] Nevertheless, most complex negotiations do involve certain significant distributional issues. Here, to reach an agreement, particularly an optimal one, it may be useful to "avoid premature 'claiming' — to concentrate on building up a big pie to share and not worry too early on about how to share that pie."[5] Still, figuring out how to handle distribution issues in a way that both parties can support is a challenge that must eventually be met.

Note, too, that at any given moment negotiators tend be thinking *either* creatively, trying to find new value, *or* distributively, trying to claim value for themselves. They rarely think about these two facets of negotiation simultaneously. Consequently, they may jump to accept a creative way around a deadlock without considering how best to gain the healthiest possible share of the benefits of the proposed solution.[6]

1. Look for Neutral Standards and Objective Criteria

The interest-based negotiator counsels that distribution issues should be taken as a problem that the parties share and for which an equitable resolution should suffice. Depending on the circumstances the parties might call on different criteria of fairness. For instance, they might link the division to what each party contributed or to what each party needs.

Sometimes, the solution to a distributional problem lies in finding a just, workable process to distribute the items in contention. Is there a fair or equal way to divide things? Might it make sense for the sides to agree to take turns in claiming benefits? Or, could one negotiator divide items into lots, and the other get first choice. Alternatively, might a third party that both respect make distributional decisions on behalf of the contending sides?

In other cases the best approach to distributional issues is to find a neutral standard or an objective criteria of some sort that supports a particular resolution. As Jeswald Salacuse wrote, "Whether you are negotiating a salary, the sale of a car, or your share of partnership profits, linking your proposals to an objective measure ... makes you more persuasive. Asking for a raise so you can make payments on your Ferrari, your Park Avenue condo, and your annual two weeks in St. Bart's is a lot less convincing than justifying your request based on the salary of your predecessor or others with your qualifications in the same industry."[7]

The trick is discovering an objective standard that speaks to your counterpart as well as to yourself. Here, a precedent of some kind could suggest how the parties determine what constitutes a fair outcome. Or, the opinion of an independent expert could be useful. As the parties set forth relevant points relating to market value, industry practice, comparable data, a cost-of-living index, or other standards that might be viewed as fair, reasonable, or legitimate, they can greatly narrow the field of possible resolutions, bringing a final negotiated agreement much closer.

The cardinal point here is that one should enter this phase of a negotiation ready to have an intelligent conversation with your counterparts about which standards ought to be relied upon. Using outside criteria can move the focus away from the push and pull of positional bargaining and help to bring about a deal that both sides find worthy of support. Being able to point to a logical precedent may also help a party to justify to others having agreed to the deal. Interest-based negotiators aim to use the mutual desire for a fair agreement to stake out, or bracket, a zone of reasonably fair possible resolutions.

To take a simple example, a buyer and a seller negotiating the possible sale of a used car might consult Kelley Blue Book values for a vehicle of that particular model manufactured in that particular year. They might go on to explore whether the car in question ought to be valued above or below the listed price because of its condition, miles already driven, past accident record, or other factors. Reference to a neutral source like the Blue Book serves the purpose of providing a useful starting point and helping to define a zone of reasonable resolutions. Similar sources are available that value an array of other items, whether antiques, artwork, baseball cards, or many other items.

Depending on the problem before them, negotiators could find relevant objective criteria that might be applied to their circumstances in many different places. Scientific data might suit one context; ethical or philosophical principles, another; a historic rationale might fit a third. However, the objective criteria that many negotiators rely on most frequently probably involves past practices of some kind. In this regard the authors of *Getting to Yes* advised: "Few things facilitate a decision as much as precedent. Search for it. Look for a decision or statement that the other side may have made in a similar situation, and try to base a proposed agreement on it. This provides an objective standard for your request and makes it easier for them to go along."[8]

The more times a negotiator can show that a particular precedent has been followed, the more influential it appears to be. The obvious counter-move is to suggest that the precedent does not really apply so well since the circumstances at issue differ in important respects. Even so, the argument that past practices ought to be followed can help the parties to work toward a fair resolution they both support.

In the business field experienced attorneys specializing in mergers and acquisitions are likely to have sometimes represented the seller and at other times the buyer in these transactions. A relevant question might be—when negotiating from the other side, what provisions did the attorney then feel were necessary to have in the purchase-and-sale agreement?

The buyer's attorney negotiating the purchase of a publicly traded company might review past agreements on file with the Securities and Exchange Commission that the seller or the seller's attorney had negotiated in the past in an effort to persuade the seller to include some of the same provisions in the current transaction. The argument would be: "If you argued in favor of a particular term being fair and necessary when you were on my side of the table in a prior deal, you ought to give me the same protections now that I'm representing a party on the side of the transaction where you once were."

Box 6.1 — Finding Relevant Standards

To find possible standards, a negotiator should ask questions like those that follow.

- How have similar problems been handled in the industry or by individuals situated in circumstances like ours?

- Is there a tradition or benchmarks of some variety that both sides could see as reasonable and applicable?

- Are there comparable values or neutral standards — things found in market rates, past agreements, community traditions, technical undertakings — that might suggest a fair resolution here?

- How about relevant provisions of law or decisions by courts or arbitral tribunals?

- How might a wise, far-seeing mediator or judge resolve the problem facing the negotiators, and why would that be a fair resolution?

Discussing potentially applicable standards and criteria moves a negotiation toward an effort to find an outcome that the different sides consider reasonably fair and logical. This may be important not only to reach an agreement, but also to have it eventually implemented. The parties are more likely to honor an agreement that seems to both to be objectively fair. Hence, negotiated resolutions that rely on standards are likely to be more durable and operational than those that are arbitrary or compelled. Using neutral standards also has the potential to bring about an agreement amicably, important for the strong working relationship that the two sides want to maintain over time, perhaps even beyond the closing of the deal.

Consider, for example, a contract negotiation in which a company wants to hire a potential employee, who would very much like to work for them. Imagine here a very large zone of possible agreement (ZOPA). That is, the employer has an ample budget to hire its target, and the employee is ultimately prepared to agree to any one of a number of possible salary figures. Of course, within that zone, those in charge of hiring for the company would prefer to pay as small a salary as possible, and the potential employee would like to earn as much as possible. Here, the negotiators could inquire, "What possible standards or criteria for salary appear to be most compelling under these particular circumstances, and why?"

In the course of a negotiation one side may suggest a particular resolution—a sales price for a business, for instance—presumably setting forth a number that would make it happy if received. To turn such a position into a search for appropriate objective criteria, an interest-based negotiator might ask, "If the number you've just proposed is the right one, help me to see why it is." Such a discussion is designed to bring a counterpart to justify a particular figure, and it tends to lead the negotiators toward a conversation about standards. You might begin to discuss, for instance, what the buyer paid for the enterprise and put into it over the years, discounted for wear and tear to the property and other depreciation of value.

2. Determining Which Standard to Use

On occasion, both sides will have similar objective criteria in mind as they consider a negotiating problem. The seller and buyer may feel that the sales of comparable houses over the past two years is a fair standard or that three appraisals by different professional appraisers ought to provide a close indication of a property's worth. If the parties do turn out to have the same, or parallel, standards in mind, a fair resolution to distributional issues may suggest itself in short order.

Quite frequently, however, the search for neutral standards or external criteria does not immediately produce an agreement on how the parties should proceed. It may be that each side has its own standard to suggest, or perhaps multiple standards, with each trying to advocate for those that are most favorable to it. One side is persuaded that one standard is reasonable, and the other may find some other criterion more on point. Or, under some circumstances a negotiator might argue that a cited precedent or norm is itself unfair or biased and, hence, ought to be disregarded.

As part of the process of discussing different objective criteria and how they might best be applied, reasons are laid out favoring one standard and casting doubt on the validity of another. More specific criteria, more directly on point, are usually more persuasive than quite general factors. But, often, one side will propose objective criteria, but the other will find flaws in them, perhaps arguing that this particular case is different, since the particular circumstances differ.

For instance, a professional baseball team negotiating with a free agent pitcher might point to the salary of another pitcher with similar statistics. The pitcher's agents might suggest that the statistics of their client are actually better than that of the pitcher the team felt was comparable. Alternatively, the player's agents might argue that their client would bring other intangible assets to the team, such as leadership or experience in pitching under pressure.

A key dimension of a negotiation may thus involve working out just what both sides can agree would be fair under the circumstances they face. Sometimes, as the parties listen to each other's perspectives, additional standards that would be mutually agreeable might be introduced. Alternatively, the parties might choose or compromise among multiple objective criteria.[9] Here, the following questions may be useful.

- Has one standard been used more frequently or accepted more broadly?
- Is it better tailored to the situation at hand?
- If the different sides continue to disagree, could they agree to select a third party charged with making a binding choice among the possibilities?

Contending with one another over different possible standards is normal and can even be enlightening. In this regard it is worth bearing in mind that being willing to remain open to persuasion by the other side is a powerful tool to elicit collaborative problem-solving.

On some occasions the available objective criteria simply do not seem to fit the current situation especially well. Sometimes, as one scholar observed, "[T]here may be no principled reason for allocation — think of child custody in a non-contested divorce with both parents having equal parenting skills, or situations where right is either on both sides or on neither."[10]

If the parties are really at odds over the objective criteria each proposes, the effort to find a neutral standard can cause serious difficulties. As Michael Wheeler wrote of the negotiation of professional sports contracts: "[A]ttempts to use 'comparables' might actually drive the negotiators farther apart if each sees the other's as self-serving. A team's invocation of lower-paid players can easily be read as an insult. An athlete, in turn, who claims he is equal to the very best is seen as a greedy egomaniac."[11]

Here, discordant notes may be introduced in what might otherwise be a quite cooperative negotiation. And yet, the challenge is to make valid points in a tactful but still clear and compelling way. Bearing in mind that one side may be sensitive about the other pointing out possible flaws in how a proposed objective standard is to be applied to the current situation may help a negotiator toward careful, even diplomatic, phrasing of important points.

Despite these occasional knotty difficulties, the effort to settle on objective criteria may still be salutary, since it brings the parties to engage in reasoned discourse about what would be a fair resolution. As one experienced lawyer put it, "Disputes over rationale can be a lot more constructive than arguments over numbers."[12]

3. Calling on Principles

Alongside discussions of objective criteria, negotiators should also keep in mind that people may want to remain consistent with past behavior or with social, religious, or ethical values that they deeply believe in. That is, they may want to stay loyal, faithful, or devoted to their own principles. Thus, another approach involves trying to work with what the other side views as proper, moral, or upright behavior. Parties may respond positively to appeals to criteria suggested by their own value systems and related traditions, precedents, or ways of doing things.

A negotiator proceeding along these lines would try to gain an appreciation for how the other side sees itself: "People will go to considerable lengths to act or say things consistent with their self-image."[13] For example, government negotiators communicating with Muslim groups that have seized hostages have had conversations about how the Koran dictates that guests ought to be treated. This approach capitalized on the fact that the extremists did hold strong normative beliefs about how people should behave and might be swayed by appeals to those ideas.[14]

Sometimes negotiators can find an organizing principle to which both sides can agree. Although the ideal time to articulate and gain assent to a principle is early in the negotiation, even after a clash or stalemate has ensued the parties might be able to agree on a principle to govern the resolution of particulars. Once the principle is established, negotiators can refer back to it in the effort to solve particular issues.

A historic example of this approach involved the sixteenth-century religious wars in Germany that ended with the historic formula in the Peace of Augsburg summarized in the phrase "*cuius regio eius religio*" ("whose the region, his the religion"), that is, a territory's ruler should choose its religion. "Broad principles," it has been observed, "are not merely inherently satisfying because of their universality; they are more helpful because they provide guidelines for the solution of a larger number of details and they remove the dangers of incoherence and conflict among many smaller criteria."[15]

B. Devising Creative Options

Once the negotiators have identified and discussed some objective criteria, they will still often have to think quite creatively in order to generate a good proposal, one that both sides will find considerably better than their walk-away alternatives. Indeed, even if the two sides have already come to a meeting of the minds on the shape of a mutually beneficial agreement, developing better options can make a barely acceptable agreement much more attractive to each party.

Too often, however, negotiators allow themselves "to be anchored by the first possibility that springs to mind."[16] Consequently, another useful step in solving negotiating problems is to generate a wealth of ideas about how to deal with the difficulties or capitalize on the opportunities that the parties confront. Often, these ideas are best presented tentatively, as "possibilities open for discussion and reexamination."[17]

The key point here is that interest-based negotiators look to surmount difficulties or maximize gains by inventing creative options. These are possible resolutions of some aspect of a negotiating problem that are unconventional, visionary, imaginative, clever, or otherwise attractive by being different or unusual. A creative option ought to meet the interests of one or both sides, speak to concerns that have been, or are likely to be, articulated, and be formulated in a fresh, perceptive, or insightful way.

Some of these ideas may be aimed at joint gains, that is, resolutions that would capitalize on interests that are shared or that dovetail, helping both parties. For example, an accounting expert and a consulting group arranging training sessions for mid-career executives might be at loggerheads over proper pay for a possible future seminar. But, those differences might be bridged by the intellectual property generated by the work to be carried out. Each might contribute to recording the session and marketing it. The anticipated long-term profits might be divided equitably between the parties, possibly to their great ultimate benefit. Furthermore, the parties might incorporate incentives in the performance deal to ensure that each side has good reasons to carry out the agreement's terms fully and to the best of its abilities. With joint gains now evident to both sides, each feels much more attracted to the agreement.

Some creative options are designed to bring one (reluctant) party around to signing onto a potential agreement—*sweeteners* or *perquisites* of some kind. These might be an incidental bonus, privilege, or fringe benefit aimed at making the deal more beneficial for one side. Perhaps a seller could offer an upgrade of some sort or secure attractive financing terms. A perquisite, offered sincerely and at the right moment, may be sufficient to conclude an agreement. These inducements may be referred to as **bargaining chips**, and seasoned negotiators often think in terms of keeping some "in their hip pocket" for use when needed. Here, one might recall how car dealers often keep sweeteners in reserve—flashier hubcaps, better tires, upgrades of a vehicle's sound system— that might appeal to a potential buyer and help to close a deal.

In thinking through creative options, negotiators are well-advised to generate a number of alternative approaches. Some might simply be kept in mind, to be used if need be, while others might be put on the table for consideration by both sides. In some cases a choice might be presented. In others the negotiator might try to select the alternative that seems particularly well-tailored to the situation.

1. Pre-Negotiation Preparation and Thinking on One's Feet

Thinking up, and even committing to paper, a broad range of possible options ahead of time can be very useful. Unveiling creative ideas at opportune moments often brings your counterparts to become excited at the prospects of working with you and building on those ideas. Pre-negotiation preparation, when there is no need to respond instantly to the other party's points, can be a productive time to think imaginatively about such options. Here, you might be able to envision or project what could be if only the different sides could agree to do this or that.

It is important, however, not to become bound to possible options conceived ahead of time. Rather, take your creative options as possibly fruitful points of discussion, to be further refined as the parties exchange thoughts on the situation and better understand the particular circumstances. One source counseled: "You may well have a good idea. But it isn't sacrosanct. It isn't a painting by Rembrandt, which could only be marred by further work. Better if you make a few strokes and then pass the brush to someone else. Encourage others to sharpen any idea, and to improve on it. Invite them to move the thinking forward."[18]

In fact, one's counterpart will usually want to share in the process of designing a resolution to the circumstances that you both face. People are often inclined to resist solutions that others have concocted, even when the ideas have real merit. And, when it comes to innovating, two or more minds may, in fact, be better than one. Then, since a negotiator rarely grasps the complete picture before talks begin, developing creative options during a negotiation allows for problem solving that is more dynamic by being extemporaneous. When negotiators share ideas, they often inspire one another toward an ever more creative resolution to an issue.

Encouraging creative juices to flow, however, is not necessarily an easy task. Particularly when subjected to the pressures of an important negotiation, people can be small-minded and let egos interfere with the inventing process. Fresh, interesting, and functional ideas that might strike a neutral observer as full of promise can be subjected to withering critical scrutiny simply because the other side came up with them. The point I would underscore is that ideas that are created together and are perceived as being "owned" jointly are often immune from being dismissed so cavalierly. This is a cardinal reason that working closely together during the negotiation to generate new ideas, or to polish and improve them, can pay real dividends.

It is sometimes said that a person can accomplish an astonishing amount if he or she pays no attention to who gets the credit for the underlying idea. In creating options, if you can leave them thinking that *your* idea is actually *their* idea, or yours together, so much the better. In this vein an Italian diplomat once quipped, "Diplomacy is the art of letting someone else have *your* way."[19]

Moreover, a negotiator must often justify an agreement to authorities, clients, or others. Being generous in attributing credit to one's counterpart for an idea, proposal, or resolution may help that negotiator to build internal support with constituents.

2. The Importance of Timing

Good effective negotiation often has a real rhythm to it, and nowhere is timing more important than in creating options. The best suggestion, offered at the wrong time, risks being rejected for reasons that have nothing to do with its merits but instead involve having "rushed the cadence."

An enthusiastic negotiator coming into the talks with a pad full of possible ideas will want to guard against hurrying into their discussion and recall how important it can be to canvass problems thoroughly, fully understand the different perspectives on the challenges or puzzles being confronted, and then generate ideas together. Those on different sides of the negotiation will want to be involved in raising key questions, thinking through their dimensions carefully and logically, and then designing interesting solutions to them.

Furthermore, once negotiators believe that a good agreement really might come together, they may be much more receptive to seriously considering creative options. But, first, the contours of the problem must be identified to everyone's satisfaction and their perspectives on it fully explored, while the negotiators gain confidence in each other and the negotiating process. The salient point here is that only after extensive discussions is it natural to move to options as solutions to the difficulties or opportunities identified.

3. Inspiring Creativity

The essence of creativity in negotiation involves envisioning a better future state of affairs and then determining how to make that vision a reality. But, what is a negotiator to do if he or she does not feel creative? Perhaps this happens repeatedly to you, or maybe one simply feels stalled at a particular moment? In either case what might be done? Rena Sharon suggested that it may be necessary "to force the mind to 'jump across' its usual pathways ... or make new connections between old pathways in order to create a new idea out of two seemingly disparate ideas."[20]

One way to do this is through word play. Jennifer Gerarda Brown illustrated this through hypothesizing a simple problem. A neighborly dispute has arisen between Jones and Smith over Smith's littered front yard, causing trash to blow onto Smith's property and detract from the appearance of the neighborhood. Brown suggests taking a core sentence concerning the dispute and emphasizing different words in order to elicit creative options for dealing with it. She wrote:

> "How can *I* get Mr. Smith to stop littering in his yard?"
> "How can I get *Mr. Smith* to stop littering in his yard?"
> "How can I get Mr. Smith to stop *littering* in his yard?"
> "How can I get Mr. Smith to stop littering in *his* yard?"
> "How can I get Mr. Smith to stop littering in his *yard*?"

Looking at the problem from those narrowed perspectives may provoke original thinking about a negotiated resolution. Brown wrote that word play of this sort: "builds upon the insight that many creative solutions are incremental. The problem will not seem so daunting when it is narrowed, and [the parties] ... can address the larger issues step by step."[21]

Another way to generate fresh thinking is to critically analyze the problem from the perspective of professionals in different fields: "By asking themselves, for example, 'what would a journalist do?', 'what would an economist do?', 'how would a psychologist view this?,' and so on, negotiators are able to form a more interdisciplinary view of their problem."[22]

Still another approach to stimulating creativity is to revise the issues under discussion so that they are aligned better with the underlying interests of the different sides. Rather than focusing on the macro problem of whether or not to build a dam, negotiators might do better to focus on such micro, subsidiary issues as the size of the dam, downstream water guarantees, an environmental trust fund to protect an endangered species, and so on.[23]

C. The Process of Brainstorming

Let us next consider some common pitfalls in the creative process, and what might be done about them. People frequently look to solve problems by immediately suggesting options as the issues are discussed, often relying on ideas thought up ahead of time. The negotiator proposing the option argues vigorously in its favor, trying to entice the other side into accepting it. The negotiator making the proposal can come to sound like a new owner trying to coax a puppy into a box it might make its home: "Look at this nice rug! And, there's some food for you. How about if I add a bowl with some water?"

The other side, however, is normally inclined to subject another's plan to critical analysis. The emphasis quickly shifts to finding flaws so as to reject the scheme. Those whose ideas have been skeptically critiqued may then take the rebuff as an affront. Their ideas have been found wanting and having suggested them now appears to have been a mistake. Hesitations about advancing new and creative thoughts multiply on both sides, and soon the process of generating new ideas bogs down.

To instil a more positive dynamic, interest-based negotiators suggest brainstorming. Although brainstorming "is a much-abused term ... sometimes used to mean little more than having an idea," for negotiators it is a term of art, denoting a structured activity "with specific ground rules and with theory underlying each step."[24]

Rather than a phase of the negotiation in which proposals are offered or commitments made, the brainstorming stage is explicitly aimed at nurturing ideas. It is informal and spontaneous, an extended exchange of thoughts about how to handle particular issues. The goal is to generate a great wealth of fresh, distinct ideas in hopes that, ultimately, one or more might be productively applied toward a negotiated resolution.

1. Different Varieties of Brainstorming

Brainstorming can occur in numerous contexts. As I started to practice law, I recall being surprised at how much of it went on. Brainstorming frequently occurs among the partners and associates within a law firm. Or, an outside counsel might brainstorm with an in-house lawyer and a handful of executives from the organization he or she represents. Brainstorming also takes place in discussions with clients. An agent might brainstorm with a principal as part of internal negotiations. Thus, before sitting down at the negotiating table, one might work to generate new ideas with a teammate or perhaps with colleagues in a business, law firm, or government agency.

Brainstorming also occurs with opposing counsel. Especially in cases that both attorneys feel really ought to be negotiated to a settlement, instead of being taken to court to be adjudicated, they often spend some time informally exchanging ideas for a resolution. Then, in a *joint brainstorming* session negotiators from the different sides work together, trying to imagine innovative ways of solving problems, overcoming obstacles, or taking advantage of opportunities. They might brainstorm innovative, elegant, or ingenious ways to capitalize on shared interests or reconcile divergent ones.

2. The Art of Brainstorming Effectively

Negotiators, while brainstorming, are not committing themselves in any way to the points being discussed. At the outset one might write in bold letters where the participants can easily see it: "Nothing said during brainstorming is a commitment by anybody or is later to be attributed to anyone — our aim for the moment is simply to produce a lot of ideas."[25]

Brainstorming negotiators are trying to go beyond a standard, conventional resolution that no one can complain about too much and reach fresh thinking. The participants are encouraged to advance wild, off-the-wall, even wholly unworkable ideas with the hope that these thoughts will stimulate better ones that may, in fact, be possible. "One of the keys to generating better ideas is simple," it has been observed, "... don't stop when you find a good one."[26]

Brainstorming should be focused in a single-minded fashion on invention. Each member of the group should work to ensure that all the participants feel quite comfortable in offering up ideas. A contribution by one negotiator should prompt suggestions by others. A host of new ideas should be tossed out, with some added to or otherwise taken further. Like a popcorn popper in action, more and more ideas should be generated over time.

To bring on new approaches to problems or opportunities, it is exceedingly important that the participants not assess the ideas as they are being articulated. Trying to merge the process of generating ideas with that of determining what will and won't work too often stifles creativity. If each fledgling idea advanced is instantly scrutinized and assessed, with many dismissed out of hand as unworkable or unrealistic, a dynamic quickly arises in which the participants come to fear criticism of their ideas and no one proposes anything very novel.

William Ury identified the leading obstacle to generating creative options as that little voice negotiators carry around in their heads that intones "That won't work." Ury counseled:

> Criticism and evaluation, while important functions, interfere with your imagination. It is better to separate [them] ... Invent first, evaluate later. Suspend judgment for a few minutes and try to come up with as many ideas as possible. Include ideas that at first seem ... wild..., remembering that many of the best ideas ... started out as wild ideas everyone disparaged.[27]

As an exploratory effort to find synergies among the thoughts of the different participants, brainstorming aims to gain intelligent, perceptive contributions from multiple negotiators. These are often encouraged by a light-hearted tone that makes it enjoyable for those involved, and, typically, a brainstorming session is more relaxed and informal than the other stages in the negotiation process.

To get one thought to stimulate another and to remind the group of the progress made in generating ideas, someone should be jotting down all the products of a brainstorming session on a flip chart or blackboard that all can see. However, no record should be kept of which negotiator suggested what during brainstorming. Indeed, participants are cautioned against even offering "congratulatory comments about how great someone else's idea is, murmurs of approval, and back-slapping." "When you signal such approval," one source argued, "you send the implicit message that you're still judging each idea as it is generated—you're just keeping the *negative* ideas to yourself. This does not encourage inventiveness."[28]

Perhaps the ideal size for a brainstorming session is a group of about a half-dozen: "large enough to provide a stimulating interchange, yet small enough to encourage both individual participation and free-wheeling inventing ..."[29] It often helps if they first prepare by themselves "before interaction with others distracts them or other people's ideas displace original ones in their own mind."[30] At times hiring a facilitator or designating one from among the brainstorming participants can help "to keep the meeting on track, to make sure everyone gets a chance to speak, to enforce any ground rules, and to stimulate discussion by asking questions."[31]

Brainstorming should be rigorously separated from the other phases of the negotiation. After a host of new thoughts have been generated, the succeeding task is thus to evaluate the ideas and select the most promising to work with further. This is a different phase, one in which the negotiators change gears to select, revise, and improve upon the best ideas generated in brainstorming. The ultimate goal, of course, is to find the best possible route toward solving the problems or issues at hand and creating a resolution that the different parties see as beneficial.

3. The Occasional Reluctance to Brainstorm

For all of its potential benefits, in some negotiations one or more of the parties may be reluctant to brainstorm. They may have little or no experience with creating ideas this way. Negotiators very concerned about an upcoming deadline may see brainstorming as too likely to waste precious time. When someone has a good idea before the negotiation begins or at an early stage, he or she may want to move directly to a proposal, leaping beyond joint brainstorming.

In situations of serious conflict the negotiators may feel constrained by the hostile circumstances, and they may view brainstorming as risky, something scorned by their respective constituencies. Politicians, diplomats, and various other professionals are "trained to be tough, to be cautious, and not to explore irresponsibly."[32]

Positional negotiators are likely to be strongly inclined to bargain with the other side in an adversarial manner. They may be very concerned with inadvertently disclosing something while brainstorming that might better be kept private. Joint brainstorming will, at the least, require sailing off on a different tack for a while.

Some negotiators may find the informal dialogue inherent in brainstorming to be awkward. Those with more introverted personalities may prefer to consider matters themselves, rather than speak out loud and spontaneously to another. Some may believe that they think more freely as well as more carefully before a negotiation than during it. And, they may shy away from tossing out what they characterize as half-baked ideas on the spur of the moment.

Even though all negotiators will not be equally receptive to inventing options this way, brainstorming has much to recommend it. Putting forward a good option can lead to the development of an even better one. Even if one has an excellent idea in mind, additional suggestions could improve it—amending this aspect, trimming back that one, taking something else even further. Brainstorming gets the parties working together in devising ideas that address mutual problems or opportunities. The more engaged the sides get in joint problem solving, the more of a stake they have in agreeing to a negotiated resolution and, later, in carrying it out.

4. Alerting One's Counterpart to Brainstorming

One cautionary note: seasoned negotiators often have a good sense for when counterparts are brainstorming as opposed to when formal proposals are being made. No matter how experienced one's counterparts, however, it is good practice to be explicit about brainstorming. It is awkward to find yourself in the position of having to retract what others considered your own prior proposal but you thought was simply tossing ideas around. Indeed, if the other side mistakes your brainstorming for a firm proposal to which you are already committed, the remainder of the negotiation may be marred by the misunderstanding.

After noting, "To reduce the risk of appearing committed to any given idea, you can make a habit of advancing at least two alternatives at the same time," the authors of *Getting to Yes* further suggested: "You can also put on the table options with which you obviously disagree. 'I could give you the house for nothing, or you could pay me a million dollars in cash for it, or ...' Since you are plainly not proposing either of these ideas, the ones which follow are labeled as mere possibilities, not proposals."[33]

Better yet, when negotiators call for brainstorming, they can reaffirm what they mean by the term. In particular, they can underscore its exploratory nature — off the record and without attribution or prejudice — while putting others on notice that you want them to embark on an informal process of generating ideas. While brainstorming, you have certainly not yet reached the stage of delineating precisely what you are prepared to do by making a formal offer or other binding commitment.

5. Alternatives to Traditional Brainstorming

Another route toward generating fresh new thoughts is called *piggybacking*. Here, a group focuses upon a promising idea with the members trying, each in turn, to suggest ways that it could be taken further.[34] A similar process has been termed cooperative overlapping.[35] The goal here is to stimulate the evolution of thinking through exchanging ideas and soliciting other views from other participants.

Both of these alternatives to brainstorming emphasize revising, looping back, and building on ideas as new contributions are made. The piggybacking and overlapping processes also differ from brainstorming in that criticism is not prohibited. Generating ideas is not kept separate from evaluating them and selecting the best among them. Instead, these are evolutionary processes aimed at using synergies among the participants and their thinking to develop better ideas.

D. When Impasses Arise

Some complex negotiations stall on issues about which the parties conflict. As negotiators try to reconcile differing interests and goals, incompatibilities can develop into deadlocks. Negotiations verge on breaking down, with the parties seriously contemplating walking away without an agreement. Let us consider, first, some common sources of impasses.

1. Claiming and Positional Deadlocks

When negotiators reach distributive issues and both aggressively claim value, they often come to an impasse. More generally, positional-bargaining strategies can readily lead to stalemates. The position of one side collides with that of the other. Each makes strong demands punctuated by pronouncements of what it will not do. Then, should the other side question these positional statements, the parties often become further attached or committed to them.

Recall that the position a negotiator takes can often be addressed in a strictly limited number of ways, perhaps in only a single way. A company wants to hire an employee, but he or she declares: "I have to have a six-figure income to sign a contract with you." If the company has budgeted only $90,000 for the position and the hiring officer announces, "We absolutely cannot pay more than $90,000," then the two positions clash, there appears to be no zone of possible agreement, and the differences appear to be irreconcilable.

The seemingly intractable position of one party then brings its counterpart to formulate its own different position, stated with equal firmness to signal its inability or reluctance to yield. The stark contrast between the parties' declarations may appear incompatible. Sometimes, as a negotiation develops, a negotiator couches the differences between the parties as an either-or choice, and each of the two alternatives appears flawed.

Negotiation theorists sometimes refer to the difficulties of negotiating "along a single dimension": "the amount of territory, the price of a car, the length of a lease on an apartment, or the size of a commission on a sale."[36] At other times, while the negotiation includes other items, one issue seems of overwhelming importance. One example would be child custody in a divorce settlement.

A hard-bargaining approach exacerbates the problem of negotiating along a single dimension. One authority noted, "In the course of hard bargaining, things are often said and done that change the climate of relations in ways that do not easily allow for a return to a less confrontational stance. A 'residue' is left behind, in the form of words spoken or acts committed, which cannot be denied and which may well change the relationship."[37]

Sometimes the impasse concerns a *last gap*: a final issue about which the parties fundamentally disagree and have become deadlocked. Although the negotiators may have already resolved numerous issues and seem very close to a final agreement, the last gap can still pose a formidable obstacle. One or the other or both parties may feel that they have already given up all that they are prepared to. Hence, the negotiator digs in and refuses to yield the last point, jeopardizing the entire agreement.

2. Psychological Barriers

Impasses also sometimes arise when one or both parties erroneously size up the situation. Here, their own psychological processes can create intractable barriers. Deadlocks usually lead to frustration, and frustrated negotiators may mis-diagnose the actual sources of an impasse as they "make inferences about each other's ... motives and behavior that are not only uncharitable but often erroneous and bound to exacerbate existing feelings of ill will and mistrust."[38]

More problems arise when one negotiator falls prey to over-confidence, believing that its counterpart is on the verge of yielding. Those on each side understand their own perspective much better than they do the other side's. Hence, each ends up under-estimating why the other might see it as rational to stand firm rather than to compromise or give in.[39]

Another psychological barrier to agreement occurs when negotiators become intent on justifying their prior behavior. For instance, a party that has turned down a settlement offer might be inclined to rationalize that decision and "stay the course" in order to avoid having to admit to an earlier mistake. Two scholars wrote: "This objective is accomplished by convincing themselves ... that the rejected proposals were even more one-sided, or that those offering them are even more untrustworthy, or that the causes for which they are struggling are even more noble, or that the prospects for better terms in the future are even more favorable, than they had seemed prior to the disputant's decision not to settle."[40]

E. Techniques for Overcoming Stalemates

The unfortunate temptation for busy people confronted with a difficult negotiating problem, whether substantive or psychological, is to quit when confronting a real deadlock, assuming that it cannot be overcome. So, the impatient negotiator hangs up the phone, deletes the e-mail message, or walks away from the bargaining table. In contrast, skillful negotiators learn to wrestle with the vexing problems they confront, even those that may initially seem impossible to resolve satisfactorily. And, the five negotiating techniques that follow might help to create a zone of possible agreement when none at first seems apparent.

1. Try to "Build a Golden Bridge"

William Ury drew on the thinking of Chinese strategist Sun Tzu to introduce to western audiences the concept of building a golden bridge.[41] That is, rather than trying to push, argue, and press the other side toward the agreement you would like, a skillful negotiator draws his or her counterparts in the preferred direction more subtly.

The other party may be resisting a possible agreement because some basic interest has been overlooked. Or, perhaps your counterpart feels that he or she has not participated sufficiently in crafting the agreement or that things have simply moved too fast, raising fears of being taken. Or, maybe the opposing negotiator fears losing face among important onlookers and wants to avoid looking over-eager, soft, or weak should he or she agree at this juncture.

Under these circumstances the more that one side exerts pressure, the more difficult it becomes for the other negotiator to agree. Yielding would simply exacerbate the underlying problem. Ury explained that, whatever disjunction exists between the thinking of the two sides, "[y]our job is to *build* a golden bridge across the chasm. You need to reframe a retreat from their position as an advance toward a better solution."[42]

By engaging the other party in creating the deal, you undermine their resistance to it. You elicit their ideas and look to build on them, while asking for constructive criticism and then trying to incorporate aspects of it into the developing proposal. By working with the other side and its interests, and by helping them to save face whenever possible, you give your counterpart a clear stake in resolving the issues at hand. In this way you construct a golden bridge toward agreement that your counterpart can be comfortable in venturing to cross.

2. Make Trades

a. Trade-Offs

Another approach to a stalled negotiation involves reciprocity. In a *trade-off* one negotiator promises to do something in exchange for another agreeing to do something else. These are often presented in an "if/then" construction: "if I were able to do x, then would you be able to do y?" For example, if I advance the annual delivery date of the widgets to August 1st, will you agree to a three-year term for the contract?

Negotiators sometimes refer to an offer by one party to do something for the other in exchange for getting something else in return as a *side payment.* If you will agree to lease our property, we will pave the parking area before you move in. Here, a negotiator looks for items that the two sides value differently: one side sees a significant benefit there, and the other can accommodate at a reasonable cost.

Side payments can take many different forms. Consider, for instance, political negotiations. In diplomacy within an international organization a country's vote on one issue might come in exchange for another's support on a different issue. In domestic politics, to get what it wants on one issue, the executive branch might agree with particular legislators or other counterparts to appoint a designated political figure or adopt a particular regulation or policy.

In the legislature a representative's vote on one matter might be traded for support from a counterpart on another. All of these are sometimes referred to as *logrolling*.

b. Trade across Issues

A negotiator confronting a stalemate can also look to see if a break-through might be possible via a *trade across issues*. The idea is that, although both sides might see value in something, one might want it much more than the other does. To illustrate, although a divorcing husband and wife would likely each see very substantial value in the house they had lived in, the one charged with being the primary care-giver for the children might value staying in the house even more highly than the other. Or, while both sides might hope some event does not happen, one might be able to handle its occurrence much more readily than the other. Individuals, for instance, might be far more risk-averse than large institutions that can spread risks among many clients or customers. Those differences might set up a trade-off that both parties support.

Alternatively, one side might want something in which the other has no interest whatsoever. One party might want publicity; the other might shun it. Perhaps a deal can be worked out in which "one side can have a public victory if it needs it, while the other receives something in currencies it values more."[43]

i. Strengths of Feeling

Trades across issues hinge on different *strengths of feeling*. That is, when one party wants one item, but another wants something else, or when they otherwise analyze and evaluate matters differently, one side might sacrifice certain things that, relatively speaking, it does not feel so emphatically about in order to gain other things that are really important to it. Hence, negotiators looking to engineer trade-offs need to attend carefully to differences "in tastes, forecasts, endowments, capabilities ..."[44]

Suppose that two people are negotiating the subletting of an apartment. Normally, a lease would begin on the first of the month, but "[i]f it is worth more to Jim to move in early than it costs Sara to move *out* early, they may agree to accommodate Jim's schedule in exchange for compensation to Sara."[45]

For another illustration, a divorcing husband and wife might find that whether they characterize payments as alimony or child support has tax consequences. But, if they are in different brackets, the advantage of terming certain payments alimony might help the higher-earning individual more than terming them child support would assist the lower earner. Consequently, it might be in both parties' interests to work out a trade in which the payments are characterized as alimony, but the lower earner receives a significant part of the savings. In that way, the parties have traded across issues, and money that might have gone to the Internal Revenue Service has been captured and allocated between them, leaving both better off.

The central point here is that when the sides are at an impasse, negotiators might usefully consider whether a mutually agreeable package could be created that capitalizes on different strengths of feeling. A negotiator aiming to construct a tradeoff might begin by posing a series of relevant questions, designed to flush out preferences: "[T]he agent for [a] ... baseball star might ask the team owner: 'What meets your interests better, a salary of $875,000 a year for four years, or $1,000,000 a year for three years? The latter? OK, how about between that and $900,000 a year for three years with a $500,000 bonus in each year if Fernando pitches better than a 3.00 [Earned Run Average]?'"[46]

This bargaining technique can really come into its own in a complex group negotiation that requires intelligent compromising on the part of the different parties. Each negotiator comes to recognize that achieving everything desired on every issue is unrealistic. However, joining to create a package that serves certain key interests of all the parties may be far better than walking away without an agreement. But, each negotiator must be willing to prioritize, with an eye to foregoing some items that serve its interests in a modest way in order to achieve other much more important matters.

ii. Time Value of Money

Economists speak of the *time value of money*, the idea that gaining a sum of money today is more valuable than gaining the equivalent amount at some future date. The reason is that the sum at issue could be invested, with the recipient gaining the fruits of that investment over time. However, although both parties might recognize the potential benefit of gaining compensation sooner rather than later, one of the negotiators might prefer immediate payment now to payment later, or vice versa.

In some circumstances a party might value payment after retirement, when he or she is in a lower income-tax bracket. In other circumstances he or she might very much want payment now, to cancel or service a bothersome debt or to make an enticing investment.[47] Note that one way to enhance the attractiveness of an offer is to have the benefits to one side accrue sooner, while the costs it must pay come due later.[48] That type of tradeoff might have a very modest effect on the one party, but cinch the deal for the other.

3. Fractionate or Enlarge the Negotiation

An impasse might also be overcome, in Roger Fisher's phrase, by *fractionating* a problem.[49] In other words, the parties could disaggregate the matters on which they are deadlocked—divide them into component parts—and see whether any of the particular pieces could be resolved. Perhaps one or more issues could be excluded from the negotiation: isolate "'the one that doesn't belong' for separate treatment or postponement."[50]

Underlying fractionating a problem is the conviction that a partial loaf is better than no bread whatsoever: "If we insist on all or nothing, and have not got the capacity to get all, we get nothing."[51] Furthermore, a negotiator markedly increases the chances of getting something by revising what is being proposed so that it is more modest. People more readily brush off or sweep aside major or extraordinary demands than they do smaller, more bite-sized proposals or requests.

In some circumstances the differences in a stalemated negotiation can be narrowed, producing a much more manageable problem, if the negotiators agree to arbitrate a portion of the dispute, while working out a resolution to the rest. Although the parties might shy away from a full-blown, costly, and complex arbitration of the entire problem, putting the resolution of a single thorny issue into the hands of a neutral third party may be the most efficient way to proceed.[52]

The opposite of fractionating is to see if a deadlock could be broken by aggregation or enlargement. In some cases issues could be added to the matters the negotiators are considering. In others the scope or magnitude of a potential project could be enhanced. Then the negotiators could inquire whether the savings associated with a more sweeping project could be employed to help the parties get beyond a stalemate.

When enlarging a negotiation, the parties should certainly bear in mind *economies of scale.* That is, when some business, or, conceivably, some government entity, expands its various outputs through large-scale production, the cost per unit of each output often falls. Thus, for example, if two parties are each producing the same item, costs might be cut if one party produced enough for two. And, where discounts accrue with volume purchases, buying needed items together could produce savings in dealing with a third party.[53]

Where the parties are deadlocked over how to divide revenues, might there be other sources of money to tap into, if thinking about the project were expanded? For example, while a country-western band and a community park might reach a stalemate on compensation for a concert, should the deal be expanded to include a division of potential profits coming from the associated intellectual property, such as an album memorializing the show, a zone of agreement might emerge where none had been apparent. Or, if the parties are stalled on the proper price, additional items might be bartered, and these new elements might make the deal appear to be attractive to both sides.

When an impasse develops with one party, consider whether it would be possible to invite in others. Perhaps you can come to a deal with them, or maybe they will bring to the negotiation a distinct set of interests, more reasonable voices, or a different mix of capabilities and objectives. "If you find yourself besieged in a public dispute by a group with a particular point of view," one authority suggests, "find others with that point of view but with whom you can deal and include them in the process. They will serve as a leveling agent and can help to bring the objecting party into the fold."[54]

Another route toward creating value involves what economists call *economies of scope*, that is, costs of production can be lower when the same basic resources are devoted to producing a number of different goods or services rather than just one. For instance, "[a] restaurant supplier who is selling and delivering fresh vegetables may be able to offer fresh fruits at very little additional cost."[55]

4. Fashion a Contingent Agreement

In some impasses a key part of the problem concerns real uncertainty about the future: the negotiators do not share a vision of what is most likely to happen. In some cases the parties may want to defer certain matters until additional information is learned. In others, however, it may be preferable to negotiate a *contingent agreement*. The deal, or some aspect of it, is tentative in that it depends upon some particular thing happening in order to become final. When future circumstances, outside of the control of the parties, may affect the deal but the two sides differ in their predictions of what is likely to happen, negotiators ought to consider fashioning a contingent agreement.

A simple example may help to clarify this point. Let us say a wife and husband prefer different types of movies, but like to watch them together. They live in a small town with one movie theater, and one likes horror movies, while the other prefers comedies. The wife recalls that one movie in each category has been playing at the theater. Which movie do they go see?

One approach would be to decide first on a process. The husband could flip a coin, the wife could call either heads or tails while the coin was in the air. The winner of the coin flip could decide which movie to see this Saturday, and the loser could decide next Saturday's show. Alternatively, the couple could agree to the coin-flip process but only if both movies would be available for the next two weeks. If one of the movies were to leave town the following weekend, the couple could decide to go, first, to the one soon leaving town, and, second, to the one that would be available both weekends, whichever movie those might be.

a. Formulaic Negotiation

Contingent agreements are one type of *formulaic negotiation,* that is, coming to an agreement on an equation, but not knowing the outcome of that equation until missing information is gathered and inserted. This highlights another approach to overcoming an impasse: focus on a fair procedure. Instead of demanding a particular result, alter the objective to creating an equitable process that will eventually settle the issue.

One such procedure involves one side creating two relatively equal portions, giving to the other the opportunity to choose first between them. Here, Howard Raiffa wrote: "Two children are arguing about how they will share a piece of cake. Their mother ... imposes a procedure ... She designates one child to divide the cake into two parts and the other child to select one part."[56] Plainly, the divider has a strong incentive to split the cake into two even pieces since the other child is the one who gets to select the piece.

The same technique can be used to resolve much more elaborate disputes. As the United Nations Convention on the Law of the Sea was being negotiated, Henry Kissinger successfully suggested a technique using the same dynamics to overcome a sticking point regarding deep-seabed mining. The private or state-run mining concerns would bid to reserve sites in international waters. However, the mining sites would be large enough that each would be divided into two with the International Seabed Authority then getting first choice as to which one to reserve for itself.[57] Thus, procedural fairness was built into the scheme to ensure that the public mining sites would be of as good quality as the private ones.

b. Types of Contingent Agreements

Some agreements are made contingent on a certain event occurring. "*If* such and such happens, *then* we agree to do so and so." In a simple contingent agreement the parties discover in the future whether x or y occurs. If x takes place, then one plan of action is instituted; if y happens, another is. Each party gets favorable terms for the outcome that it thinks most likely to come about.

Another variety of contingent agreement involves a bonus provided from one party to the other if something turns out to happen. Here, it may be possible to bridge differences by trading on the different forecasts of the sides as to what is likely to occur.[58]

For example, a team of business consultants is hired to revamp a company's sales processes. It will be guaranteed a fee, but the deal will be sweetened by an incentive bonus if sales over the next three years rise to particular levels. Or, a once-popular stand-up comedian now trying to make a comeback is quite optimistic about the crowd likely to be drawn to the bar that is hosting him. He might agree to relatively low base compensation enhanced by a bonus, the size of which would depend on the numbers of paying customers.

Another species of contingent agreement makes the deal hinge on a particular fact being confirmed as true: "*If* the necessary software is produced by the end of the year, *then* we will purchase it for x amount of dollars." Or, an agreement may be binding *only if* the negotiators obtain the approval or blessing of others — the client, the board of directors, a government regulator, an expert, or some other authority figure. For instance, the interested buyer agrees to the terms of the purchase and sale agreement for a piece of industrial property so long as a test by an accredited environmental consultant shows no evidence of hazardous waste at the site.

In sum, then, a contingent agreement might help negotiators to deal with issues or problems, or for that matter great windfalls or victories, that may or may not arise. A contingent agreement can create useful incentives — the women's professional basketball star who gains a bonus if her team makes the playoffs. And, risks can be allocated to the party that is more risk-tolerant, while rewards could flow to the party that brings about a successful ending.

Yet another contingent approach to an impasse would be to turn the immediate agreement into something experimental. Undertake a pilot project, see if it works, and if we are both happy, then we can consider a larger or more permanent agreement.

c. Possible Problems with Contingent Agreements

Those who come to a contingent agreement are, in effect, laying a wager on what will happen. But, not all parties will be comfortable gambling this way. If future events turn out as hoped or anticipated, all will be well, but if they don't, the agreement may no longer look attractive.[59]

While fashioning a contingent agreement can sometimes help parties to overcome an impasse, it is important that the contingency be spelled out clearly with a readily assessed or measured term. One source hypothesized: "A married couple might agree, 'If the weather is nice tomorrow, we'll hike. Otherwise, we'll go shopping.' The next morning, when it is cloudy but not raining, the spouse who wants to hike is likely to declare it 'nice,' while the person preferring to shop will argue the opposite."[60]

The parties will also want to see if it is possible to circumvent incentives that may not be in line with the spirit of the deal. Negotiation theorists sometimes refer to this as *moral hazard*. That is, rather than heeding the biblical injunction of doing unto others as you would have them do unto you, one party behaves in an underhanded manner that advantages itself and disadvantages its counterpart. For example, when it appears that a sports star is going to reach certain incentive goals, the team benches the athlete so it will not have to pay the promised bonuses.[61]

5. Introduce Calculated Ambiguity

As negotiators look to close a deal, they are usually programmed to work towards clarity in the commitments that each side makes. For an agreement to be durable and operational, the parties ought to clearly understand what each side is to do. "The traditional view of ambiguity in an agreement," it has been noted, "is that it implies either the presence of an unconsidered point, or a deliberate failure to come to grips with the problem."[62]

When trying to wrestle with an impasse, however, negotiators may find certain differences to be, in fact, unbridgeable. For instance, each side may feel it necessary to adhere to core principles, and those principles might clash. Alternatively, each might have to report back to constituencies that are adamant about matters that fundamentally conflict.

In such circumstances it may be possible to introduce what Henry Kissinger once termed "constructive ambiguity."[63] In negotiating treaties, diplomats might paper over irreconcilable differences with ambiguous language. In working out a labor agreement, the company and union might opt not to try to specify, say, all the circumstances in which an employee may be fired but instead rely on an inherently vague term such as "just cause."[64] The negotiators leave for the future the task of determining exactly what the ambiguous language means.

Purposefully injecting ambiguity in an agreement is not a step to be taken lightly. Unresolved issues have an unfortunate tendency to spring back to life, often at a most inopportune moment; hence, they can hang over the parties and their agreement. Still, calculated ambiguity may be necessary to overcome a major substantive impasse. And, as Christopher Honeyman concluded: "[T]here is nothing inherently wrong with gracefully admitting the impossibility of reaching, in every instance, a complete 'meeting of the minds.' Allowing an ambiguity to pass into the agreement, when there is a reasonable expectation that it will later be interpreted in terms not likely to cause a wider dispute, is just another way to get the agreement done."[65]

F. Conclusion

The ideas above illustrate how negotiators might grapple with and eventually overcome impasses. They are by no means an exhaustive list. Another approach in a stalled negotiation, for instance, would be to work on enhancing one's best alternative to a negotiated agreement (BATNA). If you gain a better BATNA, you improve your negotiating posture and get more leverage with which to work.

Note, too, that parties stuck in an impasse are often completely absorbed by their differences and may be overlooking or minimizing the progress they have, in fact, already made. The present situation may not be advantageous for either side, and if the realistic alternatives to working with one another are unattractive as well, bringing attention to the poor walk-away options may remind everyone of the importance of trying to keep working together to find some creative or compromise resolution.

Hence, deadlocked parties might usefully think together about just what an agreement could reasonably deliver to them. The negotiators could "share visions."[66] Whether the payoff would be peace or profits or some other good, refocusing on what sort of beneficial deal might be realistic and possible could inspire the parties to overcome the deadlock.

Deadlocks are also sometimes overcome by having someone new consider the problem. Occasionally, it may be possible to invite another party to enter the discussions. One or the other or both of the stalemated sides might be able to think of someone who would have an incentive or the necessary resources or the fresh insights that they so desperately need.

If agents are negotiating on behalf of principals, one approach would be to bring the clients into the negotiating process. A deadlock might be broken by getting past the other negotiator and to the real decision-maker. Should a principal not be able or willing to appear at the next negotiating session, it may be worth recalling that an attorney is obliged to pass along a written offer to his or her client. Hence, writing out a proposal may have the effect of changing the mix of people at the table. And, one might append an invitation that the parties come together to discuss the new proposal.

Another way to alter the dynamics at the table is to introduce a mediator. There may be someone who is trusted by both parties and can speak to both better than they can communicate directly with each other. A mediator might be able to improve working relations and get the sides back into a problem-solving frame of mind. In addition, a mediator might convince the different sides to reveal matters in confidence that they would be wary of revealing to one another. In this way the mediator might be able to see a route around the impasse that the parties might never find themselves.

For all of these ideas, negotiators should also bear in mind that some impasses simply cannot be overcome. Perhaps on this matter no zone of agreement exists, or problems away from the table may obstruct the negotiators in their effort to arrange a mutually beneficial resolution. For instance, clients or constituents, far from the negotiation, may prove to be more stubborn or more radical than their negotiators. This sometimes poses insuperable problems for concluding negotiated agreements.

Nevertheless, skillful negotiators wrestle with problems, while critically scrutinizing either-or choices presented to them. Mary Parker Follett, once called "the mother of negotiation theory," advised, "The clever thing to do is not to let the negotiation drift toward two mutually exclusive alternatives—your way or my way."[67] Elsewhere, she cautioned against allowing "ourselves to be bullied by an 'either-or.' There is often the possibility of something better than either of two given alternatives."[68]

Before terminating a negotiation, one should be absolutely certain that the key problems that are holding up the deal cannot be resolved or reconciled. In this regard one authority counseled: "If it appears that you are at the end, ask your counterparts to review again with you the reasons it is over.... [T]hey may grow exasperated and tell you they've been over it a million times but you must persist.... [I]t is not uncommon ... for parties to stumble upon an opening, a crack in the door..., ... a fundamental misunderstanding or a ray of hope that had eluded them until then."[69]

A final technique is to have each side try to assemble a *last best offer*. These ultimate proposals could then be compared to see if any promising leads presented themselves. A variant is final-offer arbitration in which each side agrees to put a final offer in the hands of an arbitrator, who is given the power to make the ultimate decision but must choose one or the other of the parties' offers.

In fact, even when matters appear quite bleak, with a complete breakdown threatening, there is often a route forward. People enter complex negotiations in the belief that they will be better off agreeing with each other than proceeding alone. It is true that, sometimes, after discussions, they are disabused of this notion. However, an internal dynamic often exists on each side—even though often masked, and sometimes purposely so—that nonetheless favors a deal. Since the parties often have good reasons for wanting to come to an agreement, skillful negotiation can often surmount considerable difficulties and ultimately reach a successful conclusion.

To bridge a last gap, one authority found skillful negotiators using numerous different techniques.[70] For example, the parties might agree that neither side will prevail on this last issue; instead, whatever they are disagreeing on will be transferred to a third party. If money is at issue, it might be set aside for a charitable contribution or deposited in a child's trust fund. Or, depending on the circumstances, the money might be put into renovating a house that is to be sold, or it could be dedicated to paying off court costs or legal fees.

Another approach would be to write out an agreed number of possible solutions on slips of paper, put them into a hat, and have someone draw out one of them, which both parties agree beforehand that they will be bound to accept as the final resolution. John Wade illustrated this with the following example: "[I]f the last increment is $20,000, then ten slips of paper can be placed in a hat beginning with '$2,000' and ending with '$20,000' with gaps of $2,000 written on each slip of paper. The person drawing the slip receives whatever number is on the drawn piece of paper; the residue of the last gap goes to the other disputant."[71]

When all else fails, it may be useful to reflect on the possibility that the root of the problem is that the parties have simply tried to do too much too quickly. Here, it may be useful to lower everyone's sights for the current negotiating session. Might a watered-down resolution be preferable to no resolution at all? Rather than a signed agreement, perhaps the parties need to think about coming up with a tentative joint recommendation for how to proceed or even content themselves with an informal exchange of views. This still might be a productive step forward for the parties. In sum, then, seasoned and skillful negotiators can call on a plethora of different techniques and tactics to overcome impasses. Of course, some deadlocks simply cannot be overcome, but many others are susceptible to mutually agreeable resolutions.

Notes

1. David A. Lax & James K. Sebenius, The Manager as Negotiator 89 (1985).
2. I. William Zartman & Maureen Berman, The Practical Negotiator 84 (1982).
3. Howard Raiffa, Negotiation Analysis 191 (2002).
4. Roger Fisher & Danny Ertel, Getting Ready to Negotiate 35 (1995).
5. Raiffa, supra note 3, at 205.
6. Lax & Sebenius, supra note 1, at 168.
7. Jeswald Salacuse, *The Power of Standards*, Tufts magazine (Winter 2007), http://emerald.tufts.edu/alumni/magazine/winter2007/columns/life.html.
8. Roger Fisher, William Ury, & Bruce Patton, Getting to Yes 78 (1991).
9. *Id.* at 89–90, 154.
10. Carrie Menkel-Meadow, *The Ethics of Compromise,* in The Negotiator's Fieldbook 158 (Andrea Kupfer Schneider & Christopher Honeyman eds., 2006).
11. Michael Wheeler, *First, Let's Kill All the Agents!,* in Negotiating on Behalf of Others 247 (Robert H. Mnookin & Lawrence E. Susskind eds. 1999).
12. James C. Freund, Smart Negotiating 122 (1992).
13. Roy J. Lewicki, David M. Saunders, & John W. Minton, Essentials of Negotiation 143 (2d ed. 2001).

14. Michael R. Fowler, *The Relevance of Principled Negotiation to Hostage Crises*, 12 HARV. NEGOTIATION L. REV. 292–99 (2007).

15. ZARTMAN & BERMAN, supra note 2, at 112.

16. RAIFFA, supra note 3, at 35.

17. ROGER FISHER, ALAN SHARP, & JOHN RICHARDSON, GETTING IT DONE 27 (1998).

18. *Id.* at 29.

19. WILLIAM URY, GETTING PAST NO 3 (2d ed. 1993).

20. Jennifer Gerarda Brown, *Creativity and Problem Solving*, in THE NEGOTIATOR'S FIELDBOOK 410 (Andrea Kupfer Schneider & Christopher Honeyman eds., 2006).

21. *Id.*

22. ROGER FISHER, ELIZABETH KOPELMAN, & ANDREA KUPFER SCHNEIDER, BEYOND MACHIAVELLI 35 (1994).

23. LAX & SEBENIUS, supra note 1, at 68–69.

24. FISHER, KOPELMAN, & SCHNEIDER, supra note 22, at 85, 89.

25. Roger Fisher, *An Interview with Roger Fisher and William Ury*, 18 ACAD. OF MGMT. EXECUTIVE 105 (2004).

26. RAIFFA, supra note 3, at 403.

27. URY, supra note 19, at 20.

28. ROBERT H. MNOOKIN, SCOTT R. PEPPET, & ANDREW S. TULUMELLO, BEYOND WINNING 38 (2000) (italics in original).

29. FISHER, URY, & PATTON, supra note 8, at 61.

30. RAIFFA, supra note 3, at 403.

31. FISHER, URY, & PATTON, supra note 8, at 61.

32. RAIFFA, supra note 3, at 403.

33. FISHER, URY, & PATTON, supra note 8, at 63.

34. ROY J. LEWICKI, ALEXANDER HIAM, & KAREN WISE OLANDER, THINK BEFORE YOU SPEAK 107 (1996).

35. Deborah Tannen, *The Relativity of Linguistic Strategies*, in GENDER AND CONVERSATIONAL INTERACTION 165–88 (Deborah Tannen ed., 1993).

36. FISHER, URY, & PATTON, supra note 8, at 56.

37. Jeffrey Z. Rubin, *Some Wise and Mistaken Assumptions About Negotiation*, 45 J. OF SOCIAL ISSUES 206 (1989).

38. *Id.* at 7.

39. Daniel Kahneman & Amos Tversky, *Conflict Resolution*, in BARRIERS TO CONFLICT RESOLUTION 46–50 (Kenneth J. Arrow et al. eds., 1995).

40. Robert H. Mnookin & Lee Ross, *Introduction*, in BARRIERS TO CONFLICT RESOLUTION 18 (Kenneth J. Arrow et al. eds., 1995).

41. URY, supra note 19, at 108–10.

42. *Id.* at 110.

43. FISHER & ERTEL, supra note 4, at 36.

44. LAX & SEBENIUS, supra note 1, at 90.

45. MNOOKIN, PEPPET, & TULUMELO, supra note 28, at 15.

46. FISHER, URY, & PATTON, supra note 8, at 76.

47. MNOOKIN, PEPPET, & TULUMELO, supra note 28, at 237, 260.

48. ROGER FISHER, INTERNATIONAL CONFLICT FOR BEGINNERS 124 (1969).

49. Roger Fisher, *Fractionating Conflict*, in INTERNATIONAL CONFLICT AND BEHAVIORAL SCIENCE 91–109 (Roger Fisher ed., 1964).

50. Zartman & Berman, supra note 2, at 144.

51. Fisher, supra note 48, at 13.

52. Mnookin, Peppet, & Tulumelo, supra note 28, at 232.

53. Fisher & Ertel, supra note 4, at 35.

54. Patrick J. Cleary, The Negotiation Handbook 124 (2001).

55. Mnookin, Peppet, & Tulumelo, supra note 28, at 17.

56. Howard Raiffa, The Art and Science of Negotiation 23 (1982).

57. Id. at 24.

58. Mnookin, Peppet, & Tulumelo, supra note 28, at 14.

59. Gerald Wetlaufer, *The Limits of Integrative Bargaining*, in What's Fair 47 (Carrie Menkel-Meadow & Michael Wheeler eds., 2004).

60. Michael L. Moffitt, *Contingent Agreements*, in The Negotiator's Fieldbook 456 (Andrea Kupfer Schneider & Christopher Honeyman eds., 2006).

61. Id. at 457.

62. Christopher Honeyman, *Using Ambiguity*, in The Negotiator's Fieldbook 461 (Andrea Kupfer Schneider & Christopher Honeyman eds., 2006).

63. Zartman & Berman, supra note 2, at 183.

64. Honeyman, supra note 62, at 461.

65. Id. at 466.

66. Howard Raiffa, *Analytical Barriers*, in Barriers to Conflict Resolution 140 (Kenneth J. Arrow et al. eds., 1995).

67. Deborah M. Kolb & Judith Williams, The Shadow Negotiation 183–84 (2000).

68. Mary Parker Follett, Dynamic Administration 49 (Henry C. Metcalf & Lyndall F. Urwick eds., 1942).

69. Cleary, supra note 54, at 124.

70. John H. Wade, *Crossing the Last Gap*, in The Negotiator's Fieldbook 468–73 (Andrea Kupfer Schneider & Christopher Honeyman eds., 2006).

71. Id. at 471.

Checkpoints

- To deal with distributional bargaining—that is, the apportioning of money or other items of value between the parties—interest-based negotiators look to propose an equitable resolution based on one of various criteria of fairness, such as equal division or relative contributions or needs.

- The most promising approach to distributional issues often involves finding neutral standards or objective criteria to support particular resolutions. These might be drawn from expert opinions, industry practices, market rates or values, community traditions, scientific or technical understandings, relevant comparable data, decisions by courts or arbitral tribunals, or any of a host of other standards.

- Discussing objective criteria moves a negotiation toward an effort to find an outcome that the different sides consider to be fair, reasonable, logical, and legitimate. Using neutral standards in this way has the potential to bring about an agreement, and do so amicably. This is important both to maintain strong working relations and to encourage conscientious implementation of the agreement over time.

- The challenging aspect of relying on neutral standards is that the parties will have to work out which standard or standards to rely on, and may have quite different ideas of which is the correct one to use. Here, more specific criteria, more directly on point, tends to be more persuasive than quite general factors.

- As you work with a counterpart in trying to solve a problem together, you will want to generate a large number of ideas, select among them, refine and improve them, and put the ideas together in such a way that both sides have enough interests satisfied that they agree to a negotiated resolution of the problem.

- One difficulty is that the process of selecting ideas can become competitive: I attack your ideas, which you defend, and then you attack my ideas, which I defend. The negotiation begins to sound more like a debate than an effort to put the negotiator's minds together and use both of their perspectives to come up with a workable and mutually agreeable resolution.

- Rather than fall into a pattern where each idea that is placed on the table for consideration is then dunked in an acid test of skeptical criticism, it can be useful to designate a period for brainstorming. The idea here is to generate many ideas quickly, without immediate criticism. The effort of choosing the best among them is relegated to the next phase of the negotiation.

- Impasses and deadlocks can be rooted in many different aspects of a negotiation: aggressive claiming, positional bargaining, or psychological barriers.

- To overcome an impasse, a negotiator might try to "build a golden bridge," or he or she might suggest trade-offs or trading across issues, taking advantage of different strengths of feeling.

- Fractionating or enlarging a negotiation is another possibility, as is fashioning a contingent agreement. Here, negotiators should bear in mind the possibility of coming to an agreement into which the missing information will be plugged, once it is in hand. Another approach is to introduce calculated ambiguity.

- Finally, it may be possible to share visions of a better future and what an agreement might deliver to the parties, or change the people involved in the negotiation, or create a last best offer.

Chapter 7

Overcoming Personality
Conflicts and Pressure Tactics

Roadmap

- **Personality conflicts:** Why are relationship issues highly problematic in some negotiations?

- **Varieties of negotiators:** What are the characteristics of hard and soft bargainers?

- **Partisan perceptions:** How might *partisan perceptions* adversely affect a negotiation?

- **Emotion:** Why might strong emotions arise during a negotiation? What are productive uses of emotion and problematic ones? Why do negotiators sometimes make purposeful inflammatory statements and sometimes accidental ones?

- **Pressure tactics:** What ploys do negotiators occasionally use to try to compel counterparts to do something that they are otherwise disinclined to do?

- **Threats:** How are threats made effective? What dangers are associated with threats, and what distinguishes a threat from a warning? How might a negotiator respond to a threat?

- **Deadlines:** What are the characteristics of an artificial deadline and an exploding offer? What problems are associated with using time pressures this way, and how might a negotiator counter a deadline?

- **Managing interpersonal difficulties:** Why focus on interpersonal problems? What benefits and risks are associated with venting? How might a negotiator make amends for contributing to a negative dynamic? How ought an offensive comment be handled? How about dealing with hard bargainers and uncommunicative, unimaginative, or otherwise unhelpful negotiators?

People are often inclined to proceed with a negotiation as if it were concerned exclusively with the rational adjustment of differences. This can be short-sighted since factors that have little to do with logic or cost-benefit analyses frequently come into play as well. "When people bargain," two scholars observed, "they bring their idiosyncrasies to the table—their disposition toward conflict, their biases, remembered slights or successes, and their feelings about each other."[1]

Conflicts between negotiators or the parties they represent can be rooted in grievances preceding a negotiation or they can spring up during it. People sometimes enter talks suspicious of one another's motives, particularly when they have had past difficulties. At other times, negotiations start off productively but attitudes turn sour or belligerent, relations become strained or hostile, personal antagonisms and misunderstandings crop up.

When the negotiators have established a positive rapport, problematic statements or even offensive comments might be ignored or circumvented, without lasting damage to the course of the talks. But, negotiations can descend into a negative spiral very quickly, and a working relationship can sour rapidly. Suddenly, the discussions no longer seem so productive and the fear grows that one or more of the parties will decide to walk away.

Interpersonal problems can make complex negotiating problems even more challenging to resolve. One reason that polarizing interpersonal difficulties arise so frequently is that, as one authority noted, "It takes two people to cooperate, but only one person is usually required to make a mess of a relationship."[2] It is all too easy for negotiators to get frustrated or exasperated and for relations to spiral downward. This can then cause the negotiation to fail.

In hopes of preventing knotty negotiating problems from being further tangled by poor interpersonal relations, negotiators have long been advised to "separate the people from the problem."[3] This advice, however, is not well-suited to situations when the people, and their relations with one another—how they get along and interact with one another—*are* a fundamental aspect of the problem. The danger in ignoring or circumventing such relationship issues is that they may cause the substance of the dispute to be impossible, or at least much more difficult, to handle.

A. Hard versus Soft Bargainers

The roots of some interpersonal difficulties are to be found in negotiation strategy. In particular, the pressure tactics that are an integral part of the approach of a *hard bargainer* are more likely to bring on personality conflicts than those of a *soft bargainer*.[4]

1. Characteristics of a Hard Bargainer

A negotiator pursuing a hard-bargaining approach adopts the positional method of negotiation. He or she often fully expects interpersonal conflict, may even relish it, and certainly tries to take advantage of it. The hard bargainer looks to induce or even compel or coerce his or her opponent into giving into demands. He or she projects toughness and puts forward extreme positions, while marshaling arguments to try to justify them.[5]

Hard-bargaining negotiators tend to be competitive: a key goal is to do better than their opponents. To that end, they initiate hard-hitting exchanges and look to "mix it up" with their adversaries in an argumentative style. Hard bargainers attempt to convince their counterparts that they are locked into their own positions and will not budge from them. They routinely downplay the other side's goals and interests. They try to put opposing negotiators on the defensive, cornering and pressuring them with arguments, in order to gain their acquiescence to pre-conceived solutions.

In focusing the talks on what they want to achieve, hard bargainers look to control the negotiations. Their aim is to gain the most advantageous resolution possible, and their focus tends to be on the items to be apportioned between the parties: "the cheapest price, the most profit, the least cost, the best terms ..."[6]

The motto of a doctrinaire hard bargainer might be "All is fair in love, war, and negotiation." He or she feels few compunctions about harming the relationship, if that might provide some bargaining advantage. Negotiation is seen in terms similar to those of a highly competitive game. Although illegal behavior might well be frowned upon, negotiation is otherwise seen as a largely amoral undertaking in which each side aims to maximize its gains by all lawful means.[7] Thus, to rattle the other side, a hard bargainer might badger a counterpart; another might deceive, mislead, or manipulate him or her, or even engage in insulting behavior. This is all seen as a normal part of the process of negotiation.

2. Characteristics of a Soft Bargainer

To soft bargainers, in stark contrast, a strategy founded on interpersonal conflict makes a flawed foundation for negotiation. Soft bargainers emphasize, above all else, creating, maintaining, and improving positive relations with the other side. Here, the biblical counsel is taken to heart: "Do unto others as you would have them do unto you." A soft bargainer is friendly and trusting and acts agreeably, harmoniously, even graciously, in hopes that his or her counterpart will follow suit, and that both sides will proceed in a fair-minded way toward a mutually beneficial agreement. To nurture positive relations, a soft bargainer sometimes provides the other side with substantive gains, while looking to oblige their fellow negotiator whenever possible. In return, they expect like treatment.

The rationale for soft bargaining is that one's generosity can coax the other side into reciprocating. Cultivating good terms with one's counterpart will often lead to a useful agreement. The assumption is that people enjoying friendly relations will not take advantage of one another but will instead treat each other equitably.

Friends, neighbors, and adult family members who get along well with one another might bargain softly, and "[a]s each party competes with the other in being more generous and more forthcoming, an agreement becomes highly likely."[8] However, the content of the deal may not be carefully scrutinized, and a one-sided resolution might very well result.

3. Assessing Hard and Soft Bargaining

Each of these simplified, type-cast approaches has something to recommend it, but can also prove to be quite problematic. Hence, the counsel in these pages differs in important respects from both. Sometimes hard-bargaining strategies work, in the sense that they bring about a very advantageous agreement for a negotiator who succeeds in flustering or intimidating a counterpart. And yet, hard bargaining by one side often brings on like behavior from the other. Intransigence is then matched by intransigence, and constant clashes often follow with little forward progress.

For their part, soft bargainers might elicit cooperation and readily reach agreement with fellow negotiators who have adopted a similar approach. A negotiator who feels quite weak might bargain softly, reasoning that "[y]ielding may be as effective as the blade of grass that bends and survives."[9]

However, the soft bargainer's single-minded focus on gaining and maintaining positive relations provides a real incentive for another to take advantage of them. Acceding to the other side's demands frequently ends up feeding a more hard-nosed counterpart's hunger for more gains. A soft-bargaining approach to a hard bargainer tends to degenerate into the constant appeasement of the tough-minded counterpart, who in turn keeps pushing for more.

While soft bargainers sometimes accept a poorly conceived deal, they also often opt for no negotiated resolution. They get fed up with hard responses, sensing that their counterparts are trying to exploit them. The push and pull of positional bargaining often causes tempers to flare, as one party tries to bend another to their way of thinking or their preferred resolution. The bruising dynamics of hard bargaining turn off soft-bargainers, leading them to conclude that the negotiation is not worth pursuing further. The process of negotiation comes to seem frustrating and ineffective and incapable of producing much in the way of desired benefits.

Soft bargainers often attribute the problems they perceive in their negotiations with hard bargainers to the difficult, unyielding personality of their adversaries. And, problems that might be successfully negotiated are left unresolved.

4. Responding to Hard Bargainers

So, how might a negotiator respond to a counterpart pursuing a hard-bargaining approach? If the other side adopts a highly competitive and adversarial positional approach, how might one try to turn it into a more collaborative problem-solving endeavor? Robert Mnookin and colleagues observed, "Almost anything a hard bargainer says can be reframed and restated as an interest, an option or a suggestion about a norm that might be used to resolve distributive issues. This can be a form of 'negotiation jujitsu' — deflecting the difficult tactic and treating whatever the other side has said as part of a problem-solving tactic."[10]

When the other side declares its position on something, negotiators are often tempted to make one of three moves: respond with a contrasting stance, argue against the position, or inquire further about it, attempting to clarify just what the other side has in mind. Each of these moves, however, tends to cause a hard bargainer to dig into the stance already adopted. They can get locked, ever more securely, into the arguments and frame of mind just taken. And, this often turns the negotiation into a debate over the merits of positions.

A more promising approach is to sidestep the hard bargainer's position or pass over it lightly and redirect the discussions. For instance, instead of responding to the position, one might suggest a more deliberate approach: "We seem to be moving pretty quickly here toward possible final resolutions. Before getting there, what I'd like to do is to first take the smaller step of seeing if we can arrive at a common understanding of the contours of the problem. I'm still not sure I fully understand how it looks to you, and I've also got some points to make that may help you to see how things look from our perspective." This type of effort to redirect or refocus may propel the negotiation along a very different course. The aim here is to delve behind a stated position, peel away the rhetoric to identify the issues and underlying motives at the very core of the problem.

Another way to proceed is to identify the hard-bargaining tactics and question whether this is the best path for the negotiation to take. Howard Raiffa suggested putting a choice to a hard bargainer. First, you allude to the difference between a cooperative interest-based approach and a hard-bargaining positional one: "We can share information about the strength of our interests and try to arrange a mutually beneficial deal, and find a composite contract by trying to figure out what's fair. Or we can play hardball—try to trick each other, refuse to budge until we exact a price from the other, and that sort of thing."

Then, you make clear your own preference, indicating why it is likely to work better under these circumstances: "I think we'll both be better off if we work together. If we play hardball, I think we'll be here a long time, leave a lot of value on the table, and probably hurt our chances of making more deals in the future."

Finally, you leave to the other negotiator the choice of which approach to negotiation to adopt: "I know how to play both of those games. I assume you do as well. I'd prefer the first, but I am willing to go along with you on the one you choose. By choosing a strategy, you will also be choosing the one I'm going to use when I negotiate with you ..."[11]

B. Recognizing Partisan Perceptions

Sometimes interpersonal conflict stems not from a hard-bargaining approach but from the negotiators' pre-conceived perceptions of one another. How the parties perceive matters is an integral part of negotiation, and yet people tend to view things through a lens colored, or even distorted, by what they think of the other side. That is, people tend to have *partisan perceptions.*

If we like someone, we take what they do and say one way, placing positive connotations on their behavior whenever possible. If we fear or dislike them, or perhaps if we see them in competitive or adversarial terms, we hurry toward negative connotations and conclusions. And, when someone views another with hostility, as an enemy, he or she tends to interpret their words and actions in the worst possible light.[12]

1. Problems Caused by Partisan Perceptions

a. Distorted Analysis

On account of partisan perceptions information relevant to a negotiation is often interpreted in accordance with prior expectations. Something may be overlooked or ignored because it does not fit in with those expectations. One source noted: "What you see depends in part on where you stand, who you are, and what you've seen before.... Although we often assume that we perceive and remember our experiences neutrally and objectively, people are disposed to 'see' what they expect and wish to see, and what it is in their self-interest to see."[13]

The actions and statements of those who have long been opposed or mistrusted are most readily misinterpreted. On the international stage think about the conflict between the Palestinians and Israelis or the historically difficult relations between India and Pakistan or China and Japan. When officials from one side make statements or take action, the message that they are trying to send is not always the same message that the other side receives. Furthermore, the more pronounced is the lack of trust, the more likely it is that positive statements will be discounted and the parties will look instead to actions to see if a negotiation might be productive.

Whether we are negotiating at home or abroad, our partisan perceptions can place our counterpart in a catch-22 dilemma. As Jeffrey Rubin put it, "Kind acts by one's adversary are attributed to manipulative intent, while uncharitable acts are attributed to an undesirable, untrustworthy disposition. One's own kind acts, in turn, are attributed to one's being a truly nice, kind person while one's less wonderful behavior is attributed to circumstances or to behavior by the other person that has necessitated an unkind response."[14]

What exacerbates the problem is that "we are quick to recognize others' partisan perceptions but slow to see our own. We each live thinking that what we see *is* objective reality, that we perceive the world as it really is."[15] But, this may not, in fact, be the case. And, faulty assumptions about what the other side is thinking or doing can lead to personality conflicts and even derail a potential agreement.

b. Fears of Possible Actions

When past relations have been antagonistic, one side must often contend with fears of what their counterpart might be preparing to do. It has been observed that "People tend to assume that whatever they fear, the other side intends to do."[16] Plainly, such assumptions are particularly problematic in a negotiation, often leading negotiators astray.

When in the grip of partisan perceptions, adversarial or competitive intentions are readily projected on one's counterpart. One might assume the other side to be biased, ruthless, self-centered, or Machiavellian. Such assumptions — even though supported only by vague or inadequate evidence — are often taken to be the only "realistic" way to proceed.

Assuming that one's counterpart has bad intentions and motivations may sidetrack negotiators from introducing fresh and constructive possible solutions. Negotiating while focused on fears of what might occur diverts attention from aspirations of what could happen. The negotiators are not giving each other a real chance to cooperate in creative ways.

Then, in trying to preempt the negative trait you have presumed the other side to have, you may act in such a way as to bring on a self-fulfilling prophecy. *Your* actions, stimulated by your fear of what *their* actions might be, may bring them to do just what you feared they might do. The better course is to critically examine one's assumptions of how the other side is likely to behave and the evidence on which those assumptions are based.

C. Emotion, Anger, and Offensive Comments

1. The Presence of Emotion in Negotiation

The word *emotion* refers to something felt, rather than something reasoned. The display of emotions during negotiations differs from culture to culture: in some societies emotions are routinely expressed; in others, suppressed. They also vary with different circumstances. The expression of emotions might be expected in negotiations over a divorce settlement and might surprise when negotiating the technicalities of a service contract.

Some negotiators view the surfacing of emotions as unprofessional or even as unnerving, and some believe that a professional approach to complex problems should invariably focus on logical discourse. In fact, however, the expression of a range of emotions often occurs in virtually all varieties of negotiation. These include what might be thought of as positive emotions— joy, pride, goodwill, excitement, and enthusiasm would be examples—and negative ones—such as anger, anxiety, contempt, fear, shame, sorrow, indignation, jealousy, resentment, and revenge.

Emotions are an inherent part of the human psyche and are often present even when not immediately evident. The eighteenth-century French scholar F. B. de Félice declared, "Even actions that at first glance may appear to be farthest from what are called emotional acts have some hidden sentimental motive behind them."[17] Some personalities constantly skate close to the emotional edge. As Winston Churchill once quipped of U.S. Secretary of State John Foster Dulles: "He's the only bull I know who carries his china closet with him!"[18]

Working closely with a counterpart can put a real premium on coming to understand something of their psychological makeup. Some individuals are more comfortable expressing their emotions than others. At times emotions are used tactically in a negotiation, and whether one feels it legitimate to deploy them strategically is something else that differs from one person to the next.

Negotiators should be alert to the emotions expressed by their counterparts, since people reveal important dimensions of their thinking through expressing their emotions. Displaying one's feelings can underscore the intensity of a negotiator's views. One source noted, "Showing real anger at an unfair deal— even if both sides know the offer on the table is better than your best alternative—may persuade the other side to better its terms."[19] Instead of ignoring or discouraging the display of emotions, expert negotiators listen to and read emotions. This can provide clues as to how the negotiation might best be moved forward.

2. Productive Uses of Emotion

It is possible for emotions to come into play in a negotiation in an array of productive ways. When sentiments of one kind or another surface and a counterpart empathizes, sympathizes, or reciprocates "the exchange can build a sense of connection."[20] Indeed, it has been argued that emotions "tend to evoke reciprocal or complementary emotions in others"; hence, "a disappointed or sad opponent might elicit compassion, which might in turn lead to more cooperative behavior."[21]

Furthermore, when positive emotions are expressed in a negotiation, this can get the parties prepared to deal with their most serious differences later on. Then, in the course of a negotiation something like a genuine display of indignation, supported by solid reasons, can be an effective way to change your counterpart's mind.

3. Problematic Emotions in Negotiation

The principal drawback to injecting emotion into a negotiation is that it might distort one's judgment and pose real risks for the effort to find a reasoned and reasonable agreement. Emotions can divert attention from problem-solving and bring on impulsive or short-sighted behavior. Emotional confrontations can waste time that could be spent negotiating substantive difficulties.

One scholar noted that emotions "may cause us to lose our temper, to stumble anxiously over our words, or to sulk uncontrollably in self-pity." He went on to suggest that "emotional residue may become the seeds of future conflict."[22]

One of the most potentially problematic emotions in a negotiation is anger. American humorist Ambrose Bierce once quipped, "Speak when you are angry and you will make the best speech you will ever regret."[23] U.S. diplomat and international lawyer Philip Jessup observed: "Occasionally, it is valuable to appear to be very angry, but by and large, a cold kind of approach to a problem is I think more effective. One maxim is never to lose your temper unless you intend to."[24] Anger frequently results in negotiators breaking off communications and walking away from potential deals.

An angry person may be strongly disinclined to cooperate. Instead, anger often leads negotiators either into competitive behavior or a cycle of recriminations. Each side wants to best the other, show up their counterpart, compel them to do something. An angry negotiator envisions the unconditional surrender of the other side to dictated terms. But, these attitudes are rarely realistic. In the negotiation of complex problems compromise is far more likely than surrender.

Nevertheless, strong passions do sometimes surface during a negotiation, and good negotiators must be prepared to deal effectively with them. People sometimes react strongly to one another, their statements and attitudes, or perhaps their goals, strategies, or views of the situation. The parties may become defensive and lose their inclination to collaborate. Heated exchanges, bitter feelings, and rising tempers all have the potential to cloud judgment and subvert efforts to craft sensible, rational resolutions.

4. Causes of Anger during Negotiations

On occasion, a negotiator says something that brings tempers to flare. The response then often initiates a negative, escalating spiral. Tensions rise and suspicions multiply, as hostile thoughts are exchanged. It may be easier to handle such a situation effectively if one has previously analyzed the common sources of angry exchanges in a negotiation. Objective, dispassionate insights on what causes angry comments can help to keep negotiations from degenerating into quarrels.

a. Accidental Inflammatory Statements

One prominent cause of anger during negotiations is accidental in nature: slips of the tongue, minds wandering, senseless behavior of one kind or another that rubs another wrong.[25] Negotiation often requires quick responses to another's statements and questions over an extended period. Negotiators must respond on the spot and, often, without the benefit of much forethought. Spontaneous communication is an imperfect art. Points are easily overstated, misinterpreted, or misconstrued. Tension or stress may increase the emotional ante.

In a lengthy, complex negotiation some points are bound to be mis-stated, blurted out, or phrased poorly or tactlessly. People can jump to conclusions. As a negotiation gets heated, insults, or biased, condescending, or thought-less statements can all too easily be interjected. And, as flurries of points are being made, one negotiator may seize on real or imagined slights coming from a counterpart. Negotiators can thus find themselves to have said things that they soon wish they hadn't.

As pressures multiply, and as it becomes clear that all of one's objectives are not going to be met, the urge to be contrary or contradictory may increase. Either or both sides may get caught up in the discussion and become passionate about it. Lawyers, in particular, are taught to advocate for their clients zealously. But, one person's zealous advocacy could readily be taken by another to amount to irritating hyperbole or insufferable badgering.

During negotiations the different sensitivities that people have may surface: what is firm to one may seem belligerent to another. As people try to work to-gether, their egos may clash. A negotiator's ego may become linked to his or her proposal, making it especially difficult to move on from an idea that the other side does not welcome.

One side may take personally comments made by the other. He or she may dwell on something said that was belittling or otherwise offensive. Gratuitous insults may slip into the discussions. Someone may try to engender feelings of guilt in another, blaming a counterpart for being unreasonable, and this may trigger recriminations. "Blaming someone *for* the situation," it has been said, "chills any discussion *of* it."[26]

Then, a part of the art of negotiation involves drama. A negotiator might express emphasis or passion or try to communicate some other message by appearing to be outraged, confused, or in some other particular state of mind. But such dramatized reactions can easily be seen as disingenuous or overly the-atrical, irritating a counterpart.

Anger can also well up even when the parties are genuinely intent on work-ing together to construct a mutually beneficial agreement. A negotiator may be trying to lead the talks down one path, and when that effort is thwarted by another, pulling in a different direction, frustrations can quickly develop. One side can take the other to be debating them, trying to score points in some non-productive fashion. And, frustrated people are especially prone to ex-pressing their feelings in ways that may anger others.

Finally, the base, petty, or small-minded attitudes inherent in human na-ture can surface in negotiation. Short-sighted, narrow-minded, obnoxious bullies negotiate with others, just as far-seeing, open-minded, tolerant peo-ple do. "In every profession, nationality, and organization," two authorities noted, "there are people who try to increase their importance by putting down someone else."[27] Those who routinely make demeaning, prejudiced, or insulting comments are very likely to do so when negotiating as well. The inflammatory statements that they make are part of their nature, as opposed to being negotiating tactics.

b. Purposeful Inflammatory Statements

At times a negotiator purposefully makes an inflammatory remark, reasoning that one's counterpart ought to hear a particular point, even if differences in perspective are so pronounced that it may enrage them. At other times the rationale is that the other side is trying to "get away with something" by twisting the truth and needs to be called on it. A negotiator may feel compelled to raise some aspect of a highly problematic history of past relations. Alternatively, key points to be negotiated might concern fundamental values, basic ideas of justice or fairness. When these come into play, the emotional ante can quickly rise.

While sometimes "ruffling the feathers" of an opposing negotiator may, rightly or wrongly, be seen as exerting some useful influence on that person, on other occasions deliberately saying something that will anger a counterpart may be a matter of *posturing* or *grandstanding*. Here, the offensive statement is aimed not at one's counterpart but at some other party or parties who will hear of it, directly or indirectly. Perhaps public opinion will be stirred up or a particular constituency will be pleased. For instance, a labor negotiator might pound the table or make a particularly hard-hitting statement to try to demonstrate tough-minded thinking to the union or corporation being represented. Nevertheless, this could very well antagonize the other side.

Here, thinking analytically about what exactly is going on, and why it is occurring, can be good advice. Thomas Colosi suggested:

> Ask yourself questions: Why are they doing this? Who is their audience? Is it really addressed to your team? Are they playing to the folks back home? Is it for the press? Are they having internal problems? Is the speech-maker in a precarious position with ... his or her own team? ... What kind of messages are the other members of the team communicating as the speaker harangues your side? Is the speaker trying to maximize the importance of a concession he or she is about to make or to embarrass you? Should you take it personally? Is the speaker trying to anger or intimidate you ...?[28]

Colosi also suggested that taking notes can defuse anger: "Say, 'Excuse me. I want to get this down. This is important.' If you want to manage the members' boisterous behavior at the table, ask them to speak more slowly as you write down what they are saying. *It's impossible for anyone to yell slowly!*"[29]

Alternatively, an offensive comment may be part of an elaborate ploy. A negotiator might hope to gain some tactical advantage via ridiculing or browbeating another, or through some derogatory comment, a series of jabs and barbs, or another purposeful effort to provoke. This type of gamesmanship might embolden the one who made it, or it might ruffle, disturb, or distract the other side.

Some negotiators, when angered, have trouble staying focused and thinking analytically. Offensive comments could conceivably intimidate or cow the other party. An upset or distracted counterpart could lose his or her effectiveness. Or, one side might hastily conclude a negotiation that has turned insufferable or quite distasteful. A negotiator might offend another in hopes of bulldozing his or her way to a favorable resolution.

Angering another on purpose is, however, highly risky behavior. Generally, each side is present at a negotiation voluntarily, and each usually has walkaway options. Grievously irritating one's counterpart might well cause talks to be broken off. Moreover, if an agreement is reached, it will eventually have to be implemented. Since people tend to have long memories of times when they were offended, smooth implementation of the terms of an agreement may be jeopardized.

D. Other Pressure Tactics

An opposing negotiator making inflammatory statements is not the only pressure tactic. Some scholars have identified pressure in particular forms of argument. For example, in a *consistency trap* a negotiator first looks to persuade a counterpart to agree to the logic or fairness of an innocuous-sounding standard. He or she then tries to get the counterpart to concede that the standard also applies to the present situation.[30]

Another pressure tactic is often referred to as the *good cop/bad cop routine* since police departments have long used this approach to gain information from suspects. Here, in a two-person team, while one partner takes on a negative, difficult, abrasive, and uncompromising style, the other adopts a trusting and understanding persona. The target will be softened up by the good cop, who pretends to be trying to help out the suspect and looks to use sympathetic rapport to get the person in a position to cooperate. But the bad cop insists on driving a tough bargain, to which the good cop urges the suspect to yield. The hope is that manipulating these two psychological approaches will bring an advantageous resolution.

One way to greatly diminish the effectiveness of this negotiating ploy is to let the other side know you have identified it. You might say, "O.K., so now I've heard from the good cop, and I guess I can expect the bad cop next." If you plainly see through the pressure tactic being employed, your counterparts are very likely to abandon it.

1. Threats

A negotiator who promises something is assuring a counterpart that he or she will do something the counterpart considers to be positive. The one making the promise purposefully creates an expectation that something that the other side wants to happen will, in fact, occur.

A threat, in a sense, is the reverse of a promise. It is an attempt to coerce or intimidate the other side into taking some step. A negotiator informs a counterpart that, unless particular steps are taken, it will take some action that other side will consider harmful, negative, or quite unpleasant.[31]

It might be able to take away something of value or expose the other party to some risk, hazard, or danger. Or, it might be able to cause the other side some variety of pain or embarrassment, something it acutely dislikes. (Chapter 10 on honest bargaining explores improper, or legally impermissible, threats.)

A negotiator who senses the other side's vulnerability and wants to try to take advantage of it can issue a threat. That is—perhaps in hopes of bringing the other side to the negotiating table or moving it along toward a particular negotiated resolution—one side may note the possibility of going ahead and taking the action that the other party fears.

a. Effective and Ineffective Threats

To be effective, the target must, in fact, view the threatened action as quite harmful or the threat will have little impact. For example, authorities could threaten that if an injured hostage dies, they would unleash an all-out armed assault on a barricaded building very likely to kill the hostage-taker inside. If the extremist genuinely aspires to be a martyr to some cause, however, that threat by the authorities will fall flat.

The threat must also be credible. That is, the party that is being threatened has to believe that its counterpart has both the will and the capacity to take the action. A threat is potent only if the target does, in fact, believe that the threatened action could and will be carried out.

Since parties are often inclined to overlook or ignore vague statements, phrasing a threat precisely may factor into its effectiveness. It may be useful to make very clear exactly why the threatened action would be taken.

Note, too, that legitimate threats tend to move parties more frequently than do illegitimate ones. "A threat can be legitimate," one scholar observed, "if its implementation would be morally or legally justified. Such a threat is more likely to exert influence than one that appears to be rank blackmail."[32]

b. Dangers Associated with Threats

However, making threats in a negotiation can be a dangerous move, one prone to backfiring. Sometimes one negotiator threatens another, hoping that muscle-flexing alone will get the desired result. However, often threats do not work. Not only do they typically anger the recipient, but parties often dismiss threats as mere bluffs. The threatened party may doubt that its counterpart really will follow through with the action. Carrying out the threat might make it look bad, and this might bring on trouble from that party's allies or constituents. Or, taking the threatened action—for instance, walking away from a negotiation—might end up hurting the threatening party as much as the threatened.

Moreover, people naturally resist pressure. "The question changes from 'Should we make this decision?' to 'Shall we cave in to outside pressure?'"[33] When a group considers a decision, as is often the case in complex negotiations, few of its members are inclined to suggest giving in. This may be perceived as cowardly or entail a significant loss of face.

Instead, the natural reaction to coercion is to try to leave the impression that the threat has accomplished nothing in changing behavior. If anything, it has made the situation worse. One way to do this is to issue a counter-threat. Threats can thus easily escalate, not only ending the possibility of a negotiated resolution but often creating further problems if the threats are actually implemented. In this respect, it is worth bearing mind that if a party decides to issue a threat, not carrying through will hurt its credibility, and make future threats less believable.

Threats are particularly problematic when the parties will have continuing relations. Roger Fisher and Scott Brown observed: "When I make a threat, there are three possible outcomes: I 'win' the encounter because you back down; you don't give in, so I carry out the threat; or you don't give in, and I decide not to carry out the threat. None of these outcomes is good for the relationship. None will make it easier for us to deal with differences in the future."[34]

c. Threats versus Warnings

Threats are sometimes differentiated from warnings on the following grounds. A threat is imposed by the will of the person who issues it. Its tone is confrontational: do this or else. A warning is cautionary and indicates what is likely to happen if something does or does not occur. Its tone is more neutral and respectful: it is a forecast of what the future holds in a given set of circumstances. A warning might be presented as an effort to be straightforward with the other side. The news is bad, but better to know and understand it than be blind-sided by something you never realized was approaching.

A negotiator might issue a threat toward the end of a negotiation, confronting the other side, implicitly or explicitly, with an ultimatum. That is, the threatening party would make one final, uncompromising demand that the other party do something or face substantial negative consequences. For example, a negotiator might declare, "Agree to these terms or we will break off the negotiation and file a lawsuit." In contrast, a negotiator might warn a counterpart by saying, "You should be aware that the union has voted to strike if we do not reach an agreement by midnight on June 30th."

It has been argued that something passed off as a warning is actually a more subtle and Machiavellian form of a threat.[35] My own view is that threats can usually (and usefully) be distinguished from warnings, but that some statements may contain elements of both. For instance, a lawyer might say: "I understand the difficulties your side has had in coming to a consensus about how to proceed. However, the party I represent has to move forward, and we have decided to approach your chief competitor if we do not have a deal within a week." Is that a warning or a threat? On the one hand, the negotiator has adopted a respectful tone and couches the statement as a straightforward declaration of what is going to happen if a deal is not reached. On the other hand, the decision to change negotiating partners is an act of free will emanating from that party, not a neutral act that results naturally from a particular state of affairs.

d. Responding to Threats

If you are confronted with a threat, you can respond to this type of pressure tactic a number of ways. First, it can be quite useful to pause to consider what may have provoked the threat.[36] Are longstanding or deep-seated frustrations surfacing? Does your counterpart seem to have been offended by some statement or action? If so, examining the grievances and acknowledging the other side's perspective may help to defuse the situation. Is the threat an attempt to intimidate or coerce via a display of leverage or power, or is it, possibly, a bluffing ploy aimed at compelling a resolution in short order on favorable terms? If one of these may be the case, then posing questions may clarify important aspects of the situation, including how seriously to take the threat. As one source put it, "Imagine that a contractor threatens to sue you, a supplier, over a proposed change in the delivery date of raw materials. You can try to discover the motivation for the threat by asking, 'Why would a lawsuit be a better option for you than continued talks?' "[37]

As for other possible responses, rather than arguing about whether the threat is real or a bluff, you could simply ignore the statement. Register to yourself that it has been made, and move on. Alternatively, you could indicate your skepticism about the threat without directly challenging it. For instance, a negotiator might simply respond: "Well, we'll just have to hope it doesn't come to that." Yet another option is to focus further attention on the statement by labeling it a threat. One might come right out and ask: "Should I take that as a threat, then?" Whether your counterpart denies or affirms it, a skillful negotiator can often then redirect attention back to the substance of the problem. The threat then tends to recede from the attention of the negotiators, and it may lose force or even be exposed as bootless.

Finally, another possibility is to respond with a counter-threat, underscoring useful aspects of your own BATNA, leverage, or power. This could then be coupled with a move aimed at refocusing attention on the negotiating issues at hand. For instance, one might say, "You know, we're here as negotiators, not as courtroom litigators or for that matter battlefield generals. If we have to take future adversarial steps, so be it. But, I still haven't given up hope that we can put our heads together to find a way out of these circumstances that we both can support."

2. Time Pressures

a. Deadlines: Real and Artificial

Time limits are commonplace in life and in negotiations. A labor union might announce a strike deadline. Negotiators from out of town are likely to have a limited period that they can devote to interactions at the negotiating table. If real progress has been made and hopes are high that a negotiated resolution will occur, these deadlines can often be extended or additional negotiation sessions can be scheduled in hopes of gaining a positive outcome.

Sometimes, however, since negotiators can drag their feet and negotiations can become long and tedious, an *artificial deadline* is contrived in order to gain a decision, one way or another, on the matter being negotiated. Under these circumstances, the time limit becomes a variety of pressure tactic. Such a deadline is arbitrary in the sense that it is imposed at the will of the person making it. No independent rationale exists for cutting off talks at that point and no outside events or circumstances underlie the deadline. Sometimes the implication is added that any future offers will be less favorable.

b. Exploding Offers

Plainly, no one expects a proposal to be good for ever, and attaching some time limit is often a useful and reasonable move to bring matters to a head. The context in which this turns into a pressure tactic is when a short deadline is imposed in a calculated attempt to bring about a self-advantageous resolution at once. For instance, one party might abruptly announce that a particular proposal will expire at 5:00 p.m. the following day, after which it will be withdrawn. This is sometimes termed an *exploding offer*: a particularly pronounced variety of artificial deadline "marked by an extremely tight deadline in order to pressure the other party to agree quickly."[38]

One authority suggested that exploding offers tend to be marked by several additional characteristics.[39] The person making the proposal to which the artificial deadline has been attached is in a much more powerful position than the one receiving the proposal. A student considering a summer job offer from a corporation might well feel a power asymmetry, as might a recent Ph.D. recipient considering one of the very scarce faculty positions available. An exploding offer is also often couched as a test of faith: "If you're one of us, you'll accept; if you hold out, we'll be so disgusted with you that there will be no sense in further dealings." And, the person making an exploding offer is obdurate, arbitrarily ignoring any pleas for flexibility no matter how reasonable these may be.

Exploding offers are conceived not only to hurry along a negotiation, but to restrict the counterpart's free choice. This variety of offer shows a lack of respect for the person to whom it is directed in that the hardships such an individual may be confronting are ignored. If successful, they prevent him or her from shopping around, diligently investigating the details of the proposal, or considering other similar offers.

c. Problems with Timing Pressures

A number of problems are associated with this pressure tactic of trying to compel a yes or no answer in short order. First, an artificial deadline can greatly irritate those at which it is directed. When relations have already deteriorated between the parties, an artificial deadline can be taken as an invitation to a test of strength, an extra wrestling match over a non-substantive matter. The party to whom it is directed may flout the deadline to try to call the bluff or spite its counterpart.

Second, the party facing the expiration date is very likely to suspect that the deadline is contrived and not real. As one authority has pointed out, you can easily probe a statement like "You have until midnight to accept this deal" by asking "Or else *what?*" The response to such a question may appear difficult or impossible to pull off ("Or I'll work out a deal with someone else").[40]

d. Countering Deadlines

A negotiator can handle an artificial deadline in various ways.[41] One can cite interests that might move the party that has made the proposal with the artificial deadline to withdraw or overlook it at least for a period. For instance, a company might recognize its interests in having contented employees start to work for them or in having positive reports circulate concerning its interviewing and hiring process.

Robert Robinson notes that one approach would be to express genuine interest in the proposal, explain why the deadline cannot be met, and perhaps add a "what if."[42] For instance, a job applicant might say, "I am extremely interested in your offer and wish I could accept right on the spot, but this is a major move for us and I really have to consult my spouse. What if I commit to calling you bright and early Monday morning with a final answer?"

This is, in effect, responding with a counter-offer in which what is being countered is not the substantive terms of the proposed deal but the process of coming to a final decision. If the recipient of the offer explains when he or she could give a definitive response and why waiting until that date makes sense, the other side may very well prove amenable.

When appeals to interests or empathy fail and the party making the offer continues to try to use its position of power to coerce an immediate response, another option, according to Robinson, is to accept the offer but only provisionally, making the provision something that will result in the artificial deadline passing.[43] Again, in the employment context this could involve clarifying a policy, meeting co-workers or a supervisor, or determining whether a perquisite is to be granted.

Robinson acknowledges that this is itself a "hardball tactic," and suggests that a reputable negotiator might be completely comfortable using it only if the following three conditions were met.

- "If the other side is perceived by the recipient of the exploding offer to be behaving unethically, and does not respond to appeals to reason;
- the recipient is truly interested in making a deal but needs more time to make a decision; and-or
- there genuinely are issues that need clarification, which would make the difference between accepting or rejecting the deal."[44]

E. Managing Interpersonal Difficulties

When interpersonal relations are a problem, what tactics should a negotiator bear in mind that might help to turn things around?

1. Improve Poor Working Relations

How does one handle hostility present at the outset of negotiations? A party might enter the talks nursing a grudge, or it might be quite clear from the outset that particular personalities are likely to clash. Here, negotiators could be tempted to regard the poor working relations as a given. However, it may be worth seeing if interpersonal difficulties can be managed better than in the past and if it might be possible to establish a more positive relationship at least for the duration of the negotiation.

In a negative relationship you can easily get so caught up in what you feel, in what you think you need, and in your own arguments, interests, and proposals, that you stop listening or overlook what the other side thinks, needs, and feels. This is not a state of mind conducive to creating a resolution that you both find advantageous and to which you both will agree.

One approach is to immediately see if it is possible to dissipate some of the existing tension by improving the problematic relationship so that productive negotiations can occur. I hasten to add that this counsel is better tailored for some circumstances than others. In a dysfunctional family, for instance, whose members must now negotiate with one another over some common problem, the history of inter-personal relations may be so tangled and complex that if significant progress is possible at all, it might take years of intensive therapy to occur.

Nevertheless, in many relationships, especially those of a professional or arm's-length variety, more bite-sized interpersonal problems may have accumulated that the parties might be able to identify and deal with productively. It is also worth recalling that the goal here is simply to foster a positive working relationship, that is, one in which the parties can set aside their differences sufficiently that they can negotiate with one another effectively, advancing toward an agreement both can support.

In the discussion of agendas in Chapter 3 I noted that a party will sometimes want to address relationship problems early in a negotiation. If you tackle the relationship issue head-on, restore decent relations, and then move to the substance, you may well find that the substantive issues seem much more manageable. And, an eventual agreement might serve both sides' interests better and prove more durable and optimal and more likely to lead to a positive future working environment.

But, a negotiator might wonder how exactly to bring sensitive relationship issues onto the table, early in the negotiation, in a way that does not poison the negotiation at the outset. In some circumstances a statement like this might help: "If there's one thing we can probably agree on, it may be that our relations have sometimes been less than ideal. Maybe we can at least clear the air a bit in that regard. Why don't you give me some thoughts about things that have happened that have adversely affected our ability to get things done together? Then, I'll add some of my own perceptions. Maybe we can come up with a few ideas to try to set things on a better footing as we start to negotiate this new problem."

An approach of this sort invites discussion of the relationship and shows a willingness to hear out the other party, while providing an opportunity for both sides to get certain matters "off their chests." And, while it invites the parties to think back over past behavior and re-hash some problems, it next shifts the emphasis toward future relations and how these might be arranged more productively. Although not well-suited for every case of hostility as a negotiation commences, it is an option to consider in some cases.

2. Permit a Party to Vent

When a negotiation gets under way but is immediately hampered by evident interpersonal problems, one approach is to permit, even encourage, *venting*. This refers to releasing tension by publicly expressing some point, often emotionally or passionately. In order to move forward with substantive points and reach a negotiated resolution, one or the other or both parties may feel a need to identify frustrations and voice their opinions about them.

When potentially antagonistic comments simply involve someone venting, the job of listening to your counterpart can be easier to tolerate. Perhaps some venting of your own is also in order. One authority suggests leaning back and letting the noise wash over you, all while you think to yourself how much good this is doing your counterpart and the negotiation to get all these feelings out in the open.[45]

When a party is venting, it may be very useful to find something to agree with. Your counterpart is very likely to expect you to do just the opposite — to resist, raise counter-arguments, and try to diminish their points. Listening respectfully and showing concern for their perspective may shorten the venting process and allow you, eventually, to re-frame matters into a substantive discussion of the problem.

It is important to realize, however, that while venting can clear the air, it also has the potential to make a bad situation worse.[46] This often occurs when in the course of venting one participant blames another who is at the negotiating table and who then responds in kind. Each creates arguments as to why they were right and the other was wrong. Here, voicing your anger may escalate matters, rather than simply release a pent-up emotion.

Although your venting may seem completely logical and appropriate to you, to others it may sound self-righteous or narrow-minded. The better practice, then, might be to vent to someone else and not directly to the person who angered you or to have a neutral party present prepared "to moderate self-justifications and to keep in mind each party's perspective of the situation."[47]

Should you find yourself becoming drawn so far into the venting process that you fear losing your own temper or composure or becoming distracted or incapacitated by it, one might recall that negotiation can be a form of theater. One authority counseled: "Imagine that you are an actor playing a role ... The other side is screaming at the person in your position, not at you. Let it go." In noting that "[p]arties will yell at one another for only a finite—and generally brief—period of time," he went on to observe, "[T]here is a definite limit to how long people can yell, typically only a few minutes.... After that time the parties usually cease, out of relief and embarrassment. But often, the skies clear after such an episode and the parties can move ahead."[48]

3. Alter the Negotiating Process

Another possible route toward improving working relations involves making a notable change in the negotiation process. Should forward progress have slowed as the parties engage in heated exchanges or as a defensive or self-righteous tone has emerged, it may be useful to table a particularly problematic issue. Calling a *recess* or a caucus might also help to restore positive relations.

In a recess negotiators ask for a short period to take a break, usually by leaving the negotiating room. The purpose is to cool down, clear heads, get fresh air, and prepare to come back and negotiate more effectively. Perhaps most important a recess provides time to think without the pressure of needing to formulate an immediate response. Time away from the negotiating table can help a negotiator to revisit where matters stand and to review goals and strategies.

A recess, then, differs from a break that serves as a caucus where negotiators on one side of the problem meet to discuss what has occurred. If both sides caucus, that enables them to consider the problem for a time without the pressure of having to participate in the give-and-take of ongoing discussions with each other. Taking a coffee or lunch break, meeting privately with one's client or negotiating partner, or even planning to resume the talks in another future session might give the parties needed distance from each other and provide the opportunity to return with a fresh attitude or having taken a new look at the problem.

More subtly, a change in body language sometimes proves useful in regaining positive working relations. When the parties have adopted, or slipped into, adversarial postures, a physical change of position that underscores the need to tackle the problem jointly can restore positive energy. Motion releases tension, so getting up, moving about, and then sitting down next to one's counterpart can help to break a downward spiral. A negotiator might direct attention toward a pad of paper set on the negotiating table or toward a flip chart, chalk or white board. Starting to work together in this way provides a natural reason to shift the seating arrangements. This can signal the start of a more cooperative phase.

One potent source of frustration, as working relations sour, is the feeling that one's points are not registering well with the other side. Recall here the active-listening techniques reviewed in Chapter 2. These signal the other side that, while you may not agree with them, they are being heard and understood, and a real attempt is being made to understand their perspective on the issues under discussion. So, to try to regain a positive, productive tone, a negotiator might look for opportunities to do more paraphrasing, to ask additional questions and then to pose follow-ups.

Another way to alter the negotiating process would be to make an appeal from one negotiator to another to return to your fundamental negotiation skills to try to regain momentum. One might say to one's counterpart: "Things seem to have gotten stalled. How about if we both agree to try to move away from debating each other, since that doesn't seem to be getting us too far, and see if we can work as negotiators to find something that both sides can accept?"

4. Make Amends for Your Contributions

One might also think back to what *you* might have said or done that might have played a role in causing interpersonal problems to develop. Directly acknowledging that you share responsibility for the current difficulties may bring your counterpart to be less defensive and more open to working positively with you.[49]

Beyond this, it may be possible to make amends in one way or another, and this is likely to have an even greater impact. You might clarify a prior point that may have been construed in an unfortunate way. Sometimes, making very clear that you do understand what the other side has experienced will restore a cooperative tone. Showing that one is now interested in a rapprochement via a statement of concern may also help to re-establish decent relations. At times, tensions are eased simply by acknowledging that you appreciate that different valid perspectives exist on the issues that divide you.

a. Apologies

Negotiators or the parties they represent sometimes consider apologizing to a counterpart for something that occurred, whether in the talks or in the history of relations between the parties. Their motive may be to provide sympathy, to regain positive momentum, to place themselves in a more positive light, or to work toward feeling better about themselves. The chief purpose of an apology, however, is usually to try to heal damaged relations. An earnest apology can disarm a hostile counterpart and restore a positive tone, while failing to apologize may be taken as disrespectful, something that could escalate conflict.[50]

Should a negotiator issue an apology, he or she would accept blame, while expressing regret or remorse to another for some improper statement or action, one that may have been impolite or uncalled for or in some other respect hurtful, wrongful, or injurious. The one apologizing also often references some norm about how the situation should have been handled but was not.[51]

By diminishing the other side's anger, persuading a counterpart that future behavior is likely to be different, and gaining a degree of forgiveness, an apology can often go quite a ways toward altering a negative dynamic. "The willingness to admit you were wrong, to apologize, and take responsibility for the wrongdoing," one authority noted, "may greatly enhance your credibility in the future."[52]

It is possible, of course, and sometimes useful, to express regret for a difficult or problematic set of circumstances but not delve into who exactly is at fault for the situation. Where the parties share blame, another possible move is to allude to an apology without actually apologizing. For instance, a negotiator might say something like this.

> We certainly are not here to demand an apology or anything of the sort. Who ought to apologize to whom for what is a tangled issue that we may not need to deal with. Maybe we can simply agree that some things have been said that probably would have been better left unsaid, since they were mistaken or poorly phrased, or not completely accurate. And, leave it at that.

An outright apology, however, goes considerably further, particularly if it is paired with some action or gesture aiming to repair some of the harm done.

Sometimes people shy away from an apology since they feel that blame for the situation should be shared. A party may believe that, while he or she was in the wrong on matters A and B, the other side should really be apologizing for matters C and D. However, it may be helpful to be quite specific about what you are apologizing for. This will enhance the sincerity of the apology and may bring the other side to apologize as well.

At other times people refrain from apologizing for fear that they will be admitting something or will appear meek and submissive. These hesitations suggest, however, not that an apology be eliminated from consideration but instead that one put careful thought into the particular wording of the apology. What exactly is being apologized for? What should the content of the apology include?

Often in negotiations the matter to be apologized about involves discourtesy and not legal culpability. Nevertheless, lawyers and clients as well as those potentially the target of a lawsuit should be particularly cautious about the content of an apology, so as to avoid potential liability. Here, while state laws differ, a trend seems to be developing that distinguishes "between apologetic expressions of sympathy ('I'm sorry that you are hurt') but not fault-admitting apologies ('I'm sorry that I injured you') after accidents."[53] In a civil case the latter are more likely to be admissible as proof of fault.

Box 7.1 — Useful Considerations in Formulating an Apology

A negotiator considering apologizing might consider the following questions, the answers to which will vary from one negotiation to another.

- On what matters might an apology be owed?
- How is an apology likely to be received?
- What effect might an apology have on the remainder of the negotiation?
- How might one best convey that an apology is sincere and heartfelt?
- What does one not want to apologize for, either because an apology is inappropriate or for fear of an admission bringing on liability?
- How might one best phrase the type of apology in mind?
- How might an apology be worded most appropriately and most effectively?

5. Choice of Responses When Offended

Another species of interpersonal conflict stems from offensive statements abruptly dropped in the midst of a negotiation. In daily life, when someone is offended, their personality may dictate their response. Some naturally withdraw when upset; others become combative. Some feel that bad manners are best ignored; others see themselves as on a mission to improve them. A negotiator, when offended, may be tempted to react in kind, perhaps treating the statement as a personal affront. Cutting off the talks and walking away from the negotiations is a very real possibility.

a. Make a Considered Decision about a Response

A skillful negotiator, however, will make a considered decision about the appropriate way to respond. Certainly, a thoughtful, purposeful reaction is preferable to one made blindly or precipitately. To do this requires forethought as to what options you might have should an offensive comment occur.

Negotiators who feel stress or anger can try to gain perspective by momentary detachment, which can assist them not to take comments personally. William Ury counseled, "Imagine you are negotiating on a stage and then imagine yourself climbing onto a balcony overlooking the stage. The 'balcony' is a metaphor for a mental attitude of detachment. From the balcony you can calmly evaluation the conflict almost as if you were a third party. You can think constructively for both sides and look for a mutually satisfactory way to resolve the problem."[54] By temporarily distancing yourself from the give-and-take of the discussions, you may be able to do a better job of objectively analyzing what is causing the problems and determining what might be done about them.

b. Handling an Offensive Comment

Andrea Kupfer Schneider offered a particularly useful and option-oriented approach to handling offensive comments, suggesting that a negotiator can respond in the different ways listed below.[55] To choose among them, she suggests that you review your assumptions to be sure that you are not projecting something false on another, that you appraise their motivation for making the comments—misguided or malicious—and that you then choose the response that seems most appropriate. Ignoring the comment is certainly an option, but, she argues, it "should be a conscious, affirmative decision by you that either the comment does not bother you that much or it is just not worth your time and effort to deal with it."[56]

i. Pause in Communication

If you hear something that outrages you, one response is to stop and say nothing, perhaps simply look, with a puzzled expression, at the other person. Your counterpart, uncertain as to what you are thinking, may get uncomfortable with the silence and revise what was said—perhaps even apologize.

A pause in communication will also give you a chance to collect your thoughts and not respond with a retort that you later regret. In this regard Thomas Jefferson once counseled, "When angry, count ten before you speak; if *very* angry, a hundred."[57]

ii. Acknowledge and Move On

Another approach is to sidestep problems of this sort, or as Schneider put it, acknowledge the comment, deflect it, and move on. She wrote, "[I]n response to someone asking you to [go] get coffee, you might respond, 'I'll call my secretary to bring us refreshments. In the meantime, can we review the contract?' "[58]

This might also be a moment to rely on body language to send a message without further interrupting the talks: "A raised eyebrow, an exaggerated sigh, or a roll of the eyes leaves little room for a verbal rebuttal."[59] One experienced mediator offered a less confrontational option that negotiators can use, noting: "Using the familiar 'time out' hand signal when the situation has gotten out of hand is an excellent way to control behavior without appearing to be condemning."[60]

In the midst of a particularly intense group negotiation session marked by some inflammatory statement, a short caucus between leading negotiators on different sides can be quite useful. One might point out that exchanges that seem bitter or insulting make it difficult to hold together allies or team members. In all of these cases the negotiator does not ignore the offensive comment, but acknowledges it, somehow deals with it, and moves on to re-focus the discussion on the negotiation process.

iii. Confront the Party and Statement

A third way to proceed is to confront the statement or the person who made it. Comments that one side feels are bullying, exploitative, or otherwise wholly unfair may fester, bring on deep resentment, and possibly ruin relations and even the negotiation.

One confrontational approach is to draw attention to—to "name"—what the opposing negotiator is doing. Deborah Kolb and Judith Williams wrote,

"By naming the move, you let the other party know it's not working. However clever or disguised the tactic, you see through it and remain unruffled."[61] They illustrated this point by recounting a television-rights negotiation. After finally getting the literary agent on the phone, the media executive recounted that:

> Before she could say hello, the agent started screaming abuse at her, attacking her competence and her experience. She was surprised that he would jeopardize a lucrative deal for his client, but whatever his motivation, she could not let his attitude go unchecked, and set the tone for the negotiation. 'I called to start talking deal points,' she interrupted. 'Calm down. Yelling won't help. I won't go away.'

Later, the executive learned that the tirade had been an effort to buy time, since the agent did not, in fact, yet control the television rights in question. Kolb and Williams further observed: "A humorous or mocking retort elicits a different reaction than a stinging rebuke. Few negotiators like to look foolish, and an ironic twist or sarcastic comment often exposes the absurdity of demeaning behavior better than a rapier thrust."[62]

iv. Engage the Comment

A final approach to an inflammatory remark Andrea Kupfer Schneider terms "engaging," a response that she argues has certain marked advantages. By engaging, Schneider means that you have "a conversation about the other side's purpose in making the remark and your feelings upon hearing it." After you determine their intent and have listened to their point of view, she advises sharing your own perceptions. She advised, "Explain your reaction and … reasoning" (e.g., "When I hear that comment, I usually assume … and it makes me feel, think, etc.…").[63]

Engaging leaves one's options open, since it is still possible to deflect or confront, once you have heard what your counterpart has had to say and can better determine if the statement was purposeful or a slip of the tongue and whether it was motivated by ignorance or bias. It may be preferable to doing nothing since an ignored comment may "color your future interactions," and engaging may preserve a working relationship where confronting would sour or end it.[64]

6. Handling Difficult Negotiators in a Group Negotiation

In multi-party negotiations the members of the group can often come to an agreement that encompasses less than all of those gathered at the table. A central issue, however, is how to handle the parties that might or might not be a part of the final deal. A group might include one or more individuals who are either singularly difficult to work with or are far out of sync with the thinking of the others. How might you effectively handle such a situation, and how and when do you try to cut out of the deal such a negotiator?

a. Working on Their Allies

When a representative in a group negotiation proves unusually problematic, one tactic is to focus your efforts on that person's natural allies. For example, when a company is negotiating simultaneously with several unions or perhaps the mayors of several adjoining towns or cities, and relations with one are especially difficult, it may be worthwhile to draw out the thinking of the others at the table.[65] While the especially recalcitrant negotiator may be looking to dictate the course of the negotiations, the group might make progress working with the more reasonable allies. And, they may be in the best position to sway their colleague toward accepting an eventual deal.

b. Cutting Out a Problematic Party

Another option in a group negotiation where progress is being stymied by one negotiator is simply to cut that party out of the developing deal. In determining how much deference to give that person's interests, objectives, and perspectives, an important question is whether that party has a veto power or can otherwise block a potential agreement? Is it possible to have a deal without that side of the negotiation participating? Is the problematic negotiator likely to reach out to form a blocking coalition? The more difficult it appears to be to reach an agreement without that party, the more its interests must be factored into any negotiated resolution.

Often, while the group could possibly move forward without the problematic party, its presence would certainly be missed. Here, before cutting that party out, it is worth asking the following questions.

- What is the problematic party's Best Alternative to a Negotiated Agreement (BATNA)?
- Could the other group members offer anything that would serve the party's interests sufficiently that joining the group would be better than pursuing its BATNA?
- What would such a course of action cost, and would the price be worth keeping the party in the deal?
- Has the group clearly sent the problematic party the message that it is seriously considering moving forward in any event, with or without that party present?

- What would be the most tactful and diplomatic way to communicate that message? In a caucus or in front of the group as a whole? Would any particular negotiator be the most effective spokesperson?

i. Spotting a Spoiler

A skillful negotiator should also assess whether an unusually difficult party is really negotiating in good faith try to bring about an agreement or, instead, is playing the role of a *spoiler*, that is, a party that feels as though its interests will be better served by preventing a negotiated resolution than by joining one and, hence, is looking to derail, subvert, or sabotage the negotiation. Rather than working toward a mutually beneficial agreement, a spoiler might be intent on taking a tough stand or gaining outside publicity and might not be at all interested in compromising or problem-solving. To keep from being dismissed or ejected from the negotiation, the spoiler might pretend to be pursuing a negotiated resolution, while actually trying to prevent one.

To take one example of a party playing a spoiler role, when one company looks to merge with or acquire another, creditors of the target business might prefer to have the company go bankrupt and "pick apart its assets in litigation."[66] If the creditors are brought into such a negotiation, they may be there to undermine progress and derail any potential deal that seems to be coming together.

Other negotiators identify a possible spoiler by analyzing its interests, trying to determine its underlying motivations, and being alert to tell-tale signs that it is not really negotiating in good faith. A spoiler's tactics could include getting other parties quarreling with each other or trying to delay the talks until the different negotiators become frustrated or a time limit of some variety expires.

Note that sometimes a party is simply a potential spoiler. Trying to scuttle the agreement is one option, but the possible spoiler waits to see how the negotiation develops before committing to a spoiler strategy. Here, the other negotiators may be able to coax the potential spoiler back into productive discussions, or they may ultimately conclude that cutting out the party is necessary in order to prevent the spoiler from wrecking the chances for a negotiated resolution.

F. Conclusion

The interpersonal communication problem in some negotiations is not so much a hard-bargaining approach, partisan perceptions, the need to vent, or offensive comments but a counterpart who is uncommunicative, unimaginative, or perhaps even lacking experience or competence in negotiation. How might a skillful negotiator proceed under these circumstances?

First, in trying to work with an unhelpful counterpart, one should try to make the other side as comfortable as possible and then look to make slow, steady progress. Establish positive relations, if at all possible, and should there be cultural differences, these might be openly acknowledged, maybe with the light touch of self-deprecating humor. Then, it may be especially important not to hurry into elaborate or grandiose proposals. Rather, be sure to explore the interests on both sides thoroughly. Adopt a deliberate negotiation process, taking quite small steps forward, if need be, being very specific and asking questions that can be answered simply, perhaps even with a "yes" or "no" response.

All inter-personal difficulties among negotiators amount to unhelpful baggage that can hinder or disrupt the course of a negotiation. They can poison working relations and obstruct efforts to negotiate in a cooperative and innovative manner. Sometimes they cause parties to walk away from a potential deal in frustration, hostility, or disgust. The fact is that people who are angry, stressed, or distracted are rarely at their best in terms of creativity, rationality, and other problem-solving skills. They are usually not receptive to reasoning their way to an optimal negotiated resolution.

The parties to a negotiation may find themselves contending with difficult personal conflicts among the parties brought on by offensive comments or pressure tactics. Sometimes a negotiator has a good sense for what has angered the other side, but at other times the source of the problem may be unclear. Roger Fisher and Scott Brown wrote, "Since it is impossible for us to put ourselves into the emotional 'skin' of another person, we may not try at all. But if we don't think about the other person's emotional state, we will blunder into emotional traps that we might have avoided had we taken the time to consider how we might feel in the other's position."[67]

Notes

1. DEBORAH KOLB & JUDITH WILLIAMS, THE SHADOW NEGOTIATION 20 (2000).

2. Jeffrey Z. Rubin, *Some Wise and Mistaken Assumptions About Negotiation*, 45 J. OF SOCIAL ISSUES 206 (1989).

3. ROGER FISHER, WILLIAM URY, & BRUCE PATTON, GETTING TO YES 17 (2d ed. 1991).

4. *Id.* at 7–10.

5. *Id.*

6. Gary Goodpaster, *A Primer on Competitive Bargaining*, 1996 J. OF DISPUTE RESOLUTION 326 (1996).

7. Kevin Gibson, *Ethics and Morality in Negotiation*, in THE NEGOTIATOR'S HANDBOOK 176 (Andrea Kupfer Schneider & Christopher Honeyman eds., 2006).

8. FISHER, URY, & PATTON, supra note 3, at 8.

9. Lisa Blomgren Bingham, *Avoiding Negotiation*, in THE NEGOTIATOR'S HANDBOOK 115 (Andrea Kupfer Schneider & Christopher Honeyman eds., 2006).

10. ROBERT H. MNOOKIN, SCOTT R. PEPPET, & ANDREW S. TULUMELLO, BEYOND WINNING 4, 216 (2000).

11. HOWARD RAIFFA, NEGOTIATION ANALYSIS 301 (2002).

12. ROGER FISHER, ELIZABETH KOPELMAN, & ANDREA KUPFER SCHNEIDER, BEYOND MACHIAVELLI 24 (1994).

13. MNOOKIN, PEPPET, & TULUMELLO, supra note 10, at 4.

14. Jeffrey Z. Rubin, *Psychological Approach*, in INTERNATIONAL NEGOTIATION 222 (Victor A. Kremenyuk ed., 1991).

15. MNOOKIN, PEPPET, & TULUMELLO, supra note 10, at 158.

16. FISHER, URY, & PATTON, supra note 3, at 25.

17. I. WILLIAM ZARTMAN, THE 50% SOLUTION 49 (1987).

18. Townsend Hoopes, *A Critique of the Prime Mover John Foster Dulles*, in MAJOR PROBLEMS IN AMERICAN FOREIGN POLICY 377 (Thomas G. Patterson ed., 1984).

19. MNOOKIN, PEPPET, & TULUMELLO, supra note 10, at 166.

20. KOLB & WILLIAMS, supra note 1, at 166.

21. Bruce Barry, Ingrid Smithey Fulmer, & Gerben A. Van Kleef, *I Laughed, I Cried, I Settled* in THE HANDBOOK OF NEGOTIATION AND CULTURE 84 (Michele Gelfand & Jeanne M. Brett eds., 2004).

22. Daniel L. Shapiro, *Untapped Power*, in THE NEGOTIATOR'S FIELDBOOK 264, 267 (Andrea Kupfer Schneider & Christopher Honeyman eds., 2006).

23. WILLIAM L. URY, GETTING PAST NO 31 (2d ed. 1993).

24. I. WILLIAM ZARTMAN & MAUREEN R. BERMAN, THE PRACTICAL NEGOTIATOR 23 (1982).

25. ROGER FISHER & SCOTT BROWN, GETTING TOGETHER 179 (1988).

26. KOLB & WILLIAMS, supra note 1, at 163.

27. FISHER & BROWN, supra note 25, at 151.

28. THOMAS R. COLOSI, ON AND OFF THE RECORD 54 (1993).

29. *Id.* at 55.

30. G. RICHARD SHELL, BARGAINING FOR ADVANTAGE 45–46 (1999).

31. ZARTMAN & BERMAN, supra note 24, at 180–81.

32. ROGER FISHER, INTERNATIONAL CONFLICT FOR BEGINNERS 58–59, 148 (1969).

33. FISHER, URY, & PATTON, supra note 3, at 137.

34. FISHER & BROWN, supra note 25, at 147.

35. James J. White, *The Pros and Cons of* "Getting to YES," 34 J. OF LEGAL ED. 118 (1984).

36. *How to DEAL with Threats: 4 Negotiation Tips for Managing Conflict at the Bargaining Table*, Program on Negotiation, Harvard Law School, March 10, 2016, http://www.pon.harvard.edu/daily/conflict-resolution/how-to-deal-with-threats/?mqsc=38.

37. *Id.*

38. ROY J. LEWICKI, DAVID M. SAUNDERS, & JOHN W. MINTON, ESSENTIALS OF NEGOTIATION 79 (2d ed. 2001).

39. Robert J. Robinson, *Defusing the Exploding Offer*, 11 NEGOTIATION J. 278–79 (1995).

40. PATRICK J. CLEARY, THE NEGOTIATOR'S HANDBOOK 84 (2001).

41. Robinson, supra note 39, at 280–84.

42. *Id.* at 281.
43. *Id.* at 282–83.
44. *Id.* at 284.
45. Ury, supra note 23, at 45.
46. Roger Fisher & Daniel Shapiro, Beyond Reason 157–60, 168 (2005).
47. *Id.* at 168.
48. Cleary, supra note 40, at 125.
49. Roger Fisher, Alan Sharp, & John Richardson, Getting It Done 24 (1998).
50. Jonathan Cohen, *Advising Clients to Apologize*, 72 S. Cal. L. Rev. 1019 (1999).
51. Jennifer Gerarda Brown & Jennifer K. Robbennolt, *Apology in Negotiation*, in The Negotiator's Fieldbook 429 (Andrea Kupfer Schneider & Christopher Honeyman eds., 2006).
52. Lisa Blomgren Bingham, *Avoiding Negotiation*, in The Negotiator's Fieldbook 115 (Andrea Kupfer Schneider & Christopher Honeyman eds., 2006).
53. Jonathan R. Cohen, *Legislating Apology*, 70 Univ. of Cincinnati L. Rev. 820 (2002).
54. Ury, supra note 23, at 37–38.
55. Andrea Kupfer Schneider, *Effective Responses to Offensive Comments*, 10 Negotiation J. 107–14 (1994).
56. *Id.* at 112.
57. Ury, supra note 23, at 45.
58. Schneider, supra note 55, at 112.
59. Kolb & Williams, supra note 1, at 132.
60. Karen King, *But I'm Not a Funny Person…*, 4 Negotiation J. 121 (1988).
61. *Id.* at 114.
62. *Id.*
63. Schneider, supra note 55, at 112.
64. *Id.* at 113.
65. Cleary, supra note 40, at 43–44.
66. Shell, supra note 30, at 19.
67. *Id.* at 59.

Checkpoints

- A hard bargainer puts forward extreme positions, aiming to marshal arguments to justify them, while trying to persuade the other side that he or she is locked into them.

- A hard-bargaining negotiator assumes the best route to reaching the most favorable negotiated resolution is to put counterparts on the defensive, corner them with logical arguments, and gain their acquiescence to pre-conceived solutions.

- A soft-bargaining negotiator looks to create, maintain, and improve positive relations with the other side, presuming that a friendly, trusting, cooperative approach is likely to be reciprocated and will ultimately bring about a good agreement.

- Hard bargainers sometimes achieve very advantageous terms, but often frustrate their counterparts who walk away from one-sided potential deals. Soft bargainers sometimes negotiate effectively with fellow negotiators with a similar approach, but their single-minded focus on cultivating good relations leaves them vulnerable to constantly appeasing their counterpart.

- Conflicts between negotiators or their clients can be rooted in grievances preceding a negotiation or they can spring up during it, making difficult substantive problems even more challenging to negotiate to mutually beneficial resolutions.

- The advice "separate the people from the problem" is not good counsel when the people, including their relations with one another, are a fundamental aspect of the problem.

- Partisan perceptions cause problems by distorting analysis, bringing about misinterpretations, and magnifying fears of what the other side might do. If we like someone, we take what they do and say one way, placing positive connotations on their behavior whenever possible. If we fear, dislike, or see them in competitive or adversarial terms, we hurry toward negative connotations and conclusions.

- As an inherent part of the human psyche, emotions are often present in negotiations and can be used productively or become quite problematic. When negative emotions take charge of a negotiator, impulsive or short-sighted behavior can result that detracts from reasoned problem-solving.

- Anger, one of the most potentially problematic emotions, sometimes surfaces after an accidental statement, mis-statement, slip of the tongue, or poorly phrased thought. But, anger can also arise when a negotiator purposefully makes an inflammatory remark to try to gain some tactical advantage, such as ruffling or distracting the other side.

- Negotiators may try pressure tactics to persuade a party to take some course of action that it is otherwise disinclined to take. For instance, a negotiating session might be artificially prolonged, a consistency trap might be sprung, or a good cop/bad cop routine undertaken.

- One common pressure tactic is a threat to do something the other side will intensely dislike, perhaps take away something of value, expose the other side to some risk, hazard, or danger, or cause some variety of pain or embarrassment.

- Negotiators sometimes make threats hoping that simply flexing their muscles will produce the desired result. However, threats often do not work. People naturally resist pressure, and their target might consider the threat to be a bluff. Then, threats can easily escalate since many are inclined to react to coercion by issuing their own counter-threat.

- Another pressure tactic is to introduce an artificial deadline or exploding offer, both aimed at getting one's counterpart to agree quickly. A negotiator can counter such timing pressures with interest-based arguments, appeals to empathy, counter-offers, or provisional acceptance.

- One approach to interpersonal problems that are hampering a negotiation is to encourage venting, that is, letting off steam by publicly expressing some points, often emotionally or passionately. Getting deeply held feelings voiced and in the open can help the parties to move on to productive negotiation of substantive issues. However, venting has the potential to make a bad situation worse, particularly when it involves casting blame on parties at the table.

- Another approach to improving poor working relations is to alter the negotiating process. This can be done by calling a recess or caucus, introducing more positive and cooperative body language, reemphasizing active-listening skills, or making a professional appeal, negotiator to negotiator, to try to work out a reasonable proposal. One can also make amends for the breakdown in relations, including by issuing an apology.

- When an offensive comment has been made, a negotiator should come to a considered decision about how to respond. One option is silence, a pause in communication to see if your counterpart will voluntarily revise what was said or even apologize for it. Another is to deflect the comment, that is, directly acknowledge it but then move on. Still another is to confront the party with the statement, naming what the other side is doing to show that you see through it. Finally, you can engage the comment by having a conversation about what the other party said, why they said it, and what your reaction to it is.

Chapter 8

Closing a Deal: Reaching a Worthwhile Agreement

Roadmap

- **Closing:** What characterizes the closing phase of a complex negotiation?

- **Timing:** What steps should be taken before a negotiator assembles a proposal? How do deadlines affect negotiations, and what exactly is a fading opportunity? Why might a negotiator rush to close a deal, and what is proper timing?

- **Steps to close a deal:** How can summarizing the ground covered to date help the parties to transition into a productive closing? Why should negotiators spend some time on ancillary as well as primary issues? Why is it imperative to pair skepticism with creativity as you think through a possible resolution?

- **Yesable proposition:** What are the characteristics of a yesable proposition? How do you make such an offer speak to the other side? How do you enhance the credibility of an offer, and why can it be important to explain your reasoning?

- **Making commitments:** Why is committing often such serious business, and what is meant by "buyer's remorse"? What are the ideas of casual commitment and over-commitment, and what dangers are associated with them? What helps to ensure that commitments are honored? What role might a ratifier play in a negotiation?

- **Accepting or rejecting an offer:** What factors should a negotiator keep in mind in trying to determine whether to agree to a deal or walk away from it? Why is trying to reach perfect terms too often a costly quest for the unattainable? When is agreeing not to agree the most sensible route to take? What is a ripeness issue, and when should a negotiator opt to postpone a final resolution?

- **Drafting an agreement:** Why carefully draft the terms of an agreement? What considerations are associated with the initial draft? What are the advantages to having a template or framework agreement? How might negotiators draft provisions to resolve disputes, allocate risks, or attend to special circumstances?

- **Gaining approval:** Why is gaining client or constituent approval often the culminating moment of the closing phase, and what considerations come into play?

The essence of much effective interest-based negotiation involves intelligent communication about a shared problem or opportunity. One launches a negotiation productively with an engaging opening. One then transitions into the substance by working with interests, advancing objective criteria and creative options to address distributional and other problems, and overcoming any difficulties that might crop up, whether personality issues or substantive impasses. "Pledges as to what you will or won't do," Roger Fisher advised, "should be made not at the outset of a negotiation but after differences of perception, interest, and values are fully appreciated."[1]

Intelligent communication in a complex negotiation involves gathering a great deal of information. But it also involves sifting through that information, making sense of it in relation to the present circumstances, producing cogent ideas that relate to it, and then assembling a possible resolution. Of all the challenges a negotiator faces, formulating a realistic and beneficial possible agreement is the most formidable. American statesman John Quincy Adams once observed, "You will find hundreds of persons able to produce a crowd of good ideas upon any subject for one who can marshal them to best advantage."[2] Expert negotiators first dissect and analyze a problem or opportunity and then combine different strands of thought to find possible solutions attractive to both sides.

This chapter explores *closing*[3] a negotiated agreement, the art of bringing the pieces of a deal together. This is perhaps the most intense and intellectually exciting period of a complex negotiation but it is also one fraught with risk. An agreement might develop nicely or it might fall to pieces. The more involved is the situation and the more intricate the proposed terms, the greater are the chances that things will break down before a deal is successfully closed.[4]

Through skillful negotiation, however, the parties might find terms to which each can agree. They might succeed in creating a basic deal, an agreement in principle perhaps, or they might go further still, and reach a more detailed and optimal resolution.

A. Timing during the Closing Phase

When teaching negotiation in Beijing, I was introduced to the ancient Chinese saying, "The right time and the right place leads to success." Prior chapters have focused on the importance of timing at different junctures in the negotiation process. Timing is also key when concluding a negotiation. One wants to stay true to the rhythm of the negotiation, and not rush matters.

However, one also wants the negotiation to progress smoothly and efficiently toward a conclusion and not get bogged down.

Agitating and badgering is seldom the best route to get a deal closed. A "hard sell" approach of pressuring another can easily backfire. The other side gets suspicious. It begins to see the proposal as something created by others that it is being lured into accepting. A feeling may develop that, if at your insistence the other negotiators yield, you have won and they have caved in.

Your counterpart will need time to become familiar with all the terms of the proposal and comfortable in accepting them. One of Japan's most experienced diplomatic negotiators once counseled me: "Michael-san, this is going to take nearly super-human patience." In this stage of a negotiation exhibiting patience can be an exceedingly important virtue. Since the closing phase is often concerned with identifying and managing the details of the agreement, ample time needs to be set aside to work these out. One does not want to create an agreement that is never properly implemented. Nor does one want to arrive at an acceptable agreement but not an optimal one. For these reasons a negotiator should guard against prematurely closing a deal.

And yet, too much attention to minutiae and undue tinkering with the language of particular provisions can distract the parties from their main task of making the crucial decisions needed to bring the deal to fruition. One experienced lawyer observed, "People get nervous when things move too fast; they step back to reassess the situation. But too slow a pace creates its own problems, the delay exacerbating the obstacles and providing the parties with additional time to change their minds."[5]

With proper timing, however, positive momentum can build to close the deal. I. William Zartman and Maureen Berman put it like this: "At some point during the bargaining a 'crest' occurs, after which the rest of the items are rapidly resolved and the general feeling is one of being in the 'home stretch.'" They continued: "This crest may be described in various ways: it is the point where enough is agreed upon to constitute an acceptable accord even if the remaining points are unresolved, or the point where enough is agreed on favorably to outweigh any remaining disagreements or nonagreements."[6]

1. Deadlines and Fading Opportunities

A factor that often influences timing in the closing phase of a negotiation is the presence of some sort of deadline. One or the other or both parties convince themselves that the agreement deal must be concluded by some particular date. Indeed, some deadlines are generated by a party: the deal must be done by a specified date or some walk-away option will be pursued instead.

Other time limits are related to facts or external circumstances. For example, a negotiator might point out: "It will take eight weeks to manufacture 100,000 widgets. If you must have them by June 1, we have to conclude our agreement by April 1." Another example would be an upcoming change in the tax code that creates disadvantageous tax considerations after January 1 of that year. Or, by law, a collective-bargaining agreement between a local government and police or fire fighters might have to be signed by a particular date.

What sometimes drives the closing phase of a negotiation is not so much a hard deadline as a sense that the parties face a *fading opportunity*, that is, that the chances of reaching an agreement will dissipate over time. This provides a real motive to bring negotiations to a head. Indeed, in assembling a proposal, a negotiator may look for ways to emphasize to the other party that the opportunity to agree will not last forever.

When an actual deadline approaches, the parties either come to an agreement or reject the potential deal. Or, not infrequently, they find a way to revise the time limit so as to continue to negotiate. Some deadlines turn out to be more flexible than they might first appear, and others are artificial, not real. (Recall the discussion of exploding offers in Chapter 7.)

When a genuine deadline approaches, moving too slowly may not leave sufficient time to get the deal properly closed. Sometimes a potential agreement might be lost. The opportunity to do the deal may be fleeting; the window to agree, once open, may close. Perhaps circumstances change or your counterpart has a change of heart or opts to move on to a third party. As you try to put provisions in writing or otherwise wrap matters up, the entire agreement might evaporate.

More often, the deadline is met and the deal gets done, but important details are overlooked. And, often the operational points that get passed by end up being precisely those that could have made the agreement more durable, sustainable, and long-lasting.

Negotiators should also be aware that the presence of a time limit raises the possibility of last-minute gamesmanship, something that may occur in any negotiation but is especially prevalent in positional bargaining. "As a deadline approaches," it has been observed, "parties harden their positions, spar and feint, in preparation for a last minute jump that will present the other with an offer that will be barely acceptable but too late to improve on."[7]

2. Rushing to Close

While moving too slowly to close an agreement is one common criticism of ineffective negotiators, another is quite the opposite: that many tend to move too hastily to conclude the deal. People are often concerned about the costs already sunk into the negotiation process, or they want to ensure that the deal does not melt away. Hence, they rush to close, sometimes agreeing to terms without thinking them through carefully enough and sometimes by offering to split the difference in whatever gap remains.

At other times, after a grueling negotiation process, the participants may be so delighted to have finally achieved an apparent meeting of the minds that they hurry past important details. Or, they fail to explore ideas that might make for an even better agreement. In both cases issues that a skillful negotiator might take a good bit of time to work out get polished off in short order. When " 'Let's wrap it up' becomes the byword," one lawyer noted, "... we find ourselves settling on terms that could have been improved with a little more patience."[8]

Sometimes, after much jockeying and haggling with one another, the parties tire and then in a final spasm of activity they quickly agree. One labor negotiator lamented, "We never sign a contract until 4 o'clock in the morning. Things happen so quickly that we do not know what we are agreeing to."[9] In short, more experienced negotiators often perceive more possible opportunities and more potential pitfalls, and so they construct a better and more comprehensive agreement.

B. Useful Steps in Closing a Deal

At times, negotiators under pressure to come to an agreement emphasize certitude, sometimes making sweeping, dogmatic, or categorical statements. A negotiator might declare firmly that something is absolutely non-negotiable or that a suggested resolution is the "final" one. Be skeptical of such declarations, at least at first, since they may simply reflect stress.

Nevertheless, recognize as well that a skillful negotiator has to be prepared, on occasion, to tell a counterpart "no." The meeting of minds that results in a negotiated resolution is rarely a perfect union. Some terms or resolutions that look quite attractive to one side will not meet the interests or negotiating parameters of the others. What one side wants may simply be incompatible with what their fellow negotiator needs.

Although the negotiation of complex problems frequently calls on skills of compromise, cooperation, and problem-solving, reaching a negotiated resolution also requires clear signals to be sent back and forth. Some things are impossible for a negotiator to deliver, and delineating for the other side just what cannot be done is often a vitally important aspect of closing a deal.

1. Summarizing the Ground Covered

As the parties move toward closure, it can be quite useful to take a few minutes to summarize the course of the talks to date. This helps the negotiators to pull together their thoughts and to articulate the progress that has already been made, while laying out what remains to be determined. In this way an overview can serve as a transition into the final phase of the negotiation.

The following issues might be raised at this stage.

- Where did we start, in our thinking and discussions, and where are we now?
- In light of the views and perspectives exchanged thus far, how might we now describe the contours of the problems or opportunities being negotiated?
- What have been the key challenges with which the parties have been grappling?
- How might interests on both sides be served by pushing forward to a final agreement?
- What particularly constructive ideas have been advanced that might find their way into an ultimate resolution?

Instead of a monologue on such matters, getting all present to participate in the summarizing process by adding their own thoughts can fill out such an overview in a collaborative manner.

2. Covering Blue Chip and Ancillary Issues

In closing a deal, negotiators might think in terms of the *primary*, or *blue chip*, *issues* at the heart of the negotiation as opposed to the ancillary issues, that is, the auxiliary, supplementary, or subsidiary points designed to make the agreement more durable, optimal, profitable, or wide-ranging. And, various issues may need to be dealt with especially carefully since they speak directly to the parties' most vital interests and may be considered to be potential *deal-breakers* by them. That is, the entire negotiated agreement may hinge on whether those particular points are resolved satisfactorily or not.

Skillful negotiators want to try to make very sure that any proposed agreement speaks to the primary issues in a manner the parties find fair, logical, and intelligent as well as beneficial. But, negotiators should also think carefully about how the deal might be enhanced beyond the most fundamental matters. Are there additional points that really ought to be raised and considered before any final deal is struck. Have the last small details been attended to? While apparently of lesser importance, these points may end up playing quite significant roles in determining just how successful the agreement is.

What qualifies as a blue chip and an ancillary issue will vary with circumstances and with the parties' particular goals. But, to illustrate, negotiators representing an author and a publisher might consider as primary issues the subject of the manuscript, the target number of words to be produced, its delivery date, the amount of royalties, and the expected date of publication. Ancillary issues might include provisions regarding advertising, future editions of the book, translations into different languages, or e-book sales.

Negotiators representing a supplier and a purchaser might take their blue chip issues to be price and terms of payment, the length of the deal, and when and how delivery will be made. Notable ancillary issues might involve who will bear the costs of insurance during the transfer of the items, how future disputes might best be resolved, and how the quality of the items will be assured over time.

If one side is buying a business from another, the blue chip issues might involve timing, price, and non-competition. That is, the purchaser is likely to want protection against the possibility of the seller going back into business and competing with the original company. The negotiators might find the most challenging issues to be how long the non-compete provision will last, and how exactly the business ought to be defined. The seller would be likely to want geographical limits spelled out as to where he or she could not compete, whereas the buyer might well be concerned about retaining employees. Ancillary points here might include what happens to inventory on hand at the time of the closing or whether the prior owner might agree to a part-time, short-term consulting contract to promote a smooth and profitable transition period.

3. Thinking through Problems and Opportunities

Good negotiating often involves concentrating attention, bearing down so that you, and others at the table, see more than the obvious. Doing this well tends to be an acquired skill. Over time, negotiators gain the knack for thinking carefully through potential problems and possible opportunities. They learn to turn over in their minds the different elements of a potential negotiated resolution. They analyze matters under discussion, searching for ambiguities that might be partially hidden from view. And, they look for various ways to improve a potential agreement, as it begins to come together.

A negotiator should thus step back and carefully examine a developing agreement from many different angles. Are the terms clear and crisp, or do some appear vague or convoluted? Does the proposal cover all the central matters on which the parties can agree, or is it marred by gaps? Interest-based strategists counsel that negotiators aim for an agreement that is sufficient, realistic, and operational. Testing the provisions of a potential agreement on these grounds takes time and careful thought.

In working away on these different dimensions of a complex deal, negotiators often need to call on creativity but also skepticism. To create a proposal with a real chance of being accepted, one must often be quite imaginative. Fresh, interesting ideas may be needed to gain everyone's agreement and to approach the very best resolution theoretically possible under the circumstances. At the same time, however, negotiators should also be prudent and skeptical, to make sure that what is being proposed is realistic and will stand the tests of time.

a. Contingencies

One aspect of effective negotiating during the closing phase involves concentrating attention on *contingencies* that might arise, that is, things that might just occur whether through chance, accident, or design. As skillful negotiators turn problems over in their minds, probing them for hidden difficulties or opportunities, they think through possible contingencies.

- What if x happens?
- What if y doesn't happen?
- What consequences would those developments have for the agreement?
- If we don't take into account contingency z, might we be solving a short-term problem at the risk of creating long-term trouble?

Once possible contingencies are identified, the negotiators must consider whether or how the agreement should speak to them. If the agreement is silent about particular contingencies, what might occur if this or that one arose?

However, if one goal is to address important contingencies, another is to avoid drafting an unwieldy and cumbersome agreement. One should not necessarily aim to spell out what ought to happen if a great slew of conceivable events either happen or, perhaps, fail to occur. "Even encyclopedic contracts," it has been pointed out, "do not allow for every exigency in human affairs, as many words are capable of multiple interpretations."[10] The wisest course of action may be to leave alone some contingencies as too unlikely or perhaps too difficult or controversial to take up in the agreement. Here, part of the wisdom that expert negotiators bring to the table is the ability to prioritize intelligently, to make rational judgments about what ought and ought not be addressed in the agreement.

Box 8.1 — Questions to Consider in the Closing Phase

In the closing phase negotiators should ask themselves questions like these.

- Have all points necessary for a lasting agreement been raised?

- if we are overlooking something that might turn out to be vitally important, what is it likely to be?

- if some aspect of the deal, as presently constituted, were to turn into a disaster, what would it be likely to be, and what might we do now to prevent it from happening?

- if it turned out that our side had been tricked or otherwise taken advantage of in this agreement, what aspect of the proposed deal would likely be at fault? How might we avoid such problems?

---

4. Emphasizing Their Contributions When Possible

Since people often bridle at having solutions imposed on them, even sensible ones, the aim of the interest-based negotiator is to have both sides participate in defining the nature and the contours of the problem or opportunity and then in creating a mutually beneficial resolution together. Consequently, in trying to close a deal, a negotiator is well-advised to emphasize the other side's contributions, ideas, and perspectives, whenever that can be done consonant with the other dictates of a strategy.

This is particularly important since people's feelings about a possible resolution are often influenced by which side places it on the table. It is not uncommon for negotiators to de-value suggestions made by their counterparts, perhaps because they are assumed to be self-serving. On the assumption that the other side must be trying to put one over, an overly cautious, fearful, or competitive negotiator might suspect most anything a counterpart proposes, whether an option, concession, or way to proceed.

One scholar pointed out, "When one side unilaterally offers a concession that it believes the other side should value and the other side reacts by de-valuing the offer, this can obviously make resolution difficult."[11] This psychological phenomenon, known as *reactive devaluation*, may be diminished in weight or even eliminated if the proposal relies to a significant extent on points made by the other side in the course of the negotiation.[12]

C. Formulating a Proposal

During the closing phase a negotiator looks to formulate and present to others a *proposal* in hopes that this will become the basis for the final agreement between the parties. A proposal is a potential resolution that one or more negotiators offer to counterparts and stand behind: that is, they are announcing terms to which they would agree, and they wonder if others would agree to them as well?

Box 8.2 — When Are You Ready to Close a Deal?

When do you move from talking through what may be a host of possibilities to laying an actual proposal on the table that you would agree to and that you hope the other side will find worthwhile as well? In resolving a complex problem via an interest-based approach, you will be ready to try to close the deal if you have taken the following steps.

- You have drawn out your counterparts so that you understand, in detail, their perspectives on the most important issues being negotiated, and vice versa.

- You have thoroughly explored interests, explaining various of your own core concerns and motivations and demonstrating through active-listening techniques that you grasp the other side's.

- You have worked with the other party to align interests in a mutually beneficial way, calling on useful objective criteria, brainstorming creative options, while overcoming any impasses that might have arisen.

- You feel ready to move forward toward a possible agreement, perhaps because further discussion promises dramatically diminished returns or because a deadline or other circumstance means that a final decision must now be made either to agree or walk away from the potential deal.

The culminating effort, then, is to bring together the pieces of a possible deal, one that aims to benefit both sides sufficiently that they will agree to it. Sometimes that potential resolution is devised jointly. More often, one side places a proposal before its counterparts, who must then decide whether to accept, reject, amend, or counter it.

In this final stage of a negotiation simply creating a proposal to set before the other side is usually not so difficult. One can readily imagine some resolution that looks very attractive to *us* but that our fellow negotiators will likely reject out of hand. At the same time, once we really understand the other side's key interests and perspectives, making a proposal that *they* will gladly accept is also fairly easy done, so long as we do not concern ourselves much with just how enthusiastically *we* would react to such a resolution.

What requires real thought and skill is to develop a comprehensive proposal to which the other side will want to agree, but that still provides us with a very good deal. It will serve our important interests well, but our counterparts will be drawn to it, too. They will find this proposed agreement serves their interests as well as ours. In this regard Roger Fisher often spoke of negotiators creating "an elegant solution." "The more complex the problem," he wrote, "the more influential an elegant answer."[13]

1. A "Yesable" Proposition

To assist negotiators in closing deals, the interest-based negotiation approach advances the concept of a *yesable proposition*.[14] That is, during this concluding stage a negotiator ought to try to create a proposal that is sufficiently clear and comprehensive that the other side could simply say "yes," and the deal would be done.

Agreeing to the proposition should serve the interests of both parties better than saying "no" would.[15] And, "yes" should be a sufficient, realistic, and operational answer. Presenting such a proposal presses a definitive decision on your counterpart: he or she must weigh the pros and cons and choose what to do about it.

The leading proponent of advancing yesable propositions, Roger Fisher, further explained: "We are more likely both to know what we want and to get it if we try to write out the proposed decision with such clarity that it is in a form to which the single word 'yes' would be an effective answer." He went on to note: "The more mechanically easy it is to make that decision—the more yesable the proposition with which we confront them—the more likely they are to make it."[16]

Quite unlike brainstorming, where ideas are being generated without anyone being committed to them, here you inform your fellow negotiator of what you would be prepared to do to reach an agreement. You have made the transition from discussing a variety of possibilities to advancing a concrete proposal. Of course, by doing this, you necessarily sacrifice something: "To submit one yesable proposition may be effectively to forfeit the opportunity to ask for more favorable terms."[17]

Note, too, that when interest-based negotiation theorists counsel designing a yesable proposition, they do not mean to suggest that the negotiation necessarily ends with one side advancing such a proposition and the other, accepting or rejecting it. The talks could be concluded that way, or there might very well be additional discussion as this term or that one is amended, scrapped, added, or tinkered with. By formulating a yesable proposition, you press forward the process of closing the deal.

2. Have the Offer Speak to Your Counterpart

For a given offer to qualify as a yesable proposition, there must be some fair chance that the other side will respond positively to it. Consequently, as you formulate a proposal, it is critically important to bear in mind not only the objectives you want to achieve, but the other side's perspectives on the different issues. What might it be possible for your fellow negotiator to decide to do, and how attractive would that decision appear to them?

The person advancing the yesable proposition needs to make the case that this proposal would satisfy well key interests that the other side discussed in the earlier phases of the talks. Indeed, one should emphasize the ways in which the terms speak to your counterpart's core interests. If your fellow negotiator has voiced special concern with certain issues, look to illustrate how the proposal is designed to meet their concerns.

Be sure to highlight as well all those ideas in the proposal that the other side raised or helped to develop. A focus on your *joint* thinking and your *joint* ideas can be disarming and persuasive. And, see if there are ways to minimize the disadvantages or to help the other side to save face. For example, a labor leader, politician, or diplomat may need to appear to his or her constituents as having "squeezed an important concession" from the other side or risk being dismissed by constituents "as weak and ineffective leaders."[18] Consequently, the phrasing of some provisions, the precise words used, may be quite significant.

In trying to convince another of the very positive attributes of your yesable proposition, you should consider presenting, first, those provisions that the other party or parties are most likely to look upon favorably. Too often, negotiators load the front-end of their proposal with various items that the other side is not going to be happy with or, at least, will have to swallow hard to accept.

That this is poor salesmanship may be illustrated with a simple example. How many marriage proposals would be accepted if they were phrased in terms like these?

> About this marriage idea, you have to understand that my finances are shaky. You also need to know that I may very well need guaranteed time to myself each month. Oh, and I do want my own bank account, as I aim to keep our finances separate. If you're not already

aware, my mother is a control freak, and my father is impossible to talk to. And, don't even consider a conversation with me before my first cup of coffee in the morning. Also, while I would like to get married, frankly, I'm quite worried about what will happen to the assets we bring into the marriage if things don't work out.

My point is that a "yesable proposition," like a marriage proposal, usually ought to start by emphasizing the points that will attract the other side. Other issues may well have to be raised, including some matters that a fellow negotiator will be unenthusiastic about. It is usually better, however, to lead with the positive.

In projecting what will entice the other side and what will be viewed as problematic, one might consider what a critic within your counterpart's camp might say against your proposal, and how might that criticism best be answered. This exercise can flush out interests that need to be attended to. Note, too, that the rationales you offer in presenting a yesable proposition might well form the basis for the future discussions of your fellow negotiators with their own superiors, colleagues, or constituents.

In short, a negotiator formulating a persuasive yesable proposition needs to devote thought to possible reasons the other side might reject different terms. Then, he or she needs to determine if those problems could be accounted for and the proposal buttressed without weakening it appreciably or unduly from his or her own perspective.[19] For all these reasons, a yesable proposition should be quite carefully crafted.

3. Make the Offer Credible

An important part of making a yesable proposition attractive is ensuring that it is credible. Do you mean what you say? Will the proposed actions really happen? Realize that while we usually take for granted that our side will actually do whatever we propose doing, the other side may harbor real doubts as to whether we will carry through with our commitments. One way to enhance the credibility of an offer is to make it as specific and precise as possible, while avoiding exaggerated claims. In some situations a detailed plan will help, a clear road map for the parties to follow.

In this regard note that it may be more economical to increase the credibility of an offer than to make it more generous. Roger Fisher suggested that we imagine we are prepared to provide a $100 check but the seller fears it may bounce. He wrote, "One way to try to influence the seller in such a case is to increase the amount of the check until he is persuaded to take the chance. A far less costly way ... is to improve the credibility of the check, by establishing our good credit, by getting the check certified by a bank, by putting money in escrow, or by other such device."[20]

4. Explain Your Reasoning

Finally, when clear rationales exist for elements in the yesable proposition, it may be persuasive to spell these out as you lay out the proposal. For example, some years ago, in organizing a bid to buy a large farm, I opted not simply to put a number on the table as a counter-offer to the family's listed purchase price, but to lay out for the seller in a letter the rationale for how the potential buyers had reached the amount being offered. The different family members could read and assess the way that the price in the counter-offer had been reached.

- To what use was the farm going to be put?
- What values were ascribed to the timberland and the farmland, and on the basis of what recent comparable sales in the county?
- How were the barn and other outbuildings valued, and on what basis?
- What amount did the old farmhouse seem worth?
- What points in the attached appraisal of the property seemed especially relevant to the buyers?
- Who did the home inspection, and what did it reveal about needed repairs?
- How did the numbers add up, and why exactly did the potential buyers feel the counter-offer reasonable in light of each of these factors?

Within 48 hours the sellers had accepted the counter-offer, and members of the family later declared that the letter of explanation had been a central factor in their deliberations.

D. Making Commitments

One reason that the closing phase of a negotiation tends to be its most serious is that the parties are now contemplating making real commitments to one another. They are pledging to do certain things, and, perhaps, to refrain from doing other things.

As they prepare to close a deal, negotiators naturally become increasingly focused on precisely what the agreement means for their side. Making hard-and-fast commitments focuses attention on what exactly the parties are agreeing to do. Here, the positive working relations developed earlier in the negotiation may be challenged by what is often the less cooperative tone of the closing phase. And, as the parties consider the array of formal commitments they are now poised to make, either side may be influenced by last-minute doubts, sometimes termed *buyer's remorse.*

Tensions may be raised by discussions of whether or to what extent commitments—formal or informal, binding or tentative—have already been made in the course of the talks. Here, communication between the negotiators may have been murky, and the memories and assumptions of the different sides may not match each other.

Such disputes can be super-charged by the perception that an individual's credibility as a negotiator is tied to the commitments that he or she chooses to make and to the ultimate track record in carrying through with them. Gaining a reputation for not keeping your promises can affect future negotiations with that party and perhaps with others as well.

In this regard skillful negotiators guard against what might be called *casual commitment.*[21] That is, without considering the situation carefully enough, a negotiator vows to do something that he or she ultimately regrets and, thus, perhaps, fails to honor and follow through. In many cases substantial costs promise to arise, costs that should have been, but never were, fully anticipated. Casual commitments sometimes occur when a negotiator tries to be agreeable. At other times he or she is pressed by a counterpart or by exigencies of time to move more quickly than is comfortable.

1. Guarding against Over-Commitments

Just as they avoid casual commitments, good negotiators also perceive the dangers in *over-commitment.* You are over-committed when you have told the other side that you will do something which you then end up not being willing or able to do. Perhaps other commitments interfere, or the burdens of carrying through with your promise come to appear too high.

One context in which these problems frequently arise is when an agent exceeds his or her authority or mistakenly believes that it will be possible to gain needed approval by others. A commitment might then be undercut by the unwillingness of those the negotiator represents to carry it out.

A negotiator wants the commitments made in an agreement to be seen as valuable and rock solid—something that a fellow negotiator can wholly rely upon, not something questionable, to be doubted or mistrusted. Over-committing may seriously damage the relationship between the parties, and perhaps even ruin their negotiated agreement. And, particularly egregious over-commitment or multiple instances of it may grievously harm a negotiator's reputation as one who is reliable and trustworthy, whose word can be accepted as credible.

In the closing stage a seasoned negotiator thus considers, "Are there certain terms that the other side would like to put into this agreement to which I ought not agree? Would others I answer to object? If I were to do what they would like, would I be over-committing our side of the negotiation?"

2. Ensuring That Commitments Are Honored

Negotiators expect that implementation will follow closely the terms of the deal they are hammering out. This raises the question for them: "How do we draft the agreement so as to maximize the chances that it will in fact be implemented as we now envision?" That ultimate operational question ought to be in the minds of both parties throughout the closing phase of a negotiation.

Negotiators rely on various devices to help to ensure that the commitments made in an agreement are, in fact, honored. Putting the deal into written form and drafting provisions that can be enforced in court are important steps. So, too, is carefully avoiding walking "close to the line on any of the legal rules, such as duress, deceit, vague terminology or illegality," which could provide a loophole that a party might take advantage of to shake free from a prior commitment.[22]

Sometimes negotiators arrange matters so that those who negotiated the deal have an ongoing role in its implementation. Meetings can be planned ahead of time to review progress made in putting the agreement into action.[23] Since proper implementation often requires information to flow back and forth readily, the negotiators may give thought to how to ensure that this happens regularly and productively.[24] Or, the agreement may be structured so that the parties incur costs if they do not comply with the agreement's terms.

In other cases negotiators look to bring about proper implementation of an agreement by taking advantage of useful relationships. To ensure that the deal is carried out as planned, negotiators can draw on the working relations developed with their counterpart. Beyond this, various individuals may be in a position to influence a party not to renege on a commitment. Allies, friends, associates, or business partners could "exert pressure on the wavering party to 'honor his/her commitments.'"[25]

E. The Decision to Accept or Reject a Proposal

To bring the different sides to agree to a particular negotiated resolution, ordinarily, each must believe that a net gain is to be derived from the deal. The balance of pros and cons must suggest that their over-all interests will be served by agreeing, rather than *walking away* from the deal.

1. Appraising a Possible Deal

Virtually all complex negotiations have some distributional angle, and any competent negotiator will balk at accepting an agreement that is one-sided in their counterpart's favor. Hence, a deal that one party sees as perfect, spotless, and faultless is exceedingly rare, and agreements of complex disputes and opportunities are not often clean sweeps. Seldom do we see a deal that is just overwhelmingly favorable to one party, since in those circumstances the other party would be likely to see itself as disadvantaged, at least in certain particulars, and hence would reject the proffered terms.

Consequently, trying to reach absolutely perfect provisions too often becomes a costly quest for the unattainable. Roger Fisher used to say that, if you aim to obtain the best conceivable agreement, you will almost invariably be left disillusioned since here or there in the final agreement one almost always could have received a bit more money or a term phrased slightly more favorably.

But, if a negotiator does not look to achieve the ideal outcome in that sense, what criteria might help to determine when to come to an agreement and when to walk away? Here, the following brief equation may be of use: if a proposed agreement serves key interests well, if an impartial observer would consider it a fair deal, and if it approaches the best that can be done in this situation, it is probably well worth signing.

For a more detailed analysis, to help to determine whether to accept, reject, or amend a proposal, the parties might consider the following five factors.

a. The Future Outlook

All agreements are somehow designed to alter the future conduct of the parties. To decide whether or not to sign on to a potential deal, negotiators should first look ahead and ask themselves:

- If we fail to agree, what is going to happen next?
- Does the proposal exceed our best alternative to a negotiated agreement (BATNA)?

In the closing phase a negotiator should again take stock of walk-away options, focusing attention on the best of them, so that it can be compared to the proposal now on the table. If we feel that we can serve our interests substantially better by coming to a different deal with another party, the offer should be rejected.

More typically, however, one must weigh a concrete proposal offering a definite set of advantages and disadvantages with a BATNA of which particular aspects are shrouded in uncertainty. The question "does the proposal exceed our BATNA?" may be difficult to answer. Nevertheless, a negotiator does need to come to a carefully considered judgment about it.

On occasion, a difficult challenge for negotiators is to go ahead and accept an agreement that is clearly better than their BATNA but remains less-than-ideal and falls well short of their side's aspirations. It can take real composure to make a reasoned judgment that a particular proposal is worth accepting even despite its flaws.

b. The Distribution of Pros and Cons

A negotiator's typical reaction to a proposed agreement in a complex situation is mixed. Our enthusiasm for the things we might gain is tempered by our more sober reflections about what we will have to do to get them. In deciding whether to close a deal, you should realize full well that you are often going to need to give something to get something.

To ensure that the benefits of the proposed deal outweigh the drawbacks, a negotiator should ask the following questions.

- What do you want from this negotiation?
- How badly do you want it?
- How much are you willing to give up in order to get what you want?
- What benefits might flow to us from the proposal being considered?
- What drawbacks might such an agreement entail?
- Does the proposal sufficiently address the key issues and serve the core interests that have been discussed?

The more carefully you have thought through your priorities with respect to goals and interests, the easier it is to make intelligent decisions about whether it is worthwhile to yield one item in order to get something else. Here, in the first instance a negotiator aims to have his or her own side's interests well-satisfied. As for the other side's interests, these must be met well enough that they will agree and then have sufficient incentive to carry out the agreement.

c. The Nature of the Commitments

As for the terms of the deal, each party should be aware of precisely what it is being called on to do, and what its counterparts are supposed to be doing as well. Are these realistic? In this regard recall that having solid arguments that a deal is fundamentally fair, perhaps in light of how it measures up to objective or neutral standards, may be quite significant in convincing constituents that a proposed settlement is worth accepting.[26]

Negotiators should thus consider, skeptically, whether the agreement really can be carried out, as it is currently drafted.

- What does each party commit to do, and are these commitments clear, fair, and realistic?
- How easily can the provisions of the agreement be put into operation?
- Would the agreement be stronger if it encompassed more situations or was elaborated with more details?
- Are we relying on others to carry out aspects of the deal, and do they have the motivation, the resources, and the frame of mind needed to carry through with these plans?

In sum, is the agreement "easy to implement, with responsibilities clearly assigned, time frames defined, and visible milestones of progress staked out — as well as durable, capable of withstanding differences in assumptions and unforeseen events?"[27]

d. Implementation

For an agreement to be successful, its terms must be carried out. Hence, in scrutinizing a possible deal, one ought to give thought to its proper implementation. Here a negotiator might ask the following.

- How long is the proposed agreement due to last?
- What exactly are the incentives for each side to carry through with what it has pledged to do? Could those incentives be strengthened?
- What might we commit to do to try to ensure that the agreement endures as long as we hope that it will?
- When are the different actions to be taken? Does the agreement go too far too fast?
- How confident are we that this agreement will be carried out as envisioned?
- Are we pledging to do things that are unlikely to happen? Does the deal seem rugged and durable, or are aspects precarious, ephemeral, or doubtful?
- If costs or profits are associated with implementation, are they divided in a way that serves our interests and is sufficiently equitable that the agreement is unlikely to fall apart over time?
- Are there third parties who might work to sabotage or block implementation of the agreement or foment future discord among the parties unless thought is given to satisfying some of their interests as well?

e. Expanding the Pie

It is not unusual when the parties reach a meeting of the minds, for the initial deal to be a *sub-optimal agreement*: that is, one that could be better from the perspective of at least one party without being made worse from the perspective of another. This is a problem, not simply for the party whose interests are not being served as well as they might be, but for both sides since the more contented or enthused the parties are, the more likely they are to carry out the agreement effectively and conscientiously throughout the agreed-upon term.

Frequently, an agreement can be improved upon for both sides in a bilateral negotiation or for multiple parties in a group negotiation without detracting from its attractiveness for any other party. In this regard negotiators sometimes refer to a *Pareto optimal frontier*. Named after Vilfredo Damask Pareto, the Italian economist who popularized the idea in the early twentieth century, this describes the line on a graph that illustrates that no joint gains are left and any improvement in the outcome for one side would entail a decrease in the benefits to another side.[28]

To focus attention on whether a proposed agreement could be readily improved upon, negotiators might ask the following.

- Does the proposal appear to be close to an optimal outcome?
- Would there be some way to make all of us better off?
- Would there be a way to make the agreement fairer in the eyes of both parties or a neutral observer?
- Could we improve the deal for one side without making another worse off?
- Because we value things differently, could we make some mutually advantageous tradeoff?

Note, however, that at some point a law of diminishing returns may intercede. That is, the costs of pursuing a bit better agreement may outweigh the benefits of hammering one out.

2. Deciding to Turn Down a Potential Deal

Especially after spending long and perhaps grueling periods preparing and then negotiating, both sides tend to want to conclude the process by reaching an agreement. Indeed, some negotiators get swept away with the effort to find attractive joint gains. A word of caution is thus in order. Negotiators should not allow their instincts to collaborate to cloud their better judgment. A negotiator should aim to communicate effectively so as to leave the negotiating table confident that he or she attained the wisest possible outcome under the circumstances.

The cardinal point is that, sometimes, deciding not to agree may be the most sensible route to take. The costs of a proposed agreement may overshadow its benefits, or the risks of a potential deal may be intolerable. A negotiator may become convinced that the most sensible course of action is to pursue his or her BATNA.

If one views negotiation in terms of having an intelligent conversation about a shared problem or opportunity, discussions that end in no deal, while perhaps disappointing, should not be taken as abject failures. Instead, they stand as considered decisions not to move forward together under the present circumstances. The manner in which the talks have been carried out will often then determine whether the decision to walk away occurs amicably or not and whether the parties are motivated to renew negotiations on this or some other subject in the future.

3. Opting to Postpone a Final Resolution

A negotiation session need not end in a final deal even if the parties are enthusiastic about eventually reaching an agreement with each other. As the negotiators attempt to assemble the pieces of a potential agreement, they ought to have in mind the question: "Would we benefit by having more information before we try to agree on a final resolution?" If key pieces of information are missing, a competent negotiator ought to consider carefully whether agreeing would be premature.

If a more realistic, operational, and optimal agreement could very well be achieved in the near future, postponing a final decision might be the most sensible course of action. The best approach might be to sketch out the areas of tentative agreement and those where significant issues remain, and then determine who is going to get missing information that might make for a better and more complete future deal.

When the parties opt to postpone a final resolution, it remains to decide when to meet again to see if the deal can be finalized and closed and to determine who will do what in the interim. When a negotiation is suspended in this way, the subsidiary issues that ought to be considered include the following.

- Which of the parties is going to get the missing information?
- Should the other party have an opportunity to verify it?
- How ought the processes of information gathering and verification work?

Another valid concern may be that, while the negotiators "fill in the blanks" the situation will deteriorate, rather than stay frozen over time. This raises the question: is there anything that might be done to keep the negotiating challenges from becoming more difficult to resolve when the parties meet again?

F. Drafting an Effective Agreement

Although simple deals sometimes remain oral agreements, in the vast majority of the more complex scenarios with which we are centrally concerned any agreement is committed to paper. Note, too, that with respect to matters involving property, state laws include some version of the common law Statute of Frauds that mandated that all land contracts for sale or lease of more than a year in duration must be in writing to keep them from being voidable.

Putting the agreement the parties have reached in their negotiation into writing is a critically important aspect of the closing phase since deals are more likely to be properly implemented if written out. It can also be a difficult one. Even terms that seemed relatively simple when the parties talked about them can become much more complicated when the negotiators turn to drafting them. The commitments being made on one or the other or both sides are more starkly apparent when written out. Items readily agreed to when first discussed can later bring on much more searching and contentious interactions.

When a team is negotiating on behalf of an organization, it may be especially useful for each side to draw on different talents and expertise as provisions are drafted. Look to elicit comments from your colleagues, checking particular points with them and re-confirming technical matters with those who have special experience or expertise.

1. Drafting Mechanics

As for the mechanics of drafting, on some occasions negotiators together write the terms of at least the most important provisions of their agreement. Alternatively, one negotiator will turn the oral agreement into an initial draft, which the other side will then review and critically analyze. Sometimes multiple drafts are created, and a duel of drafts can ensue, with the negotiators working to reconcile provisions worded differently.

The negotiator who writes the first draft can craft provisions in ways that suit his or her side. The drafter might omit certain items and spell out others in great detail. He or she might opt for clear and precise language with respect to one provision and much more ambiguous phrasing with respect to another. And, the drafter has considerable control over how quickly (or slowly) the first draft is produced.

Any experienced counterpart, however, is likely to be well aware of these advantages. The recipient of the first draft will likely be on guard to prevent the agreement from being one-sided or the drafters from introducing new issues into the text. (Box 8.3 explores certain of the advantages of drafting an agreement as well as the expected protocol for working with a counterpart on it.)

Box 8.3 — Who Drafts the Agreement

In advising negotiators to volunteer to be the one who drafts the agreement, two lawyers observed, "Just as a diner who seriously wants to pick up a check will usually end up paying, a lawyer who insists on drafting an agreement will usually prevail. Lawyers are not exceptional in preferring to avoid unnecessary work, particularly the tedious work of drafting documents." They went on to explain, "If you draft the document, the other side should be given an opportunity to correct it and to discuss any language not faithfully incorporating the agreement that has been reached. But many lawyers are not thorough editors, so the opportunity to write the first draft becomes the power to choose critically important language. If an adversary writes the first draft, you should be prepared to go over it line by line, and, if necessary, to rewrite every word." Michael Meltsner & Philip Scrag, *Negotiating Tactics for Legal Services Lawyers*, in WHAT'S FAIR 211 (Carrie Menkel-Meadow & Michael Wheeler eds., 2004).

---

2. Starting with a Template or Framework Agreement

In the course of constructing a complex agreement, negotiators sometimes draw up and work on and off of a skeletal draft of what they hope will eventually turn into the final document. The template might start with at least the headings for key provisions. For example, those for a joint venture might include "finance, location, production, distribution, organization, management, accounting and control, conflict resolution, employment policy, review of operations, and contingency planning, as well as others depending on the specific context."[29]

At first, the template will have many blank areas, representing issues that need to be worked out. During the negotiation points are filled in, with the negotiators inserting key words or phrases. Bits and pieces of language might be added that can be further refined when an actual rough draft is formulated. In this way each side gets the opportunity during the talks to sharpen and improve the document. Note that this approach requires one or more negotiators to act as a scribe, ideally someone "good at reducing complex statements to a pithy essence that can be jotted down for all to see," while continually "check-ing his understanding against the contributor's meanings."[30]

Creating a template and working on it together can be a crucially important dimension of a negotiation: "Working on a draft helps to keep the discussions focused, tends to surface important issues that might otherwise be overlooked, and gives a sense of progress. Drafting as you go also provides a record of dis-cussion, reducing the chance of later misunderstandings."[31] Using a template can also prevent some unnecessary jockeying over drafts of an agreement since some of the phrasing has already been hammered out.

3. Content: Determining the Proper Provisions

In the course of a negotiation of any complexity, the parties are likely to have mentioned or alluded to many different points. One's discussions with the other side may be envisioned as "'two' negotiations: the verbal negotia-tions and the negotiations over what words to choose to accurately reflect the intentions of the parties. The *written* words are what count to a judge, arbi-trator or implementer of the deal."[32]

During the drafting process the negotiators will be faced with the issues of how many of the details of their prior discussions should be included in the writ-ten agreement and which of the points discussed should become the subject of provisions. They may have had quite different views on whether certain fore-seeable events might just occur or are very unlikely to do so. With respect to certain issues, assurances of some kind may have been made. The best word-ing for particular terms may have been come up repeatedly, with amendments, additions, and subtractions proposed, but no clear meeting of the minds.

Turning the tangled discussions into clear, coherent, and mutually agreeable provisions usually turns out to be easy with respect to some matters, about which consensus emerges without too much difficulty, but much more chal-lenging with respect to other more contentious issues. It is important to real-ize here that negotiators (and courts later considering agreements) often take the act of placing a negotiated deal into written form as superseding the ear-lier discussions. Putting something in writing underscores the negotiator's in-tent to make it legally enforceable. The points that are written out then gain stature as those of cardinal importance, and those overlooked in the written agreement are assumed to be of little significance.

In Chapter 9 we will consider cultural differences in negotiation. For now, note that this is an approach to agreements found in many western countries, but other cultures may view this subject in a markedly different fashion. Many Japanese negotiators, for instance, favor agreements that, to a western eye, might appear simple and spare, highlighting broad principles but leaving details to be worked out in the future. In this tradition what was said during the negotiation may be of great weight, even if not reflected in the final document.

4. Aiming for a Clear and Coherent Agreement

The wording of an agreement should also be reviewed quite carefully and rigorously edited to circumvent potential problems. The overall structure is worthy of thought as well: the order of the provisions and the way they interrelate should be logically constructed. In a tight, coherent agreement the pieces fit together nicely.

One advantage to carefully drafting a detailed agreement is that putting provisions into words to which everyone agrees often forces more precise thought about the commitments on each side, what exactly the agreement is aiming to accomplish and how it is to be carried out.[33] On occasion, negotiators must cloak irreconcilable disagreement in ambiguous phrasing, but in general one looks to draw up crystal-clear provisions that leave no doubt as to what is expected.

As the negotiators review a written draft, they might focus on the following questions.

- Does the agreement spell out exactly what is expected of the parties, or is it vague?
- Are the key points covered well, including all necessary details?
- Is there unfortunate jargon or redundant or repetitive phrases that might be eliminated?

5. Illustrative Provisions

a. A Dispute-Resolution Clause

Once reached, an agreement must still be implemented, with the parties honoring the commitments they have made. An array of potential problems—some generic and some specific to a particular agreement—could very well arise. Consequently, negotiators ought to take time to peer into the future and try to anticipate problems that might arise. The next task is to consider how the agreement ought to be drafted to maximize the prospects for it being properly carried out.

When the parties contemplate ongoing interactions, incorporating a *dispute-resolution provision* is advisable. This directs the parties as to how to handle any conflicts that might arise under the terms of the agreement. For instance, the parties might be directed to undertake *mediation* or *arbitration* should negotiations fail to resolve their disputes. In mediation a dispute is referred to a neutral third party who attempts to assist the parties in resolving it by helping them to create a mutually agreeable resolution. Arbitration differs in that here a dispute is referred to an impartial third person, chosen by the parties to the dispute, who agree in advance to abide by the arbitrator's award. That award is issued after a hearing at which both sides have an opportunity to present arguments and evidence. The dispute-resolution clause might spell out various logistics involved in the arbitration or mediation process such as to what organizations the parties are to turn to select the mediator or arbitrator.

The signal point here is that a neutral third party is introduced to manage serious differences that arise in implementation. Once problems have cropped up, perhaps with accompanying tension or mistrust, figuring out how best to resolve disputes can be complicated and can sour or embitter relations. The better approach is to capitalize on the positive feelings as a deal is being finalized and negotiate a dispute-resolution process before particular problems arise.

Whatever the details of the system, it ought to provide, first, for multiple opportunities for the parties to meet and try to talk out their differences. If those efforts fail, then a fair and efficient route to arrive at a final, binding outcome should be in order. Placing a clause in the agreement stating, for example, that failure to reach the negotiated agreement of a dispute will lead to binding arbitration provides a real incentive for the parties to work out their disagreements, so as to avoid losing control of the process.[34]

b. Allocating Risks

As the agreement is being carried out, matters may also go off-track if events assumed by the negotiators do not occur as expected. The underlying problem may be cataclysmic or quite mundane, but it upsets the expectations of the parties.

Sometimes events of public significance intervene. The economy could be plunged into a recession, a flood or fire might occur, or environmental or other laws or regulations could change dramatically. Alternatively, particular problems might arise with respect to the private transaction at issue. For example, the condition or longevity of a product might not meet the buyer's expectations. A piece of property might contain some hidden hazard or turn out to be contaminated. In all such cases what one or both of the parties expected to occur is not happening, engendering tension or conflict. In crafting an agreement, the parties may want to consider various such risks and allocate between the parties responsibility for dealing with their effects. Various devices exist to place responsibility on one side or the other or both.

Where a party is concerned about the potential consequences of a natural disaster for performance under the terms of the agreement—floods, tsunamis, hurricanes, typhoons, and alike—a negotiator might consider a *force majeure* clause. This excuses a party for failing to perform its obligations for causes that are beyond its control and could not have been avoided even if the party had exercised due care.

In other circumstances one party might be willing to make a **guarantee**, that is, a formal, usually written, assurance about something that concerns its counterpart. Guarantees are designed to provide protection of some kind. They can take the form of an assurance that a product will be of a specified quality or will perform satisfactorily for some given period. In a money-back guarantee, if the assurance turns out to be false, the buyer receives back the purchase price in exchange for the defective product.

Sometimes, a party provides another with a **warranty**, that is, an assurance that some fact is correct or true. For instance, a seller might warrant that he or she holds good title to the article to be sold or that it will function correctly. If the warranted fact proves untrue, the party who made the promise covers any losses that might accrue as a consequence.

Some warranties are designed to adjust the terms of the agreement should problems arise after purchase. The seller might agree to compensate the buyer by replacing the product, repairing it, or providing a full or partial refund. Here, the precise wording of a warranty is often of great moment. A warranty that provides that a product will be replaced only for manufacturing defects is of limited usefulness if the defect could be the result of buyer misuse.[35] In some circumstances a provision might be drafted to help the parties to determine if a problem is indeed a manufacturing defect or a matter of misuse.

Risks are also allocated when a party issues a **covenant**, that is, a promise that something shall be done, or, occasionally, that a party shall refrain from doing something: "An affirmative covenant might require a board of directors to submit a plan for shareholder approval. A negative covenant might contain a promise not to pay dividends prior to closing."[36]

Covenants can be thought of as exit options: "statements which, if not satisfied, relieve a party of its obligation to complete the transaction." One source went on to note: "[C]ontracts can provide for customized remedies in the event of nonsatisfaction. This tailors the remedies the parties receive should some term or condition not be met and ensures that the deal can then go forward rather than derailing into litigation over damages."[37]

c. Particular International Considerations

Negotiators fashioning international deals may need to contend with political, social, or economic instability. A war or revolution might break out or an exchange rate could shift markedly in a country where one or both parties are to undertake different activities. Where some variety of unrest or substantial fluctuation is a real possibility, the parties might be concerned at what will happen to their agreement if, say, hostilities break out or a coup occurs, followed by substantial political changes? Sometimes a party hires a risk consultant to outline potential problems and the probability that they will arise. The parties then need to consider how their deal might be affected should particular events take place.

Parties to an international transaction need to focus attention as well on any differences between their respective legal and political systems. What taxes will have to be paid? Would the use of a tax haven be possible and advisable? How about dispute resolution? In the last resort will international commercial arbitration be used to reach a binding settlement?

The money that passes from one party to the other may be complicated when the countries use different currencies. A government might have currency-exchange controls that aim to regulate the passage of foreign and local currencies into and out of their country. Who is to be paid in which currency, and what is to be done about any currency fluctuations that arise during the term of the agreement? Could a third party, such as a bank, take on some of the risk of currencies changing in value? What would that cost, and how should the expenses be divided between the parties?

This leads to the broader point that the role of government in society can differ sharply from one country to the next. A foreign government may be deeply involved in economic activities that would be in private hands in many western societies. And, government officials may not be focused on maximizing profits so much as on public or partisan goals such as aiding employment statistics or gaining positive publicity for a particular political figure. A seasoned negotiator working in an international context will be alert to how such matters might affect the subject-matter of the agreement. Under some circumstances it might be possible to craft a provision in the agreement that speaks to a potential problem regarding possible government action or inaction.

The parties in an international negotiation must also focus some attention on the legal system under which the terms of the agreement will be interpreted. The major families of law—common law, civil law, socialist law, and Islamic law—differ in many respects. The negotiators may well want to hire local counsel to advise on such particular matters as the relevant labor codes and contract, corporate, tax, and environmental laws.

Since two or more courts may have jurisdiction over a dispute and two or more legal systems may have jurisdiction over a contract, choice-of-law issues can arise. Do the parties want to try to specify what laws will govern different aspects of the deal or how the terms of the agreement ought to be interpreted? These are just a sample of the considerations that negotiators should bear in mind as they construct an agreement in a complex international transaction.

G. Gaining Client or Constituent Approval

In virtually all complicated negotiations the negotiators must gain the consent of their clients or constituents before the resolution they have proposed becomes final and binding. Here, the ultimate commitment — the conclusive decision to approve or disapprove the negotiated deal — is not the negotiator's but lies in the hands of others, sometimes referred to as *ratifiers* or *closers*.

This reality ought to be taken into account as the negotiators interact, finalize the deal, draft its terms, and prepare to announce the resolution they have reached, usually privately at first but occasionally publicly. The negotiators will often need to have a final internal negotiation with those who sent them to the table to ensure that they fully understand the terms of the agreement and are prepared to approve and, perhaps, sign it.

The manner in which a potential agreement is ratified can vary markedly from one set of circumstances to another. The power structure of a business might be laid out such that the president, managing partner, chief executive officer, or board of directors has the authority to assent to, or reject, a deal. A union's rank-and-file typically has ratification powers; hence, a vote might have to be held before a labor agreement can be finalized. Under the U.S. Constitution a treaty must be approved by two-thirds of the Senate before the President can ratify the work of the negotiators.

The need to gain client or constituent approval can play into negotiation strategy. For example, negotiators ought to be aware of what have been called the *salami tactics* sometimes evident at the end of a negotiation. That is, one side tries to gain just a bit more, an additional concession or two, blaming the last-minute demand on its ratifiers, who must be kept content or, purportedly, there will be no deal. (This issue is discussed further in Chapter 10 on negotiation ethics.)

In short, then, the process of obtaining final assent occurs differently in diverse varieties of negotiation and from one client to another and sometimes one culture to another. Sometimes negotiators will have been in close touch with their clients as the terms of the agreement have been worked out. Here, when the negotiators shake hands on the deal, the resolution already reflects their constituents' views. On other occasions the most the negotiators can do is to reach a tentative agreement that each will take back to their clients to be approved or disapproved. In either case, securing client or constituent approval tends to be a weighty issue, hanging over the closing phase of a complex deal.

1. Sharing Credit and Saving Face

Prior chapters have touched on why a negotiator might want to be generous in sharing credit with fellow negotiators for ideas and proposals generated during brainstorming and other problem-solving efforts. The same is true in the closing phase as each side looks to gain assent to a deal that has been, or is being, negotiated. In short, the agreement may appear more palatable to constituents if their side is seen as having contributed in important ways to creating it.

When a party is trying to gain final approval of a potential resolution, it will naturally emphasize those aspects of the agreement that serve its interests. Experienced negotiators realize that in some circumstances the opposing side may exult in its gains, perhaps even publicly.

For example, when union negotiators bring a tentative agreement back to the full membership to be approved, one federal mediator observed, "Typically, the union crows about its big victory over management while management remains silent ... to assure some degree of face-saving for the union." He continued: "If after every deal, management publicly boasted that they had carried the day, the union members might believe them, reject the contract, and send their bargainers back to the table to extract more concessions from the company. By showing some restraint, the company allows the union to save face and secures a final agreement."[38]

2. Looking to the Future

This chapter has emphasized the central challenge negotiators face of creating an agreement that will actually be implemented in much the way envisioned when negotiated. Will the parties end up doing what the agreement called for? Will one party have to enforce its terms in the courts, or will the relationship, perhaps forged in the negotiations themselves, be strong enough to encourage proper implementation or to resolve difficult issues that arise?

Another aspect of looking to the future involves whether *to leave something on the table*. This phrase signifies granting your counterpart a final concession rather than trying to secure that item for your side. This issue is especially significant when parties expect to be negotiating with one another in the future on a series of other matters. Leaving something on the table can serve as a token of good will from one party to the other. Or, it might enable a fellow negotiator to save face. A negotiator can also request reciprocity in the future, reminding the other party in the next negotiation of that ultimate concession the last time they met.

In this regard Roger Fisher once recounted to me that a distinguished Japanese negotiator had told him that he very much approved of much of the counsel offered in *Getting to Yes*. However, one matter about which he strongly disagreed was the subtitle—*Negotiating Agreement Without Giving In*. The Japanese negotiator observed that in closing a deal his standard policy was to search actively for some last point on which to yield. He would purposefully leave something on the table for the other party to take so as to end the negotiation with the other side in his debt.

Although the second edition of *Getting to Yes* did not change the subtitle, Fisher and colleagues advised negotiators to be generous at the end:

> When you sense that you are finally close to an agreement, consider giving the other side something you know to be of value to them and still consistent with the basic logic of your proposal. Make clear that this is a final gesture; you do not want to raise expectations of further concessions. Such an improved offer can sometimes break through any last-minute doubts and clinch the deal.

They concluded: "You want the other side to leave the negotiation feeling satisfied and fairly treated. That feeling can pay off handsomely in the implementation of an agreement as well as in future negotiations."[39]

One final point. Since the manner in which matters are brought to a close can influence future relations, from time immemorial people have performed rituals of different sorts to underscore their commitment to an agreement.[40] The protocols differ in diverse cultures: some parties might simply shake hands; others might share a bottle of alcohol; still others might enjoy a meal or other closing ceremony. Speeches might be made, and certain agreements might be publicized in a press release or at a press conference. Think of all of these as ways not only to mark the occasion of an important agreement, but to encourage its eventual implementation along the lines the negotiations planned. A closing ceremony may have real tangible value for continuing relations.

Notes

1. Roger Fisher, *A Code of Negotiation Practices for Lawyers*, 1 NEGOTIATION J. 108 (1985).
2. LLOYD PAUL STRYKER, THE ART OF ADVOCACY 115 (1954).
3. The word *closing* is used in two different senses, one more formal than the other. In the informal sense negotiators close a deal when they put different terms together and ar-

rive at a resolution to which both can agree. In the other sense of the term, the closing is the ultimate meeting in which the parties come together to formalize their agreement usually by signing and exchanging legally binding documents. This chapter uses closing in the first sense of the word.

4. John H. Wade & Christopher Honeyman, *A Lasting Agreement*, in The Negotiator's Fieldbook 486 (Andrea Kupfer Schneider & Christopher Honeyman eds., 2006).

5. James C. Freund, Smart Negotiating 80 (1992).

6. I. William Zartman & Maureen Berman, The Practical Negotiator 188 (1982).

7. *Id.* at 196.

8. Freund, supra note 5, at 88.

9. Robert B. McKersie, *Agency in the Context of Labor Negotiations*, in Negotiating on Behalf of Others 192 (Robert H. Mnookin & Lawrence E. Susskind eds., 1999).

10. Wade & Honeyman, supra note 4, at 491.

11. Robert H. Mnookin, Why Negotiations Fail 22–23 (Stanford Center on Conflict and Negotiation Working Paper, 1995).

12. Lee Ross, *Reactive Devaluation in Negotiation and Conflict Resolution*, in Barriers to Conflict Resolution 27–42 (Kenneth J. Arrow et al. eds., 1995).

13. Roger Fisher, *Negotiating Power*, 27 Am. Behavioral Scientist 157 (1983).

14. Roger Fisher, International Conflict for Beginners 15–26 (1969), and Roger Fisher, Elizabeth Kopelman, & Andrea Kupfer Schneider, Beyond Machiavelli 96–98 (1994).

15. James K. Sebenius, *What Roger Fisher Got Profoundly Right*, 29 Negotiation J. 162 (2013).

16. Fisher, supra note 14, at 15, 56.

17. *Id.* at 17.

18. Alexander G. Nikolaev, International Negotiations 96 (2007).

19. Fisher, Kopelman, & Schneider, supra note 14, at 96.

20. Fisher, supra note 14, at 117.

21. Inis L. Claude, Jr., States and the Global System 54–67 (1988).

22. Wade & Honeyman, supra note 4, at 494.

23. Keith Lutz, *Negotiation Examples in Business: Putting Your Negotiated Agreement into Action*, Program on Negotiation, Harvard Law School, Jan. 19, 2016, http://www.pon.harvard.edu/daily/negotiation-skills-daily/we-have-a-deal-now-what-do-we-do-three-negotiation-tips-on-implementing-your-negotiated-agreement.

24. *The Deal is Done—Now What?*, Program on Negotiation, Harvard Law School, Oct. 8, 2013, http://www.pon.harvard.edu/daily/conflict-resolution/the-deal-is-done-now-what/.

25. Wade & Honeyman, supra note 4, at 494.

26. McKersie, supra note 9, at 190.

27. Roger Fisher & Danny Ertel, Getting Ready to Negotiate 105 (1995).

28. Howard Raiffa, The Art and Science of Negotiation 158–64 (1982).

29. Howard Raiffa, Negotiation Analysis 207 (2002).

30. *Id.* at 401.

31. Roger Fisher, William Ury, & Bruce Patton, Getting To Yes 172 (2d ed. 1991).

32. Thomas R. Colosi, On and Off the Record 57 (1993).

33. Fisher, supra note 14, at 78.

34. Dean G. Pruitt, *Strategy in Negotiation*, in International Negotiation 85 (Victor A. Kremenyuk ed., 1991).

35. Peter C. Cramton & J. Gregory Dees, *Promoting Honesty in Negotiation*, in What's Fair 117, 133 n. 13 (Carrie Menkel-Meadow & Michael Wheeler eds., 2004).

36. Robert H. Mnookin, Scott R. Peppet, & Andrew S. Tulumello, Beyond Winning 134–35 (2000).

37. *Id.*

38. Patrick J. Cleary, The Negotiation Handbook 21 (2001).

39. Fisher, Ury, & Patton, supra note 30, at 175.

40. Wade & Honeyman, supra note 3, at 494.

Checkpoints

- The closing phase of the negotiation is the time when skillful negotiators make clear what they will commit to do and what they will not or cannot do. Assembling the pieces of a potential deal is the most intense and intellectually exciting period of a complex negotiation but also a risky one since the effort might fall to pieces.

- An experienced negotiator stays true to the rhythm, or cadence, of a negotiation, neither rushing to close and overlooking key matters nor getting bogged down in minutiae and undue tinkering with the language of different provisions.

- Skilled negotiators also gain the ability to take a proposed resolution and examine it from many different angles before finalizing a deal. They think in terms of possible contingencies — things that might occur whether through chance, accident, or design — and figure out how to handle them. As an agreement comes together, the terms often need to be appraised critically and skeptically in order to improve them and ensure that they are sufficient, logical, durable, and operational.

- To help negotiators to formulate a proposal, the theory of the yesable proposition is that the process of closing a deal will be advanced if you articulate a proposal that serves interests of both sides, that is phrased clearly and specifically, and that is so comprehensive in scope that the other side could simply say, "Yes. We're agreeable to those terms."

- In assembling such a proposition, you should not simply attend to your own needs but step into the shoes of your counterpart. What do they care about, how could the offer be made attractive to them, and how might it be phrased so as to maximize its chances of being accepted?

- In presenting a yesable proposition, a negotiator should look to call on advocacy skills. What you are advocating is not how admirably the proposal is tailored to your own interests but how it ought to suit the other side. Making the offer credible and carefully laying out the reasoning that underlies it can help to bring the other side to accept a proposed deal.

- How your proposal is organized and presented may well contribute to whether it plays a conclusive role, or even simply a useful one, in concluding the talks. Sell your fellow negotiators on the advantages offered by the potential agreement you have in mind, from their perspectives, before you focus on the aspects of the agreement that will be burdensome for them to fulfill.

- The closing phase of a negotiation is about making commitments. The experienced negotiator does not commit casually and does not over-commit. Instead, he or she puts the deal into written form, carefully and clearly drafts legally binding provisions, and takes advantage of useful relationships to help to ensure proper implementation.

- In appraising a possible agreement to determine whether to accept it, reject it, or continue to negotiation, a negotiator should look into the future: is the proposed deal better than his or her BATNA? Do benefits outweigh drawbacks? Commitments should be scrutinized to ensure that they are fair, with clear and realistic terms, so that proper implementation occurs. And, negotiators should strive for an optimal agreement — the best possible resolution under the circumstances.

- In putting the oral agreement between the parties into written form, negotiators need to determine how many details to include and which of the points discussed should become written provisions. A well-drafted agreement is clear and coherent and leaves no doubt as to what is expected. It should have a logical overall structure with the provisions well-ordered and inter-relating properly. In some negotiations the decision maker will be present and able to offer a definitive response. In others the proposal will have to be brought back to other authorities — the chief executive officer, the board of directors, the president, etc. — for final approval. Often, the negotiators will need to defend the proposed agreement and generate enthusiasm for it.

Chapter 9

Contending with Cultural Differences: Navigating Cross-Cultural Complications and Opportunities

Roadmap

- **Current importance of culture:** Why has contending effectively with cultural complications and opportunities never been more important for negotiators than is true today?

- **Cultural distinctions:** What is meant by *culture* and *deep culture*? Why might culture be considered an elusive and complex term, and what varieties of culture exist? What differentiates a high- from a low-context culture and a sub- from a supra-culture?

- **Culture and communication:** How do cultural variables affect communication, verbal and non-verbal? How can the cultural context in which a negotiation occurs influence what is said and left unsaid? What problems are associated with translation and the use of interpreters?

- **Debating the influence of culture on negotiation:** What is the debate over the significance of cultural influences for negotiation? What are the views of the advocates, and how do the skeptics respond?

- **Cultural and social norms:** How is appropriate behavior related to culture, and what is cross-cultural noise? How does culture affect deeper notions of the good life and the proper ordering of society, and how might culture influence the way a person reasons?

- **Cultural ambiguities and other difficulties:** In what ways might generalizations about a culture be inaccurate? Why are there so many individual variations within cultures, and how might multiple cultures influence any particular individual?

- **National negotiating characteristics:** What are examples of national negotiating characteristics, and why might these be worth attending to in a cross-cultural negotiation?

- **Culture and negotiation strategy:** How might cultural factors be incorporated in a negotiation strategy? How might sensitivity to cultural differences help a negotiator to develop a positive working relationship with a counterpart? Why might it be important to help a counterpart to save face? How do legal cultures differ, and how might those differences affect a cross-cultural negotiation?

We ordinarily think of cultures as varying substantially from region to region, an African culture distinct from an Asian one, or differing from one country to another, a Russian culture versus a French one. In fact, many people today live in countries that contain multiple cultures. Complex multi-cultural transactions now occur not only in international business and foreign policy but as individuals negotiate with each other at home. A cross-cultural domestic negotiation in the United States might involve, for instance, a dispute involving neighboring Vietnamese-American and African-American communities or those living on a Native American reservation and others owning adjacent farmland.

With the revolutions in transportation and communication associated with globalization many professionals have found that cross-cultural interactions have grown in number and importance. These days people in many lines of work confront the challenge of dealing with culturally heterogeneous counterparts. For negotiators, contending effectively with cultural complications and opportunities has never been more important than it is today in a world that is more tightly knit than in past eras.

International negotiations, which often bring on a host of cross-cultural issues, are rising rapidly in number. Academics—professors and students alike—routinely teach, study, and research abroad or in conjunction with foreign colleagues. Some doctors and engineers, many advisors and consultants, even missionaries and military personnel, routinely find themselves interacting internationally. Small and medium-sized businesses, as well as large ones, now depend on suppliers abroad. Some look to form joint ventures with companies in other countries. Business executives see exciting new markets in the developing world, in regions that are unifying, and in economies that are expanding. Since many of these interactions include negotiations, the cultures of distant places are of more immediate concern than ever before.

We used to associate cross-cultural negotiation chiefly with the work of diplomats. But, in recent decades the practice of international relations has leapt far beyond the traditional interactions of foreign ministries. Private sector and nongovernmental personnel, whose expertise is in such technical fields as health, agriculture, and science, may find themselves working with foreign counterparts and, hence, undertaking negotiations with people grounded in divergent cultures.

Legal and government matters now routinely reach out across state boundaries. Officials trying to solve common problems or respond to sudden crises find that they need to work closely with one another. Complex civil litigation often has international dimensions. When settlement discussions occur in these cases, cross-cultural negotiation occurs. Indeed, with much crime occurring internationally, police, prosecutors, and defense lawyers are now often thrust into contact with foreigners.

Diplomatic contacts have skyrocketed as well. The nearly two-hundred sovereign states send thousands of diplomats abroad each year to grapple with issues that spill over borders. Differing cultural orientations come into play in bilateral dealings between governments as well as in multilateral interactions, including those occurring in scores of international organizations. A key reason for a government to train a professional diplomatic corps is to enable officials working on a daily basis with international affairs to become closely familiar with other cultures and to use cross-cultural skills in negotiations abroad.

Adept negotiators understand how to view a situation from the perspective of their counterpart. If we are to change another person's mind, we must first focus on what is in it. Likewise, if we need to work with another to capitalize on a shared opportunity or fashion a mutually beneficial resolution to a common problem, we need to understand just what he or she is thinking. In the negotiation of complex problems, gaining insights into the mindsets and thought processes of our counterparts can be vitally important.

Seasoned negotiators working in a cross-cultural environment will thus give some thought to how differences in culture might affect how each side approaches the subject of the negotiation. One authority declared, "Culture is to negotiation what birds flying into engines are to flying airplanes ... practical impediments that need to be taken into account (and avoided) ..."[1]

We will also see, however, that cultural differences can bring about opportunities for making deals as well. Precisely because one negotiator views interests in a way quite distinct from a counterpart from another culture, the two may be able to realize joint gains. To illustrate, a Minister of Foreign Affairs from a highly competitive democratic society might badly need a diplomatic resolution that can be characterized, publicly, as a victory for his or her country. Behaving in that way might be considered off-putting or impolite braggadocio if undertaken by a counterpart from a more formal, reserved, and traditional society. The two sides might agree, however, on terms that ensure that the one gets its public victory but in exchange for a concession that its counterpart finds valuable.

Negotiators ought to be prepared to contend with cultural ingredients in all of the phases of negotiation. If cultural differences exist, handling them in a strategically sound manner should be one focus of preparing to negotiate, initiating talks, moving to substance, solving problems, overcoming impasses, and closing a deal. Effective twenty-first century negotiators need to be able to identify cross-cultural challenges and then to navigate successfully through them. To help with these tasks, this chapter explores an array of issues regarding how to negotiate well across cultures.

A. What Is Meant by Culture?

1. How the Concept Is Used

Culture can be a slippery, elusive concept, an abstraction used in different ways by people in distinct fields. One person might understand culture to be a type of learned behavior, while another might conceive of it chiefly in terms of shared values. A pair of anthropologists found more than 160 definitions of culture.[2] And, one scholar termed it "one of the two or three most complicated words in the English language."[3]

I use the term to refer to distinctive sets of values and attitudes, norms and beliefs, that usually evolve slowly with the experience and tradition of particular groups. These then play a role in determining a group's self-image or identity. To some extent, they help to guide the actions and orient the behavior of many of the group's members as they cope with the problems of daily life. "Each person," it has been noted, "does not belong to a single culture—rather, we are all members of many cultures simultaneously."[4]

a. The Influence of Deep Culture

Deep culture refers to a society's values, ideology, philosophy, religious ideas, and collective memory, featuring its understanding of past experiences and history.[5] A people's assumptions, their rituals and symbolism, their myths, stories, and traditions have cultural dimensions. And, over time, those adhering to a particular culture transfer their core ideas to the incoming cohort or next generation.

One's cultural orientation comes to "form unwritten and often nearly invisible, instructions on how to act in the world."[6] One scholar pointed out that "culture is *learned* behavior, although the learning is often out of awareness" and that it is sanctioned behavior as well in that those who contravene cultural norms may experience disapproval or even punishment, while those who abide by cultural norms are accepted or otherwise rewarded.[7]

In this way culture does not so much determine the way that people think, as it often influences what is considered fitting, legitimate behavior by most of them. Since culture provides patterns of thinking, or psychological predispositions, it affects an individual's sense of rights and duties, what is upright versus immoral, normal versus peculiar. Culture can influence the meaning that people ascribe to events, and it can help them to determine how to defend, criticize, or rationalize various actions.[8]

b. The Evolution of Cultures

Cultures are not static, crystallized, or unchanged. Rather, they are, in the phrase of Oliver Wendell Holmes, Jr., the skin of living thoughts.[9] While cultures typically resist abrupt changes, they do evolve over time, though at varying speeds in different societies. Specific experiences can stimulate the process of cultural change, as can broader trends such as urbanization, modernization, regionalization, or globalization. Although governments have often found it extremely difficult to instigate sweeping cultural change, on occasion, government policies have helped to alter cultures.[10]

2. The Varieties of Cultures

Plainly, by the definition laid out above, quite different varieties of culture exist. Experienced negotiators involved in cross-cultural exchanges will be constantly asking themselves how the values, beliefs, and traditions that are a product of their own culture differ from those that are likely to characterize their counterparts' patterns of thinking? Culture might very well affect one's understanding of events, interests, or objectives. One authority on culture recounted that under a blazing sun in China "two Englishmen sweated and puffed while playing tennis. When they finished, a sympathetic Chinese friend asked: 'Could you not get two servants to do this for you?'"[11]

Around the globe, however, significant cultural commonalities exist alongside great cultural differences. Canadians negotiating with Pakistanis might be expected to confront far more challenging cross-cultural difficulties than a Jamaican negotiator working with one from across the Caribbean Basin in Belize. Where cultures share features or are complementary, these similarities might assist the parties in fashioning a negotiated resolution, a point that is true of talks involving governments as well as businesses or individuals.

One scholar analyzed the negotiations concerning the 1951 San Francisco Peace Treaty between the United States and Japan and concluded that complementary cultural traits had smoothed the way toward agreement: "The willingness of the Japanese to adjust uncomplainingly to their surroundings, an acceptance of hierarchy in social life, and familiarity with dependency (*amae*) relationships proved compatible ... with the optimistic and manipulative American approach to nature, egalitarianism in relationships, and readiness to accept a role of responsible leadership."[12]

Furthermore, although dissimilar cultures are most often taken to be obstacles to a negotiation, they can sometimes provide opportunities for the respective sides to reach a resolution agreeable to both. Variations in culture can broaden the thinking of negotiators. People from distinct cultures often seem inclined to frame problems in different ways, to look in different places for the sources or causes of conflict, and to direct their minds toward different varieties of solutions. Hence, it may be possible to come to more creative and effective negotiated resolutions by drawing on insights offered by people from more than one culture.

a. Regional and National Cultures

When people speak of culture, it may be that more often than not they have regional or national cultures in mind. Certainly, points are often made about the cultures of regions—Asia, Africa, the Caribbean, the Middle East, South America, and so on—as well as about national cultures, say, the culture of the Netherlands and how it differs from that of Britain or Germany.

People point to broad cultural traits, indicative of how societies are organized and what those within that culture might be thinking. To illustrate, Latin American societies are often said to exhibit fatalism: "Life and its circumstances are accepted as givens, the individual's task is to adjust to, rather than manipulate, surrounding forces."[13] The cultures of South American and Central American countries are also thought to feature *personalism*—an emphasis on close one-on-one relations in general and patron-client relationships in particular.

Ideas about culture also include much more specific ideas about how negotiators from that culture might operate. For example, Glen Fisher described the Latin American ideal of leadership as follows: "The successful individual is a forceful, even audacious, personality, eloquent in expression, one who is clearly in charge and to whom other people defer, one who guards honor and who takes care of those who enter his web of personal relationships and reciprocal responsibilities."[14]

Across Latin America various aspects of society are so organized as to depend heavily on personal contact, including hierarchical relationships in which a superior gains the allegiance of a subordinate and then, in turn, is expected to look after that person's interests. Since relationships are so critically important, people aim to develop such a level of trust with their closest colleagues that they are confident that those others will act in their best interests.

An important aspect of professional life in Mexico thus involves the concepts of *ubicación* and *confianza*. Within Mexican business circles, cardinal importance is attached to being properly plugged in to the key social, political, or business networks. Great stock is put in managing relations and affiliations with others. Skillful people maneuver toward their established goals using their connections and their relationships of trust and confidence with others.[15]

b. High-Context and Low-Context Cultures

Anthropologists and others analyzing cultures across the world sometimes categorize national cultures by whether they are high- or low-context in nature.[16] A high-context culture is closely oriented toward groups in society. To retain social harmony, people tend to be circumspect in what they say, often hinting at what they mean. The culture favors indirect and implicit expression of views. Honor, status, and hierarchy are often felt deeply.

In contrast, a low-context culture features much more explicit communications much more regularly. That people directly say what they mean reflects an orientation that, relatively speaking, tends to be less focused on community and more on individualism. Assertive business-like attitudes, such as the expression 'time is money,' would resonate with people grounded in a high-context culture, while face-saving might often hold particular significance in a low-context one. One scholar observed: "In some cultures, action will be direct, conflict widely accepted, and problems met head-on; in others, action will be indirect, conflict not openly acknowledged, and problems dealt with only obliquely, through allusions."[17]

Since the cultural context in which a negotiation takes place may hold the key to what then occurs, the differing fundamental orientations in high- and low-context cultures can pose a real challenge to effective communication. When I first taught law in Japan, an official at the Japan-U.S. Educational Commission recounted to me that, some years before, an American Fulbright Scholar, with exceptional Japanese language skills, had attended a faculty meeting at a Japanese university. Afterwards, he spoke with one of his Japanese faculty colleagues of what had transpired: one professor had made this statement; another had said that; a third had responded as follows. Finally, the American scholar summarized where the train of thought had led and the consensus he believed the faculty had reached. Here, however, his Japanese colleague had to correct him: the decision had, in fact, been just the opposite. His colleague observed, revealingly: "You understood all the words, and misconstrued all the silences!"[18]

Since communication in a high-context culture can thus differ fundamentally from that in a low-context one, even a wholly accurate translation or transcript can be an inadequate guide to meaning. This has strategic significance: for instance, one might be especially leery of undertaking an e-mail negotiation with a counterpart from a high-context culture.

c. Ethnic, Religious, and Occupational Cultures

For all of the attention garnered by regional and national cultures, people frequently refer to other species of cultures altogether. Think, for instance, of the cultural orientations of religions: a Muslim or Buddhist culture can readily be distinguished from a Christian or Hindu one.[19] Some identify cultural traits with ethnic groups within a country: for instance, one might view an Hispanic-American culture as distinct in important regards from an African-American one, which, in turn, differs from an Asian-American culture.

Professionals also may share important cultural attributes, so much so that they are sometimes said to form their own cultures. Diplomats might discover that they share common values, attitudes, and beliefs, just as officers in the militaries of Latin American countries might find cultural bonds rooted in their profession, as practiced in that region. In fact, many professionals, from accountants to judges to anti-drug police to international lawyers, confront similar problems, have common core experiences, share thoughts with one another on occasion, and come to develop sets of norms alike in many respects.

Even long-time employees in large institutions might speak of its particular culture. The culture of the United Nations staff, for instance, would focus attention on certain shared values, attitudes, and beliefs. And, in a world in which fifty-one of the one-hundred largest economies belong to multinational corporations, as opposed to forty-nine belonging to countries,[20] corporate culture—say, the culture of IBM versus that of Toshiba—may be well worth examining.

d. Sub-Cultures and Supra-Cultures

Some have conceived of sub-cultures existing within a country that has its own national culture, and these "may complement or contradict the national … culture, for it can favor values that may be very different, even conflicting."[21] For example, Honduran culture might be envisioned as including a number of sub-cultures, including the values, attitudes, and beliefs of the Honduran armed forces, long a major actor not only in national security matters but in the country's political and business life. Or, if one considers, not the main islands of Japan but the distant prefecture of Okinawa, long an independent kingdom before being assimilated into the Japanese state, aspects of the sub-national culture of the people there would differ notably from the culture of people living in or around Tokyo or Osaka or another large Japanese city.

Other cultures existing within a country might better be termed supra-cultures, since they are cross-national in nature. The most obvious example is a regional culture: people speak, for instance, of an Asian, African, or European culture. Another example would be religious cultures—the culture of Catholicism or of fundamentalist Islam. These would affect certain believers within a country but would be extra-national in scope. And, in different circumstances supra-cultures, like sub-cultures, might conflict with other characteristics of a national culture or run parallel to them.

B. Communication, Language, and Culture

Prior chapters have noted how the essence of the interest-based negotiation approach might be likened to having an intelligent conversation about shared problems or opportunities. When the conversation includes people from distinctive cultures, cultural variables might deeply influence key aspects of communication.

1. Non-Verbal Communication

Think again of the American scholar trying to follow the discussion at the Japanese faculty meeting and then consider the broader issue of just what silence suggests in diverse cultures. Does responding to a statement with silence imply *agreement* with it on the assumption that the party would otherwise express disagreement? Or, does it imply *disagreement,* since accord with the statement was never declared? Is sudden silence indicative of a cooperative effort to circumvent potential conflict, or might it be a signal of brewing hostility or aggression? Might silence instead connote mistrust, frustration, or some other emotion? How frequently does it reflect one thing as opposed to another? The answers vary from culture to culture.

Or, consider body language once again. The messages conveyed by a person's gestures, facial expressions, and other movements can differ sharply in diverse cultures.[22] Shaking one's head in a way that would convey "no" in the west would instead mean "yes" to someone in India. A negotiator who communicates something with a hand covering the mouth might be thought to be polite in one culture but deceptive in another.

A thumbs-up sign offered by an American or Canadian to convey optimism about the current or future situation might be taken as an obscenity in parts of Asia and Africa. The giggle of a Caribbean negotiator might indicate humor, while that of a Japanese negotiator could signal embarrassment.[23] In short, the meaning of gestures comes to us via the prism of culture.[24]

In typical western cultures people often feel that they are communicating better when both sides are making regular eye contact. In the west, as one makes and hears points, the simple act of looking at the other negotiator, as opposed to gazing elsewhere, can help the sides understand one another and work toward establishing trust. You might assume that a counterpart's mind is wandering if he or she fails to maintain eye contact while you are speaking. And if one's negotiating partner looks away when explaining a point or making a proposal, some might suspect doubt or deceit. And yet, these might well be erroneous conclusions to draw when interacting in an Asian culture in which eye contact bears with it a distinctive set of connotations.

2. Verbal Communication

Turn next to verbal communication. Linguistic shortcomings can bring on significant problems. That many of those who hail from different cultures also speak different languages greatly complicates communication. How do you effectively and precisely convey your ideas to someone who does not speak your language or at least lacks the fluency and cultural awareness of a native speaker?

What one negotiator means to express may not be captured by the other. The words that one negotiator uses may even be *culture-bound* in the sense that no exact equivalent exists in the other negotiator's language. Much more frequently, problems of translation occur, when differences that are linguistic and cultural cause one negotiator not to grasp exactly what the other means.

Though occasionally negotiations are carried on in two or more languages, much cross-cultural negotiation occurs in the language of one of the parties. Unfortunately, people sometimes have inflated ideas of their abilities in a foreign language, and a negotiator may not, in fact, be sufficiently fluent to negotiate well. Although one could try to avoid slang that might confuse someone from another culture or bring them to interpret the words quite differently than intended, the problem runs considerably deeper than that. In an array of particular circumstances what one person means to express, the other may not fully comprehend.

a. Differences in Meaning

Consider, for instance, idiomatic expressions. The proverb "A rolling stone gathers no moss" is usually given a positive interpretation by Americans and a negative one by Japanese.[25] "The Japanese equivalent of 'individualistic' has a negative nuance while in English it is positive."[26] A linguist likewise noted: "For Japanese, the proverb, *'deru kugi wa utareru'* (the nail that sticks out gets hammered back in) reflects how a group member should not stand out. In fact, translating the compliment in English, 'She's a real individual!' to Japanese becomes an insult: ... 'What a person with strong individuality!' ... [with the connotation] 'She's weird (different) and selfish (does what she wants without conforming).'"[27]

A non-native speaker's mastery of a foreign language in its cultural context may not be nearly as extensive as is necessary to negotiate effectively. They may lack "the ability to distinguish nuances, decode metaphors, or decipher cultural subtleties key to understanding the full import of what is said, or avoiding misunderstandings."[28] "[C]ommunicating with another culture," one scholar explained, "is not just a matter of learning the other side's vocabulary; it also requires an understanding of its values, perceptions, and philosophies. Different cultures operate on the basis of different unspoken assumptions, and each may interpret the same phenomenon in very different ways."[29]

b. Use of Interpreters

To minimize such problems, parties to important negotiations often use interpreters. Many translators are highly professional; some of them are remarkable linguists in their own right. Professional interpreters have created a code of ethics to work by. However, even a simultaneous translation by a skilled interpreter with a close understanding of the cultures of the negotiators at the table can be problematic.

Among the difficult questions that accompany the use of interpreters are the following.

- How does one control any partiality the interpreter might feel for one side or the other in a negotiation?
- How can the parties even determine when the translation is being shaded in a way that might influence what is occurring?
- How is an interpreter to handle side comments or emotional outbursts? Are these ignored or explained, with full intensity or in a muted form?
- When does an interpreter add information that was not said but may be needed for clarity?
- When does one offer the listener a literal translation, and when a translation with a cultural interpretation added that may better capture the spirit of what was said?[30]

Simultaneous translators aim to select the best word or phrase in one language to match that in another, and yet some words come with what has been termed a "mini-mindset" marked by real cultural differences.[31] Terms like *fair play*, *public interest*, *human rights*, or *civil service* may connote quite distinct things to different peoples. Consider the difficulties in translating a euphemism like *collateral damage*. A literal translation would likely confuse, but a very accurate rendition would require explanation that might encompass moral values, ideologies, philosophical points, and so on. Sometimes even several sentences or more of explanation might be inadequate to bridge profound cultural differences, yet a simultaneous translator has no time for that. Hence, the precise communication so necessary for effective negotiation can get "lost in translation."

In sum, then, an interpreter is not necessarily a neutral figure, mechanically translating words from one language to another. The *modus operandi* of interpreters varies, as does their effectiveness. Consequently, where the stakes are high, it may be worthwhile for each side to have its own interpreter so as to increase the chances that the true meanings of each side's words are conveyed as accurately as possible to its counterparts.

c. Gamesmanship

Another problem arises when negotiators on one team mistakenly assume that those on the other cannot understand their side comments to one another. Sometimes a negotiator who does have some foreign language abilities feigns ignorance in the language to see if it provides a tactical advantage. For instance, teammates might say something to each other or a colleague or a client that they really do not mean for their counterparts to hear. Or, negotiators who do have very good second-language skills might use an interpreter simply to give them more time to think before having to respond.[32] Having cultivated the appearance that one cannot speak or understand a language well may also enable a negotiator to plead misunderstanding when he or she wants to take back or reformulate a point.

d. Language as a "Layer of Culture"

One highly significant dimension of cultural differences is thus linguistic. A person's language might very well help to shape the way that a negotiator is thinking about goals, interests, and alike. In calling language "another important layer of culture," Guy Olivier Faure and Gunnar Sjöstedt pointed out that "One function of language is to structure reality and to order experience. Therefore, the language of an individual significantly influences his or her perceptions and thinking."[33]

C. The Significance of Culture for Negotiators

If culture is such a broad and flexible concept, applied by different people to quite distinct groups, to what extent is it significant for negotiation today?

1. The Advocates: Culture as Vitally Important

For years scholars and practitioners have debated the extent to which culture affects the manner in which people negotiate. One school of thought has long contended that cultural characteristics are a vital aspect of international negotiations as well as some domestic, but cross-cultural, ones. American diplomat Glen Fisher wrote: "[P]atterns of personality do exist for groups that share a common culture.... [I]n the process of being socialized..., the individual picks up the knowledge, the ideas, the beliefs and values, the phobias and anxieties of the group."[34]

The advocates argue that cultural differences do very much affect how people think and, thus, influence the course of many negotiations. One authority noted that people often view matters "according to their subjective attitudes, ... their likes and dislikes, their attachments and inclinations, their predispositions, hopes, fears, aversions, habits, and logics—in short, according to their culture."[35] Consequently, understanding—"decoding"—the messages counterparts are sending may depend on close familiarity with their cultures.

Furthermore, the advocates hold that ascribing characteristics to particular nationalities, if done carefully and appropriately, is a valid analytical tool and one that ought to be regularly employed. Is it not common sense to expect the culture of a business executive from India to affect a negotiation differently than the culture of an Israeli or Saudi counterpart? Harvard anthropologist Clyde Kluckhorn compared descriptions of culture to a map which serves "as an abstract representation of a particular area. If a map is accurate, and one can read it, one doesn't get lost. If a culture is correctly portrayed, one will realize the existence of the distinctive features of a way of life and their interrelationships."[36]

a. Culture and Proper Behavior

Those who see culture as a vitally important component of many negotiations note that talks may be hampered by *cross-cultural noise*: that is, background distractions somehow tied to cultural differences that may obstruct effective negotiation by causing one side to feel disgust, tension, irritation, or awkwardness.[37] To take one example, when someone from the Middle East converses with a westerner at a distance normal for an Arab culture, the westerner might "feel so uncomfortable that the substance of the conversation is all but lost."[38] Culture influences comfortable conversational distance, that is, how far apart people normally stand or sit from one another when they interact.

Certainly, cultures differ on whether and when it is fitting to hug, kiss, bow, and shake hands. Cultural distinctions can help to determine what negotiators wear and what topics of conversation are accepted or taboo. Protocols followed when people negotiate can be important, and not exclusively in diplomatic or government circles. Learning the etiquette of a foreign society can lead to more productive cross-cultural negotiations.

Consider the formality with which people interact. An American might be comfortable being on a first-name basis with a counterpart much more quickly than someone from France, Japan, or Switzerland. In some societies people customarily address one another using titles (Dr. Michel, Professor Dominguez, or Ishikawa Sensei). Those who properly employ the language might confine the use of informal pronouns to family members and close friends (for example, *vous* versus *tu* in French and *usted* versus *tú* in Spanish). Here, to avoid giving offense, one might aim to match the formality of one's counterpart. Start with more formal interactions, and move to informal forms of communication only after having received signals that this is now expected.[39]

Or, think of the rituals that people from various cultures see as an important aspect of negotiation. Cultural factors might determine the precise manner in which gifts or business cards ought to be exchanged or banquets and other formal ceremonies carried out in order to avoid offense and augment the working relationship. The growing literature on doing business abroad reflects the conviction that an important part of a negotiator's preparation involves understanding something of what behavior a counterpart is likely to consider appropriate and inappropriate.[40] Here, one might think of what it means in one culture versus another to be at ease with or to conflict with someone. For instance, a quick-paced, purposive style might be comfortable in one culture, off-putting in another. In one cross-cultural encounter a humorous remark might be heartily enjoyed by both sides, while a negotiator from another culture might find joking senseless and improper in those circumstances.

In helping a visiting professor to buy a car, I learned that the tone of normal bargaining interactions at an auto dealership in the United States might be considered most impolite in Japan. "[W]hat is viewed as a conflictual negotiation by Japanese," one scholar observed, "may not be seen as such by Americans. Similarly, what is often seen by American negotiators as a delaying device can simply be for Japanese the time needed to know the other party better."[41] For many Japanese being polite might well be judged as a far more important aspect of a relationship than being straightforward, while in the United States being straightforward might well be considered one key aspect of being polite.

In short, then, skillful negotiators working across cultural divides look to gain a feel for what is suitable behavior in another culture and prepare themselves to minimize the effects of cross-cultural noise. Indeed, negotiators who in renegotiation have identified likely sources of cross-cultural noise may be able to circumvent or ameliorate its effects when the talks get under way.

b. Cultural Understanding

To avoid giving offense is but one aspect of skillful negotiation between people of separate cultures. Cross-cultural issues run much deeper than matters of polite behavior and proper etiquette. They can delve into the philosophical: a party's views of life and the proper ordering of private and public affairs. What you value, how you understand your interests, what priorities and goals you set, the way in which you interact with a counterpart, whether you are primarily long-term or short-term oriented, cultural values might affect all of these important features of negotiation.

One source maintained: "Too often in the past, cultural variables were thought of as 'quaint customs' that one merely had to 'learn about' in order to succeed in foreign settings— … remember to bow when meeting the Japanese, take a gift when you are entertained at someone's house, and don't make this or that gesture that means something-or-other lewd in such-and-such a country."[42] Another scholar identified cultural relations as much more than "an awkward encounter between contrasting languages, manners, and habits … which hand one eats with or whether showing the soles of one's feet is considered to be seemly." Instead, cultural factors may play into differing assumptions about the nature of the world, about whether a good society puts the group or the individual first, and whether disputes should be resolved "on the basis of abstract justice or social harmony."[43]

Some have argued that the notion of setting time aside for a direct discussion of how to resolve differences or take advantage of opportunities has its origins in western cultures.[44] One consequence could be that people from a particular culture might see the core objectives of a negotiation differently from those in another. One negotiator might expect little more than an exchange of views, perhaps featuring symbolic statements or formal rhetorical arguments, whereas one deeply influenced by another culture might anticipate a pragmatic, cooperative, outcome-oriented problem-solving session.[45] Where cultural expectations regarding the central point of the negotiation differ starkly, an important aspect of your strategy might involve bringing your counterparts to see the same possibilities that you do in initiating discussions with each other.

Cultural considerations might also affect the preferred site to negotiate and the time to be allotted for talks. Culture might influence whether a negotiation is conceived of as an intensely private affair or one that ought to be at least partially exposed to the public view. Those chosen to negotiate, or to lead a negotiation team, might have varying expectations of conventional negotiation behavior based on whether a culture has a highly refined sense of hierarchy or is more egalitarian in orientation. Even the proper size of a negotiating team might be viewed differently in distinct cultures. For instance, a multinational corporation headquartered in the west might arrive in China with a team of three negotiators and confront fifteen to thirty Chinese counterparts.[46]

All this suggests that understanding how people within a given culture view negotiation — its customary objectives and processes — can be very valuable information. In a negotiation with cross-cultural dimensions learning something of the contents of the particular cultural baskets that might be influencing one's counterparts is an inherent part of good preparation. And, a rich and growing literature exists on inter-cultural communication, offering negotiators the chance to "do their homework" and learn something ahead of time about the culture of many possible counterparts.[47]

To the advocates, it is self-evident that an adroit negotiator working in a cross-cultural context ought to be identifying significant cultural variables and working with them as he or she plots out a negotiating strategy. Seasoned negotiators pick up on cues and signals sent by their counterparts, both verbal and non-verbal, about the subjects they are discussing. Ignoring or overlooking the cultural context in which those cues and signals are sent is short-sighted.

c. Culture and Reasoning

Some advocates have suggested that cultural differences might even influence the mode of thinking typically found in a country. For instance, a French negotiator might be likely to rely on Cartesian logic, the formal reasoning traced back through French intellectual history to René Descartes, in which problems are split into subsets and tackled by a *deductive negotiation approach*, that is, one in which the negotiators attempt to agree on general principles that may then guide the resolution of specific issues. Various other nationalities, including the Chinese and Germans, are also said to often negotiate deductively.

In contrast, a typical American negotiator might be quite pragmatic, routinely elevating substance over form, focusing much attention on tangible, and perhaps technical, points. This approach to negotiation would be *inductive*, that is, the negotiator would concentrate on resolving a series of particular issues, looking to solve one problem after another, each on its merits. Rather than trying to reach a consensus on general principles, negotiators would look to draft provisions addressing specific issues. These would then form the superstruc-

ture for the general agreement.[48] One scholar observed, "For Americans, negotiating a deal is basically making a whole series of compromises and tradeoffs
on a long list of particulars. For Chinese, the essence is to agree on basic general principles which will guide and indeed determine the negotiation process
afterwards."[49]

After remarking that the parties to an international negotiation frequently
find that they are pursuing "different paths of logic," Glen Fisher observed:
"[A] breakdown [in negotiations] may result from the way that issues are con-
ceptualized, the way evidence and new information are used, or the way one
point seems to lead to the next." He continued by asking, "Do cultures ... tend
to impart to the members of the society, distinctive ways of putting ideas together, associating causes and effects, seeking knowledge and understanding,
using evidence and reasoning? Could it be that a line of reasoning that would
be persuasive in the U.S. would be ineffective in another culture?"[50]

Note in this regard that abstract issues are particularly prone to bring on
cross-cultural misperceptions.[51] What is viewed as legitimate and illegitimate is
one abstraction of great moment to negotiators. Thinkers grounded in diverse
cultures have advanced differing answers to the question of how legitimacy is
obtained and conferred. Some point to legitimacy through law, others to morality, still others to religion or ideology or politics. What a party views as legitimate will reflect their "notions of decency, fair play, morality, order, precedent,
international law, and history."[52] This would then influence a negotiator's reactions to specific issues. For example, under what circumstances, if any, is a
compromise solution like *splitting the difference*—that is, resorting to an equal
division to bridge a gap between two numbers—considered to be legitimate?

Since people in one society might call on principles of justice less familiar
to those in another, culture might strongly influence determinations of what
seems fair. People from one culture might equate fairness with equal gains or
equal concessions by each side, while those from another might focus on how
the needs of each party are met.[53]

In sum, then, the advocates see cultural variables as affecting many aspects
of negotiation. To negotiate effectively across cultures, you should aim to gain
a sufficient understanding of your counterpart's culture that you can formulate an effective strategy to minimize the obstacles posed by cross-cultural differences and take advantage of cross-cultural similarities and opportunities.[54]

2. The Skeptics: Culture as Confusing and Misleading

Another school of thought, however, takes a much more cautious view of
the usefulness of cultural analyses in negotiation. I. William Zartman, a skep-

tic on the role of culture in negotiation, offered the riposte: "Culture is indeed relevant to the understanding of the negotiation process — every bit as relevant as breakfast and to much the same extent."[55]

This group of thinkers sees culture as a notoriously difficult concept for negotiators to put to practical use. All too often, pointing to cultural differences serves as a convenient scapegoat for negotiations that failed to reach agreement, very likely for other reasons altogether. In fact, cultural influences might affect one negotiation quite differently than another, depending on a range of factors including whether the cultures clash, co-exist, or complement each other.

Note, too, that a counterpart from another culture might try to use cultural factors tactically to gain an advantage of some kind. For example, a negotiator "may make his foreign counterpart believe that he is acting according to social habits and traditions when in fact he is playing with these strategically."[56]

a. Generalizations about Culture

To the skeptics, the essence of the problem is that generalizations about cultures can be confusing and misleading. Zartman argued: "African culture is what Africans ... do, and they do it because they are Africans.... Exceptions are treated as deviants, Africans who do not act like Africans."[57] Certainly, people within a culture sometimes act at variance with the cultural traits that they are presumed to exhibit. Individuals can be socialized in many diverse settings, they may be affected by cultural conditioning differently, and they can be subject to a range of cultural factors, some of them conflicting.

Furthermore, the skeptics point out that a country may contain such significant cultural differences that trying to determine how to contend with purported national negotiating characteristics may be futile. Two scholars noted: "Few of us, if asked to characterize an American negotiating style, would be able to do so, arguing that the differences between Texans and Bostonians, Hawaiians and Tennesseans are so vast that it makes no sense whatsoever to attempt a single characterization."[58]

Similarly, Chinese negotiators might be expected to be under the sway of some separate and distinct cultural influences, if they hailed, say, from Hong Kong as opposed to Beijing, or Taiwan as opposed to Shanghai. And, wouldn't we expect the typical characteristics of negotiators to vary substantially from place to place in Canada, India, Russia, and a host of other large and diverse countries?

This problem is even more pronounced with respect to a regional culture. Are there too many variations between countries or sections of countries to speak with any confidence of an Asian, African, European, or Latin American culture? This issue was highlighted for me when, after teaching for an extended period in Japan, I was leading a negotiation workshop for mid-career officials in Hanoi, and a group of Vietnamese diplomats asked if we could meet after work one day to try to puzzle out some aspects of Japanese culture. It turned out that they all felt quite awkward interacting with Japanese diplomatic counterparts, much more so than with Americans.

The diplomats contended that, for all of the tragic history between Vietnam and the United States, core aspects of our cultures are sufficiently similar that Americans and Vietnamese can readily negotiate with one another. They argued that we establish personal and working relationships in similar ways, intuitively understand where one another is coming from on many subjects, and even laugh easily at the same jokes. To them, the formality and restrained emotions of the Japanese—despite being fellow Asians—made them much more challenging negotiating partners than Americans.

While reference is often made to Asian culture, or even the culture, say, of Southeast Asia, people within those areas are quick to see the many distinctions among their cultures. Ambassador Tommy Koh declared that he sometimes felt that others in Southeast Asia considered his country, Singapore, to be the "barbarians" of the Association of Southeast Asian Nations (ASEAN): fact-based, westernized, straightforward, inherently transactional, linear thinkers, Aristotelian in logic.[59]

b. Individual Variations within Cultures

Various of these difficulties are compounded by the subtlety of many cultural cues. These frequently amount to no more than general guidance on how to view the world and how to act in it. Moreover, in any given encounter individual variations might very well temper or contradict those typical tendencies. Clyde Kluckhorn observed:

> No individual thinks, feels, or acts precisely as the 'blueprints' which constitute a culture indicate that he will or should. Nor are all the 'blueprints' meant by the society to apply to each individual. There are sex differentials, age differentials, occupational differentials, and the like. The best conceptual model of the culture can only state correctly the central tendencies of range and variation.

Kluckhorn argued that most people, most of the time, adhere to cultural patterns in order to have a positive social life and to affirm solidarity with groups important to them. However, he also acknowledged that in an individualistic society people are likely to resist cultural patterns more frequently than in a collectivistic one more focused on group harmony. Ideas of liberty, spontaneity, and non-conformism—the value placed on thinking for oneself—all of these may counteract the patterns of culture in one country, whereas in another those who fail to heed cultural strictures may be ostracized.[60]

Alternatively, might a negotiator's behavior be better explained by other aspects of their personality, or strategy or, perhaps, by their perceived leverage or lack thereof? If a party is risk averse, to take one example, how can that be confidently attributed to culture? Perhaps the caution that the other side perceives is linked to the context in which they are negotiating, for instance, their understanding of the risks associated with their bargaining position.[61]

Rather than cultural differences being at the root of negotiating behavior, something about the particular problem may be eliciting behavior that might very well not be apparent in other circumstances. Consider a heated exchange. Is this culturally derived, or, perhaps, "there is something about you—or, more precisely, about the two of you negotiating together—that tends to bring out this kind of aggressive negotiating behavior ..."[62]

In short, in many international negotiations the culture of the participants is but one of many variables. Rarely is it the most important factor, and determining how it will affect any particular negotiation can be extraordinarily difficult.

c. The Impact of Multiple Cultures

Further complicating matters, a negotiating counterpart might be influenced not by traits of national or regional culture, but by other cultural dimensions altogether. These could be drawn from graduate schooling undertaken abroad, such as in the United States or Europe. They could come from the professional characteristics associated with people in a particular line of work. Law-enforcement officials negotiating for the transfer of fugitives or evidence across national boundaries might capitalize on the shared professional values and beliefs of what might be termed an international police culture. Indeed, some have identified common cultural characteristics existing among farmers, professors, prosecutors, and many others.[63]

Perhaps even more important, it can be exceedingly difficult to disentangle and analyze the multiple cultural influences at work on any particular individual at a given time. If culture comes in regional but also national forms, and is even visible in sub-national forms, how does one determine which cultural basket is likely to predominate on a particular issue or question or in one phase or another of a negotiation?[64]

At any one moment a mainland Chinese negotiator might be operating under the influence of communist culture, yet at another juncture elements of more traditional Chinese culture might surface. If one is preparing to negotiate with a business in Bali, Indonesia, should one expect the negotiator to exhibit Asian cultural traits, Southeast Asian traits, Hindu characteristics, or Indonesian or even Balinese ones, or—perhaps most likely—a complex mixture of all of them? And, how can that mix be accurately estimated or predicted so as to determine how a foreign negotiator should behave when visiting Bali?

In a complex negotiation, then, how does one determine when a cultural factor is likely to drive another party? Should a counterpart be expected to exhibit the characteristics of a Basque negotiator or a Spanish or European one? When might Mayan cultural characteristics predominate over Guatemalan or Latin American ones? One authority noted, "Often one's identity is a composite, or identities overlap. It is a question of which comes first, and when. Is one, for example, Chinese Malaysian, or Malaysian Chinese?"[65]

In observing that many distinct cultural worlds can intersect, sometimes in complementary and sometimes in contradictory fashion, one scholar concluded: "[T]his is precisely what makes contemporary international negotiations so complex; they are multi-cultural arenas in which national culture is but one component and not always the crucial one."[66]

To the skeptics, all of these difficulties in employing cultural concepts suggest, at the least, that negotiators be quite cautious as they try to work cultural ingredients into their negotiation strategies. The impact of national and other cultures on a counterpart is uncertain. A negotiator should enter cross-cultural talks with guarded expectations of how cultural influences might affect the other side. This school of thought counsels that trying to tailor a negotiation strategy to account for cultural differences could be fraught with unforeseen hazards.

D. National Negotiating Characteristics

"[P]eople who negotiate," it has been observed, "make attributions about each other all the time, whether group attributions are accurate or not."[67] So, what exactly are the cultural attributes of this people or that one? If the way in which members of distinct cultures negotiate often differs, how exactly does it do so? Certainly, determining cultural traits specifically and accurately, while avoiding biases and stereotypes, can be a complex endeavor. I. W. Zartman argued:

> Instead of asking, How do the Fijians negotiate?—a question that usually allows the author to illustrate preconceived notions about Fijian culture with well-selected examples from negotiation behavior, never asking whether anyone else acts the same way or whether any

Fijians act any other way—one must ask, out of a conceivable range of ways ... [to negotiate], which one is associated with Fijians..., and what is it in being Fijian ... that determines the choice of particular behaviors?[68]

National negotiating characteristics are traits commonly associated with the negotiators of particular countries: how they tend to strategize, what tactics they often use, how they might typically tackle a class of problems or follow a line of reasoning or train of thought. Some negotiators working across cultures find information on these characteristics to be quite valuable. For example, what would constitute a legitimate offer, one that would open the door to further negotiations? This might differ substantially from one place to another: "starting at a quarter of the market price to buy a jewel in Senegal would not surprise anybody.... [I]f this were done in Sweden, the seller would just walk away."[69]

Although the scholarly literature on national negotiating characteristics is far more extensive with respect to certain peoples than others, negotiators looking to research how counterparts from other countries might tend to negotiate can delve into a growing body of written work on the subject. To explore further the issue of national negotiating characteristics, let us look next at one representative case, to gain a sense for the type of information available to negotiators interested in investigating the cultures of their counterparts.

1. A Profile of a Typical Japanese Negotiator

Much has been written about Japanese negotiators. To illustrate the sorts of national negotiating characteristics that scholars and practitioners sometimes highlight, consider what some have identified as notable traits of a typical negotiator from Japan.

a. Common Characteristics

Analysts of Japanese negotiation emphasize the use of numerous questions to elicit information, of frequent apologies to set a desirable tone, and of an inclination to counter the proposals of others, rather than initiate by being the first to lay out an offer. In certain respects Japanese negotiators may also be more risk-averse than negotiators from other cultures, including a pronounced unwillingness to share information in the course of the negotiation that might turn out to have problematic dimensions.

Indeed, some have argued that a typical Japanese negotiator is likely to adopt a calm, implicit, understated, imperturbable, and not especially voluble negotiating style. One authority notes, "Zen Buddhist teaching places great value on silence and on the communication of ideas and feelings by nonverbal means."[70] A Japanese negotiator might be expected, on occasion, to use silence tactically during a negotiation to communicate feelings without using words that might cause unnecessary offense.[71]

Negotiators from Japan are often thought to be quite reluctant to say "no" directly or to interrupt or confront a counterpart. The ideal of a proper, polite Japanese negotiator would perhaps be more serious, reserved, and formal than would be the case for a negotiator from Australia, Israel, Mexico, Vietnam, the United States, or various other countries.

b. The Group or Organizational Consensus

Furthermore, Japanese negotiators are often acutely aware of the need on their part to gain an organizational or group consensus to support their negotiating strategy and any ensuing proposed agreement.[72] When serving as agents for a large entity such as a business or government department, Japanese negotiators might be expected to reflect this cultural trait in various ways. Opening positions as well as the preferred wording of provisions in an agreement would often be the result of extensive discussions within the organization. One of the central purposes of the negotiation might be understood as working towards engineering an internal, organizational consensus regarding a possible external agreement and its particular terms.

c. Thought Processes and Strategy

The Japanese are another nationality, we are told, that tends to negotiate deductively. They look to first come to a simple agreement with a counterpart and then, through extended negotiations, to try to build it into a much more complex deal, as conditions are inserted and mutually beneficial elaborations and tradeoffs made.

Yet another national negotiating characteristic often associated with Japanese negotiators involves a tendency toward what might be termed the indirect transmission of offers. In a conventional western approach to negotiation, a negotiator prepares a proposal and then reviews each facet of it with the other party, working together to approve, amend, or eliminate particular provisions.

In Japan the preferences of the opposing negotiator are often deduced not by direct questions about each proposed provision but via a more subtle and involved approach. Over the course of the talks, a Japanese negotiator often advances not one proposal, but a series of offers, and he or she looks to gauge the priorities of the other side by their differing reactions to elements within the proposals.

For example, offer *A* includes provisions *x*, *y*, and *z*. Offer *B* encompasses provisions *v*, *x*, and *z*, and offer *C* focuses on provisions *v*, *w*, and *x*. By looking to see which offer, *A*, *B*, or *C*, seems to garner most interest from the other side, and why, the Japanese negotiator gains insight on what is important to his or her counterpart. The emphasis is not so much on intently questioning the other side, but on analyzing its reactions to a pattern of separate proposals put forward.

E. Culture and Negotiation Strategy

How, then, might cultural factors be incorporated into a negotiation strategy? It has been suggested that cross-cultural negotiators steer clear of *stereotypes* but factor *prototypes* into their strategizing.[73] A stereotype is a simplified, standardized, and often pejorative generalization about how another is likely to behave based on how the speaker believes that people of a group that person belongs to often think or act. A stereotype might be advanced concerning how Europeans or Africans or Catholics or Muslims are likely to respond to some situation. A prototype also refers to typical qualities of a particular set of people, but focuses on "cultural averages on dimensions of behavior or values,"[74] and is often phrased in neutral, rather than negative, terms.

Katie Shonk suggested incorporating prototypes into a cross-cultural negotiation in the following terms:

> [I]t is commonly understood that Japanese negotiators tend to have more silent periods during their talks than, say, Brazilians. That said, there is still a great deal of variability within each culture—meaning that some Brazilians speak less than some Japanese do.
>
> Thus, it would be a mistake to expect a Japanese negotiator you have never met to be reserved. But if it turns out that a negotiator is especially quiet, you might better understand her behavior in light of the prototype. In addition, awareness of your own cultural prototypes can help you anticipate how your counterpart might interpret your bargaining behavior.[75]

Next, in a cross-cultural encounter it is especially important to be alert to how the parties' understandings of their interests might vary by culture. One scholar wrote, "In some cultures land is considered the most desirable commodity, in others leisure time or a retinue of servants might be considered the mark of the good life."[76] Where people from distinctive cultures interpret their interests differently, trade-offs may bring about joint gains.

Consider an example. Coming from a culture that greatly values the concept of self-determination, I may particularly sympathize with and admire the Kurdish people, the largest nation without a state, and I may identify with their efforts to gain their own sovereign state. A Turkish rug dealer may view the Kurds' efforts to obtain sovereign statehood in a largely negative light, as threatening the unity and territorial breadth of the Turkish state. Then, with respect to a particular negotiating issue, I may particularly value bringing home a Kurdish rug. For his part the dealer would like to reduce the number of Kurdish rugs in his store's inventory, since they are more difficult to sell in Turkey. We soon reach a mutually beneficial deal.

In thinking about how to work productively with a fellow negotiator, one might consider which aspects of the culture of one's counterpart complement one's own culture or run counter to it. This might then have strategic implications. For one, initiating positive working relations might be especially challenging where cultures clash, perhaps with historic animosities greatly exacerbating the tension. Imagine, for instance, the difficulties inherent in launching a binational claims commission or other dispute settlement institution between Japan and Russia or India and Pakistan.

Consider, too, the cultural implications involved in closing a deal. In some countries communication styles can be quite indirect. It might be considered polite, and would certainly not be unusual, to hear superficial assurances that everything is in order or on track, when in fact it might not be. This could raise issues for a negotiator from a more direct and assertive culture regarding how best to structure an agreement to minimize problems of implementation.

Box 9.1 — Preparing to Negotiate Across Cultures

One preparing for a cross-cultural negotiation might focus attention on certain of the following questions and on how one's strategy might best deal with the answers.

- What aspects of the culture of my counterparts might pose particular challenges or offer opportunities that I should bear in mind?

- What type of agreement is the other side most likely to be interested in — a specific and highly detailed contract or a statement of general organizing principles?

> - Might cultural variables determine some of my counterparts' expectations for our working relationship? Might they also influence the way in which the other side projects resolving any future differences or problems that arise?
> - In my counterpart's culture is compromising and give-and-take ordinarily expected as part of a negotiation, or in that culture does the word *negotiate* ordinarily connote relationship building or some other objective?
> - Might my counterpart be likely to have other culturally derived conceptions concerning the process of negotiation itself — its purposes, its tactics and strategies, its pace, timing, and phases — that might affect the proceedings?

There follow several specific topics regarding culture and negotiation strategy with accompanying ideas that a negotiator anticipating a cross-cultural encounter might find useful.

1. Developing Positive Working Relations

Soon after meeting someone, many people try to size up the extent to which that person is polite, upstanding, gracious, or well-mannered or, in contrast, underhanded, boorish, or devious. Since judgments of one sort or another are often formed very early in a relationship, negotiators concerned with establishing a positive tone at the outset of talks or laying the foundation for productive working relations must concern themselves with making a good first impression.

It is often especially challenging, however, to establish a constructive working relationship in a cross-cultural encounter. For instance, it may very well be more difficult to empathize across cultures, including identifying with the internal decision making process with which your counterpart must deal. One source noted of relations between negotiators hailing from different cultures: "the contrast between their perceptions will be greater, and each will find it more difficult to appreciate how the other sees things."[77]

Part of putting oneself into the shoes of one's counterpart involves imagining how matters would look from the perspective of that culture, and then tailoring one's strategy accordingly. For example, when I was teaching in Japan, my law students reasoned that, in initiating a business relationship with a U.S. company, the negotiator for a Japanese business might want to be quite direct and assertive about its abilities. They felt that an emphatic tone would be most advisable in "selling" the company to Americans, while a humble, deferential, and self-deprecating tone might go over much better when one Japanese company was negotiating with another.

One might also consider here the need for westerners to establish a more personal relationship when negotiating in a North African or Arab culture. Before working out the details of a purchase or sale, good manners dictate a genuine attempt on the part of the negotiators to get to know one another. Buying a carpet in a Marrakesh *souk* might entail sitting down with the owner of the rug shop, drinking tea, and conversing for a period about families, backgrounds, experiences, perceptions, aspirations, and home lives. Indeed, various cultures emphasize the value associated with negotiators developing a relationship of warmth, understanding, and even perhaps of some trust, a process that cannot easily be hurried along.

Clearly, one issue of culture and negotiation strategy involves how to develop positive working relations across cultural boundaries. Showing an interest in better understanding your counterpart's culture is one form of respecting your counterpart and his or her perspective. Calling upon some phrases in the other's language projects your interest in who they are. Perhaps a fascination you show in the details of their society's history or culture can be an important step in building productive working relations. All this suggests that it may be very possible to gain good will and circumvent potential problems by learning about, or simply being aware of and sensitive to, the differences in your culture and theirs.

Note, too, that people are often fascinated by cultural differences, and they also tend to respond positively to those who can be amused at their own foibles and idiosyncracies. Another approach would be to tackle cultural differences by raising one or two of them in one's opening, perhaps lightening the conversation with self-deprecating humor. Then, should cultural variables clash in the body of the negotiation, one might take some of the sting out of the conflict by referring back to that initial and light-hearted conversation.

2. Helping One's Counterpart to Save Face

In many countries the concept of *face-saving* brings harmony to daily life. The central idea is that people have an important psychological need not to look bad, weak, foolish, or incapable before themselves and others, especially those whose positive opinion they value. Statements that threaten face naturally differ from one culture to another and one set of circumstances to another. In various societies, however, those concerned with face would feel diminished if a negotiating counterpart let them down, compelled them to back down publicly, broke a cardinal precedent, or behaved in some other disagreeable, disreputable, or dishonorable way.[78]

The authors of *Getting to Yes* observed, "In the English language, 'face-saving' carries a derogatory flavor. People say, 'We are doing that just to let them save face,' implying that a little pretense has been created to allow someone to go along without feeling badly." They continued: "This is a grave misunderstanding of the role and importance of face-saving. Face-saving reflects a person's need to reconcile the stance he takes in a negotiation or in an agreement with his principles and with his past words and deeds."[79] Elsewhere, William Ury continued with this theme:

> Face-saving is at the core of the negotiation process. There is a popular misconception that a face-saving gesture is just a cosmetic effort made at the end of a negotiation to boost the other person's ego. But face is much more than ego. It is a shorthand for people's self-worth, their dignity, their sense of honor, their wish to act consistently with their principles and past statements — plus, of course, their desire to look good to others.[80]

Although the idea of face-saving is common to many peoples around the world, it has long been especially associated with Asian cultures. In Japan, for instance, how one looks in the eyes of others is such an important aspect of culture that people refer to building face or crushing face as well as saving it.[81] One would build face by doing things that make another look good, upstanding, capable, and legitimate in the eyes of their peers, and one would crush face by acting in such a way that another is completely humiliated.

Finding ways to respect and enhance one's counterpart can be an important aspect of many varieties of negotiation — domestic as well as international. It can assist the parties to interact productively with one another and help them toward mutually acceptable resolutions. Realizing this, one scholar argued that, in general, a Chinese negotiator would be "inclined toward protecting the face of the other party before his/her own."[82]

In any event, one engaged in a cross-cultural negotiation whose counterpart hails from a society in which issues of face are especially significant should be alert to the dangers of ignoring or detracting from the face of a counterpart as well as the opportunities to build and save face for that person.

3. Legal Cultures

We have seen how, in closing a deal, skillful negotiators look ahead to its implementation, trying to ensure that the agreement lasts and that its terms will eventually be carried out as envisioned. Additional complications arise where the legal culture of one's counterpart differs markedly from one's own.

In some countries taking matters to court to be resolved is discouraged or frowned upon. Adjudicating disputes may be viewed as a shameful admission of an inability to get along well with others in the community. Or, the court system may be slow or inefficient, its personnel may be corrupt, or they may be inexperienced in dealing with complex civil lawsuits. A foreigner trying to operate within the legal system may face bias and discrimination as well as considerable expense. Here, whether the agreement is carried out as planned may be a function in the first instance of the relations between the parties.

To the eye of a lawyer in the United States or Great Britain, a contract may be a thing of beauty—with provisions skillfully and intelligently crafted. The words are potent with meaning, and the parties to the contract have confidence that the courts, if called on, stand ready to enforce the provisions. When one operates in a country with a very different legal culture, the contract may be simply a means toward an end, one route toward having the agreement carried out but perhaps not the most important one.

The manner in which conflicts are typically resolved within a society is thus another issue worthy of attention for cross-cultural negotiators. Of course, some legal systems work reasonably well in resolving disputes and others do not but, beyond this, legal cultures differ markedly. For instance, in some societies people view legal principles as moral obligations; in others those principles simply express ideals.[83] People from one culture might find going to court embarrassing and highly unfortunate, while those from another might see it as a necessary vindication of rights, a normal function of ordering society, and one setting a positive precedent for all of society.

It has often been observed that Asian cultures tend to be considerably less litigious than American culture. The reluctance to call on courts to settle disputes may bring Asians to a correspondingly greater reliance on trying to negotiate resolutions. This, in turn, may bring about distinctive cultural expectations concerning exactly what a contract is designed to do.

Asian negotiators tend to aim toward devising written contracts that are more spare and streamlined than found in a society like the United States. In arguing that Americans associate negotiation with hammering out the detailed terms of a contract, Jeswald Salacuse noted that "Americans view a signed contract as a definitive set of rights and obligations that strictly binds the two sides ..." He noted that for Japanese and Chinese, however: "[T]he 'deal' being negotiated is ... the relationship between the parties. Although the written contract expresses that relationship, the essence of the deal is the relationship, and it is understood that the relationship may be subject to reasonable changes over time."[84] Thus, rather than focusing on elaborate, detailed, and legalistic contractual provisions, these Asian negotiators are likely to emphasize the underlying understanding between the parties and the use of negotiation within a trusted relationship to resolve future differences.

In developing a negotiation strategy, a party operating abroad ought to carefully assess and then take into account the realities of operating in that particular legal culture, whatever they are. And, the overriding goal of eventually having the contract's provisions carried out needs to be factored into different aspects of the negotiation, including the development of the working relationship. People with a real aversion to going to court may also not want to alienate those who are important to them. Consequently, the negotiator who establishes strong, long-term relationships may be in a better position than one who emphasizes detailed contract provisions.

F. Conclusion

Skillful negotiators are sensitive to cultural variations, and try to keep cultural factors from complicating what may already be quite difficult substantive issues. If something odd occurs as you communicate with the other side in a cross-cultural encounter and you feel unsure or suspicious about what is going on, do not immediately dismiss your counterpart as irrational or engaged in some clever negotiating tactic designed to take advantage of you. Realize that another very real possibility is a clash of cultures. You may be able to clarify what is, in fact, occurring by thinking or asking about relevant cultural differences.

While it is obviously important for negotiators to think about the cultures of their counterparts and the ways in which culture could affect communications with them, those adept at cross-cultural negotiation will also consider how their own culture might puzzle or confuse others. That is often a much more challenging question to answer than it might appear at first glance since it is difficult to analyze objectively one's own culture. Matters that might seem to you to be common sense or reflections of human nature may actually be derived from your upbringing within a particular culture.

Hence, an American negotiator, for instance, might be well-advised to think carefully about the distinguishing dimensions of American culture and how their reflection in his or her approach might affect an upcoming cross-cultural negotiation.[85] To take one example, solving problems has long played a large role in the American cultural orientation. When Americans think of social issues, their minds move quickly toward debating the best policies to deal with those issues. For example, the mention of drugs stimulates many Americans to turn instinctively to the issue of what should be done about them. Is the best policy legalization or improved law enforcement? Should more funds be devoted to interdicting drugs in transit or to public education campaigns? What will solve the problem? One from another culture might think about the issue of drugs from a contrasting viewpoint. Perhaps a central assumption is that no "solution" exists: the problem of illegal drug use is insoluble. It is beyond human capabilities to fix or alter much and will always be with us.

Or, consider conflict. Americans are accustomed to thinking and talking in terms of resolving it ("conflict resolution"), managing it ("conflict management"), transforming it ("conflict transformation"). The emphasis is on using our intelligence to manipulate conflict in positive directions. In summarizing the quite different approach of a prominent Chinese philosopher, one scholar wrote: "At core, said Sun Tzu, conflict is not just *in* the nature of things, it *is* the nature of things. Conflict is as sure a thing as sickness and health, day and night, joy and sadness, risk and opportunity."[86] When a Chinese-American conflict occurs, these contrasting cultural orientations might very well influence the ensuing negotiation.

Skillful negotiators also bear in mind, however, that trying to act in a culturally sensitive manner can fail or even backfire. Extensive cultural understanding is quite difficult to attain. Even a negotiator who sets out to match the negotiating approach of a foreigner may not be able to do so effectively.[87] Cultures are so distinct and complex that one's effort to align oneself with the way people from another country act may seem false or even ridiculous to them. In a 1960 speech at the United Nations Soviet Premier Nikita Khrushchev took off his shoe and pounded it on the lectern as he made a point. His son later revealed that his father knew of the passionate public political debates that occurred in so many western countries and was trying to act the way he imagined westerners might.[88]

One species of problem that occasionally arises in cross-cultural interactions is termed **cultural hyper-correction**. That is, a negotiator intent on demonstrating cultural awareness or sensitivity might go too far to be effective in trying to negotiate just the way that someone from the other culture might, a phenomenon sometimes short-handed as, for example, "out-Japanese-ing the Japanese." Cultural hyper-correction can upset expectations and puzzle an opposing negotiator. As one scholar put it, "It is far from obvious that when in China, a Western negotiator is expected to behave like a Chinese negotiator would. Such behavior might raise more questions than it answers and end up confusing the other party."[89]

Another problem occurs when a cross-cultural negotiation involves a mutually aggravating spiral of contrasting cultural approaches. The term **complementary schismogenesis** stands for the idea that the culturally derived behavior of each negotiator drives his or her counterpart toward increasingly exaggerated expressions of their own contrasting cultural approach in a mutually intensifying spiral.[90] For example, as one authority put it, "When Americans and Japanese experience cross-cultural communication problems, the Americans will use more and more talk to try to resolve the conflict, and the Japanese will use less and less talk to avoid the problem."[91]

Today, however, cross-cultural negotiations occur in an extraordinary variety of situations. The potential for cultural misunderstandings has never been greater, yet those engaged in negotiations of this sort may lack the skills, training, and background to bridge distinct cultures effectively. Biases, stereotypes, and over-generalizations continue to hamper perceptions of foreign cultures. All these and the other issues highlighted above pose real challenges for negotiators in the twenty-first century. This chapter is designed to open the eyes of those negotiating complex issues to significant cross-cultural considerations and offer ideas about how to craft a negotiating strategy so as to handle them effectively.

Notes

1. I. William Zartman, *A Skeptic's View*, in CULTURE AND NEGOTIATION 19 (Guy Olivier Faure & Jeffrey Z. Rubin eds., 1993).
2. Guy Olivier Faure, *International Negotiation*, in INTERNATIONAL NEGOTIATION 400 (Victor A. Kremenyuk ed., 2d ed., 2002).
3. RAYMOND WILLIAMS, KEYWORDS 87 (1983).
4. HOWARD RAIFFA, NEGOTIATION ANALYSIS 284 (2002).
5. GLEN FISHER, MINDSETS 44 (2d ed. 1998).
6. Faure, supra note 2, at 400.
7. FISHER, supra note 5, at 44.
8. *Id.* at xi, 39, 54.
9. *Towne v. Eisner*, 245 US 372, 376 (1918).
10. JULIE M. BUNCK, FIDEL CASTRO AND THE QUEST FOR A REVOLUTIONARY CULTURE IN CUBA 215–22 (1994).
11. HARRY C. TRIANDIS, CULTURE AND SOCIAL BEHAVIOR 181 (1994).
12. RAYMOND COHEN, NEGOTIATING ACROSS CULTURES 12 (1991).
13. FISHER, supra note 5, at 52.
14. *Id.* at 53.
15. WILLIAM HERNÁNDEZ REQUEJO & JOHN L. GRAHAM, GLOBAL NEGOTIATION 209 (2008).
16. COHEN, supra note 12, at 25–27, 50–51.
17. Faure, supra note 2, at 405.
18. Michael R. Fowler, *Transplanting Active Learning Abroad*, 6 INT'L STUD. PERSP. 165 (2005).
19. Jeffrey R. Seul, *Religion and Conflict*, in THE NEGOTIATOR'S FIELDBOOK 323–34 (Andrea Kupfer Schneider & Christopher Honeyman eds., 2006).
20. Ramon Muller, *Foreword to the Third Edition*, in THE ABA GUIDE TO INTERNATIONAL BUSINESS NEGOTIATIONS xi (2009).
21. Faure, supra note 2, at 396.
22. ROGER E. AXTELL, GESTURES (2d ed. 1998); JOHANNES GALLI, INTERCULTURAL COMMUNICATION AND BODY LANGUAGE (2000).
23. ROY J. LEWICKI, DAVID M. SAUNDERS, & JOHN W. MINTON, ESSENTIALS OF NEGOTIATION 198 (2d ed. 2001).
24. Faure, supra note 2, at 406.

25. KENJI KITAO & S. KATHLEEN KITAO, INTERCULTURAL COMMUNICATION 45 (1989).

26. GLEN FISHER, INTERNATIONAL NEGOTIATION 61 (1980).

27. HARU YAMADA, AMERICAN AND JAPANESE BUSINESS DISCOURSE 33 (1992).

28. Sanda Kaufman, *The Interpreter as Intervener*, in THE NEGOTIATOR'S FIELDBOOK 537 (Andrea Kupfer Schneider & Christopher Honeyman eds., 2006).

29. Jeswald Salacuse, *Making Deals in Strange Places*, 4 NEGOTIATION J. 10 (1988).

30. Kaufman, supra note 28, at 538–40.

31. FISHER, supra note 5, at 36.

32. Kaufman, supra note 28, at 539.

33. Guy Olivier Faure & Gunnar Sjöstedt, *Culture and Negotiation*, in CULTURE AND NEGOTIATION 4 (Guy Olivier Faure & Jeffrey Z. Rubin eds., 1993).

34. FISHER, supra note 26, at 37.

35. J.E. Walsh, *Foreword*, in CULTURAL FACTORS IN INTERNATIONAL RELATIONS 9 (Ram P. Anand ed., 1981).

36. Clyde Kluckhorn, *The Study of Culture*, in THE POLICY SCIENCES 87 (Daniel Lernere & Harold D. Lasswell eds., 1951).

37. FISHER, supra note 26, at 53–57.

38. FISHER, supra note 5, at 55.

39. ROGER FISHER & DANIEL SHAPIRO, BEYOND REASON 98 (2005).

40. TERRI MORRISON, WAYNE A. CONWAY, & GEORGE A. BORDEN, KISS, BOW, OR SHAKE HANDS (1994).

41. Faure, supra note 2, at 410.

42. Nancy L. Roth, Todd Hunt, Maria Stavropoulos, & Karen Babik, *Can't We All Just Get Along*, 22 PUB. REL.S REV. 151–61 (1996).

43. Raymond Cohen, *An Advocate's View*, in CULTURE AND NEGOTIATION 22 (Guy Olivier Faure & Jeffrey Z. Rubin eds., 1993).

44. FISHER, supra note 26, at 20.

45. Faure & Sjöstedt, supra note 33, at 9.

46. Faure, supra note 2, at 402.

47. See, for instance, THE ABA GUIDE TO INTERNATIONAL BUSINESS NEGOTIATIONS (James R. Silkenat & Jeffrey M. Aresty eds., 2000).

48. FISHER, supra note 5, at 41, 56.

49. Jeswald Salacuse, *Making Deals in Strange Places*, 4 NEGOTIATION J. 10 (1988).

50. FISHER, supra note 26, at 49–50.

51. FISHER, supra note 5, at 5.

52. ROGER FISHER, INTERNATIONAL CONFLICT FOR BEGINNERS 128 (1969).

53. Faure & Sjöstedt, supra note 30, at 9.

54. ALEXANDER G. NIKOLAEV, INTERNATIONAL NEGOTIATIONS 252 (2007).

55. I. William Zartman, *A Skeptic's View*, in CULTURE AND NEGOTIATION 17 (Guy Olivier Faure & Jeffrey Z. Rubin eds., 1993).

56. Faure, supra note 2, at 413.

57. Zartman, supra note 55, at 19.

58. Jeffrey Z. Rubin & Frank E. A. Sander, *Culture, Negotiation, and the Eye of the Beholder*, 7 NEGOTIATION J. 253 (1991).

59. Address by Tommy Koh, Harvard Program on Negotiation Great Negotiator Award Speech (Apr. 10, 2014).

60. Kluckhorn, supra note 36, at 87.

61. Faure, supra note 2, at 402.

62. Jeffrey Z. Rubin, *The Actors in Negotiation*, in INTERNATIONAL NEGOTIATION 98 (Victor A. Kremenyuk ed., 1991).

63. GUNNAR SJÖSTEDT, ED., PROFESSIONAL CULTURES IN INTERNATIONAL NEGOTIATION (2003).

64. Zartman, supra note 55, at 19.

65. FISHER, supra note 5, at 170.

66. KEVIN AVRUCH, CULTURE AND CONFLICT RESOLUTION 44–45 (1998).

67. Carrie Menkel-Meadow & Michael Wheeler, *Social Influences and Impacts*, in WHAT'S FAIR 366 (Carrie Menkel-Meadow & Michael Wheeler eds., 2004).

68. Zartman, supra note 55, at 21.

69. Christophe Dupont & Guy-Olivier Faure, *The Negotiation Process*, in INTERNATIONAL NEGOTIATION 46 (Victor A. Kremenyuk ed., 1991).

70. Helmut Morsbach, *Aspects of Nonverbal Communication in Japan*, in INTERNATIONAL COMMUNICATION 241 (Larry A. Samovar & Richard E. Porter eds., 1988).

71. ROBERT M. MARCH, THE JAPANESE NEGOTIATOR 140–41 (1990).

72. KITAO & KITAO, supra note 25, at 51–53; FISHER, supra note 26, at 34.

73. Katie Shonk, *How to Resolve Cultural Conflict: Overcoming Cultural Barriers at the Negotiation Table*, Program on Negotiation, Harvard Law School, March 7, 2016, http://www.pon.harvard.edu/daily/conflict-resolution/a-cross-cultural-negotiation-example-how-to-overcome-cultural-barriers.

74. *Id.*

75. *Id.*

76. RAIFFA, supra note 4, at 285.

77. ROGER FISHER & SCOTT BROWN, GETTING TOGETHER 26 (1988).

78. Steven R. Wilson, *Face and Facework in Negotiation*, in COMMUNICATION AND NEGOTIATION 197 (Linda L. Putnam & Michael R. Roloff eds., 1992).

79. ROGER FISHER, WILLIAM URY, & BRUCE PATTON, GETTING TO YES 28 (2d ed. 1991).

80. WILLIAM L. URY, GETTING PAST NO 120 (2d ed. 1993).

81. Karen Elwood, *Facing Up to Face*, Daily Yomiuri [Japan], 30 Nov. 2006, at 17.

82. Bee Chen Goh, *Typical Errors of Westerners*, in THE NEGOTIATOR'S FIELDBOOK 298 (Andrea Kupfer Schneider & Christopher Honeyman eds., 2006).

83. NIKOLAEV, supra note 54, at 283.

84. Salacuse, supra note 49, at 10.

85. EDWARD C. STEWART & MILTON J. BENNET, AMERICAN CULTURAL PATTERNS (1991).

86. Peter S. Adler, *Protean Negotiation*, in THE NEGOTIATOR'S FIELD BOOK 22 (Andrea Kupfer Schneider & Christopher Honeyman eds., 2006).

87. ROY J. LEWICKI, DAVID M. SAUNDERS, & JOHN W. MINTON, ESSENTIALS OF NEGOTIATION 201 (2d ed. 2001).

88. URY, supra note 80, at 42–43.

89. Faure, supra note 2, at 403.

90. DEBORAH TANNEN, CONVERSATIONAL STYLE 31 (2005).

91. YAMADA, supra note 27, at 44.

Checkpoints

- With revolutions in transportation and communication and other dimensions of globalization, professionals in law, business, and other fields must often negotiate across cultures. All negotiators find insights into what their counterparts are thinking valuable, and cultural variables often deeply influence mindsets and thought processes. While culture is rarely the most important factor in a negotiation, it does often play a significant role.

- Cultures are distinctive sets of values and attitudes, norms and beliefs, that usually evolve slowly with the experience and tradition of particular groups. These then play a role in determining a group's self-image or identity. To some extent, they help to guide the actions and orient the behavior of many of the group's members as they cope with the problems of daily life.

- Culture provides people with unwritten instructions on how to act in daily life, what is fitting, appropriate, legitimate behavior. It affects an individual's sense of rights and duties, what is upright versus immoral, normal versus peculiar. Culture can influence the meaning people ascribe to events, and it can help them to determine how actions ought to be defended, criticized, or rationalized.

- There are national cultures and regional ones, high-context and low-context cultures, ethnic, religious, and even occupational cultures, such as the culture of diplomats.

- Individuals may be influenced by many separate cultural variables; sub-cultures and supra-cultures exist alongside national cultures, for instance. Given the complexities of cultural influences, their impact on any particular negotiation is uncertain. Determining which cultural value might be influencing a negotiator at any particular moment can be daunting. More often than not, cultural factors simply provide tentative indicators of what people are thinking or how they are reacting. Nevertheless, this may be quite useful if it gives a negotiator insights into how the other party views particular matters related to a negotiation.

- Cultural differences affect the way that people interact with each other, both verbal and non-verbal communication. The cultural context may determine whether the meaning of a particular statement — *"she's a real individual,"* for instance — could be a positive or negative statement in one culture or another.

- One school of thought, the advocates, finds culture vitally important for negotiation. Understanding something of the culture of one's counterpart can help negotiators to handle cross-cultural noise, to grasp what the other side values, how it understands its interests, and what priorities and goals it sets. Cultural variables may even affect an individual's line of reasoning, whether problems are analyzed inductively or deductively and such abstractions as legitimacy, justice, and fairness.

- Another school of thought, the skeptics, emphasizes the problems and difficulties associated with putting cultural concepts to practical use. Generalizations about culture can be confusing and misleading. Individual variations abound, and multiple cultures affect individuals. These may then temper or contradict different aspects of how people within that culture view the world. Negotiators at work on complex problems that contain cross-cultural dimensions might bear in mind important cultural differences and then try to take them into account in a thoughtful way as they create and implement their negotiating strategies.

- A skillful negotiator might consider the culture of his or her counterparts and think through their expectations for the working relationship, the processes of negotiation, and the type of agreement to aim at. This might then help the negotiator to create an effective strategy, one that handled the particular cultural differences and complementarities well.

Chapter 10

Ethical Negotiation: Distinguishing Proper from Improper Behavior

---

Roadmap

- **Locating standards to use:** What standards might negotiators call on as they try to determine what is proper and improper behavior? What are the legal, ethical, moral, and practical approaches?

- **Disclosure and deception:** What issues are raised by failing to disclose particular matters? What problems can arise when a negotiator sets out to deceive a counterpart? When should negotiators be especially on guard, watching carefully for possible deception?

- **Legitimate and illegitimate behavior:** What is meant by *dirty tricks, puffing,* and *bluffing*? Why might a negotiator misrepresent his or her authority?

- **Major error:** What should an honest negotiator do when a counterpart thoroughly misconceives something or makes a major error in calculations?

- **Principals and agents:** How does a principal-agent relationship raise issues of negotiation ethics? What are fiduciary relations? What potentially contrasting perspectives might a principal and an agent have? Why and how do principals design incentives to try to ensure that an agent acts to advance their best interests?

- **Bad Faith:** What is meant by negotiating in good faith and bad faith?

People consider an honest person to be one who does not engage in various anti-social activities: he or she does not shop-lift, for instance, cheat on examinations, or make off with the contents of the neighbor's garage. An honest negotiator does not lie to counterparts or take unfair advantage of them. And yet, as straightforward as that may sound, negotiators often puzzle over the great variety of ethical issues that arise as they work with each other, deciding to use or to avoid certain tactics or to behave one way and not another.

In all advanced negotiations significant quantities of information must be exchanged with both sides expecting that shared facts are accurate and not false or fabricated. On occasion, however, negotiators confront the impulse to be dishonest to try to progress toward their objectives. Negotiators may be especially prone to ethical lapses in the following circumstances:

- when facing stakes that are especially high,
- when confronting clients or constituents who are angry, demanding, or pressuring,
- when seized by feelings of envy or competitive instincts to recoup a notable loss or to try to get the better of one's counterpart,
- when mistrust of the other side, particularly of its veracity, has developed, or
- when time is short and the negotiator badly wants to conclude a deal quickly.

Complicating matters further, some who would not consider themselves to be dishonest in ordinary life may be proceeding on the assumption that their role as a negotiator permits, or even requires, different behavior. A feeling of *caveat emptor*, "let the buyer beware," sometimes lies behind that, as does the view that misleading the other side about one's intentions on various matters is an inherent part of bargaining.[1] For example, part of trying to get the best deal I can, a bargainer reasons, involves keeping from you the point at which I really will settle. And, if I am justified in avoiding straightforward communication about that, might there be an array of other circumstances where I would be justified and better off with less than candid plain dealing?

Another problem is related to the idea of *partisan perceptions* examined in Chapter 7. A negotiator, especially one who dislikes or distrusts a counterpart, sometimes justifies his or her own dishonest actions on the assumption that the other side is doing, or preparing to do, the same thing. The self-serving rationale for such behavior is "Don't take me for a naive fool. Everyone does it."

Many of the more interesting questions regarding negotiation ethics turn out to be closely tied to circumstances. With respect to a great variety of particular issues, a negotiator's ethical obligations may not be so easy to discern and fulfill. Consider, for instance, the following issues, issues that negotiators who believe themselves to be honest and upstanding might still resolve somewhat differently.

- Ought you negotiate one way with partners, colleagues, or family members, and another way in an arm's-length transaction with people you do not know? Does an honest negotiator proceed differently with friends and with strangers?[2]

- What facts pertinent to a negotiation is it proper to fail to disclose or to try to conceal from one's counterpart? What are the boundaries of legitimate confidential information?
- Should you try to get considerably more in a negotiated agreement than what you privately see as your fair share? Do you always try to maximize your side's take when you negotiate, or in certain circumstances should you self-impose particular limits? But, what circumstances exactly and what limits?
- When your counterpart asks for your rationale for designating a particular price or wanting a particular provision, is it proper to provide a different reason than is actually motivating you?
- When is it ethical to delay negotiations indefinitely or to act as a spoiler trying to block a potential agreement?
- When a counterpart chooses to take you into confidence about some matter related to the negotiation, under what circumstances, if any, could you later divulge that information, and to whom?
- How about the impact of a negotiated resolution on third parties who are not represented at the bargaining table? To what extent does one have an ethical obligation to bear their interests in mind or invite them to participate?

Or, consider the ethical issues that arise with respect to the implementation of a negotiated agreement. International lawyers consider the Latin phrase *pacta sunt servanda*—promises made ought to be honored—to amount to a foundational rule of dealings between governments in international society. Many negotiators would identify with that same principle: one arrives at a negotiated deal expecting that the agreement's terms will be carried out. Nevertheless, when would extenuating circumstances justify breaking an agreement? In what situations should one feel ethically bound to keep a promise, and when might prior promises be ignored without contravening ethical responsibilities?

Since questions regarding what honest negotiating entails often arise abruptly, without leaving much time to consider what ought to be done, people should think ahead of time about how best to deal with issues that may arise. Here, some see a difficult trade-off: "The stricter your ethical standards, the higher the cost you must be willing to pay to uphold them in any given transaction. The lower your ethical standards, the higher the price may be in terms of your reputation."[3]

The fact is that those involved in complex negotiations usually have multiple opportunities to stretch, distort, ignore, or flout the truth. The French philosopher Michel de Montaigne observed, "If, like truth, the lie had but one face ... we would accept as certain the opposite of what the liar would say. But the reverse of truth has a hundred thousand faces and an infinite field."[4] This chapter focuses on several contexts that consistently raise questions of negotiation ethics. It identifies certain tactics that a negotiator might encounter or be tempted to use, and it explores how a responsible negotiator might want to behave.

A. Different Standards

One's personal theory of what constitutes honest negotiation should be consistent and grounded in one's values. An honest, upstanding negotiator should, if called on, be able to explain and defend with a persuasive rationale how he or she has handled an ethical issue. Let us turn, then, to various standards that negotiators might find helpful.

1. Legal Principles

Some standards relevant to honest and dishonest bargaining involve legal principles. Here, negotiators ask, "What am I legally permitted to do in trying to fashion the best possible outcome for my side of the negotiation, and what would be legally proscribed?" Among the specific issues that might arise in a negotiation are the following.

- How much candor does the law require?
- What negotiating behavior might prove to be actionable at law?
- What amounts to fraudulent or coercive behavior or unlawful misrepresentation?
- What might cause a court to negate an agreement and even perhaps institute punitive damages?

Federal and state legislatures have passed laws that aim to affect the behavior of negotiators in cases involving a range of subject-matters including family law and securities law. For instance, in the sale of residential real estate potential sellers may be legally obligated to reveal significant problems they know about their own house. Consumer and banking laws mandate that one side disclose particular matters to the other or provide the potentially more vulnerable party with an opportunity to rescind an agreement for some limited period of time.

The common law of tort and contract limits lawful bargaining behavior as well.[5] Thus, fraud could affect negotiations of many varieties. A negotiator makes a fraudulent statement when he or she says something about a material fact knowing that it is untrue. The other party must also rely on that statement in a way that a court views as reasonable, and he or she must have been damaged later by that reliance. A court could void an agreement that was gained fraudulently, and the negotiator caught lying could be liable for damages.

A negotiator's use of improper threats might also bring a court to void an agreement.[6] If a negotiator threatened another, or the party that negotiator represented, with a crime or a tort or with criminal prosecution, that would be improper.[7] A court could even consider certain threats to undertake civil litigation to be improper, such as if the lawsuit involved the seizure of property.[8]

A negotiator aiming to determine proper and improper behavior by legal standards alone might reason that anything unlawful is unethical, but where the law is silent or allows particular behavior, it is presumed to be ethically sound. Others might reason, however, that the law simply establishes a minimal baseline regarding a discrete number of issues, but it does not identify and prohibit any great range of questionable tactics.

Certainly, no law compels the disclosure of a wide range of matters relevant to negotiations. For example, declarations of the value or price of something are not ordinarily considered to be statements of fact, but instead are assumed to be mere opinions, referenced in setting out a bargaining stance. In short, while various legal provisions in contract, corporate, property, and other bodies of law apply to negotiation, the law does not extensively regulate negotiation per se. Rather, more often than not, the bargaining process is left to operate on its own.

A scholar of negotiation ethics observed, "What Oliver Wendell Holmes' 'bad man' can get away with under the law does not hold a candle to what a 'bad' or immoral negotiator can still do without fear of legal sanction, in large measure because so much of what negotiators do, they do in private, where no one can see them."[9]

2. Ethical Guidelines

One consequence of the limitations of legal regulation is that societies may expect honest negotiators to follow more involved, elaborate, or demanding ethical standards than those found in the law. (By ethics I mean the principles or rules of conduct that a society expects its members to follow in this situation or that one.)

Legal proscriptions do not elucidate the best practices that might be associated with an expert negotiator and contribute to his or her positive reputation and, in that way, effectiveness. But, ethical considerations might shed some light on this. Something may not be explicitly unlawful, but other negotiators might still frown upon or scorn it as unethical.

"The purpose of ethics...," one authority declared, "is to curb excessive self-interest and to encourage regard for the rights of others."[10] One approach to ethics in negotiation would be to scrutinize the consequences of the behavior at issue. An ethically sound action would be one with defensible results.[11]

In thinking through ethical matters, attorneys across the United States tend to start with the American Bar Association's Model Rules of Professional Conduct or some closely related variant found in a state bar association's code of ethics. Such sources require lawyers not to lie about *material facts*, that is, information that a negotiator would reasonably see as quite significant in determining how to proceed in the negotiation.[12]

An attorney who says, "We won't agree to any deal that gives us even a penny less than *x*," is assumed to be giving an opinion, not stating a material fact. But, a lawyer representing a local bank that might be sold to a larger regional competitor ought to be truthful about the bank's finances. These clearly would be material facts in the negotiation. And, if a lawyer becomes aware that he or she has made a material misstatement, there is an obligation to correct what was misrepresented.[13]

Accountants, real estate agents, and various other professionals have codes of ethics, just a lawyers do, to which they are pledged to abide. Certain provisions are relevant to negotiation. Although these codes do not extensively regulate negotiation ethics, if their provisions are violated, a professional society might sanction or otherwise discipline a negotiator for unethical conduct.

If acting unethically can bring on real problems, acting ethically can have positive repercussions. It might, for instance, make professionals more content with their jobs.[14] To illustrate, imagine a business that trained its sales people to use the *bait-and-switch technique*. The idea here is to interest a purchaser in something by alluding to an extraordinarily favorable sales price, but then, once you have gained their interest, "discover" that all of those items have just been sold and try to substitute some alternative at a much higher price.

Passage of a law prohibiting this sales technique would be problematic: among other issues, reliable evidence might be difficult to gather. However, even though not illegal, people in that community might well consider the bait-and-switch routine to be an underhanded negotiation practice, and sales people might be happier in their jobs if they were not pressed to act this way.

Beyond the professional codes of behavior, one might turn to culture to try to determine if some particular negotiating behavior were in accord with the customs and norms of society or contravened them. From our discussion in Chapter 9 we ought to bear in mind that ethical considerations differ from one culture to another. Culture might affect a variety of ethical norms, such as the veracity expected in a negotiating partner. One scholar observed: "In some cultures, it is acceptable to marshal forcefully, but truthfully, all the arguments for one's own side and to avoid giving gratuitous help to the other side. In other cultures it is acceptable to exaggerate or even to bend the truth here and there—but not too much. In still other cultures a really big whopper, if accomplished with flair and humor, is something to brag about and not to hide after the fact, especially if it is successful.[15]

In sum, then, over and above legal principles, negotiators might try to discern ethical guidelines. Some of these are set forth in professional codes of conduct, but others depend upon cultural considerations of how one ought to act within that society in different situations.

3. Moral Standards

As I use the terms, *ethics* speaks to a society's vision, its value judgments, of what is good and worthwhile or bad and wrongful conduct. It thus helps to delineate proper and improper behavior for its members. I distinguish this term, however, from a *moral* perspective on negotiation, which I take as implicating the personal aspirations of individuals to be good, responsible people.

Although different individuals will define goodness and responsibility differently, many negotiators might associate good, responsible negotiating with dealing fairly with others and not exploiting their ignorance. A moral perspective asks not "What can I do and avoid being penalized for it, legally or socially?," but "What *should* I do to behave as an upright negotiator?"

The underlying rationale for calling upon moral standards is that, because you are now negotiating, you ought not become a different person with a different set of moral values. "What is wrong to do to another person," it has been said, "is not excused by the act of negotiation."[16] No one should be able to buy your morals. You should not alter who you are and what you stand for simply because you are now negotiating, as opposed to undertaking some other activity. Zealously representing a client does not obligate a lawyer or any other negotiating agent to lie on his or her behalf.

One reason that negotiators might consider their morals in determining what to do in a given situation is that their behavior does not simply affect their client and their counterpart. It can affect them personally as well. Their very identity may be linked to their morals, as may their psychological well-being, including their satisfaction with their jobs. Many people want to be proud of who they work for, what they stand for, who they are. Straying from or stretching the truth can thus have negative personal ramifications. One authority noted, "[A] liar often *does* diminish himself by lying, and the loss is precisely to his dignity, his integrity."[17]

Individuals thus sometimes call on their own senses of what constitutes moral behavior, what is the right thing to do in different circumstances. Here, one would apply the dictates of one's conscience and convictions to a question involving negotiation ethics. For example, a negotiator might revert to the biblical counsel: "Do unto others as you would have them do unto you."[18] How would you want someone to treat you, should you be placed in that same situation?

Another moral approach to issues of honesty in negotiation has a negotiator think about how they would appear to themselves or to others.[19] After engaging in a tactic that might be questioned on ethical grounds, were you to look at yourself in the mirror would you be ashamed of what you had done? What if your parent, child, or mentor watched you in action? How would they feel about your actions?

Morals can be influenced by people's visions of the type of society in which they want to live. In determining points on their moral compass, some might ask, "What if everyone were to act this way? Would that be socially problematic?"

Even when the opposing negotiator is acting deceptively or unethically, a person of high morals would resist the temptation to follow suit. Indeed, he or she would be honest even if dishonesty offered clear advantages in the short- or long-term. Furthermore, one's morals might guide behavior not only during the process of negotiation, but during pre-negotiation when a party sets out its goals. Some possible objectives, offering potential advantages of one sort or another, might be eliminated from consideration on moral grounds.

Nevertheless, moral behavior provides its own advantages as well. One authority declared: "[Y]ou need to keep your record clean both to maintain your self-respect and to avoid gaining a reputation for slippery dealing.... [A]s soon as you begin acting unethically, you lose the right to protest other people's conduct. Their behavior may give you a legitimate claim to extract concessions, or it may form the basis for a legal case. Once you join them in the gutter, you forfeit your moral and legal advantage."[20]

These points suggest that, even where the law might not prohibit a particular negotiating tactic or practice condemn it as wrong, a negotiator might nonetheless refuse to advance it on moral grounds. Your own exemplary behavior can positively influence others.[21] Dishonorable undertakings by negotiators can have the opposite effect. Our cumulative actions, over various ethical issues and multiple negotiations, directly affect our society. "Our goodness is not defined by whatever we profess in the abstract," it has been observed, "but rather is enacted step by step in each of the small things that we do at the bargaining table."[22]

4. Practical or Utilitarian Considerations

As one considers a question of negotiation ethics, quite pragmatic considerations might enter the calculations as well. Here, the negotiator focuses not on whether some possible action is impermissible, but whether it is inadvisable.

For eminently practical reasons negotiators might, for instance, decide against deceiving another about some point. A lawyer or other agent may well negotiate with many counterparts over the years. Cultivating one's good name, becoming widely known for honest, straightforward dealing, where one treats others with respect and dignity, can pay substantial dividends in future negotiations. It can be exceedingly useful to enter a negotiation highly esteemed by one's fellow negotiators, with a positive, honorable reputation for integrity, and then to live up to those expectations during the discussions.

Empirical studies of legal negotiation suggest that a lawyer who acts ethically and respectfully toward others is more likely to be seen as an effective negotiator by counterparts than one who does not.[23] Treating the other side honestly may be taken as a prerequisite to the close cooperation needed to resolve a complex problem or opportunity.

As one works with counterparts attempting to reach mutually beneficial agreements, having the other side see you as a trustworthy counterpart is quite an asset. Good will cultivated with one's negotiating counterpart can have rippling positive repercussions. Socrates once advised, "Regard your good name as the richest jewel you can possibly be possessed of …"[24]

Since intelligent professionals when dealing with significant matters tend to be wary and skeptical, trust is difficult to gain and can evaporate with questionable behavior. After an act of deception, a counterpart may very well come to recognize that he or she was, in fact, misled. Those who find that they were deceived tend to feel wronged, manipulated, and resentful.

When one treats another unethically, that party may "hold grudges, look for ways to get even, and spread rumor or gossip that may make it difficult for the negotiator to achieve future objectives."[25] In addition, if both sides are busily engaged in deceiving one another, any resulting agreement will likely have missed a number of possible joint gains.[26] Indeed, if even suspicions of deceit arise during a negotiation, this is likely to greatly constrain communication and undercut efforts at cooperative problem-solving.

Furthermore, if one side misrepresents, and the other side catches on, the misled counterpart might then inject its own misrepresentation, initiating a spiral of deception that has real potential to undermine the negotiation. If, instead, the truth is learned at some future date, the prior lie is bound to harm relations between negotiators or their clients, and it may affect implementation of the deal.

More broadly, a reputation for being shifty, crooked, double-dealing, or untruthful could diminish a negotiator's future effectiveness and be quite difficult to shed. Sir Henry Wotten once defined an ambassador as "a man of virtue, sent abroad to lie for the good of his country."[27] When reminded of this, British ambassador Sir Harold Nicolson observed, "Yes, but he must also return to negotiate another day."[28] All those aware of a negotiator's unsavory reputation will be on guard to keep from being taken advantage of.

The balance sheet of engaging in ethically questionable negotiating behavior suggests that various tactics may have long-term costs that come to outweigh any short-term benefits that might have accrued. One authority observed, "Rarely does one negotiate in the absence of future consequences. Even if you and I meet once and once only, our reputations have a way of surviving the exchange, coloring the expectations that others will have of us in the future."[29] Another source concluded: "A bad reputation, loss of credibility, and an unwillingness for others to deal with us are far more serious than anything we can gain by taking short-term advantage of our opponent."[30]

The practical or utilitarian approach thus urges negotiators to consider carefully their reputations and the effect that deceptive behavior could have on their ability to negotiate effectively in other circumstances. One considering practical or utilitarian considerations might ask the following questions.

- Is it sensible or wise to take ethically questionable actions in a negotiation?
- Might these grievously damage one's reputation for honest dealings and straightforward behavior?
- Might it serve some immediate aim but at considerable future costs?

B. Disclosure, Non-Disclosure, and Deceit

What am I to tell the other side, and what may I properly try to withhold from them? Perhaps the ethical issues that arise most frequently in negotiation involve disclosure versus non-disclosure as well as the distorting of facts or other forms of deceit. It is useful to think of full disclosure to deliberate deception as a continuum, one that regularly poses issues for negotiators as to what to reveal to a counterpart, how to phrase their statements, when to omit to say something, and what exactly to withhold from the other side.[31]

Box 10.1 lays out the various issues that might crowd into a negotiator's mind in the course of even a very simple transaction.

Box 10.1 — Illustrating Problems of Disclosure and Non-Disclosure

Eleanor Holmes Norton illustrated representative ethical problems of disclosure and non-disclosure by considering the example of the sale of a used set of barbells. She asked:

> If someone may misrepresent her settlement point as $100 when it is actually $50, may she misrepresent the information on which the settlement point is based, such as the original purchase price? What about claiming that the barbells are of high quality when, according to Consumer Reports, they are actually of middle to low quality? Suppose that the negotiator has decided that she can settle for as low as $50, if necessary, because she used the new barbells about ten times after she purchased the set. Is the prospective buyer entitled to this information? Should it be offered only if asked? May it be misrepresented if asked? Apart from truthfulness, what of fairness? Suppose the seller discovers that the buyer has no idea what barbells should cost and does not ask what the seller paid for them? Should the seller volunteer this information? Should she ask for twice as much as she might from a more experienced buyer and use hard-sell or arm-twisting techniques?

Eleanor Holmes Norton, *Bargaining and the Ethics of Process*, in WHAT'S FAIR? 275–76 (Carrie Menkel-Meadow & Michael Wheeler eds., 2004).

Negotiators are not expected to exhibit full candor. A counterpart might take advantage if a vulnerability were exposed and thoroughly disclosing all information to the other side might hurt one's bargaining position. Experienced negotiators thus bear in mind the distinct possibility that, on some points, the other side is not being entirely straightforward, but is sidestepping, obfuscating, spinning matters one way or another, or, simply, lying. We have seen that some engaged in bargaining may feel that shading the truth is a permissible part of the process of negotiation. Negotiators must thus try to distinguish true statements from half-truths and falsehoods.

1. Lies

Negotiators reason constantly about their opponent's intentions, buttressing their reasoning with facts, logic, estimates, inferences about body language, and trying to glean information from a host of telltale signs or statements. But, here, a negotiator might employ deception to influence a counterpart to draw some erroneous conclusion. Or, he or she might say something which, though literally true, is carefully formulated so as to mislead the other side.

In asking "where should you draw the line?," one experienced positional negotiator observed that, on occasion, "You *want* your counterpart to believe you're more immovable on price than you really are. You don't *want* him to realize the relative unimportance to you of the point you're about to concede, so that your concession will motivate him to make a substantial move on another front."[32]

Thus, in carrying out their strategies, negotiators may be tempted to dissemble, embellish, spin the truth, or make misleading statements, all to gain some advantage in the negotiation. The most common and direct form of deception, however, is an outright lie, that is, a statement contrary to what the speaker believes to be true. Negotiators lie "to misinform the opponent, to eliminate or obscure the opponent's choice of alternatives, or to manipulate the perceived costs and benefits of particular options that the opponent may wish to pursue."[33]

Given the private nature of much negotiation, it is certainly possible that a negotiator will tell lies that will never be discovered.[34] Nevertheless, concocting lies is often a complicated undertaking, and one that can quickly become stressful. In fact, the more intricate the lie and the further the lie recedes in the past, the more difficult it is for the liar to recall just what was said. Consequently, a Roman sage counseled wryly, "A liar should have a good memory."[35]

Moreover, not infrequently, one lie leads on to another. One scholar wrote, "It is easy, a wit observed, to tell a lie, but hard to tell only one. The first lie 'must be thatched with another or it will rain through.' More and more lies may come to be needed; the liar always has more mending to do." She concluded by observing that the strains "become greater each time—many have noted that it takes an excellent memory to keep one's untruths in good repair and disentangled."[36]

Then, some take lying to be addictive.[37] Initially, a person lies on a particular occasion, perhaps to shield another (a so-called "white lie") or to gain some major benefit "just this once." But, over time, lying can easily become a habit, and one used on more and more occasions for more and more different reasons. One can gravitate toward being a customary, persistent, habitual liar, just as one can stand out as a customary, persistent, habitual truth-teller.

And, misrepresentations in negotiations often have real potential to bring on serious problems. Noted French statesman François de Callières declared, "A lie always leaves a drop of poison behind."[38] Deceiving a counterpart threatens working relations and could spoil the chances for a negotiated resolution to the problem or opportunity being addressed.

For all of these reasons, even simply as a pragmatic matter of weighing pros and cons, one can certainly question whether lying and deceiving in negotiation really do add up to an advantageous balance sheet of serving vital interests and purposes, or whether they end up complicating and undercutting them so often that it is a risky gamble to rely on them.

2. Omissions

A lie is an act of commission: one chooses to say something to mislead another. But sometimes negotiators decide not to say something. When does this pass ethical muster, and when does it fall short?

One aspect of non-disclosure involves confidentiality. Clients have the right to rely on the discretion of their negotiator, who may legitimately be instructed not to disclose certain matters. Furthermore, a "lawyer has no ethical duty to disclose information to an adversary that may be harmful to his client's cause ..."[39]

Think, then, of negotiators involved in their client's efforts to sell something. Even if pursuing a cooperative strategy, the negotiators would not ordinarily disclose knowledge they might have that potential purchasers could obtain that same item more quickly or cheaply from a competitor. In a market transaction most would see their role as advancing the interests of their client and would not feel it incumbent to provide negotiating counterparts with all of the information in hand. Indeed, depending on the circumstances, that could be confidential information that an attorney would properly reveal only with the client's consent.

Nevertheless, many issues regarding non-disclosure are considerably more difficult to resolve. One source notes, "Research has shown that people are more inclined to lie by *omission* (not revealing the whole truth) than by *commission* (falsely answering a question when asked) ..."[40]

Imagine the sale of a small business. Ought the owner to inform the buyer that a valuable employee plans to leave before the sale is consummated, or is it the buyer's responsibility to ferret out such matters in investigating whether to make a purchase offer? What if the planned departure would come after the sale? How about if the employee's plans to leave are more tentative? Those setting out to negotiate honestly might still resolve such situations differently in accordance with their own theories of negotiation ethics.

3. Guarding against Being Deceived

A deceptive negotiator knows a point of significance, but, in hopes of gaining an advantage, stays silent about it, glosses over it, or otherwise misdirects attention in order to encourage the other side to believe something else. Experienced negotiators are well aware that lies and omissions of this sort frequently occur as people interact with one another.

In this regard it is well worth bearing in mind that "Individuals come to a negotiation with significantly different views about the nature of ethics and how it applies to negotiation."[41] As one authority put it, "[S]ome people will hold truth telling so inviolate that they would never give a false answer to a direct question; others might do so if the reward was sufficiently tempting, and others would have few qualms about making false statements."[42]

You may or may not have a good sense for which category your counterpart falls into, but it is prudent not to be too sure that your estimate is correct in any particular set of circumstances. The cautionary words of Italian political philosopher Niccolò Machiavelli may be worth recalling here: "[M]en are so simple and so ready to obey present necessities, that one who deceives will always find those who allow themselves to be deceived."[43]

So, how should people avoid allowing themselves to be deceived? In daily life from a young age forward, we all have experience in trying to uncover lies. We become suspicious by what people say and how they say it: dancing around topics, carefully choosing words when there is no apparent need for diplomacy. We also may attend to body language: someone dodges eye contact or smiles crookedly. Or, the tone of a conversation abruptly changes for murky reasons: someone suddenly appears evasive, ill-at-ease, uncomfortable.

Beyond these generic points about spotting lies, when should negotiators be especially on their guard, watching carefully for possible deception?

a. A Compelling Motive to Deceive

People often have a clear purpose in mind when they stretch the truth. If a false statement is very likely to influence you, your counterpart may be tempted to exaggerate.[44] Furthermore, a negotiator who is hyper-competitive or who feels cornered or desperate has a real motive to deceive another, as does one who has much riding on closing a particular deal. When one hears a potentially deceptive statement, one would do well to consider how motivated the other side is to deceive you on this point. Where strong motivations are present, be especially wary.

b. Difficult to Verify Matters

Another set of problematic circumstances involves matters that are particularly difficult to verify.[45] Sometimes time pressures restrict or eliminate the possibility of checking up on something the other side has said. Some issues, such as what a party prefers or how committed it is to a future action, are inherently somewhat speculative or ambiguous. And, an array of other matters might latter be readily excused or explained away as a mistake or an oversight or a mis-communication, as opposed to deliberate deception.

With respect to all of these matters a negotiator should be on guard, anticipating the possible presence of deceptive statements. These are more likely to crop up with respect to matters that are not easily proven one way or the other.

c. No Continuing Relations

One potentially problematic scenario is when continuing relations between the parties appear to be unlikely. Some negotiators routinely act in upstanding ways because of the moral compass they use to navigate issues in daily life. Others are much more punctilious about sticking to the truth when clear incentives exist to do so. A few care little about their reputation, perhaps because it is already so bad that no real stigma attaches to making it worse!

Consider, then, the following incentives to behave honorably, incentives that will be more or less compelling depending on particular circumstances. Many negotiators will be especially concerned with preserving a positive reputation so long as they expect to work with their counterpart in the future. Alternatively, reputation may weigh heavily where, if they deceive this counterpart, that information might get back to others whose opinion might very well affect them. "We should find less deception in small, close knit communities or in dense social networks," it has been argued, "than we do in large, loosely connected populations."[46]

Where continuing relations are unimportant and word of what is happening in this negotiation is unlikely to travel very far, one should particularly guard against being taken in by deception. Here, a negotiator might see less to lose from attempting to deceive his or her counterpart.

4. Uncovering or Warding Off Deceptive Practices

What, then, can negotiators do to uncover or ward off deceptive practices? One possible antidote to deceptive practices involves working to make the relationship into one that will likely have future consequences. One authority advised: "Try to get recommendations, referrals, and introductions that will show the other side that the relationship with you matters. This move somewhat mitigates the incentives to behave unethically that would otherwise apply."[47]

It may also be quite helpful to negotiate in person, face-to-face, rather than via telephone. Most negotiators are better at picking up on signals that something is awry when seen first-hand. Body language and facial expressions may provide telling indications if the truth is being stretched. And, although negotiating by e-mail creates a written record, providing one disincentive to deception, it also provides the ability to phrase matters very shrewdly, opening up other possibilities to mislead. In short, a negotiator may be more reluctant to deceive when interacting in person than by more impersonal forms of communication.

Sometimes a negotiator suspects deceit, wants to assess how straightforward the other side is being, or feels that a counterpart is trying to circumvent a particular topic perhaps in order to avoid making a material misrepresentation. In some cases a negotiator can respectfully ask for proof or documentation of some particularly important point.[48] As a skillful negotiator turns to closing a deal, he or she will look for ways to verify key points and to ensure that an apparently beneficial resolution does not hinge on a questionable fact being true.

a. Using Questions to Counter Deception

While all of the above may be useful considerations, experienced negotiators counter deception most frequently through the use of questions that help them to critically appraise what they are hearing from the other side. To gain an accurate view of the situation and to avoid being taken advantage of, you need to determine, as best you can, what is reality, what are the actual facts, and what are conjectures, misunderstandings, muddled thoughts, or items that are being avoided. Skillful questioning can help to prevent or expose deception or omissions by a cagey or evasive counterpart.

A suspicious negotiator can press another to answer questions designed to elicit the truth. When a negotiator senses a departure from the truth or spots something that seems contradictory or raises doubts, he or she can remark on the puzzling statement and ask additional questions to try to clarify what is going on. One technique is to pose a series of questions, mixing in some to which the answer is already known. Another is to point out contradictions in the other party's answers and demand better, more complete, explanations.[49]

And yet, a negotiator who is trying to use questions to determine the truth of some matter is engaged in a task that can be difficult and delicate. A litigator posing questions in a courtroom has a key advantage over a negotiator in that witnesses are publicly charged with telling the truth, or even, in the American tradition, "the truth, the whole truth, and nothing but the truth." Although this does not preclude witnesses lying, in many proceedings the formal act of being placed under oath coupled with the possibility of committing perjury through a lie on the witness stand helps to bring out what actually happened.

A negotiator lacks these advantages. He or she must put a question to a counterpart, listen carefully to the response, if any, form a judgment as to its truthfulness, and fashion follow-up inquiries, all while trying, if possible, to preserve constructive working relations, something that may entail avoiding giving offense with too many intrusive questions.

Note, too, that just as you can ask probing questions, trying to discover the truth of something, so can your counterpart. The fact that a negotiator need not answer a question might frustrate when you are the questioner. However, this also protects you when you are being questioned and would prefer to change the subject or dodge an inquiry.

Here, on occasion, you may want to deflect a question or you may even be tempted to stretch the truth yourself in order to gain or retain some perceived advantage. When you are the one on the "hot seat," one scholar counseled, "Remember, there is no commandment in negotiation that says 'Thou shalt answer every question that is asked.'" But he continued by suggesting the following rule of thumb: *"Whenever you are tempted to lie about something, stop, think for a moment, and then find something—anything—to tell the truth about."*[50]

b. Correcting Unethical Approaches

While it is often important to confront and deal with the unethical behavior of a counterpart, rather than ignore it, doing so in a moralizing or self-righteous way can end up being counter-productive. One scholar advised: "When possible, it's best to give the other side wiggle room, a chance to save face, to correct unethical approaches to negotiation without complete disgrace." She continued, "Operate as if the other negotiator is capable of ethical conduct while making it clear that you are not oblivious to unethical tactics ..."[51]

C. Other Particular Ethical Issues

1. Dirty Tricks

Negotiators sometimes label especially sharp, crooked, or underhanded practices as dirty tricks. Although culture can certainly influence what might or might not be considered a dirty trick, negotiators from many different societies would likely consider these practices to be immoral, unethical, and in

some cases and places illegal. An honest negotiator would not use these strat-
agems, but all should be alert to their occasional use.

One dirty trick is to purposefully introduce into the negotiation an erroneous document, perhaps falsified data, misleading financial information, or
a spurious warranty or guarantee. Another tactic, sometimes directed against
a negotiator who is seen as nervous, inexperienced, or unprepared, is to confuse him or her purposefully. Trickery might involve introducing misleading
information, providing indigestible quantities of detailed or technical matters,
or focusing such attention on "'irrelevent' minutiae or side issues" that the
other negotiator's thinking becomes obscured.[52] The slippery negotiator then
takes advantage of the other side's muddled thinking to try to gain some preferred resolution.

A disreputable dirty trick would be to spread false rumors or scandalous
gossip about the other side for a purpose such as eliminating an attractive walk-
away option it has. Or, an underhanded negotiator might threaten to expose
something embarrassing or otherwise make a counterpart look bad in front
of their clients or superiors or within their professional network unless some
concession were made.

Unlawful dirty tricks would include offering a bribe, stealing the other side's
notes when their backs were turned, or bugging their caucuses to learn their
private thoughts. Realize, also, that an unscrupulous business executive might
undertake negotiations as a cover for making off with trade secrets or other
targets of industrial espionage. (If the contents of a business plan or any other
private information are to be revealed during negotiations, a confidentiality
agreement could help to guard against the material being disseminated to others and provide recourse if it were distributed.)

More juvenile versions of dirty tricks involve making an opposing negotiator physically uncomfortable. For instance, one might purposefully spill something on a counterpart, place him or her in a low-slung chair, or arrange seating
so that the opposing negotiator faces a window with sunshine streaming in or
sits next to a vent blowing hot air. To try to wear down the other side, a negotiating session might be artificially prolonged or the types of abusive personal attacks examined in Chapter 7 might be employed.

Dirty tricks should be shunned for contravening legal principles and ethical or moral standards as well as for practical, utilitarian considerations. Many
have the potential to backfire or to stir up the other side beyond any conceivable advantageous return. The more egregious examples might also bring on
liability, or in the case of lawyers and others acting under codes of professional
ethics, discipline for unethical behavior. A negotiator who uncovers a dirty
trick will question the perpetrator's morals and sense of ethical behavior. Con-

sequently, negotiators who value their positive reputations would not stoop to resorting to dirty tricks.

2. Puffing

We have seen that negotiators sometimes shade their real views one way or another. They might magnify or minimize the actual worth of an item to be sold or traded. They might extol the benefits of a deal in glowing terms. These practices present closer questions of negotiation ethics.

Realize, first, that putting a more favorable spin on a point or fact is often tied to leverage considerations, for instance, how badly someone wants something, by what date they need it, or whether they have an attractive walk-away option. When a party feigns a lack of interest in some item or leaves the false impression that it is no hurry to come to a negotiated resolution, it may fear that, if it acted otherwise, the other side would see the leverage it held and capitalize on it.[53]

Puffing involves talking up or exaggerating points that benefit your side of the negotiation. Most societies grant negotiators the leeway for some hype or overstatement as they jockey over a price or other terms of a deal. A negotiator might gush with enthusiasm or airily advance opinions about something's great worth or predictions about the outstanding performance that can be expected. Buyers can puff as well, for instance, blustering about how they can compromise no more or claiming that time is running out when these constraints are actually overstated. In short, many negotiations include a sales pitch of one kind or another.

Puffing is such a common part of the give-and-take of negotiation that negotiators are not expected to rely on such statements.[54] Even if courts wanted to regulate puffing closely, it would be exceedingly difficult to do so. Often many valid or plausible opinions exist on something's worth, and sellers are expected to lean toward valuing highly whatever they are selling. Consequently, Judge Learned Hand declared, "There are some kinds of talk which no sensible man takes seriously, and if he does he suffers from his credulity."[55]

While much puffing is legally permissible, a court might ask: was the party put in a quite unfair position by what was said? In egregious cases or in those involving markedly unequal bargaining power, talking up something's value might go so far as to constitute fraud. Furthermore, if one side holds itself out as having special knowledge or expertise, and the other, less-knowledgeable party reasonably relies on that, then liability for a misrepresentation becomes more likely.[56] But where both parties are more or less equally grounded in the subject, a negotiator is given the leeway to extol the virtues, say, of the product being sold.

Note, however, that unrestrained puffing can still prove problematic for other reasons. A substantially inflated sales pitch might lead the other side to mirror its counterpart's behavior. Losing the truth in a cloud of exaggerations can stymie progress, hurt relations between the parties, and bring on retaliatory and unproductive behavior. If sufficiently annoyed, a party could even choose to walk away from the transaction. Curbing excessive hyperbole is thus often good policy.

3. Bluffing

In Chapter 1 we defined bluffing as pretending something to be the case when it is not in order to see if the other side is foolish, inexperienced, or concerned enough to accept what is said at face value. Bluffing often arises with respect to the terms a negotiator will settle for in an agreement. Indeed, some negotiators consider this a wholly legitimate matter to bluff about. Others, however, have personal scruples against participating in such bluffing or feel that it is counter-productive. Hence, they might, for instance, dodge questions about settlement terms rather than try to fool the counterpart about their views.

In other contexts a bluff sometimes takes the form of a false promise or a false threat. These are false in the sense that the bluffer really "never intends to follow through on the stated consequences."[57] At other times a bluffing negotiator alludes to benefits or other virtues of a potential deal that are made to sound plausible and attractive, but that the bluffer knows are untrue or unlikely. For instance, the chance for a beneficial future relationship might be dangled before the other party, even though it will never happen.

To generate better leverage, a negotiator might mislead a counterpart about the existence of other offers. That is, the negotiator might be tempted to leave the wrong impression about its Best Alternative to a Negotiated Agreement (BATNA), suggesting, explicitly or implicitly, that its BATNA is better than it really is. Indeed, deceiving another as to alternatives occurs so frequently that negotiators should be on their guard whenever the other side voluntarily starts to talk about its BATNA.[58] In most cases what is ultimately being masked here is the point at which a party will actually walk away from a deal.

Sometimes a negotiator sets forth some *false demand*. That is, the negotiator asks for something that he or she really does not care about but that would be costly for the other side to grant. The purpose of this tactic is, later, to "concede" on this issue in order to get something in return that the negotiator really does want. An analogous situation occurs when a negotiator adds something to the agenda, not on its merits, but in order to make a concession at the other side's insistence in exchange for a tradeoff.

A bluffing negotiator might also try to lead a counterpart along toward the wrong conclusion about constraints of some kind: perhaps a term relating to price or timing. One authority noted that a negotiator who says, "'You know I can't do that' means 'I want you to believe that the cost would be too high for me to do that.'"[59] In all such matters a negotiator could be telling the truth or could be bluffing. Part of the art of effective negotiation involves using logic, judgment, or experience, or reading body language or tone of voice or other signals, to determine which is more likely to be the case.

In sum, then, bluffing is an accepted part of bargaining in many societies. Experienced negotiators expect some bluffing to occur in many different circumstances. It is true, however, that some negotiators might view it as unhelpful gamesmanship, albeit a common part of bargaining. And, bluffing might very well undercut the cooperation needed to come to a mutually beneficial resolution. Rather than condemning bluffing as intrinsically unethical, I would suggest that a negotiator who chooses to bluff do so sparingly, having thoughtfully considered the circumstances, and being quite cognizant of the possible harm that may be done if the bluff is exposed, including the possibility that he or she will be perceived as having proceeded unethically.

4. False Statements as to Authority

In many negotiations an important question is whether the agent has the authority to come to an agreement at least within some specified range of possible outcomes. Negotiators are often authorized to accept deals on certain terms but are instructed to return for further consultations with respect to other possible terms. Issues of negotiation ethics arise when a negotiator purposefully misleads the other side as to the extent of his or her authority.

When counterparts press experienced negotiators, asking if they are authorized to settle on these terms or those, the response is often less than straightforward. The targets of such questions may not want to lay out the extent of their instructions or the reach of their authority to accept an agreement. The reason is that, if a negotiator reveals the minimum amount needed to gain an agreement, the other side is very likely to press for a deal on those terms, rather than ones more favorable.

Seasoned negotiators know that it is not uncommon to receive assurances that your counterpart is fully authorized to negotiate an agreement with you. Nevertheless, once you have worked out what was apparently a final compromise and seem to have a deal, your counterpart backs off and introduces some other person who actually has final decision making authority and whose input on the agreement is supposedly needed. The hope is that using this tactic will gain some final points by a party that would rather concede them then jeopardize the deal.

I do not recommend this tactic. It is quite possible that the tactic will cause real offense, and the potential deal could disintegrate at the last minute. When it is used against me, however, I view it as a peccadillo rather than a major ethical lapse. In fact, this ploy, while annoying, can be readily parried. Perhaps the best approach is simply to turn to points that your side is not 100 percent satisfied with and enthusiastically add them to the matters to be re-negotiated. The putative agreement is thereby transformed back into a draft. The prospect of reopening a number of issues with both sides suggesting changes and more rounds of future tradeoffs may well cause the other side to hasten back to the prior resolution. If not, then one's counterparts are put on notice that they will be asked for substantial changes as well. And, note, it is always possible that, after additional tinkering with or amending the terms of the prior possible resolution, both sides could find the new deal to serve their interests better than the prior one did.

5. Major Errors and Misunderstandings

A more telling ethical issue arises when one's counterpart makes a significant error in calculations during the negotiation. Perhaps the other side does not grasp the significance of what has occurred and is prepared to settle even though you can see that the terms are patently unfair in your favor. If the other negotiator is ignorant or confused, does one look to clarify or to capitalize on the situation?

In general, one lawyer negotiating with another would not be responsible for correcting the other side's misunderstanding of facts, since, as the Model Rules state, a lawyer has no "affirmative duty to inform an opposing party of relevant facts."[60] An exception would occur, however, if one side made a mistaken statement, and the silence of the other effectively confirmed that the statement was true. Here, a duty to correct a misimpression exists for "omissions that are the equivalent of affirmative false statements."[61]

Another key consideration in these circumstances is that a court can void a contract on the grounds that a mistake was made, just as it can in cases of fraud and misrepresentation. Furthermore, even if the issue is never litigated, the party that made the major error might not carry through with its obligations under the agreement. One's counterpart might well feel angry, betrayed, or foolish and might look to retaliate. This could happen in implementation, or in some future negotiation, or through maligning your reputation. Those potential negative consequences are so severe that quietly taking advantage of another's major mistake is not only morally suspect but may be short-sighted as a practical matter.

D. Ethical Issues Regarding Principals and Agents

Chapter 2 introduced the common scenario in complex negotiations of an individual negotiating on behalf of an organization or other client. That principal-agent relationship raises a number of interesting issues regarding negotiation ethics. In one form or another these center on the different duties that an agent owes a principal. Consider, for instance, the following questions.

- What interests does the agent bring to the negotiation, and how do these interact with the principal's interests?
- In a given negotiation has an agent, in fact, loyally advanced the principal's interests or have the agent's own interests somehow intervened?
- How vigorously does the agent try to gain the very best possible deal for his or her principal? For instance, once a deal acceptable to their principal is reached, how much harder does an agent push to find an even better, more optimal, resolution?
- To what extent does an agent try to transform the principal's understanding of his or her interests?
- Under what circumstances should an agent oppose a principal's wishes and resign if the principal does not yield?

"The client 'owns' the problem," it has been noted, and "will reap the primary benefit ... or bear the primary brunt ... of the outcome."[62] The negotiator is also likely have personal values, attitudes, and beliefs about how particular problems ought to be resolved and opportunities pursued. Perhaps he or she will even have convictions relevant to some aspect of the negotiation regarding how society ought to function. Agents do have their own sets of interests, separate and apart from those of their principal. Among other matters, they may well be concerned to a greater or lesser degree with managing their time and other transaction costs as well as with their own professional reputations.

Conflicts can arise with respect to negotiation ethics as these varying concerns contend with each other. For example, although unscrupulous behavior at the bargaining table today could possibly advantage their principal in this negotiation, this could come at a considerable cost to a negotiator's own reputation for integrity and credibility, and thus hinder their ability to negotiate effectively in the future. And, while agents ought to defer to principles on various matters, negotiation ethics is not one of them: "If the principal proposes an unethical course of conduct, the agent's voice ought to be heard loud and clear in opposition."[63]

1. Fiduciary Relations

When a lawyer is acting as an agent, he or she is in a *fiduciary* relationship with the principal. Here, the agent is to represent the principal with the utmost good faith, working to serve the principal's best interests at all times. The concept of a fiduciary dates to Roman law and describes a relationship in which one acts, first and foremost, for the benefit of another in trust, confidence, and good faith.

Note, too, that, as a practical matter, an agent who wants to be re-hired needs to be responsive to a principal's wishes. Even where negotiators are serving a client on a long-term basis, staying in close touch with the client's goals and expectations is often crucially important. Moreover, an agent who puts his or her personal interests above those of the principal could be liable for significant penalties. He or she might have to forfeit all personal gain, including fees, and also cover any losses flowing from the wrongful conduct.[64]

The agent should ensure that the principal makes the final decisions that determine how his or her interests should be advanced or otherwise best handled. Among the implications of this is that a lawyer negotiating on behalf of a client is obligated to communicate offers and counter-offers to the principal as well as explicating relevant legal principles and legal rights and duties that might be relevant to a settlement.[65]

One negotiating on behalf of another is by no means precluded from trying to attain a fair result or one good for the community or for society but the chief aim is to achieve the ends that the principal lays out. And yet, the agent's paramount objective is to reach the very best deal possible for the principal. This suggests that "good" representation involves considerably more than the agent mechanically pursuing certain goals outlined by the principal.

In particular, an expert negotiator should also be concerned with what the client ought to want, if properly educated and thinking clearly and rationally about the situation. The principal's views of the negotiation may be shortsighted, perhaps driven by a desire for an immediate return or by an emotion like revenge. Agents may find it easier to distance themselves from the situation and help the principal to see what might really be most valuable. Ultimately, however, the principal should be fully in charge. If the principal's viewpoint remains unaltered, the agent must bow to the principal's vision or resign as agent.

2. Incentive Structures

Principals are often concerned that their negotiators may not always be motivated to act in their own best interests. To take one of many possible examples, divorce attorneys, if paid an hourly fee, would have a financial incentive to magnify the parties' differences and spar with one another on behalf of their clients, rather than quickly and dispassionately settle the case.[66]

Indeed, the manner in which the agent bills the principal may bring about various incentives for an agent to act in ways that are at odds with the principal's interests. This can be readily seen in the sale of a house where, typically, a realtor will be paid only if he or she arranges a sale. Consider the following illustration:

> Suppose that with very little effort, maybe 25 hours of work, Betty could sell Sam's house for $250,000. With a 6 percent commission, this would generate a $15,000 fee — $600 an hour. Assume that with a great deal of effort, perhaps 100 hours of work, the house could be sold for $275,000. Sam would pay Betty an additional fee of $1,500 on the extra $25,000. From Betty's perspective, the marginal effort may not be worthwhile. She works 75 extra hours for only $1,500 — which works out to $20 an hour.[67]

Another common difficulty in principal-agent relationships is that the principal may be disinclined to spell out the details of an acceptable agreement, since he or she wants the agent to strive for an optimal deal. If the principal commits too early to the specifics of what is acceptable, the agent may work less creatively and assiduously to find the best possible agreement.[68]

To counter divergent interests of this sort, principals sometimes design incentives to attempt to ensure that the agent tries as hard as possible to fulfill their wishes. A bonus might be paid should a favorable agreement be negotiated. The size of the bonus might be correlated to a sliding scale of some variety: the more attractive the provisions, the larger fee is paid. Or, in some cases an agent could have a share of the deal to ensure that he or she works diligently on the principal's behalf. Alternatively, the client might offer additional work if the deal is secured or assist with favorable publicity for the agent for a job well done.[69]

3. Ethical Problems Associated with Mid-Stream Reporting

Chapter 2 introduced the idea of mid-stream reporting by an agent to his or her principal. Note in this regard that agents have first-hand information of what has transpired in the negotiation, while principals often learn things second-hand, usually as filtered through the prism of the agent's analysis. Ordinarily, the agent paints a picture for the principal of what has happened and how the negotiations have been proceeding.[70]

A key problem is that, consciously or subconsciously, the agent may "spin" the description of what is going on one way or another. The story, as told by the agent, may be one that enhances his or her own competence, while circumventing or downplaying errors, and perhaps while also featuring prominently any arguments advanced by the other side that seem unreasonable or illogical.

All of this can raise issues of negotiation ethics. A conscientious negotiator ought to report to the principal frequently enough that meaningful dialogue can occur about such matters as goals and strategies, understandings of interests, and potential terms. Then, an upright negotiator offers an honest appraisal of what has really occurred. It is certainly in the negotiator's self-interest to be sure that the client hears of his or her triumphs at the bargaining table, but some commentary as well on mistakes or shortcomings can underscore that the client is hearing a frank appraisal that is not entirely one-sided.

E. What Is Meant by Negotiating in Good and Bad Faith?

In conclusion, then, when people refer to negotiating in good faith or in bad faith, what exactly do they have in mind?[71] First, when proceeding in good faith, an organization sends someone to negotiate who has the necessary knowledge, abilities, and experience to handle the job. Purposefully selecting an unqualified negotiator in order to mislead, frustrate, or confound the other side, delay any resolution, or obfuscate aspects of the situation would amount to negotiating in bad faith. A good-faith negotiator is, in fact, interested in seeing if a deal can be worked out and negotiates honestly and fairly toward that end. An upstanding negotiator ensures that the information he or she presents in the course of the negotiation is completely accurate: "If you state something as a fact, it should be a fact."[72]

A bad-faith negotiator might operate under false pretenses, pretending to negotiate while actually stalling, gathering information, looking to act as a *spoiler*, or pursuing some other agenda. Beyond this, some consider that, once a concession is made, it is bad-faith bargaining to later remove or reverse it. Successive offers by a buyer are expected to continue to increase, and those by a seller, to decrease. Howard Raiffa went so far as to identify as a principle of good-faith bargaining that "once a concession is made, it is not reversed."[73]

Occasionally, however, a party introduces what is sometimes termed a *negative concession*, that is, the negotiator moves away from what the other side wants, not toward it. In my view the real problem with removing a concession is not so much that the tactic is done in bad faith as that it is too often self-defeating. Since the side to which a concession is made expects it to stick, later reversing the concession will greatly increase the chance that no negotiated resolution will occur.

In short, then, a good-faith negotiator is an honest bargainer. He or she does not engage in dirty tricks, falsify information, or lie to a counterpart. Then, one aspect of avoiding lies involves duly implementing the agreement made. A promise should be "hard currency," not something granted casually. It is vitally important to upholding a good reputation that a negotiator keep the commitments that have been made. And, if changing circumstances require that a prior pledge be broken, it is important to advise those who will be affected, speedily and apologetically, with a full explanation of what has occurred. These, I would say, are the central ingredients of good-faith bargaining.

Notes

1. James J. White, *The Pros and Cons of 'Getting to YES,'* 34 J. of Legal Educ. 118 (1984).
2. See *How to Negotiate with Friends and Family: When you add loved ones to your business negotiation, dealmaking can get complicated*, Program on Negotiation, Harvard Law School, Feb. 2, 2016, http://www.pon.harvard.edu/daily/dispute-resolution/how-to-negotiate-with-friends-and-family/.
3. G. Richard Shell, Bargaining for Advantage 205 (1999).
4. Sissela Bok, Lying 3 (1978).
5. Russell Korobkin, Michael L. Moffitt, & Nancy Welsh, *The Law of Bargaining*, in The Negotiator's Fieldbook 183 (Andrea Kupfer Schneider & Christopher Honeyman eds., 2006).
6. Gerald R. Williams, Legal Negotiation and Settlement 92 (1983).
7. *Restatement, Second, of Contracts*, § 175 (1981).
8. *Id.* at § 175, Comment (b).
9. Carrie Menkel-Meadow, *What's Fair in Negotiation? What Is Ethics in Negotiation?*, in What's Fair xxiii (Carrie Menkel-Meadow & Michael Wheeler eds., 2004).
10. Eleanor Holmes Norton, *Bargaining and the Ethics of Process*, in What's Fair 284 (Carrie Menkel-Meadow & Michael Wheeler eds., 2004).
11. Roy J. Lewicki, David M. Saunders, & John W. Minton, Essentials of Negotiation 164 (2d ed. 2001).
12. A.B.A., Model Rules of Prof. Conduct, Rule 4.1: Truthfulness in Statements to Others.
13. Geoffrey C. Hazard, Jr., *The Lawyer's Obligation to Be Trustworthy When Dealing with Opposing Parties*, in What's Fair? 168 (Carrie Menkel-Meadow & Michael Wheeler eds., 2004).
14. Art Hinshaw, Peter Reilly, & Andrea Kupfer Schneider, *Attorneys and Negotiation Ethics*, 29 Negotiation J. 282 (2013).
15. Howard Raiffa, Negotiation Analysis 112 (2002).
16. Jonathan R. Cohen, *The Ethics of Respect in Negotiation*, in What's Fair 260 (Carrie Menkel-Meadow & Michael Wheeler eds., 2004).
17. Bok, supra note 4, at 46.

18. The verse in the King James Bible reads: "Therefore all things whatsoever ye would that men should do to you, do ye even so to them: for this is the law and the prophets." Matthew VII, 12.

19. Howard Raiffa, The Art and Science of Negotiation 350–51 (1982).

20. Shell, supra note 3, at 228.

21. *Id.* at 353.

22. Carrie Menkel-Meadow & Michael Wheeler, *Bargaining Tactics*, in What's Fair? 201 (Carrie J. Menkel-Meadow & Michael Wheeler eds., 2004).

23. Cohen, supra note 16, at 260.

24. Catherine H. Tinsley, Jack J. Cambria, & Andrea Kupfer Schneider, *Reputations in Negotiation*, in The Negotiator's Fieldbook 202 (Andrea Kupfer Schneider & Christopher Honeyman eds., 2006).

25. Roy J. Lewicki, Alexander Hiam, & Karen Wise Olander, Think Before You Speak 216 (1996).

26. Raiffa, supra note 18, at 345.

27. Willem F. G. Mastenbroek, *Development of Negotiating Skills*, in International Negotiation 382 (Victor A. Kremenyuk ed., 1991).

28. Kenneth W. Thompson, *New Reflections on Ethics and Foreign Policy*, 4 J. of Pol. 991 (1978).

29. Jeffrey Z. Rubin, *Some Wise and Mistaken Assumptions About Negotiation*, 45 J. of Social Issues 201 (1989).

30. Lewicki, Hiam, & Olander, supra note 25, at 238.

31. White, supra note 1, at 118.

32. James C. Freund, Smart Negotiating 62 (1992).

33. Roy J. Lewicki & Robert J. Robinson, *Ethical and Unethical Bargaining Tactics*, in What's Fair? 223 (Carrie Menkel-Meadow & Michael Wheeler eds., 2004).

34. James J. White, *Machiavelli and the Bar*, in What's Fair? 91 (Carrie Menkel-Meadow & Michael Wheeler eds., 2004).

35. Suzanne Brock, Idiom's Delight 10 (1988).

36. Bok, supra note 4, at 25.

37. Shell, supra note 3, at 204.

38. Francois de Callières, On the Manner of Negotiating with Princes 32 (1919).

39. Alvin B. Rubin, *A Causerie on Lawyers' Ethics in Negotiation*, in What's Fair 354 (Carrie Menkel-Meadow & Michael Wheeler eds., 2004).

40. Hinshaw, Reilly, & Schneider, supra note 14, at 281.

41. Kevin Gibson, *Ethics and Morality in Negotiation*, in The Negotiator's Fieldbook 177 (Andrea Kupfer Schneider & Christopher Honeyman eds., 2006).

42. *Id.*

43. Niccolò Machiavelli, The Prince 64 (1950).

44. Freund, supra note 32, at 68.

45. Peter C. Cramton & J. Gregory Dees, *Promoting Honesty in Negotiation*, in What's Fair? 124 (Carrie Menkel-Meadow & Michael Wheeler eds., 2004).

46. *Id.* at 125.

47. Shell, supra note 3, at 226.

48. Maurice E. Schweitzer & Rachel Croson, *Curtailing Deception*, in What's Fair? 176 (Carrie Menkel-Meadow & Michael Wheeler eds., 2004).

49. Lewicki, Saunders, & Minton, supra note 11, at 178–79.

50. SHELL, supra note 3, at 228 (italics in original).

51. KATHLEEN KELLEY REARDON, THE SKILLED NEGOTIATOR 96 (2004).

52. PHILIP H. GULLIVER, DISPUTES AND NEGOTIATIONS 118–19 (1979).

53. LEWICKI, SAUNDERS, & MINTON, supra note 11, at 170.

54. Korobkin, Moffitt, & Welsh, supra note 5, at 184.

55. *Vulcan Metals Co. v. Simmons Manufacturing Co.*, 248 F. 853, 856 (2d Cir. 1918).

56. Korobkin, Moffitt, & Welsh, supra note 5, at 184.

57. Lewicki & Robinson, supra note 33, at 223.

58. ROBERT H. MNOOKIN, SCOTT R. PEPPET, & ANDREW S. TULUMELLO, BEYOND WIN-NING 274 (2000).

59. I. William Zartman, *Introduction*, in THE 50% SOLUTION 33 (I. William Zartman ed., 1976).

60. A.B.A., MODEL RULES OF PROF. CONDUCT, Comment to Rule 4.1.

61. *Id.*

62. Chris Guthrie & David F. Sally, *Miswanting*, in THE NEGOTIATOR'S FIELDBOOK 279 (Andrea Kupfer Schneider & Christopher Honeyman eds., 2006).

63. FREUND, supra note 31, at 180.

64. ALVIN L. GOLDMAN, SETTLING FOR MORE 12–13 (1991).

65. MNOOKIN, PEPPET, & TULUMELLO, supra note 58, at 86.

66. Cramton & Dees, supra note 45, at 123.

67. MNOOKIN, PEPPET, & TULUMELLO, supra note 58, at 77.

68. Roger Fisher & Wayne Davis, *Authority of an Agent*, in NEGOTIATING ON BEHALF OF OTHERS 71 (Robert H. Mnookin & Lawrence E. Susskind eds., 1999).

69. Lawrence E. Susskind & Robert H. Mnookin, *Major Themes and Prescriptive Implications*, in NEGOTIATING ON BEHALF OF OTHERS 278 (Robert H. Mnookin & Lawrence E. Susskind eds., 1999).

70. Joel Cutcher-Gershenfeld & Michael Watkins, *Toward a Theory of Representation in Negotiation*, in NEGOTIATING ON BEHALF OF OTHERS 24 (Robert H. Mnookin & Lawrence E. Susskind eds., 1999).

71. Since the National Labor Relations Act imposes a duty to bargain in good faith, 29. U.S.C. § 158(d) (2003), U.S. courts have gone further in defining good-faith negotiation in the labor context and have done so more strictly and in more detail than in other fields. For instance, in the particular circumstances of collective bargaining, a take-it-or-leave-it offer or a delaying tactic could form the basis for a claim that bargaining in good faith did not occur. Russell Korobkin, Michael L. Moffitt, & Nancy A. Welsh, *The Law of Bargaining*, in THE NEGOTIATOR'S FIELDBOOK 187 (Andrea Kupfer Schneider & Christopher Honeyman eds., 2006). Here, however, I am referring simply to the vernacular use of the terms "good faith" and "bad faith" negotiation.

72. Roger Fisher, *Negotiating Inside Out*, 5 NEGOTIATION J. 39 (1989).

73. RAIFFA, supra note 19, at 50.

Checkpoints

- People call on different standards to construct their theories of what constitutes an honest negotiator. Some involve legal principles; others, ethical guidelines, moral standards, or practical or utilitarian considerations.

- A negotiator makes a fraudulent statement when he or she says something about a material fact knowing that it is untrue, and the other party relies on it in a way that a court views as reasonable, and that party is later damaged by that reliance.

- Cultivating a reputation for honest, straightforward dealing may pay substantial dividends in future negotiations, while a reputation for being shifty, double-dealing, or untruthful could diminish the negotiator's future effectiveness and be quite difficult to shed.

- The ethical issues that arise most frequently involve disclosure versus nondisclosure as well as the distorting of facts or other forms of deceit.

- Negotiators are not expected to exhibit full candor for fear they will be taken or their bargaining position will be undercut. However, an honest negotiator does not lie to counterparts nor take unfair advantage of them. Suspicions of deceit are likely to greatly constrain communication and undercut efforts at joint problem-solving.

- A deceptive negotiator believes one thing but in hopes of gaining some advantage says something different to encourage the other side to believe something else. Or, perhaps, he or she simply keeps silent, withholding knowledge of the true state of affairs in hopes of encouraging a false belief.

- Negotiators should be especially careful to avoid being taken in by deception where continuing relations with their counterpart are unlikely, where the other side has a compelling motive to deceive, or where the matters being discussed are quite difficult to verify.

- The best ways to uncover or ward off deceptive practices are through questions and requests for proof and documentation. The parties can also try to structure the agreement so that it does not hinge on a questionable fact being true.

- Dirty tricks are especially sharp, crooked, or underhanded practices. Puffing involves negotiators shading their real views or putting a more favorable spin on a point or fact. Bluffing is pretending something to be the case when it is not in order to see if the other side is foolish, inexperienced, or concerned enough to accept what is said at face value.

- The duties that an agent owes a principal can raise ethical issues, such as when the agent does not act as a fiduciary but pursues his or her own interests contrary to those of the principal.

- The central ingredients of good-faith bargaining are to negotiate honestly and fairly to see if a deal can be reached, without engaging in dirty tricks, falsifying information, or lying to a counterpart.

Chapter 11

Conclusion: Formulating and Implementing Effective Strategies

---

Roadmap

- **Thinking about strategies:** What is a negotiating strategy? What considerations ought a negotiator bear in mind, and what elements might be included in such a strategy?

- **Creating an effective strategy:** In the circumstances being faced, is it better to lead or to react? Should the negotiation be envisioned as a checklist of items to be dealt with one-by-one, or should it be viewed as a package deal in which no single item can be negotiated to a resolution until the parties see how all of the items fit together?

- **Components of a negotiating strategy:** What are the key components of an effective negotiating strategy? What strategic issues arise in the different phases of a negotiation?

- **Special circumstances:** Why is it important to identify special circumstances and tailor one's negotiating strategy to handle those issues? For instance, how might a negotiator respond to preconceived drafts and pattern bargaining?

- **E-mail negotiations:** What are the singular aspects of e-mail negotiations, and what are the advantages and disadvantages to negotiating by e-mail?

- **Renegotiation:** What is a renegotiation, and why do parties renegotiate? What distinguishes the chief varieties of renegotiation: post-deal, intra-deal, and extra-deal renegotiations?

- **Multi-party negotiations:** What special difficulties characterize multi-party negotiations? What considerations ought to be in mind as parties are convened and settle on a decision-making process? What common communication problems afflict groups, and how might they best be dealt with? How might negotiators set ground rules, adopt particular roles, and formulate task forces to organize a group? Under what circumstances might caucusing be useful?

A negotiating strategy should be a detailed plan for a negotiation, made up of various tactics, thoughtfully assembled, and aimed at achieving specified objectives. Thinking strategically is certainly one of the most vital but intricate dimensions of advanced negotiation, and this concluding chapter focuses on how negotiators might best formulate and implement effective strategies. In creating a strategy, experienced negotiators dig deep into their knowledge of the theory and practice of negotiation. Thus, each of the preceding chapters offers a host of ideas that could be incorporated into a negotiating strategy. Since it draws on all that has gone before, we consider strategy last.

To negotiators, however, strategy should be at the forefront of their thinking from pre-negotiation on. Entering a negotiation with a carefully plotted, comprehensive strategy can be immensely useful, building confidence and bringing about positive results. To create an effective strategy, one must first critically analyze the negotiating problem or opportunity. One must think deeply about issues, constraints, and possibilities, not as a dry intellectual exercise but with the orientation of a practitioner. What is to be done about it? How might it best be approached?

To formulate a first-rate strategy, a negotiator must identify realistic goals—possible objectives that will very much please his or her side if attained—and then look to create a sophisticated plan with which to approach the negotiation. Although some conceive of positional or interest-based negotiation as strategies in and of themselves, I prefer to view them as basic methods of negotiation. Each of these fundamental approaches includes a toolbox of concepts that can contribute important elements to a negotiator's strategy.

Skillful negotiation is, in part, a matter of conceiving useful and coherent strategies, but it also involves implementing them. If one challenge is to create a good plan, another, quite different one, is to execute that strategy well. Even when the elements of a negotiation strategy are straightforward, recalling its details and carrying them out smoothly and effectively can be very challenging.

This is especially true when the parties are dealing with complex problems. Here, one can easily lose focus. Contending thoughts are often exchanged rapidly, surprises of one sort or another may upset expectations, and the discussions often jump about from point to point as the parties look to put their distinct strategies into effect. It can be difficult or impossible to predict just how the negotiation will develop.

What further complicates matters is that, at times, clinging too closely to a negotiation strategy conceived ahead of time can hinder progress toward a creative, mutually beneficial resolution. As you start to negotiate, as you understand better the parties' varying perspectives and their different needs and goals, the strategy with which you entered the negotiation may come to appear inadequate. Hence, you may be compelled to discard or alter elements of a strategy or even move to another plan altogether. Indeed, it may be useful to have created an alternative strategy that could be called on in particular circumstances. Or, perhaps one wants to plot out different paths that one's strategy might take with respect to potentially problematic issues.

Despite these challenges, taking the time to think strategically is critically important to gaining the best possible result in complex negotiation. You ought to start the talks with a sophisticated plan, responsive to particular points and including various tactics, all aimed at helping you to achieve your goals. It is much easier to adjust a strategy in the midst of a negotiation than to devise one for the first time once the talks are already under way. Think of a strategy, then, as a road map for the negotiation. If your preferred route is obstructed or impassable, you will need to find another. But, having plotted an attractive course can be an immensely valuable part of sound preparation.

A. Creating an Effective Strategy

Let us consider next some key factors that negotiators might find useful in creating an effective strategy.

1. Leading Versus Reacting

One initial question is whether to try to lead and influence the other side or whether to wait to see what the other negotiator does and react to it. Unprepared or inexperienced negotiators are often unsure about what to do in a broad range of circumstances, while more experienced or better prepared counterparts usually act with purpose.

Skillful negotiators generally want to guide a negotiation in a way that is most likely to help them to reach their goals. Their strategy often calls on them to do a number of things, perhaps even ideally in a particular order. Seasoned negotiators tend to be confident in their own abilities to gain their objectives and may fear that their fellow negotiators could enter the talks less able to propel it forward productively. Their counterparts may be less competent, less creative, or less knowledgeable as well as intent on achieving other goals. Hence, they look to move the talks in a particular direction, if at all possible.

Sometimes, however, a strategy focused on countering the other side has much to recommend it. To take one example, in a cross-cultural encounter an opposing negotiator might expect you to be exceptionally assertive, even brash and pushy. Here, one might establish a productive working relationship by doing just the opposite of what is expected: taking a more deliberate, deferential, introspective, and reactive approach.

In other circumstances a negotiator might fashion a strategy with a reactive dimension. For instance, depending on the context, one might much prefer to have the other side make a first offer. This might be sensible if the negotiator is wholly unable to estimate the counterpart's BATNA and reservation price. Or, one side might be much less certain about the value of items at stake in the talks. Consider, for instance, an employment negotiation in which "the interviewer knows more about the possible salary range than the job candidate does."[1]

Although a skillful negotiator features each approach at different times, I would suggest that, more often than not, leading is preferable to reacting in a complex negotiation. However, if you decide that in this particular set of circumstances you would rather sit back, let the other party move forward, and respond to what they have to say, you should be able to articulate just why that strategy is better-suited for the negotiating problem you face.

A related issue involves whether or not to choose one's strategy on the basis of your assumptions about how the other side negotiates. Some negotiation theorists advise that, if you see your counterparts as hard bargainers, you move into a like posture, but if you see them as collaborative, you fashion a cooperative strategy.

I find this counsel to be not just reactive, but problematically so. By presuming that our counterpart will not work cooperatively with us, we risk giving rise to a self-fulfilling prophecy. In a complex negotiation you should usually aim to be proactive. This includes seeing if it is possible to lead the negotiation along a collaborative path, if that would otherwise be your preferred approach.

2. Checklist versus Packaging Negotiations

Another threshold strategic issue involves whether or not you envision the negotiation in terms of a checklist of issues to be ticked off one after another as you resolve them with your counterpart? Alternatively, do you see an eventual agreement taking the form of a package deal? If so, you might discuss matters thoroughly but then hold them in solution until you create a comprehensive proposal that might work. In creating negotiation strategies, one ought to consider carefully the nature and relative advantages and disadvantages of *check-list* and *packaging*, or *horse-trading, negotiations.*

a. The Nature of a Checklist Negotiation

In a checklist approach the parties negotiate a series of issues, individually, to mutually agreeable settlements. Although certain of the items may be temporarily set aside to be returned to later, the effort is to deal with each matter on its own merits, without explicitly linking one issue to another. Once all of the items on the checklist have been resolved, the parties have come to their agreement.

Consider a handful of examples of common checklist negotiations. Politicians or their legal counsels might move this way through a proposed bill or regulation, moving from one provision to the next, trying to find workable compromises or common ground on each. Two attorneys negotiating the terms of a merger or purchase-and-sale agreement might proceed through a draft document in a checklist manner. They would start at the beginning of a draft, with the language of each provision then scrutinized and either approved or critiqued and reformulated.

In reviewing a draft collective-bargaining agreement, negotiators for a union and a business could also opt for a check-list mode. A typical labor negotiation might include not only wage rates but "issues of pension plans, paid vacations, hours of work and overtime, toilet facilities, the powers of supervisors, complaints procedures, leisure facilities, rules of operation of certain machinery, employee information about and participation in business decisions and ongoing administration, and the like."[2] The two sides might take up these items, one by one, looking to negotiate a resolution on each issue.

A checklist approach is what one author, experienced in collective bargaining, had in mind when he wrote that the constant aim of negotiators is to make the list of agreed, or "initialed," items longer and that of unsettled, or "open" issues shorter.[3] (*Initialing* the items on a checklist involves representatives of each side formally agreeing to a resolution of a particular matter, signified by each negotiator placing his or her initials next to the agreed provision.)

b. The Nature of a Packaging Negotiation

A contrasting variety of negotiation might be called a packaging, or horse-trading, negotiation. Here, the parties take on a particular issue, gain an understanding of the perspectives of each side—the interests implicated and perhaps some options that spring to mind—then suspend the discussion—negotiators might refer to *tabling* it—and move on to the next issue. Only after the parties' perspectives on all the issues have been thoroughly aired, do the negotiators turn to devising proposals. These would take the form of a package deal covering all or many of the different issues or items.

For example, imagine a farm family in which an elderly parent is moving to a retirement community. She plans to use the proceeds from sale of the house and farmland to cover her future expenses, and she has asked her two adult children, both with their own farms, to decide how the other assets she will not be taking with her should be divided between the two of them. Her daughter might propose a package to her brother: "You and your wife receive the three appaloosa horses, four sheep, fourteen chickens and their chicken house, the '67 pickup, the old tractor, and the portable generator. My husband and I get the two palomino horses, the four hogs, the small herd of dairy cows, the bull, and all the tools in the barn."

The key point is that a negotiator cannot settle on any of the constituent pieces until he or she sees the shape of the entire package. Isolating the horses and trading three appaloosas for two palominos might not be a fair deal, but the packages, each including horses as one component, might be viewed as a fair swap. Hence, a negotiator intent on formulating a package deal will stipulate that until the parties are in accord on an overall deal, no commitments will be made. Any suggestions about individual matters are nothing but tentative thoughts until a final resolution is approved by both sides: "Until *all* is agreed upon, *nothing* is agreed upon."

Note, too, that a negotiator looking to amend a package proposal that has been placed on the table will either tinker with this term and that one or respond with a substantially different counter-package proposal.

c. Advantages to a Checklist Approach

In certain circumstances negotiators might prefer a checklist approach. One would be where the matters being negotiated are separate and distinct or where the internal logic of the negotiation suggests that it is sensible to take them one at a time and resolve each on its own terms.

A negotiator pursuing a strategy that involves building momentum by tackling easier issues first might also favor a checklist approach. In most complex negotiations some agenda items are readily resolved and others, much thornier. Moving through a negotiation by checking off one point after another might be a way to propel matters forward, while helping to build positive working relations that might be drawn on when the parties grapple with the truly difficult matters ahead.

Another scenario conducive to checklist negotiating would be where the list of items to be negotiated is exceptionally long and unwieldy, for instance, a large group of representatives of different governments trying to codify international law on some subject, say, the rights of tourists and other aliens when traveling abroad. The fact that dozens or even hundreds of issues exist often inclines parties toward a checklist approach.

Alternatively, a party might really care about the resolution of one or two issues out of many to be discussed. He or she might be concerned that the other side will learn of that intense interest and hold resolution of it "hostage": that is, refuse to budge until substantial concessions are granted on other issues. To forestall such a scenario, the negotiator might prefer to proceed in a checklist fashion: knocking off items one by one without special emphasis being placed on any one of them.

d. Advantages to a Packaging Approach

In contrast, a packaging approach would be a natural choice when items are inter-related and the resolution of any one matter really needs to be set aside until a comprehensive deal can be struck. The negotiators would rather wait to see if the package is sufficiently attractive to agree to it.

The packaging route may also be especially appropriate when the negotiators are tackling sophisticated problems in which reaching a deal is likely to depend on making trade-offs. Neither side will get everything that it wants, but the parties aim for a resolution that is mutually beneficial since each gets certain items that it strongly favors.

A packaging approach may be more challenging to put into effect, but also may encourage more creativity and bring about a more nuanced resolution. Two scholars argued that when negotiators work down a list of issues, trying to resolve them one at a time, they are "almost guaranteed to leave value on the table for all parties" since they "will typically reach mid-range settlements on each of the issues" on which their interests are opposed, rather than fashion creative trade-offs that maximize the value each receives.[4] While assembling a package may take longer than moving through a checklist, it provides "a greater opportunity for flexibility and creativeness and a greater chance to avoid a winner-take-all situation and to provide for a balanced distribution of payoffs ..."[5]

Finally, note that a given negotiation might well contain elements of checklist and horse-trading negotiations. For instance, negotiators could begin to move through an agenda checking off one item after another, but then come to realize that a final agreement might hinge on packaging a number of separate items together. Hence, they might start in checklist fashion and transition to packaging, or they might checklist some items but fashion a package that satisfies both sides on others.

3. The Components of a Negotiating Strategy

The decisions to lead or react and to adopt a checklist or a packaging approach underscore how important it is that negotiators think very carefully about the characteristics of the problem or opportunity they face and craft a strategy accordingly. Instead of taking a one-size-fits-all approach, negotiators should design a strategy that is neatly tailored to the situation before them. A negotiator preparing a strategy might first consider the following questions.

- What is the nature of the problem or opportunity before us? Is there a history worth recalling, and is it remembered similarly or differently on each side?
- What exactly is our side trying to accomplish, and why?
- What are the principal challenges facing the negotiators? Ought special circumstances be taken into account?
- What is the style and personality of our counterpart?
- What strategy do we expect the other side to pursue?

These questions provide context for the central issue to be considered: *in light of the particular circumstances we face, what would be the most creative, sophisticated, and comprehensive plan that could effectively help us to reach our goals?*

In creating a negotiating strategy, one should recall first that a number of significant strategic issues typically arise early in the negotiation process. In pre-negotiation a party will want to articulate and prioritize among its goals. Some thought might also be devoted to how to capitalize on one's leverage and power, or diminish that of one's counterpart. Here, one notable strategic issue involves analyzing one's best alternatives to a negotiated agreement (BATNA) and estimating the other side's BATNA. Negotiators confident that they have very good BATNAs can set their sights higher, and those with very poor BATNAs may need to think carefully about what it is realistic to achieve. Should one party have a clearly superior BATNA, it will enjoy leverage that its counterpart lacks.

Remember, too, that in many situations negotiators will perceive strategic implications in the agenda, and will feel that the issues are best addressed in a particular order. A strategy rooted in an interest-based approach might very well speak to how best to draw the other side into the process of thinking together about the problem or opportunity that both parties face. Thus, certain ideas might aim to promote positive working relations. Note, too, that it may be strategically important to try to set a particular tone early on. And, some negotiators might consider what would be the ideal seating arrangements or the best body language as the talks commence.

For an interest-based negotiator, a strategy might also include ideas about how best to explain one's interests to the other side and to discover your counterpart's interests. Be sure not to overlook the significance here of questions, many aimed at filling in missing information. Such a strategy might also identify some objective standards that both sides can recognize as having some legitimacy or logic to them.

A strategy might reference promising creative options, including issues regarding the best time and manner in which to raise them. And, it might encompass a brainstorming phase aimed at generating fresh ideas. A negotiator's strategy might also reference some ideas on how to change a negative tone or overcome likely problems or impasses. Then, strategic considerations should feature quite detailed thoughts on how best to close the deal. Box 11.1 lays out a series of questions that could help a negotiator to organize his or her strategic thinking.

Box 11.1 — A Negotiation Strategy Checklist

- How about an agenda? In what order do I want to tackle the issues?

- What is the best way to go about creating the type of working relationship I want?

- What tone do I want to try to set, and how might I try to establish it?

- Is there a seating arrangement I prefer? Are there points regarding body language I should bear in mind? How about useful props (easel, blackboard, PowerPoint, etc.)?

- What information is missing? What questions, posed in what order, might help to uncover key points?

- What about BATNA? Do I want to discuss mine and/or theirs?

- If I am pursuing an interest-based approach, how can I best engage the other side in a discussion about interests, eliciting their interests and elucidating those of mine that I want to share?

- What objective standards, creative options, and other problem-solving devices might prove useful, and how and when do I plan to raise them?

- Do I want to suggest a joint brainstorming session, and how do I foresee it being conducted?

- Do I have particular thoughts on timing? Are there matters that would be best not to delve into immediately? Is there anything I prefer to set aside waiting for an opportune moment to arise?

- How do I expect to formulate an offer, proposal, or yesable proposition? What will the other side be most excited about achieving? What will they be most concerned about? What is the best order to list its elements?

B. Identifying Special Circumstances

As one prepares, it can be quite useful to try to encapsulate in a few words what especially stands out about the upcoming negotiation. What is the context in which you will be negotiating? For instance, are these talks among people who know each other quite well, such as partners in a small business or members of an extended family? Alternatively, will this negotiation be conducted among unfamiliar or arm's-length negotiators or even across significant cultural divides? Is there a need to overcome a past hostile relationship?

Let us consider next a handful of other special circumstances that frequently arise in complex negotiations.

1. Preconceived Drafts and Pattern Bargaining

Sometimes negotiators justify a refusal to move by claiming that their hands are tied. One version comes with a reference to company policy or to the standard contracts that their business "always" uses. Whether the counterparts' statements are real or a bluff, a party may feel hemmed in when presented with a preconceived draft agreement. At times, too, a negotiator confronts a weighty tradition within that industry of arriving at parallel agreements. *Pattern bargaining* refers to negotiations among different firms that follow a particular prototype or model. Agreements within the industry are quite similar, though not absolutely identical, since the particular needs of the parties may bring slight deviations. Let us consider each of these circumstances in turn.

First, what ought a party do when in the initial stages of a negotiation a counterpart presents a standard contract or even a complete draft agreement and insists it be approved as is or rejected? The obvious argument for the other side is that the current situation is sufficiently unusual that typical practices ought not apply. This can be phrased positively: "Rather than rely on what someone else has done in some past set of circumstances, let's 'roll up our sleeves' and work out an even better agreement."

When one side presents the other with a complete package resolution, the perception may be that it is attempting to cut out the other party from joining to create a mutually beneficial resolution together. One side is presenting its preferred deal, without first listening to the other's perspectives. The negotiator who fields the preconceived draft usually then assumes the role of becoming the great critic of what has been set forth. A contentious and counter-productive tone frequently results. Perhaps the side presenting the draft can be persuaded that this is a potential pitfall and that jointly and thoughtfully engineering a new agreement would be a better way to proceed.

2. E-Mail Negotiations

Another context that arises with increasing frequency in a world ever more reliant on technology involves negotiations that are not conducted in the traditional face-to-face manner. For reasons of speed and convenience a growing number of negotiations are carried out electronically, mostly or entirely through the exchange of e-mails. Some negotiators welcome e-mail exchanges; others find them frustrating. All negotiators, however, ought to recognize their distinctive features and consider how best to adapt their strategies to the e-mail context.

a. Singular Aspects of E-Mail Negotiations

The e-mail form of conversation is singular in that the parties rely on a series of written messages exchanged, at least potentially, in much more rapid sequence than one would find in past eras in sending letters to and fro. If both negotiators are simultaneously on-line, the messages might be read and responded to at once. However, they might also be ignored or set aside until convenient. Although e-mails are delivered instantaneously, at least in theory, uncertainty often remains as to when the recipient will get on e-mail and next check their messages so as to be able to respond. If no response is forthcoming, the negotiator having sent the e-mail may get frustrated and may also, correctly or incorrectly, be inclined to read some message into the lack of a quick turn-around.

Another reason that e-mail is a singular form of conversation is that the participants in an e-mail exchange do not have the ability to adjust their message, mid-stream, to the way in which it is being received. Two authorities observed: "While norms of turn-taking in face-to-face conversation typically allow only one or a few comments to be made before others have their turn, an e-mail message sender can make numerous points all at once ... without the receiver having the opportunity to respond or clarify."[6]

It may also be the case that negotiations conducted in person tend to be more wide-ranging, as the parties converse with one another, discussing different aspects of the situation they confront. In contrast, e-mail negotiations are often more tightly focused, as each negotiator has to write out each question and each response, a feature that tends to circumscribe their messages. This has real consequences for many phases of a negotiation. In e-mail exchanges a negotiator may need to make a very conscious effort to explore interests and brainstorm creative options and may never achieve as thorough a job as he or she would in a face-to-face encounter.

Certain aspects of e-mail negotiations may be positive or negative, depending on the circumstances or the particular negotiators involved. For instance, some people are inclined in e-mail negotiations to volunteer more information in more detail more quickly, simply to speed communication. Other negotiators are reluctant to have their thoughts recorded in a message that could be forwarded to others or printed and preserved for posterity, and hence they are more circumspect in an e-mail than in person. But, restricting one's communications can make it doubly difficult to grasp interests, find common ground, and work together to create options and find the best possible resolution.

b. Advantages to Negotiating by E-Mail

Other aspects of e-mail negotiations are more clearly advantageous or disadvantageous for negotiators. Among potential benefits is that, when parties have negative relations, face-to-face meetings can be volatile, with aggressive communication leading, ultimately, to an unproductive session. Negotiating by e-mail can encourage the parties toward more thoughtful and less reactive exchanges.[7]

E-mail also allows both parties the opportunity to think and reflect without the pressure of the instant response that might be expected in a face-to-face negotiation. The fact that both sides have a precise written record of their points may further understanding, particularly when the negotiators are engaging in logical discourse about the problem or opportunity they face.

And yet, a negotiator may need to consciously take advantage of the time he or she potentially has to think and formulate a thoughtful response. It is all too easy to fall into the pattern of receiving an e-mail, glancing over it quickly, and dashing off a response.

c. Disadvantages to Negotiating by E-Mail

As for disadvantages, taking the time and spending the resources to meet in person demonstrates an optimism and dedication to the potential negotiated agreement that can build momentum toward a collaborative resolution. Further, an experienced negotiator can be especially persuasive in person. When you are conversing, posing follow-up questions may seem quite natural, while in writing they may look like a cold interrogatory. Then, when does one need to slow down, to repeat a point, to remind a counterpart of something noted before? A blank computer screen is of no help in discerning such matters. And, as we saw in Chapter 3, visual cues, such as reading the body language of a counterpart, can be extraordinarily valuable.

Beyond this, effective complex negotiation may require intensive discussion, whether of interests or perceptions, or in the course of brainstorming or otherwise creating options. Consequently, certain negotiations are really much better suited for face-to-face discussions than for e-mail exchanges. To take one of many possible examples, consider a negotiation over the proper formula to compensate the chief executive officer of a major corporation with a bonus should the firm's performance warrant it.[8] Should the bonus take the form of money or shares of stock? Should it be tied to increasing share prices or to other aspects of corporate life, such as diversity targets? How ought the formula to account for factors beyond the control of the firm's top executives, such as broad trends in the stock market or substantial changes in commodity prices? How would stakeholders, such as the corporation's shareholders, react to different possible bonus formulas? Discussing such complex issues in person seems far preferable to exchanging scores of e-mails, particularly in light of the private and potentially controversial aspects of the matters at hand.

i. Problems of Working Relations and Tone

Establishing positive working relations and even trust is far easier in person than through the written word. Being gracious or even just polite can be especially difficult in the e-mail context. One can usually demonstrate sincerity and honesty more readily by speaking to another than by writing a counterpart a message. And, most people are much more able to make humor work when they say something than when they type it out. Practicing sound active-listening techniques is also quite challenging when typing out e-mail messages. What seems friendly and reassuring in person may seem like belaboring a point when written out.

One confined to written messages can also find it much more difficult to establish a positive tone. Communicating in person can humanize a dispute, and this can be a very useful step in working out differences. It may also be the case that in face-to-face discussions negotiators more readily see their counterparts as individuals and are less likely to hurry to stereotype their views.[9]

In addition, the body-language and other cues that are routinely sent and read when negotiating in person are of no help in an e-mail exchange. No one can be seen nodding their head, leaning forward to catch a point, or otherwise physically responding to what is being said. When one fails to see or hear the other negotiator, it can be hard to tell when a particular point has registered. The tone of the negotiation and of each communication within it must come through the words selected to send to the counterpart's computer screen. Proceeding without the benefits of seeing the postures or facial expressions of one's counterparts or hearing the tones of their voices, makes effective communication substantially more difficult. Important but delicate matters, for instance, subtleties of emotion, usually pass by without notice.

ii. Writing and Reading Problems

Another problem is that while it is unfortunate how infrequently we read something that is well-written, even more seldom do we read a well-written e-mail. Most professionals can write better than they do. People tend to respond to e-mails, even important ones, in a hurried and careless fashion. One scholar wrote, "One cannot write well without taking the time to read what one has written, looking and listening for errors and obscurities, checking the rhythm of the prose, testing to see whether one can understand what one has written, whether it says exactly what one meant it to say. It takes time to take an interest in the nuances of meaning that words and phrases convey and to deliberate about how best to make an intended point."[10] The process of writing well is time-consuming: it cannot be done in haste. Composing e-mails brings out the worst traits of most writers.

If few of us write as well as we could, fewer still read well. This, too, requires just the time and concentrated effort that seems to be in exceedingly short supply when people communicate by e-mail. Inis Claude observed, "The tendency to do things quickly, casually, and superficially affects our reading as it affects so many of our other activities; careless reading may be as serious a problem as careless writing. If we read the instructions on our medicine bottles as carelessly as we read academic literature, we should spend most of our time in emergency rooms having our stomachs pumped out."[11]

Furthermore, in lengthy e-mails the sender may be providing more information than the receiver can easily process.[12] A particularly long e-mail may also be seen as off-putting: many people don't like to read long passages, which may also be seen as piling on an argument or taking too extensive a turn in the conversation.[13] Another consequence of this is that the recipient of a lengthy e-mail message may absorb only a part of it, focusing on the first or last point, or the aspect he or she most strenuously disagreed with, or some problem early in the message that was never hashed out as it might have been in a face-to-face exchange.

d. Negotiating Effectively by E-Mail

Proceeding by e-mail can lend a fragmentary feel to a negotiation. Each side must go back and "pick up the thread" before writing the next response. Points can get lost as the parties constantly drop and then, after some time has elapsed, pick up their communication. Memories are fallible, and yet negotiators may have neither the time nor the inclination to review the entire e-mail chain before sending the next message.

The balance sheet of pros and cons to negotiating by e-mail suggests that negotiators think carefully about whether to proceed this way and then how to tailor their strategy to this specialized form of communication. To help to counter some of its evident problems, those negotiating by e-mail should force themselves to think clearly and then to put their ideas into precise language that cannot readily be misinterpreted. E-mail certainly puts a premium on writing clear, detailed, well-organized and easy-to-read messages. It pays to carefully edit and proofread them to ensure that the phrasing might not imply something unintended.

But all this is hard work. One's writing skills are often taxed by the challenge of taking the thought in your own mind and transferring it to your fellow negotiator's mind without slippage, that is, without significant ambiguities or omissions creeping in to mar communication. All of this ought to be factored into the decision as to whether or not to negotiate by e-mail.

3. Renegotiations

"A key challenge in negotiating any agreement," it has been observed, "is not just 'getting to yes,' but also staying there ..."[14] A simple fact of life for negotiators is that agreements of many different varieties must ultimately be renegotiated. Indeed, this is one reason that negotiators think carefully about, and sometimes puzzle over, the proper duration of their agreement. A lengthy one may seem to provide a useful measure of stability and security, but, as circumstances change, an opportunity to renegotiate may be beneficial, too.

a. Examples

Examples of renegotiation abound. Various American airline and other companies have asked their employees to renegotiate their labor agreements in order to avoid the impending bankruptcy that might cost the employees their jobs. Professional baseball teams have become convinced that one of their young players will become a star. The team wants to bind the player to a long-term contract, and the player wants a higher salary and values the security of a lengthy deal. Consequently, one side or the other has suggested renegotiating the existing agreement.

In the 1960s and 1970s various Latin American governments borrowed large sums to finance development projects, not expecting a sharp economic downturn that affected their ability not only to pay back the loans but to service the accumulated interest. In the 1980s private banks as well as international lending institutions like the World Bank and International Monetary Fund permitted the governments to renegotiate the terms of those loans.

b. Why Renegotiate?

Sometimes the original agreement includes an option to renew. This essentially invites the parties to renegotiate the terms when the terminal date arrives. At other times, the agreement, as originally contemplated by the negotiators, no longer suits one or both sides, and someone proposes that a renegotiation is called for. No matter how lengthy and detailed the first discussions, no matter how clever the original negotiators or how talented and skillful they are at creating a deal and clearly drafting its terms, unforeseen circumstances arise and the prior agreement comes to appear inadequate.

Sometimes the altered circumstances involve a change in the parties. A new management team takes over a business, for instance, and for one reason or another finds certain terms in a prior agreement out of sync with its new policies or objectives. Alternatively, one side may feel that the other let it down, failed to follow through or otherwise deal fairly or honorably with respect to some facet of the agreement. Perhaps relevant information was concealed, or an important condition was violated, or a strong expectation was upset.[15] In their view this justifies renegotiating their agreement.

At that point, if the parties still want to enjoy the benefits of the agreement, they will need to renegotiate. This process, however, poses special challenges. A request for a renegotiation might be quite problematic for the relationship. One side might see the other as trying to renege on its promises. The party that feels a need to renegotiate might be defensive. Either of these developments might bring sudden tension to a relationship that may once have been quite positive and that may need to be cooperative again for the new agreement to work well.

One issue often highlighted in the context of renegotiation is how to balance long-term and short-term interests. On the one hand, significant benefits might flow from continued cooperation over the years. On the other, certain gains were expected over the short-term, and these might be jeopardized by renegotiating the existing agreement. Note, however, that a renegotiation need not necessarily be thought of in terms of a zero-sum game in which one party makes all the gains, while the other takes all the losses. Instead, there may be some horse-trading as the parties adjust for past performance and aim to reach an even better future agreement.

c. Varieties of Renegotiation

As one tailors a strategy to suit the renegotiation context, it may be useful to think in terms of three varieties of renegotiation.[16]

i. Post-Deal Renegotiation

Jeswald Salacuse has suggested terming a first category a **post-deal renegotiation.** This occurs when the period of the original agreement is drawing to a close. The parties come together to see if they can renew their agreement, though perhaps altering the terms of the deal with different provisions that might spell out new rights, duties, responsibilities, or incentives.

Sometimes the original agreement includes a term that specifies that at some date or when some event occurs, the parties will come together again to try to renegotiate the agreement. A process is thus already in place to ensure that the parties have the chance to see if the deal can last longer than its original term. At other times, the original agreement runs its course, and the parties have been sufficiently happy with their experiences or hopeful about the future that they opt to renegotiate.

To prepare for a post-deal renegotiation, a negotiator should thoroughly review the history of the agreement at issue. Questions to be reviewed in preparation might include the following.

- To what extent was the agreement carried out as envisioned by the original negotiators?
- How did relations between the parties evolve as the agreement was being implemented?
- What were the benefits of working together, and what problems arose?
- If the relationship were to continue, what issues are likely to arise in the future?
- What goals would you have for a new agreement, and what is your current BATNA?
- How might a renegotiated deal improve on the original agreement, enhancing cooperation, increasing profits, or otherwise serving the parties' interests better.
- Should the parties insert a post-deal renegotiation clause?

ii. Intra-Deal Renegotiation

Salacuse differentiates a second variety of renegotiation which he labels an **intra-deal renegotiation.**[17] The original negotiators may have been concerned that unforeseen, or only partly foreseen, events might arise that would make their agreement unfair or difficult or impossible to carry out. Hence, some agreements will actually state that the deal may be renegotiated midway through its term if certain specified circumstances occur. An intra-deal renegotiation might be envisioned as a course correction in the middle of a voyage.

Imagine, for example, the owner of a newly renovated historic building located on the waterfront in a port city with multiple vacancies to fill with stores and businesses but operating in a depressed economy. An entrepreneur appears who would like to rent office space for a language-training school being opened, but is highly uncertain about its prospects. The potential lessee might agree to take the space at a certain monthly rent figure, but request an intra-deal renegotiation provision. Should the annual revenues of the language-training school, as reflected in its yearly tax return, drop below a designated figure, or in the event that a natural disaster, including a tropical storm or hurricane, floods the environs and damages the building, the lessee would be released from its obligations and the parties could renegotiate to see if it were possible to conclude a revised agreement taking into account the new circumstances.

iii. Extra-Deal Renegotiation

The third type of renegotiation that Salacuse identifies is an ***extra-deal renegotiation***.[18] The idea here is that one party asks to renegotiate without relying on any specific provision in the original agreement that gives them the right to do so. Since a party can be completely blind-sided by such a request, and since those requesting the renegotiation may feel a significant *loss of face* in not simply carrying out the terms of the original agreement, these tend to be the most difficult, stressful, and emotional renegotiations.

Salacuse suggests that, if a party requests an extra-deal renegotiation, it is important, right away, to look into the changed circumstances that led to the request and to assess how important a continuing relationship might be. So long as a renegotiated relationship would be likely to remain quite productive, the parties will often want to negotiate with one another to see if a fruitful future relationship can be created.

4. Multi-Party Negotiations

Negotiations that involve multiple parties pose yet another special set of challenges. Multi-party, multi-issue negotiations can readily become unwieldy, diminishing the chance for a negotiated resolution. Hence, a negotiator's strategy ought to take into account the group context. Let us consider next some particularly notable issues.

a. Convening the Parties

The very process of initiating a multi-party negotiation can be quite problematic. For potentially productive negotiations to take place, one may need to gain the assent of a host of different, and often contending, actors. And yet, parties may resist joining a negotiation so long as the status quo is not too painful and some hope for a unilateral resolution still exists.[19]

The processes of pre-negotiation, explored in Chapter 2, can be of great importance in the context of a large group negotiation. For a sizeable conference with an array of participants, not only must issues and parties be identified, but a chair and other leaders might have to be selected, negotiating committees, sub-committees, and work programs sorted out, and, on occasion, a negotiating text produced.[20]

Whether a large conference or a much smaller group, the point remains that the more parties end up at the bargaining table, the more elusive or complicated becomes the task of finding a mutually beneficial resolution that serves the key interests of those present. In fact, the number of parties that need to be sufficiently satisfied by a proposal for an agreement to emerge may pose a challenge as significant as the substantive issues to be discussed.

A key initial issue in a multi-party negotiation involves who exactly merits a seat at the table, and who does not? This, in turn, requires thought as to what the meeting is aiming to do and what end-product a successful negotiation would produce. Are you looking to draft and sign something together — a plan, a letter, a memorandum of understanding, a contract, a treaty? Or, are you simply hoping to gain a consensus on a decision to do something in the future? Perhaps you would just like to spur people along toward thinking more deeply about some issue or problem.

The next question faced by those organizing such a negotiation is whose needs must be reckoned with in order to reach a negotiated resolution of some value? Are there constituents or stakeholders whose interests might be affected by a deal or, perhaps, by the lack of an agreement? Then, the aim is to reach out to those parties whose presence might be necessary or useful. The over-arching point to bear in mind is that it may be impossible to reach a lasting or optimal settlement if significant actors are not present.[21]

To try to ensure that the key parties are invited to join the negotiation, one suggestion is "to ask each party who else should be at the table until you keep getting all the same names."[22] However, it is also worth bearing in mind that the larger the group, the more unwieldy it quickly becomes. With more parties, more interests need to be taken into account, more time must be taken to hear out all the different points of view, and more problems with group dynamics can crop up. Thus, determining who to target as a potential member of the negotiation and who to exclude may require real thought.

b. Coming to a Decision: Vote or Consensus

Groups should put some thought into procedural issues as well: how is the negotiation process to function? Some parties may want decision-making to occur by majority vote; others will prefer *consensus*. While just what consensus ought to mean in the particular circumstances faced may turn into another point to be negotiated, the general idea is that a consensus decision "has the support of a large and representative majority and is not rejected by any members."[23] Note, however, that such a definition can potentially hold "the ultimate results hostage to the most reluctant party on the most difficult issue."[24]

Another approach is to underscore that consensus does not necessarily mean unanimity. One acknowledged expert in large group negotiations is Tommy Koh of Singapore, who chaired the Rio Earth Summit, the third UN Conference on the Law of the Sea, and the conference that produced the charter for the Association of Southeast Asian Nations (ASEAN). When Ambassador Koh chaired large diplomatic gatherings, he would direct discussions toward formulating a consensus, attempting to out-flank possible objectors when possible. His ultimate tactic, however, was to claim that a consensus existed, and if opposed, put the matter to a vote.[25]

c. Working with Diverse Perspectives

The more parties are negotiating, the more diverse their goals and interests may be. Arriving at a mutually beneficial resolution is thus correspondingly more difficult than in bilateral negotiations. With multiple parties involved, coordinating and contending with the thinking of the various people at the table may be quite problematic.

Another possible impediment is that the parties may define success in the negotiation differently. As in a one-on-one negotiation, some might be absorbed with the immediate consequences of a potential agreement, while others could be much more concerned about long-term implications. One negotiator might be focused, single-mindedly, on serving his or her party's particular interests. Another might also be emphasizing satisfying the interests of all or most of the members of the assembled group. Frustration may result should these different visions clash — one individualistic and the other group- or community-oriented.

Trying to resolve complex multi-party negotiations via positional bargaining may be especially difficult. Parties dig in to pre-conceived stances, debate one another about the problem before them, and try to sell others on their inability to budge from their respective positions. At the same time, interest-based negotiation can be quite difficult as well. Here, each negotiator is faced with the challenge of absorbing and recalling as much as possible about the perspectives of all of the other parties. Gaining a good sense of the different interests, goals, and walk-away options of multiple parties can be daunting. Reaching a consensus on the fairness of particular objective standards may be very difficult, and the group may be overwhelmed with different views on creative options.

The distractions associated with group negotiations can bring even a committed interest-based negotiator to stray from the sound fundamental practices used in one-on-one talks. With so many people at the table, active-listening techniques may be ignored and the parties may give up on the complex task of trying to understand how the situation appears to all of their counterparts. Efforts to work together creatively to overcome impasses can slow or stop altogether. Indeed, as frustrations grow, so do the inclinations to dismiss the situation as hopelessly deadlocked and give up. Once they come to grips with the possibility of going home empty-handed, certain negotiators may begin to revel in impasses, rather than bear down to try to overcome them.

Then, when the parties turn to formulating proposals aimed at closing a deal, more challenges arise. Certainly, when moving to creating a yesable proposition, a party will have to envision it from multiple different points of view. A key question that a negotiator must consider is this: "How can I craft my proposal so that accepting it is more attractive than the status quo, ideally for all of the other parties but at least for the others whose acceptance is essential to the deal?"

On account of these formidable difficulties, interest-based negotiation may be all too readily abandoned in a group setting for a more positional method. It may be far more difficult to implement an interest-based negotiation strategy in a multi-party negotiation than in one-on-one talks; however, the limitations of positional bargaining suggest that it is often especially useful to do so.

d. Communication Problems

A bilateral negotiation is dominated by the relationship between the primary negotiators, though one must often take into account as well relations between the parties, with outsiders, including stakeholders, and between the negotiating agent and the principal or client. Multilateral negotiations are even more complex, often considerably so. With many more negotiators involved, their goals and strategies, assumptions and expectations, and even their patterns of thought often conflict. People often refer approvingly to the "dance of negotiation," but the members of a group negotiation often find coordinating dance moves difficult and stepping on each other's toes, all too easy.

Moreover, not only does the number of relationships soar, but the relative importance of the different parties to reaching a final deal may vary markedly. This context means that groups are especially prone to getting stuck as they consider a complex problem. Let us consider next some particular communication problems.

i. Ensuring the Parties Are Heard

A host of communication problems often arise in, or are exacerbated, by the group setting. Some negotiators who are quite comfortable and engaging in a one-on-one setting are much less so as the numbers around the table increase. It may be harder to strike up a positive dynamic with a negotiator who is absorbed with who is listening and how they are appraising what is being said.

Often, a one-on-one negotiation is conversational in the sense that the parties attempt to discuss in an intelligent way their shared problem or opportunity, taking turns in making points. Although, naturally, some people talk more and others listen more, nevertheless in a normal conversation the participants tend to contribute their thoughts sequentially. With only two negotiators present, each, consciously or subconsciously, is likely to feel obligated to join in the conversation and also, on regular occasions, to give way to their counterpart and hear him or her out.

Here, the dynamics of a group negotiation often differ sharply. In some groups too many people are talking at the same time, each trying to control, steer, or dominate the conversation. The negotiators are often not hearing each other, figuratively and sometimes literally. The discussions come to be disorganized, with various members off on tangents: "Thinking that bounces around at random produces random results."[26]

A contrasting problem afflicts other groups. Some negotiators are quiet, interjecting a thought only occasionally. Some may be put off or intimidated by the prospect of speaking to or before the whole group, while others may choose to sit back and watch the negotiation unfold, rather than actively contribute much to it. Drawing quiet negotiators out may thus be another group negotiation challenge.

Sometimes, the more people are in the room, the more guarded each tends to be with what they say, at least to the group as a whole. Hence, it is more difficult to gain an understanding of the interests of the different parties and then to move on to productive problem-solving, the creation of attractive and innovative options and gaining a consensus on fair objective criteria. Here, the use of caucuses, a subject to which we will turn our attention shortly, can be quite helpful.

ii. Contending with Domineering or Grandstanding Parties

A different problem involves parties who feel that their views are not being properly attended to by others within a large group. To be sure that they are heard, such negotiators may be inclined to talk louder or to pound home their points more assertively or repetitively. Egos can quickly become involved. And, with voices raised, debates often begin. Problems of *grandstanding* can be acute in a group setting as particular negotiators are tempted to *play to the gallery*.

Then, as the group contends with the substance of different problems, some negotiators may feel that they are being ganged up on, that multiple parties are joining forces against them. This, too, is not conducive to interest-based problem-solving. Ensuring that everyone is heard, while avoiding the tendency for a few to overwhelm the discussions, can be an important dimension of the process of negotiation when multiple negotiators try to engage in interest-based problem-solving.

In short, the civility that comes more naturally when one person interacts directly with another may not be nearly as apparent in a group negotiation. The goal is, in the words of Singapore's Ambassador Koh, to foster a "spirit of camaraderie" among the parties.[27] This may, however, take considerable effort and skill to accomplish, if it is possible at all.

iii. Group Process Fatigue

Dealing with the other members of a sizeable group, while trying to move its members toward a mutually beneficial resolution, can be an extraordinarily tiring and frustrating process. As one source put it: "We point out defects in each other's bright idea, instead of trying to build on it. We are typically unclear about what collective thinking is supposed to produce. We suffer from distraction."[28]

One sign of what is sometimes termed *group process* fatigue occurs when particular members of the group stop actively participating in a prolonged negotiation.[29] Some negotiators prefer to defer to others who they feel are more expert on the issues. Others may experience peer pressure to conform to the group's wishes. Or, some might believe that their voices are not valued by the other negotiators at the table.

Drawing these participants back into the process may be essential to reaching a negotiated agreement. Skillful negotiators use different techniques to re-orient a group toward a productive discussion of how to resolve their common problems. Taking a short break is one way to combat group process fatigue. Another is to elicit directly the views of negotiators who have withdrawn from the interactions. Or, one might caucus with particular members to better understand their perspectives on what is going on.

Another approach is to encourage the members of a group to think about a specific aspect of the problem they face and possible collaborative resolutions. This process could be initiated by posing a new question for the group to consider. Yet another technique is for a negotiator to offer up his or her own thoughts "and invite others to use them, build on them, or correct them."[30] Each of these tactics is aimed at getting a stalled or slowed group moving forward again.

e. Organizing a Sizeable Group

Cataloguing and critically analyzing the generic problems that often afflict group negotiations bring us next to strategy. Negotiators embarking on multiparty talks would do well to think through in advance what makes for a positive and effective decision-making process, and what more often than not results in an ineffective and negative experience for a group trying to come to a decision. Prior thought on how best to organize the group can counter an array of foreseeable difficulties and help to bring about an effective negotiation.

At the outset of a group negotiation it can be very useful for the negotiators to focus on the special challenges they face, given their numbers and the complexity of the tasks they face. Ideas can be elicited about how to preempt common group problems. Here, perhaps the best practice is to have the parties agree to particular points beforehand, as a matter of principle, before any specific problems arise.

i. Setting Ground Rules

In this regard some groups establish **ground rules**, that is, principles agreed upon by the different parties, usually before substantive negotiations begin, aimed at governing the discussions in some orderly manner. For example, to counteract the confusion of having everyone talking simultaneously, the parties might agree not to interrupt each other while at the negotiating table. Or, the parties might decide to confine their caucuses to a designated time period, perhaps five or ten minutes, if at all possible.

ii. Adopting Particular Roles

To assist in an effective negotiation process, a group might choose to have particular negotiators take on special roles. For instance, with so many people participating, groups easily lose track of time, and yet they almost always aim to decide a number of things in a limited period. One source identifies the "Murphy's Law" of negotiations: "they tend to take as long as the time period that is allotted for them."[31] Using time wisely, ensuring that the group airs all relevant issues and listens to and works with the perspectives of all of its members can require real effort on the part of those who assume leadership roles.

When a group is assembled, it might choose to put one member in charge of watching the clock and supervising time management so as to ensure that all the issues are fully discussed and that a decision really does get made in the allotted period. That individual might be designated the "time-keeper," who periodically keeps the parties aware of the time that remains or that is being spent on particular agenda issues or caucuses.

Yet another organizational idea would be to have one member of the group take notes of the key points made. A written record creates a history or a group memory. This can help the representatives to analyze the course of the negotiation, to note the progress that has been made, and to avoid overlooking significant points and issues. When it comes to trying to assemble a negotiated resolution, the negotiators can draw on the record. A written reminder of points made can help the group to meet different interests and goals.

As a potential deal begins to come together, some time ought to be set aside as well for thinking about possible problems that might crop up. For a group to reach a good, lasting agreement, negotiators need to be asking "what if" questions. What if *this* happens? What if *that* happens? How might the developing agreement be derailed at the implementation stage and what might be done now to shore it up?

Let us move next to a cautionary point, coupled with a suggestion for how it might be dealt with. As thinking within a group gains momentum, it can become increasingly difficult to disagree with the course of action the majority is advocating. To counter this, one group member could be assigned the task of "devil's advocate." Giving someone the role of objecting with the strongest arguments possible, is a useful tool to relieve peer pressure. One source noted, "The Catholic Church long ago established the role of devil's advocate to urge the case against the canonization of a saint. Without such an established and legitimate role, few within the Church might wish to speak ill of someone nominated for sainthood."[32]

iii. Setting Up Task Forces

Negotiators may sometimes be inclined to break down a large group into task forces, each assigned to work on a particular piece of a problem. To set up properly functioning task forces, the problem needs to be carefully analyzed and divided into its component parts, the best people to deal with each piece need to be identified and brought together, and their work eventually needs to be assembled and presented in a useful form to the whole group.[33]

Twenty-five people are likely to have more ideas to share with each other than five are, but twenty-five may be an unwieldy number to think carefully together about resolving a host of difficult issues. Setting up task forces might be an especially apt move when the group has a large number of discrete issues to contend with. Another scenario conducive to task forces is when multiple issues need to be resolved under strict time constraints, putting a premium on getting things accomplished efficiently as well as effectively.

The technique of dividing a large group into sub-groups tends to work best when those organizing them can see potential synergies. Does the knowledge and experience of the negotiators vary significantly? Do particular members of the group have the expertise and interpersonal skills to work together especially well on particular issues?

Note, too, that it is important to set aside sufficient time for the smaller groups to report back to the larger group. Each task force will need to explain its thinking and recommendations, yet give the other negotiators a chance to share additional ideas and perhaps amend the task force's work.

f. Using Caucuses

One of the most interesting strategic matters in group negotiations involves caucuses. Sometimes colleagues or teammates caucus internally, that is, with one another, and sometimes negotiators caucus externally, with one or more negotiators from the other parties.

Internal discussions are conducted privately: the other negotiators should not be able to watch or overhear you. And, the desire for privacy of the participants in an external caucus should be respected as well. Proper protocol is to give the caucusing negotiators the separate space they want. In general, you join only if invited. Should an important reason bring you to want to break in on an external caucus among other negotiators, you ought to announce your presence as you approach the caucusing group and deferentially ask the others if they mind your joining their deliberations for a moment.

So, under what circumstances might caucuses be helpful? What purposes could they serve? When might it be useful for negotiators to call for a caucus, but when might it prove to be counterproductive? Thinking ahead under what conditions a caucus will be called, who will call it, and how it will be called is an important part of sound preparation.[34] Indeed, one especially important matter of teamwork is how best to signal to one another when one team member believes that a caucus is needed.

Colleagues sometimes use an internal caucus to discuss privately what has been happening at the table and what the group should do next. The occasional caucus can be helpful as teams of negotiators share thoughts about what they have heard. Such caucuses provide the chance to trade ideas, insights, and reactions as well as to ensure that the team is thinking alike about the most salient points discussed thus far. The negotiators may foresee new issues arising that involve what information should be shared and what should be withheld from one's counterparts.

Caucuses are also an excellent opportunity to review strategy. How has the team's plan been implemented? What remains to be done? What should be taken on next? Does the original strategy still appear to be the best route to attaining key goals? Should that plan be altered in any respect? Ought team members be reminded of this or that point?

Despite the potential importance of these matters, negotiators are sometimes quite reluctant to call for an internal caucus. Perhaps they fear breaking the flow of the discussion, or they might imagine that caucusing could leave the impression that their side is indecisive, unprepared, or uncomfortable thinking on its feet. Negotiators trying to establish or maintain a cooperative spirit may shy away from a caucus, which tends to underscore the separate interests and reasoning of the different sides. When matters are progressing nicely, abruptly taking a break could stop forward momentum and prove ill-timed. Furthermore, calling too many caucuses can frustrate counterparts.

Nevertheless, as colleagues contend with new ideas, information, and proposals, caucuses are often extremely useful. Rather than slowing the over-all negotiation, they may ultimately enhance its efficiency. You and your partners, speaking for a few moments privately, can cut to the core of outstanding issues. In contrast, when you are uncertain about each other's reactions or those of people away from the table to something new and unexpected, communication tends to be significantly more hesitant and guarded.

In the case of external caucuses, as a negotiation progresses into problem-solving, overcoming obstacles, and formulating proposals, a separate caucus, away from the main body of negotiators, can be a critically important part of the process of bringing parties to agree with each other.

Such a caucus can serve a number of purposes. First, coalitions frequently form during caucuses. One key task in a caucus is to try to bring potential allies around to your own viewpoint as to how best to proceed. Often, those parties that are thinking alike have a limited ability to resolve a complex problem when there are others around the table viewing matters quite differently. It can thus also be very useful to caucus with a counterpart whose interests do not seem closely aligned with your own. Here, a brief private conversation may enable negotiators to find a way to reconcile differences.

Another reason that caucuses can be valuable is that people may be reluctant to reveal things to the group as a whole that they will be much more inclined to tell particular counterparts in a caucus. Some of that information could be quite important in trying to engineer an agreement or overcome an impasse. Or, at times, a negotiator can establish a better rapport, more informal and perhaps more productive, with a counterpart in the more private setting of a caucus. In addition, other negotiators might be taken aside "to explain things in terms to which they are individually receptive."[35]

Nevertheless, external caucuses are not risk-free. Apart from the danger of losing momentum, interrupting talks among the whole group for caucusing by a few may raise tensions. Those not included in the caucus may feel left out, as though deals are being cut behind their backs. Or, the perception may take hold that the negotiation is getting bogged down in small side meetings.

One way to minimize such problems is to establish a ground rule before the negotiation starts, permitting caucuses but limiting their duration to a target of a certain number of minutes. Then, if caucusing seems to be unduly slowing a negotiation, the other parties can point to the ground rule and request that the group re-assemble as a whole.

The larger point, well worth underscoring in this chapter, is that planning for internal and external caucuses can form a significant part of a strategy tailored for a multi-party negotiation.

C. Reviewing What Occurred and Improving Future Strategies

Creating ever more effective, ever more sophisticated, negotiating strategies, is a skill that one can continue to improve upon, really throughout one's life. Perhaps the single most important step to become better prepared to negotiate at your best involves the critical appraisal of past preparation efforts. As two authorities wrote, "Unless negotiators develop a habit of reviewing their negotiations and consciously articulating lessons…, most of that hard-earned knowledge fades away."[36]

No matter how extensive your pre-negotiation preparation was, you often find that you anticipated some things incorrectly, you misunderstood certain points, perhaps some errors, or even some bias, slipped into your preparatory analysis. Then, with all negotiations—even those that went quite well and produced excellent results—negotiators can usually look back and see certain matters that could have been handled more adroitly.

I can think of no better way to cap a concluding chapter on negotiation strategy than by laying out a self-quiz, designed to help negotiators to focus their thinking on what went well and what might be improved in future negotiation preparation.

Self-Quiz to Take After an Important Negotiation

I. Ultimate Lessons: What worked so well that you might try it again in a future negotiation?

II. Preparation: When you entered the negotiation, what did you think it was about? In retrospect, did the negotiation center on those matters or other ones?

At the outset of the negotiation did you have an excellent grasp of the interests of both sides, of possible creative options, and of potential objective criteria? Were there any flaws here? As you entered the negotiation, were you less confident about facts and figures than a model negotiator would have been? How might your preparation have been improved?

III. Course of the Negotiation:

A. Process: Setting aside for a moment the outcome reached, whatever it may have been, how would you characterize the process of negotiating? How did you and your counterpart go about communicating with each other?

B. Turning Points: What were the key junctures in the negotiation? Who said what to whom, and what consequences flowed from that?

C. Counterpart's Performance: What worked well for the other side, and what could they have done more effectively?

D. Your Performance: What did you do that might have helped you to reach a good agreement, and what was said or done that might have hampered that? In looking back over the negotiation, were you quieter than a model negotiator would have been? Conversely, might you have dominated or overwhelmed the discussions such that you may have discouraged your counterparts from contributing thoughts or missed points that a better listener or a more attentive negotiator might have heard or elicited?

E. Internal Negotiations: (i) Teamwork: If you were negotiating alongside another, did you work well with your teammate or partner? If you were to carry out a negotiation like this one again, what might make you an even more effective team?

(ii) Principal/Agent Concerns: If you were negotiating for another, how did your internal interactions, those that occurred within your side of the negotiation, appear in retrospect? Did you have a good understanding of the goals and interests of your client? If you were called on to write a brief memo to your client, what points would you emphasize about the negotiation?

If you ought to report to a principal on what occurred in the negotiation, think carefully about how to most effectively report in after a negotiation. For instance, would it be preferable to have an oral debriefing or an after-the-fact memorandum? Would it be useful to write a memorandum to your own file as well? Which points might best be highlighted to the client?

IV. Concluding the Negotiation:

A. Commitments: As you look back on what you asked the other negotiator(s) to do, was it appropriately realistic, given their likely negotiating parameters and their goals and interests? Why was the final proposal a good one that ought to have been accepted, or why was it so flawed that rejecting it was the only sensible course of action? If the latter, then how should your own side "pick up the pieces" and move on? What exactly ought to happen next?

B. Worst Critic Exercise: Imagine a person who stands as your worst possible critic on your own side of the negotiation. What criticism might such a person have of the resolution—whether an agreement or a decision not to agree—and how might you respond?

C. Implementation: As implementation of the agreement occurs, what issues are likely to arise? Which ones are likely to demand continuing attention over time? What items will prove difficult for one side or the other to comply with, and what might have been done differently to head off potential problems?

Notes

1. Katie Shonk, *When to Make the First Offer in Negotiation*, Program on Negotiation, Harvard Law School, Oct. 8, 2015, http://www.pon.harvard-edu/daily/negotiation-skills-daily/when-to-make-the-first-offer-in-negotiation/.

2. Philip H. Gulliver, Disputes and Negotiations 56, n. 15 (1979).

3. Patrick J. Cleary, The Negotiation Handbook 27 (2001).

4. David A. Lax & James Sebenius, *Deal crafting*, 18 Negotiation J. 14–15 (2002).

5. Jeffrey Z. Rubin & Bert R. Brown, The Social Psychology of Bargaining and Negotiation 147 (1975).

6. Raymond A. Friedman & Steven C. Currall, *Conflict Escalation*, 56 Hu. Relations 1329 (2003).

7. Anita D. Bhappu & Zoe I. Barsness, *Risks of E-Mail*, in The Negotiator's Field-book 397 (Andrea Kupfer Schneider & Christopher Honeyman eds., 2006).

8. See *Schumpter: Executive Pay*, The Economist, April 23, 2016, p. 60.

9. Roger Fisher & Daniel Shapiro, Beyond Reason 61 (2005).

10. Inis L. Claude, Jr., *Valedictory, Mea Culpa, and Testament,* in Community, Diversity, and a New World Order 313 (Kenneth W. Thompson ed., 1994).

11. *Id.* at 310–11.

12. Bhappu & Barsness, supra note 7, at 398.

13. Friedman & Currall, supra note 6, at 1329.

14. Jeswald Salacuse, *Renegotiating Existing Agreements,* 17 Negotiation J. 311 (2001).

15. David A. Lax & James K. Sebenius, The Manager as Negotiator 277–79 (1986).

16. Salacuse, supra note 14, at 312–326.

17. *Id.* at 316–322.

18. *Id.* at 321–326.

19. I. William Zartman, *Regional Conflict Resolution,* in International Negotiation 305 (Victor A. Kremenyuk ed., 1991).

20. Gilbert R. Winham, *The Prenegotiation Phase of the Uruguay Round,* in Getting to the Table 54, 58 (Janice Gross Stein ed., 1989).

21. I. William Zartman, *Prenegotiation,* in Getting to the Table 12 (Janice Gross Stein ed., 1989).

22. Lisa Blomgren Bingham, *Avoiding Negotiation,* in The Negotiator's Fieldbook 117 (Andrea Kupfer Schneider & Christopher Honeyman eds., 2006).

23. Ronald J. Fisher, *Prenegotiation Problem-solving Discussions,* in Getting to the Table 227 (Janice Gross Stein ed., 1989).

24. James K. Sebenius, *Dealing with Blocking Coalitions and Related Barriers to Agreement,* in Barriers to Conflict Resolution 159 (Kenneth J. Arrow et al. eds., 1995) (italics in original omitted).

25. Address by Tommy Koh, Harvard Program on Negotiation Great Negotiator Award Speech (Apr. 10, 2014).

26. Roger Fisher, Alan Sharp, & John Richardson, Getting It Done 99 (1998).

27. Koh, supra note 25.

28. Fisher, Sharp, & Richardson, supra note 26, at 99.

29. Bingham, supra note 22, at 118.

30. Fisher, Sharp, & Richardson, supra note 26, at 12.

31. Roy J. Lewicki, Alexander Hiam, & Karen Wise Olander, Think Before You Speak 40 (1996).

32. Roger Fisher & Scott Brown, Getting Together 82 (1988).

33. Howard Raiffa, Negotiation Analysis 399 (2002).

34. Thomas R. Colosi, On and Off the Record 40 (1993).

35. I. William Zartman & Maureen R. Berman, The Practical Negotiator 209 (1982).

36. Fisher & Shapiro, supra note 9, at 177.

Checkpoints

- A negotiating strategy is a detailed plan, made up of various tactics, assembled by a negotiator and aimed at achieving specified objectives. Negotiators ought to try to formulate thoughtful, sophisticated plans, drawing on their knowledge of the theory and practice of negotiation and crafted to maximize the chances of reaching their objectives.

- A strategy should be considerably more involved than simply designating a particular method — positional or interest-based — as the approach you aim to take. Among the fundamental questions are whether you will lead or react and whether you envision the negotiation as a checklist of separate issues or a package covering all or many different issues?

- One negotiator's strategy might include thoughts on how to capitalize on his or her leverage or power or diminish that of a counterpart. Another's might encompass a particular agenda and look to set a particular tone. A strategy drawing on the interest-based approach could involve thoughts on how best to explain one's interests and discover your counterpart's interests. It might reference objective standards and creative options. Strategic considerations often include thoughts on how best to close the deal.

- Since the parties to an advanced negotiation are constantly interacting, often in unforeseen ways, negotiators must think "on their feet," adapt to their counterpart, and react flexibly and intelligently to what is occurring. One does not want to become too wedded to a pre-conceived strategy, and it may be quite useful to create alternate strategies ahead of time to draw on in different circumstances.

- Determining what stands out about an upcoming negotiation can help a negotiator to tailor a strategy to particular circumstances. For instance, the negotiator might face the challenges of negotiating across cultures or with a need to overcome a past hostile relationship. Another set of circumstances that frequently arises involves renegotiation.

- Yet another increasingly common special context is an e-mail negotiation. Here, negotiators should be cognizant of the difficulties inherent in communicating by e-mail and look to counter them whenever possible.

- One common special context for complex problems is a group negotiation. Groups often have a hard time determining just what they want to accomplish. The larger the group, the easier it is for the voices of some of the negotiators to be drowned out, while others can drone on interminably, adding layers of frustration to the proceedings.

- In a group negotiation one representative might be intent on finding a fair and equitable resolution for all or most involved in the negotiation, while another is focusing exclusively on gaining the best possible resolution for the party that he or she represents.

- More parties also usually means more diverse goals, interests, and walk-away options for the negotiators to bear in mind; efforts to find suitable objective criteria and to agree on creative options may be quite challenging, and any yes-able proposition must be envisioned from multiple perspectives.

- Communication within large groups is often especially problematic: people tend to be more guarded in what they say, and, for an interest-based strategy to succeed, domineering negotiators or those who are grandstanding may need to be managed, while negotiators inclined to give up or withdraw may need to be drawn back into the talks.

- Sizeable groups may benefit from the extra organization brought to the talks by setting explicit ground rules or adopting particular roles (such as time-keeper or note-taker). A large group may need to be broken down into specialized task forces charged with bringing specific ideas back to the other members.

- In internal caucuses colleagues trade ideas, insights, and reactions to ensure that the team is thinking alike about key points. External caucuses can help negotiators to form coalitions or otherwise bring potential allies around to your viewpoint. You can sometimes build rapport in a caucus or learn things that a negotiator is reluctant to reveal to the group as a whole.

Mastering Negotiation
Master Checklist

The list that follows reviews the topics covered in each chapter and enables the reader to check his or her understanding of the questions posed in the text and of the most vitally important points found there. Readers who do not recall answers to certain of the questions posed below are urged to review the comprehensive discussion in the chapter in question to enhance their detailed understanding of each topic.

Chapter 1 • Choosing the Best Approach for a Negotiation

☐ **What Is a Negotiation?:** *How might the term,* negotiation, *best be defined, described, and differentiated from other like terms?*
  - Negotiations are discussions between different parties that aim to adjust differences, conclude a transaction, take advantage of an opportunity, or manage or resolve a dispute or conflict. Ordinarily, the parties are interdependent in the sense that each is looking to gain something and each has something to give that the other wants. The hope is to craft a mutually beneficial outcome that both sides believe to be better than their alternatives.

☐ **Detailing the Positional-Bargaining Approach:** *What is positional bargaining, why is it a familiar approach to negotiation, and what marks the process of positional bargaining?*
  - In positional bargaining, after both sides make contrasting declarations of what it will take to reach an agreement, they look to narrow the gap through a series of compromises, as each negotiator tries to gain concessions from the other.

☐ **Identifying Positional Bargaining:** *How do positional bargainers use starting and fallback positions, and haggle, dicker, and bluff?*

- In trying to pull the other side toward one's position, a positional negotiator wants to make the smallest possible concessions to the other side so as to arrive, ultimately, at the most advantageous resolution.
- In positional bargaining each negotiator is inclined to exaggerate the worth of what he or she has given up, while down-playing the concessions received, while each tries to deceive the other as to what it will actually settle for.
- The chief aim of the negotiators throughout this process is to stick as closely as possible to their opening stance and to move to their fallback positions reluctantly.

☐ **Appraising the Positional Approach:** *What advantages and disadvantages are associated with positional bargaining?*
- Positional bargaining is a familiar approach that is perhaps best suited for dealing with a simple problem, one where the stakes are small, or one in which there is not likely to be any continuing relationship.
- Positional-bargaining tactics have the disadvantages of inviting reciprocal treatment and stifling creativity.
- Positional bargaining might be a problematic approach for negotiations divided into numerous issues, those with many parties, those in which long-term relations are quite important, or those where emotions are running high.

☐ **Detailing the Interest-Based Negotiation Approach:** *What is interest-based negotiation, what is its logic, and what are its pros and cons?*
- Interest-based negotiation focuses on using interests—defined as what the negotiators want and need, what concerns and motivates them—as the building blocks toward a mutually beneficial agreement.
- Typically, positions can be satisfied in a limited number of ways, perhaps a single way; shifting to a focus on interests can significantly expand the number of resolutions that the parties might find beneficial.

Chapter 2 • Pre-Negotiation: Arranging and Preparing for a Negotiation

☐ **Choosing to Negotiate:** *Are there good reasons to negotiate, do the advantages outweigh the disadvantages, and is a dispute or conflict ripe to be resolved?*
- In pre-negotiation the parties determine if they want to negotiate with each other. If so, they begin to prepare, working out some logistical matters together, while readying themselves to negotiate.
- The different sides appraise the pros and cons of undertaking negotiations, while analyzing, in conflict situations, whether the situation is ripe to negotiate. They think through who would participate in a

possible negotiation, what the talks should cover, and what matters might best be excluded. They explore what subjects the parties will negotiate, by what medium, and over what time period.

☐ **Negotiating on Behalf of Another:** *Why do agents so often negotiate for principals, and what issues regarding parameters, instructions, and authority are likely to arise?*

• When an agent negotiates on behalf of a principal, he or she faces the constraints of negotiating parameters, instructions, and authority. The key issue is how much flexibility the principal will permit the negotiator; in some circumstances tight restrictions make sense, while in others permitting the negotiator leeway will help the parties to arrive at an optimal agreement.

• In advising a client on negotiating matters, the negotiator might press the client not to lay out a position to try to achieve, but instead to focus on the range of interests that might be satisfied. A negotiator will have more flexibility to work with the other side creatively if the aim is to have the ultimate agreement serve the client's underlying interests, rather than meet a detailed position.

• In complex negotiations, even where a principal has granted an agent broad authority, the negotiator will often want to obtain the client's approval before finalizing the deal.

☐ **Preparing to Negotiate Well:** *How does a negotiator best prepare before a negotiation? Why does an organization confronting a complex negotiation so often assemble a negotiating team? What are the special challenges associated with team negotiations, and how should a team be selected and prepared?*

• A negotiator organizes pre-negotiation preparation to uncover useful facts, analyze the problem or opportunity, plan how to make points effectively, and think through the difficult issues of creating value and dividing items.One assembles a negotiating team, rather than sending a single negotiator, when the different team members bring with them distinct expertise, backgrounds, viewpoints, constituencies, or interpersonal skills.

• Common problems associated with team negotiations include difficulties of coordinating the team into a reasonably united front as well as the slower pace of the talks, as more voices are raised and as the people bring different perspectives and diverse goals and strategies.

☐ **Internal and External Negotiations:** *What distinguishes an internal from an external negotiation, and what are the special difficulties associated with internal negotiations?*

- As opposed to the external negotiations that occur between different parties, internal negotiations take place within an organization, prior to and often during the external negotiation, with the aim of coordinating the team, including ironing out different perceptions of interests, objectives, and strategy.
- A leading problem in internal negotiations is that people or factions within an organization may have quite different understandings of the organization's interests or goals, and when numerous people are consulted for their views regarding an external negotiation they typically assemble a position, which can then be difficult for the negotiator to work with.

☐ **Identifying Appropriate Goals:** *How should a negotiator set explicit goals and aim for good yet realistic outcomes, while avoiding common errors and accounting for such complexities as multiple goals and the need to prioritize among them?*

- Rather than passing lightly over their goals, negotiators should set out objectives that, if achieved, will satisfy their key interests and please their constituencies. They should bear in mind, however, that over-stretching and reaching for unrealistic goals might increase the chance that no negotiated resolution occurs.
- Negotiators should be sure not to lose sight of the objectives they were pursuing as they entered the negotiation, while remaining open-minded about adding new goals or redefining them in light of their interactions with the other side.

Chapter 3 • Initiating Talks: Launching a Negotiation Productively

☐ **Building Productive Relations:** *Why spend time cultivating a strong working relationship? What type of working relationship might a negotiator hope to have with the other side, and what could be done to foster such relations?*

- A constructive professional relationship with their counterpart helps negotiators to work efficiently and effectively and to overcome obstacles and challenges, while creating a reservoir of good will that may help the agreement to be implemented and bring the negotiators to work together again in the future.
- A positive working relationship does not require a negotiator to accept a counterpart's values or arguments or approve of how the other side has been acting; instead, it connotes the ability to communicate well about the circumstances the negotiators confront, including especially the differences the parties must contend with.

- To develop good relations, a negotiator is proactive in trying to develop rapport by methods such as drawing on the similarity principle, demonstrating respect for the other side, and showing reliability, while avoiding imposing preconditions such as the need to first make substantive concessions in order to have good relations.

☐ **Gaining Your Counterpart's Trust:** *Why exactly is trust an asset for a negotiator, and distrust a problem? How might a negotiator demonstrate trustworthiness and guard against being distrusted? How might a negotiator avoid misplacing trust, and how and why might it be advisable to try to proceed independent of trust?*

- A negotiator considered trustworthy by the other side has an asset of real value to draw on, while distrust can be a formidable problem, increasing the odds against a successful resolution and, should a deal occur, requiring special arrangements to try to ensure that the agreement is properly implemented.

☐ **Setting a Tone:** *What tones might a negotiator look to promote, how might a negotiator try to set a particular tone, and how might this help to bring about a productive opening?*

- A negotiator can try to set any number of different tones in his or her opening, and a productive tone can help the parties over later "rough sledding," as potentially problematic statements are passed over lightly and do not become major obstacles.

- Skillful negotiators can use humor—ideally spontaneous and light-hearted in nature—to set a positive environment, recover one that has turned negative, or smooth over an awkward moment; however, attempts to inject humor are also inherently risky, and it is important to be sensitive to how the humor might appear to others.

☐ **Creating an Agenda:** *How and why might negotiators choose to create an agenda listing the issues to be discussed in the order that they will be raised?*

- Many negotiators find it useful to determine, early on, whether the problem or opportunity that the parties face might be divided into discrete issues to be addressed in a particular sequence, that is, they look to establish an agenda.

- In framing the issues in diverse ways and in a particular order, an agenda can be advantageous or disadvantageous to a particular party. Every agenda has strategic implications.

☐ **The Importance of Posing Questions:** *Why is posing intelligent questions an important part of initiating substantive communication with your counterpart, and to what ends do negotiators use questions?*

- Rather than jumping into efforts to entice or manipulate the other side, negotiators confronting complex problems are well-advised to start to interact with their counterparts by establishing an intelligent conversation about the problem or opportunity before them.
- From the opening phase of a negotiation forward, seasoned negotiators use questions to learn about facts, understand the perceptions of the other side, and gain feedback on key issues, while countering possible deception.
- Considerable thought should be put into formulating different varieties of questions, discarding potentially counter-productive ones, and determining the most appropriate timing for posing particular questions.

☐ **The Importance of Listening:** *How and why do skillful negotiators listen effectively, and what exactly is meant by active listening?*
- Experienced negotiators tend to have excellent listening skills: they give the other side the time, space, and attention needed to answer questions fully, they draw out their fellow negotiators, and really listen to them so as to gain true understanding.
- Active listening entails posing open-ended questions, clarifying answers with follow-up inquiries, and paraphrasing the other side's points to demonstrate that they have been fully absorbed.

☐ **Using and Reading Body Language:** *How do people communicate through their expressions and actions, and how might one be alert to body language?*
- From the opening phase of a negotiation on, negotiators should attend to their own and their counterpart's body language so as to avoid sending false signals or overlook clues as to how the talks are progressing.

Chapter 4 • Getting Down to Substance: Working with Interests

☐ **Moving Beyond Positions into Interests:** *Why should negotiators look to move past the initial positions declared by the parties to explore their underlying interests, and what is the significance of objective and subjective interests?*
- Where the term "positions" signifies what the parties initially pronounce as their stance, desired resolution, or declaration of what it will take to reach an agreement, the term "interests" refers to the underlying concerns of the parties: what they need, what they want to happen, what will make them secure, and what they fear or worry about.
- An objective interest is something that, in fact, promotes the welfare of that side of the negotiation. In contrast, a subjective interest is a personal preference or concern.

☐ **Prioritizing, Analyzing, and Working with Interests:** *How does a negotiator go about understanding and then engaging with the interests of both sides? What is the spectrum of interests that negotiators may hold in relation to one another, and how might these be worked with to bring about an agreement?*

- In appraising the interests of the different parties, negotiators should bear in mind that interests can be separate or shared, and tangible or intangible; they can dovetail with one another or conflict. Interests can also reflect the needs and values of the parties.

- In learning about or estimating the interests of the other side, negotiators should not just list the interests at issue, but try to gain a sense for how their counterparts prioritize their interests. What seems to be most and least important?

☐ **Discussing Interests Productively:** *How should a negotiator discuss interests constructively with a counterpart? Why is it so important to gain a close understanding of interests and to probe to better grasp interests?*

- Although an opposing negotiator may not enter a negotiation wholly comfortable with discussing interests, one's opening can help to overcome this reluctance by setting a constructive tone, encouraging a problem-solving climate, and establishing strong working relations.

- Negotiators should aim for a close understanding of the other side's interests and should be prepared to probe to better grasp them, using such techniques as "why," "for what purpose," "what if," and "why not" questions.

- The better your grasp of their interests, the more keen is your vision of what you can offer up to satisfy them and what you can gain for yourself.

☐ **Sharing Information:** *How much and which information should a negotiator share with the other side? Why does a negotiator reveal some and withhold other information? What is the sugarcoating problem? Why might a negotiator misrepresent some of his or her concerns?*

- Do not get so caught up in working with the other side's interests that you end up giving short shrift to your own interests. Instead, identify the most important concerns that you want your counterpart to understand and focus on as you work with them to create a mutually beneficial outcome, and figure out how to make those interests of yours come alive for your counterpart.

- Put some thought as well into which of your interests you prefer to keep to yourself at least for the moment. Why are these private concerns, and under what circumstances, if any, might you opt to reveal them?

☐ **Creating an Interest-Based Resolution:** *Why exactly does a negotiator look to serve the interests of his or her counterpart, and how can interests be assembled in an agreement?*
  • To avoid frustration and redundancy, be prepared to move on from your discussion of interests once you feel that you grasp the actual matters at stake — the underlying needs, concerns, and motivations.

Chapter 5 • Analyzing Walk-Away Alternatives, Leverage, and Power

☐ **Assessing Walk-Away Alternatives:** *What are the concepts of a Best Alternative to a Negotiated Agreement (BATNA) and a reservation value? Why are they so integral to interest-based negotiation?*
  • The acronym BATNA stands for Best Alternative to a Negotiated Agreement. It is the most promising course of action for a negotiator, if he or she cannot reach agreement with the other side.
  • A reservation value is the least-attractive proposal for which a negotiator would still decide to come to an agreement, a point just past the one at which a negotiator really does not care whether he or she accepts the offered agreement or opts to pursue his or her BATNA.
  • Negotiators ordinarily keep their reservation value confidential to guard against their counterpart creating a low-ball proposal, one barely sufficient to gain an agreement.

☐ **BATNA Analysis:** *How does analyzing the parties' BATNAs assist in determining when to accept or reject a particular proposal? What are the implications of underestimating and overestimating a BATNA? How might BATNA analysis affect negotiation strategy?*
  • If one side's BATNA is, in fact, considerably stronger than the other side seems to think it is, the negotiator with the attractive BATNA will normally want to reveal and discuss it.
  • If the other side seems to have over-estimated my BATNA, or if I have a very weak BATNA and my counterpart does not know it, I will try to avoid a BATNA discussion.
  • A negotiator saddled with a weak BATNA should be prepared, if need be, to settle for a less-advantageous deal than if he or she had a much stronger walk-away alternative.
  • The extent to which a poor BATNA ought to affect a negotiator's goals is a matter of negotiation strategy that hinges, in part, on whether one's counterpart is likely to know, or find out, how deficient the BATNA really is.

☐ **Factoring Leverage into the Negotiation:** *What is the concept of leverage? How does a negotiator appraise the leverage of different parties? How might leverage be used and countered?*

- Leverage refers to a negotiator's ability to move the other side toward doing what he or she wants, ultimately increasing the negotiator's chances of attaining his or her goals.
- The extent of a negotiator's leverage is usually a function of how strongly or urgently his or her counterpart wants or needs something and how vulnerable each party is.
- The balance of leverage between the parties is often a key variable in a negotiation. There is the leverage that A may have with respect to B, but also B's leverage with respect to A. Who in the end has more leverage?
- When your counterpart seems to have more leverage, an experienced negotiator looks for ways to counter it; for instance, if you improve your BATNA, you undercut your evident need to come to an agreement with this party.

☐ **What Brings Power to a Negotiator?:** *What are the fundamental elements of negotiating power? How does authority affect a negotiator's power? What are some of the means by which one obtains influence over others? Why are considerations of power specific to the task at hand? How does one's negotiating capabilities affect one's power? What complexities make appraising negotiating power challenging?*

- One source of negotiating power is authority: a person's position may provide him or her with the ability to make certain decisions, and these will be viewed within that society as legitimate.
- Apart from authority, one side may have the means to influence another in a negotiation through other factors. However, considerations of power tend to be specific to the task at hand. That is, the power to gain one result may not translate to the power to gain another.
- Finally, negotiating power also hinges on the skill, knowledge, and expertise of the negotiator. A powerful negotiator has better ideas or more experience concerning how to prepare and proceed effectively.

Chapter 6 • Problem-Solving: Putting Objective Criteria and Creative Options to Work and Dealing Effectively with Impasses

☐ **Dealing with Issues of Distributional Bargaining:** *Why is dividing up, or allotting, items of value among the parties a notable challenge in many negotiations? What are examples of neutral standards or objective criteria,* *and how can these help to resolve distributional problems? How might the negotiators determine which one to use, and what problems might arise in this regard?*

- To deal with distributional bargaining—that is, the apportioning of money or other items of value between the parties—interest-based negotiators look to propose an equitable resolution based on one of various criteria of fairness, such as equal division or relative contributions or needs.

- The most promising approach to distributional issues often involves finding neutral standards or objective criteria to support particular resolutions. These might be drawn from expert opinions, industry practices, market rates or values, community traditions, scientific or technical understandings, relevant comparable data, decisions by courts or arbitral tribunals, or any of a host of other standards.

- Discussing objective criteria moves a negotiation toward an effort to find an outcome that the different sides consider to be fair, reasonable, logical, and legitimate. Using neutral standards in this way has the potential to bring about an agreement, and do so amicably. This is important both to maintain strong working relations and to encourage conscientious implementation of the agreement over time.

- The challenging aspect of relying on neutral standards is that the parties will have to work out which standard or standards to rely on, and may have quite different ideas of which is the correct one to use. Here, more specific criteria, more directly on point, tends to be more persuasive than quite general factors.

☐ **Devising Creative Options:** *Why can thinking creatively be so critically important in a complex negotiation? Why is it also particularly challenging, and what can negotiators do to stimulate the creative process?*

- As you work with a counterpart in trying to solve a problem together, you will want to generate a large number of ideas, select among them, refine and improve them, and put the ideas together in such a way that both sides have enough interests satisfied that they agree to a negotiated resolution of the problem.

☐ **The Process of Brainstorming:** *What do negotiators mean by the term* brainstorming? *How is it done most effectively, and why is it sometimes resisted? Why is it so significant to alert the other side that you are now brainstorming?*

- One difficulty is that the process of selecting ideas can become competitive: I attack your ideas, which you defend, and then you attack my ideas, which I defend. The negotiation begins to sound more like a debate than an effort to put the negotiator's minds together and use both of their perspectives to come up with a workable and mutually agreeable resolution.

- Rather than fall into a pattern where each idea that is placed on the table for consideration is then dunked in an acid test of skeptical criticism, it can be useful to designate a period for brainstorming. The idea here is to generate many ideas quickly, without immediate criticism. The effort of choosing the best among them is relegated to the next phase of the negotiation.

☐ **When Impasses Arise:** *What different negotiation dynamics tend to bring on impasses? What are effective techniques for overcoming stalemates?*

- Impasses and deadlocks can be rooted in many different aspects of a negotiation: aggressive claiming, positional bargaining, or psychological barriers.
- To overcome an impasse, a negotiator might try to "build a golden bridge," or he or she might suggest trade-offs or trading across issues, taking advantage of different strengths of feeling.
- Fractionating or enlarging a negotiation is another possibility, as is fashioning a contingent agreement. Here, negotiators should bear in mind the possibility of coming to an agreement into which the missing information will be plugged, once it is in hand. Another approach is to introduce calculated ambiguity.
- Finally, it may be possible to share visions of a better future and what an agreement might deliver to the parties, or change the people involved in the negotiation, or create a last best offer.

Chapter 7 • Overcoming Personality Conflicts and Pressure Tactics

☐ **Varieties of Negotiators:** *What are the characteristics of hard and soft bargainers? How might* partisan perceptions *adversely affect a negotiation?*

- A hard bargainer puts forward extreme positions, aiming to marshal arguments to justify them, while trying to persuade the other side that he or she is locked into them.
- A hard-bargaining negotiator assumes the best route to reaching the most favorable negotiated resolution is to put counterparts on the defensive, corner them with logical arguments, and gain their acquiescence to pre-conceived solutions.
- A soft-bargaining negotiator looks to create, maintain, and improve positive relations with the other side, presuming that a friendly, trusting, cooperative approach is likely to be reciprocated and will ultimately bring about a good agreement.

- Hard bargainers sometimes achieve very advantageous terms, but often frustrate their counterparts who walk away from one-sided potential deals. Soft bargainers sometimes negotiate effectively with fellow negotiators with a similar approach, but their single-minded focus on cultivating good relations leaves them vulnerable to constantly appeasing their counterpart.

☐ **Interpersonal Conflict:** *What commonly brings on interpersonal conflict in negotiations?*
- Conflicts between negotiators or their clients can be rooted in grievances preceding a negotiation or they can spring up during it, making difficult substantive problems even more challenging to negotiate to mutually beneficial resolutions.
- The advice "separate the people from the problem" is not good counsel when the people, including their relations with one another, are a fundamental aspect of the problem.

☐ **Recognizing Partisan Perceptions:** *What are partisan perceptions, and why can recognizing them be important?*
- Partisan perceptions cause problems by distorting analysis, bringing about misinterpretations, and magnifying fears of what the other side might do. If we like someone, we take what they do and say one way, placing positive connotations on their behavior whenever possible. If we fear, dislike, or see them in competitive or adversarial terms, we hurry toward negative connotations and conclusions.

☐ **Emotion, Anger, and Offensive Comments:** *Why might strong emotions arise during a negotiation? What are productive uses of emotion and problematic ones? Why do negotiators sometimes make purposeful inflammatory statements and sometimes accidental ones? What ploys do negotiators sometimes use to try to compel counterparts to do something that they are otherwise disinclined to do?*
- As an inherent part of the human psyche, emotions are often present in negotiations and can be used productively or become quite problematic. When negative emotions take charge of a negotiator, impulsive or short-sighted behavior can result that detracts from reasoned problem-solving.
- Anger, one of the most potentially problematic emotions, sometimes surfaces after an accidental statement, mis-statement, slip of the tongue, or poorly phrased thought. But, anger can also arise when a negotiator purposefully makes an inflammatory remark to try to gain some tactical advantage, such as ruffling or distracting the other side.

☐ **Other Pressure Tactics: Threats, Time Pressures:** *How are threats made effective? What dangers are associated with threats, and what distinguishes a threat from a warning? How might a negotiator respond to a threat? What are the characteristics of an artificial deadline and an exploding offer? What problems are associated with using time pressures this way, and how might a negotiator counter a deadline?*

- Negotiators sometimes make threats hoping that simply flexing their muscles will produce the desired result. However, threats often do not work. People naturally resist pressure, and their target might consider the threat to be a bluff. Then, threats can easily escalate since many are inclined to react to coercion by issuing their own counter-threat.
- Negotiators may try pressure tactics to persuade a party to take some course of action that it is otherwise disinclined to take. For instance, a negotiating session might be artificially prolonged, a consistency trap might be sprung, or a good cop/bad cop routine undertaken.
- One common pressure tactic is a threat to do something the other side will intensely dislike, perhaps take away something of value, expose the other side to some risk, hazard, or danger, or cause some variety of pain or embarrassment.
- Another pressure tactic is to introduce an artificial deadline or exploding offer, both aimed at getting one's counterpart to agree quickly. A negotiator can counter such timing pressures with interest-based arguments, appeals to empathy, counter-offers, or provisional acceptance.

☐ **Managing Interpersonal Difficulties:** *Why focus on interpersonal problems? What benefits and risks are associated with venting? How might a negotiator make amends for contributing to a negative dynamic? How ought an offensive comment be handled? How about dealing with hard bargainers and uncommunicative, unimaginative, or otherwise unhelpful negotiators?*

- One approach to interpersonal problems that are hampering a negotiation is to encourage venting, that is, letting off steam by publicly expressing some points, often emotionally or passionately. Getting deeply held feelings voiced and in the open can help the parties to move on to productive negotiation of substantive issues. However, venting has the potential to make a bad situation worse, particularly when it involves casting blame on parties at the table.
- Another approach to improving poor working relations is to alter the negotiating process. This can be done by calling a recess or caucus, introducing more positive and cooperative body language, reemphasizing active-listening skills, or making a professional appeal, negotiator to negotiator, to try to work out a reasonable proposal. One

can also make amends for the breakdown in relations, including by issuing an apology.

- When an offensive comment has been made, a negotiator should come to a considered decision about how to respond. One option is silence, a pause in communication to see if your counterpart will voluntarily revise what was said or even apologize for it. Another is to deflect the comment, that is, directly acknowledge it but then move on. Still another is to confront the party with the statement, naming what the other side is doing to show that you see through it. Finally, you can engage the comment by having a conversation about what the other party said, why they said it, and what your reaction to it is.

Chapter 8 • Closing a Deal: Reaching a Worthwhile Agreement

- ☐ Timing During the Closing Phase: *What characterizes the closing phase of a complex negotiation? What steps should be taken before a negotiator assembles a proposal? How do deadlines affect negotiations, and what exactly is a fading opportunity? Why might a negotiator rush to close a deal, and what is proper timing?*
  - The closing phase of the negotiation is the time when skillful negotiators make clear what they will commit to do and what they will not or cannot do. Assembling the pieces of a potential deal is the most intense and intellectually exciting period of a complex negotiation but also a risky one since the effort might fall to pieces.
  - An experienced negotiator stays true to the rhythm, or cadence, of a negotiation, neither rushing to close and overlooking key matters nor getting bogged down in minutiae and undue tinkering with the language of different provisions.
- ☐ Useful Steps in Closing a Deal: *How can summarizing the ground covered to date help the parties to transition into a productive closing? Why should negotiators spend some time on ancillary as well as primary issues? Why is it imperative to pair skepticism with creativity as you think through a possible resolution?*
  - Skilled negotiators also gain the ability to take a proposed resolution and examine it from many different angles before finalizing a deal. They think in terms of possible contingencies—things that might occur whether through chance, accident, or design—and figure out how to handle them. As an agreement comes together, the terms often need to be appraised critically and skeptically in order to improve them and ensure that they are sufficient, logical, durable, and operational.

☐ **Formulating a Proposal:** *What are the characteristics of a yesable proposition? How do you make such an offer speak to the other side? How do you enhance the credibility of an offer, and why can it be important to explain your reasoning?*

   • To help negotiators to formulate a proposal, the theory of the yesable proposition is that the process of closing a deal will be advanced if you articulate a proposal that serves interests of both sides, that is phrased clearly and specifically, and that is so comprehensive in scope that the other side could simply say, "Yes. We're agreeable to those terms."

   • In assembling such a proposition, you should not simply attend to your own needs but step into the shoes of your counterpart. What do they care about, how could the offer be made attractive to them, and how might it be phrased so as to maximize its chances of being accepted?

   • In presenting a yesable proposition, a negotiator should look to call on advocacy skills. What you are advocating is not how admirably the proposal is tailored to your own interests but how it ought to suit the other side. Making the offer credible and carefully laying out the reasoning that underlies it can help to bring the other side to accept a proposed deal.

   • How your proposal is organized and presented may well contribute to whether it plays a conclusive role, or even simply a useful one, in concluding the talks. Sell your fellow negotiators on the advantages offered by the potential agreement you have in mind, from their perspectives, before you focus on the aspects of the agreement that will be burdensome for them to fulfill.

☐ **Making Commitments:** *Why is committing often such serious business, and what is meant by "buyer's remorse"? What are the ideas of casual commitment and over-commitment, and what dangers are associated with them? What helps to ensure that commitments are honored? What role might a ratifier play in a negotiation?*

   • The closing phase of a negotiation is about making commitments. The experienced negotiator does not commit casually and does not over-commit. Instead, he or she puts the deal into written form, carefully and clearly drafts legally binding provisions, and takes advantage of useful relationships to help to ensure proper implementation.

☐ **The Decision to Accept or Reject a Proposal:** *What factors should a negotiator keep in mind in trying to determine whether to agree to a deal or walk away from it? Why is trying to reach perfect terms too often a costly quest for the unattainable? When is agreeing not to agree the most sensible route to take? What is a ripeness issue, and when should a negotiator opt to postpone a final resolution?*

- In appraising a possible agreement to determine whether to accept it, reject it, or continue to negotiate, a negotiator should look into the future: is the proposed deal better than his or her BATNA? Do benefits outweigh drawbacks? Commitments should be scrutinized to ensure that they are fair, with clear and realistic terms, so that proper implementation occurs. And, negotiators should strive for an optimal agreement—the best possible resolution under the circumstances.

☐ **Drafting an Effective Agreement:** *Why carefully draft the terms of an agreement? What considerations are associated with the initial draft? What are the advantages to having a template or framework agreement? How might negotiators draft provisions to resolve disputes, allocate risks, or attend to special circumstances?*

- In putting the oral agreement between the parties into written form, negotiators need to determine how many details to include and which of the points discussed should become written provisions. A well-drafted agreement is clear and coherent and leaves no doubt as to what is expected. It should have a logical overall structure with the provisions well-ordered and inter-relating properly.

☐ **Gaining Client or Constituent Approval:** *Why is gaining client or constituent approval often the culminating moment of the closing phase, and what considerations come into play?*

- In some negotiations the decision maker will be present and able to offer a definitive response. In others the proposal will have to be brought back to other authorities—the chief executive officer, the board of directors, the president, etc.—for final approval. Often, the negotiators will need to defend the proposed agreement and generate enthusiasm for it.

Chapter 9 • Contending with Cultural Differences: Navigating Cross-Cultural Complications and Opportunities

☐ **What Is Meant by Culture?:** *Why has contending effectively with cultural complications and opportunities never been more important for negotiators than is true today? What is meant by* culture *and* deep culture? *Why might culture be considered an elusive and complex term, and what varieties of culture exist? What differentiates a high- from a low-context culture and a sub- from a supra-culture?*

- With revolutions in transportation and communication and other dimensions of globalization, professionals in law, business, and other fields must often negotiate across cultures. All negotiators find insights into what their counterparts are thinking valuable, and cultural variables often deeply influence mindsets and thought processes. While culture is rarely the most important factor in a negotiation, it does often play a significant role.

- Cultures are distinctive sets of values and attitudes, norms and beliefs, that usually evolve slowly with the experience and tradition of particular groups. These then play a role in determining a group's self-image or identity. To some extent, they help to guide the actions and orient the behavior of many of the group's members as they cope with the problems of daily life.

☐ **Communication, Language, and Culture:** *How do cultural variables affect communication, verbal and non-verbal? How can the cultural context in which a negotiation occurs influence what is said and left unsaid? How is appropriate behavior related to culture, and what is cross-cultural noise? How does culture affect deeper notions of the good life and the proper ordering of society, and how might culture influence the way a person reasons? In what ways might generalizations about a culture be inaccurate? Why are there so many individual variations within cultures, and how might multiple cultures influence any particular individual?*

- Culture provides people with unwritten instructions on how to act in daily life, what is fitting, appropriate, legitimate behavior. It affects an individual's sense of rights and duties, what is upright versus immoral, normal versus peculiar. Culture can influence the meaning people ascribe to events, and it can help them to determine how actions ought to be defended, criticized, or rationalized.

- There are national cultures and regional ones, high-context and low-context cultures, ethnic, religious, and even occupational cultures, such as the culture of diplomats.

- Individuals may be influenced by many separate cultural variables; subcultures and supra-cultures exist alongside national cultures, for instance. Given the complexities of cultural influences, their impact on any particular negotiation is uncertain. Determining which cultural value might be influencing a negotiator at any particular moment can be daunting. More often than not, cultural factors simply provide tentative indicators of what people are thinking or how they are reacting. Nevertheless, this may be quite useful if it gives a negotiator insights into how the other party views particular matters related to a negotiation.

- Cultural differences affect the way that people interact with each other, both verbal and non-verbal communication. The cultural context may determine whether the meaning of a particular statement—

"she's a real individual," for instance — could be a positive or negative statement in one culture or another.

☐ **The Significance of Culture for Negotiators:** *What is the debate over the significance of cultural influences for negotiation? What are the views of the advocates, and how do the skeptics respond?*

- One school of thought, the advocates, finds culture vitally important for negotiation. Understanding something of the culture of one's counterpart can help negotiators to handle cross-cultural noise, to grasp what the other side values, how it understands its interests, and what priorities and goals it sets. Cultural variables may even affect an individual's line of reasoning, whether problems are analyzed inductively or deductively and such abstractions as legitimacy, justice, and fairness.

- Another school of thought, the skeptics, emphasizes the problems and difficulties associated with putting cultural concepts to practical use. Generalizations about culture can be confusing and misleading. Individual variations abound, and multiple cultures affect individuals. These may then temper or contradict different aspects of how people within that culture view the world.

☐ **Culture and Negotiation Strategy:** *How might cultural factors be incorporated in a negotiation strategy? How might sensitivity to cultural differences help a negotiator to develop a positive working relationship with a counterpart? Why might it be important to help a counterpart to save face? How do legal cultures differ, and how might those differences affect a cross-cultural negotiation?*

- Negotiators at work on complex problems that contain cross-cultural dimensions might bear in mind important cultural differences and then try to take them into account in a thoughtful way as they create and implement their negotiating strategies.

- A skillful negotiator might consider the culture of his or her counterparts and think through their expectations for the working relationship, the processes of negotiation, and the type of agreement to aim at. This might then help the negotiator to create an effective strategy, one that handled the particular cultural differences and complementarities well.

Chapter 10 • Ethical Negotiation: Distinguishing Proper from Improper Behavior

☐ **Different Standards:** *What standards might negotiators call on as they try to determine what is proper and improper behavior? What are the legal, ethical, moral, and practical approaches?*

- People call on different standards to construct their theories of what constitutes an honest negotiator. Some involve legal principles; others, ethical guidelines, moral standards, or practical or utilitarian considerations.
- A negotiator makes a fraudulent statement when he or she says something about a material fact knowing that it is untrue, and the other party relies on it in a way that a court views as reasonable, and that party is later damaged by that reliance.
- Cultivating a reputation for honest, straightforward dealing may pay substantial dividends in future negotiations, while a reputation for being shifty, double-dealing, or untruthful could diminish the negotiator's future effectiveness and be quite difficult to shed.

☐ **Disclosure, Non-Disclosure, and Deceit:** *What issues are raised by failing to disclose particular matters? What problems can arise when a negotiator sets out to deceive a counterpart? When should negotiators be especially on guard, watching carefully for possible deception?*

- The ethical issues that arise most frequently involve disclosure versus non-disclosure as well as the distorting of facts or other forms of deceit.
- Negotiators are not expected to exhibit full candor for fear they will be taken or their bargaining position will be undercut. However, an honest negotiator does not lie to counterparts nor take unfair advantage of them. Suspicions of deceit are likely to greatly constrain communication and undercut efforts at joint problem-solving.
- A deceptive negotiator believes one thing but in hopes of gaining some advantage says something different to encourage the other side to believe something else. Or, perhaps, he or she simply keeps silent, withholding knowledge of the true state of affairs in hopes of encouraging a false belief.
- Negotiators should be especially careful to avoid being taken in by deception where continuing relations with their counterpart are unlikely, where the other side has a compelling motive to deceive, or where the matters being discussed are quite difficult to verify.
- The best ways to uncover or ward off deceptive practices are through questions and requests for proof and documentation. The parties can also try to structure the agreement so that it does not hinge on a questionable fact being true.

☐ **Other Particular Ethical Issues:** *What is meant by dirty tricks, puffing, and bluffing? Why might a negotiator misrepresent his or her authority? What*

*should an honest negotiator do when a counterpart thoroughly miscon-
ceives something or makes a major error in calculations?*
- Dirty tricks are especially sharp, crooked, or underhanded practices.
  Puffing involves negotiators shading their real views or putting a more
  favorable spin on a point or fact. Bluffing is pretending something to
  be the case when it is not in order to see if the other side is foolish, inexperienced, or concerned enough to accept what is said at face value.
- ☐ **Ethical Issues Regarding Principals and Agents:** *How does a principal-
  agent relationship raise issues of negotiation ethics? What are fiduciary relations? What potentially contrasting perspectives might a principal and
  an agent have? Why and how do principals design incentives to try to ensure that an agent acts to advance their best interests?*
  - The duties that an agent owes a principal can raise ethical issues, such
    as when the agent does not act as a fiduciary but pursues his or her
    own interests contrary to those of the principal.
- ☐ **What Is Meant by Negotiating in Good and Bad Faith?:** *What is meant
  by negotiating in good faith and bad faith?*
  - The central ingredients of good-faith bargaining are to negotiate hon-
    estly and fairly to see if a deal can be reached, without engaging in dirty
    tricks, falsifying information, or lying to a counterpart.

**Chapter 11 • Conclusion: Formulating and Implementing
         Effective Strategies**

- ☐ **Creating an Effective Strategy:** *What is a negotiating strategy? What considerations ought a negotiator bear in mind, and what elements might be
  included in such a strategy? In the circumstances being faced, is it better to
  lead or to react? Should the negotiation be envisioned as a checklist of items
  to be dealt with one-by-one, or should it be viewed as a package deal in which
  no single item can be negotiated to a resolution until the parties see how all
  of the items fit together? What are the key components of an effective negotiating strategy? What strategic issues arise in the different phases of a negotiation?*
  - A negotiating strategy is a detailed plan, made up of various tactics, as-
    sembled by a negotiator and aimed at achieving specified objectives. Ne-
    gotiators ought to try to formulate a thoughtful, sophisticated plan,
    drawing on their knowledge of the theory and practice of negotiation
    and crafted to maximize the chances of reaching their objectives.
  - A strategy should be considerably more involved than simply desig-
    nating a particular method—positional or interest-based—as the
    approach you aim to take. Among the fundamental questions are

whether you will lead or react and whether you envision the negotiation as a checklist of separate issues or a package covering all or many different issues?

- One negotiator's strategy might include thoughts on how to capitalize on his or her leverage or power or diminish that of a counterpart. Another's might encompass a particular agenda and look to set a particular tone. A strategy drawing on the interest-based approach could involve thoughts on how best to explain one's interests and discover your counterpart's interests. It might reference objective standards and creative options. Strategic considerations often include thoughts on how best to close the deal.

- Since the parties to an advanced negotiation are constantly interacting, often in unforeseen ways, negotiators must think "on their feet," adapt to their counterpart, and react flexibly and intelligently to what is occurring. One does not want to become too wedded to a preconceived strategy, and it may be quite useful to create alternate strategies ahead of time to draw on in different circumstances.

☐ **Identifying Special Circumstances:** *Why is it important to identify special circumstances and tailor one's negotiating strategy to handle those issues? For instance, how might a negotiator respond to preconceived drafts and pattern bargaining? What are the singular aspects of e-mail negotiations, and what are the advantages and disadvantages to negotiating by e-mail? What is a renegotiation, and why do parties renegotiate? What distinguishes the chief varieties of renegotiation: post-deal, intra-deal, and extra-deal renegotiations? What special difficulties characterize multi-party negotiations? What considerations ought to be in mind as parties are convened and settle on a decision-making process? What common communication problems afflict groups, and how might they best be dealt with? How might negotiators set ground rules, adopt particular roles, and formulate task forces to organize a group? Under what circumstances might caucusing be useful?*

- Determining what stands out about an upcoming negotiation can help a negotiator to tailor a strategy to particular circumstances. For instance, the negotiator might face the challenges of negotiating across cultures or with a need to overcome a past hostile relationship. Another set of circumstances that frequently arises involves renegotiation.

- Yet another increasingly common special context is an e-mail negotiation. Here, negotiators should be cognizant of the difficulties inherent in communicating by e-mail and look to counter them whenever possible.

- One common special context for complex problems is a group negotiation. Groups often have a hard time determining just what they
  want to accomplish. The larger the group, the easier it is for the voices
  of some of the negotiators to be drowned out, while others can drone
  on interminably, adding layers of frustration to the proceedings.
- In a group negotiation one representative might be intent on finding a fair and equitable resolution for all or most involved in the negotiation, while another is focusing exclusively on gaining the best
  possible resolution for the party that he or she represents.
- More parties also usually means more diverse goals, interests, and
  walk-away options for the negotiators to bear in mind; efforts to find
  suitable objective criteria and to agree on creative options may be
  quite challenging, and any yesable proposition must be envisioned
  from multiple perspectives.
- Communication within large groups is often especially problematic:
  people tend to be more guarded in what they say, and, for an interest-
  based strategy to succeed, domineering negotiators or those who are
  grandstanding may need to be managed, while negotiators inclined
  to give up or withdraw may need to be drawn back into the talks.
- Sizeable groups may benefit from the extra organization brought to
  the talks by setting explicit ground rules or adopting particular roles
  (such as time-keeper or note-taker). A large group may need to be
  broken down into specialized task forces charged with bringing specific ideas back to the other members.
- In internal caucuses colleagues trade ideas, insights, and reactions to
  ensure that the team is thinking alike about key points. External caucuses can help negotiators to form coalitions or otherwise bring potential allies around to your viewpoint. You can sometimes build
  rapport in a caucus or learn things that a negotiator is reluctant to reveal to the group as a whole.

Appendix 1

Linguistics and Negotiation

A. Choosing Effective Language

How do linguistic matters affect negotiation? In a sport like fencing or judo, even in a game like chess, you engage your counterpart in a particular way. Rules, traditions, and training dictate much of the moves and maneuvers during the contest. A similar phenomenon marks much effective interest-based negotiation when the parties are confronted with a complex problem and are looking to work together to create a mutually acceptable resolution.

Many of us feel most comfortable and so are most receptive to reasonable and intelligent discussion when negotiations are proceeding along familiar paths. Consequently, there is often a rhythm to the way in which many negotiations progress, from introducing the parties to setting the agenda, from exploring interests to discussing objective criteria and creating options.

There is also an important linguistic element to the effort to work toward a mutually satisfactory resolution of a shared problem or opportunity. People tend to feel awkward when terms or phrases are used that are not fully understand. (One reason that *Mastering Negotiation* includes a glossary is to help its readers toward feeling comfortable as they negotiate.) Most important, people come to believe in a joint problem-solving process—they become engaged, creative, and open-minded about it—when they receive a series of reassuring signals from the other side.

Here, much hinges on the language that the negotiators choose to use. Just as great importance can be attached to *what* is said, so it can also attach to *how* it is said. Let us turn, then, to some familiar ways in which negotiators make points, some turns-of-the-phrase that may be useful to negotiators grappling with complex problems.

1. Clarifying Phrases

Sometimes negotiators employ clarifying phrases, trying to ensure that they understand what their counterpart is saying. They might start a sentence with the words "what if" or "assuming that." Examples of other such phrases include:

- "I hear you saying ..."
- "What do you mean by saying ...?"
- "What is most important to you?"
- "You clearly feel very strongly that ..."
- "Do I have this right? Your perception is ..."
- "I'm not sure I'm following you when you say ..."
- "Tell me, then, is this the way things look to you ...?"
- "It seems that you see this situation as hinging on ..."
- "Can you flesh out what you've said about ..."
- "If I were you, I think I might be concerned about ..."
- "Help me to understand where you're coming from on this ..."
- "Is there anything I'm missing, or do I have the essence of it?"
- "I'd like to see, in some more detail, exactly why you want that ..."
- "You make an interesting point. Explain it some more for me ..."
- "Of everything we've talked about thus far, what seems most important to you?"
- "Let me see if I understand what you're saying and what you're most concerned about ..."
- "I'm not sure I've been communicating all that clearly about x. What have you all heard me saying?"
- "Let's see if we can hone in on just what are the contours of the problem that we're trying to solve here ..."
- "Perhaps this is a good time to clarify exactly how the agreement we're working on here seems to be developing ..."
- "I have a much better sense of where you're coming from, but before we move on, is there anything else that you think ought to be added to what we've discussed so far? ..."

Such phrases mark the interactions of experienced active listeners. Recall how interest-based negotiators put great stock in drawing out the other side, posing follow-up questions, and ensuring that they know that you are engaged in what they have to say. So, skillful negotiators use clarifying phrases frequently, as they try to gain a good understanding of their counterpart's interests and then try to work with them to resolve problems and create options that both sides can support.

Chapter 3 noted the importance of signaling the other side that, while you may not necessarily agree with their point, you have heard and fully understood it. Here, the following phrases may be useful.

- "Of course, *our* perspective on what you're saying may differ from yours, but I do think I now understand your key concerns here."
- "We'll have to think about the extent to which we agree with you, but we definitely see what you're saying."
- "Give us some time to consider these points you've made, but we certainly can now grasp how things look from your perspective."
- "From what you've said, if I were over on your side of table, I'd probably be thinking …"

Chapter 3 noted how useful it may be, when a negotiator wants to proceed in a packaging mode, not a checklist one, to clarify that no final commitments are being made until the full proposal can be reviewed and approved.

- "The way I see us proceeding involves developing the terms of an overall package agreement. I would propose, then, that no particular point be considered finally resolved until the whole agreement is crafted to both of our satisfaction."

2. Guiding Phrases

At other times, negotiators use carefully chosen language to try to guide the discussion forward. Examples of phrases commonly used by negotiators to guide talks along particular paths follow.

- "Let's take stock …"
- "to echo what was just said …"
- "building on that idea, we could then …"
- "Could we take a step forward by suggesting …"
- "What would be wrong with doing it like this …?"
- "Next, we'd really like to hear your thoughts on …"
- "We appreciate your being aware of our interest in …"
- "So, how can we get there? How might we achieve that …?"
- "Let me summarize where I think we have gotten so far …"
- "_____ has made an important point that I would like to come back to …"
- "How about if we go back and look at that agenda, and see where we are …"
- "To see if I understand what has happened, I'd like to ask a few questions …"
- "I definitely agree with what we've been saying about … Now, how about …?"
- "What I particularly appreciate about that idea is … Could we take your idea even further by …?"
- "I understand much better now how your side sees this, let me try to explain our viewpoint on it …"

- "I'm going to need to get back to you on that one, after I look into it further, for now how about if we move next to ..."
- "Let's talk about what we think is likely to happen if we can't reach an agreement. What we will do, and what will your side do?"
- "Let's look to the future now and see if we can figure out how to keep some of these problems from coming up all over again? ..."
- "Could we agree that, for a while now, the tone of this negotiation has shifted, and we've started to interact in some less productive ways than before? How about if we get back to seeing if we can find an agreement we both like and can support?"
- "You've made some good points about what might not work. How about turning to some of your own ideas? What would you suggest that might improve on the ideas we've gotten out so far?"

3. Challenging Phrases

Even when one side wants to challenge what the other has said, seasoned negotiators have ways of signaling their counterpart as to strong feelings about a subject but without giving unnecessary offense. Again, the particular language employed can be significant. The following are some common challenging phrases:

- "If you look at it from my perspective ..."
- "Here's where I'm not following the logic ..."
- "Can you do any better, and help me out with ...?"
- "If that's the right number, help me to see why it is ..."
- "We're not prepared to do that right now, but how about ..."
- "Help me to see why you think that would be a fair and reasonable outcome?"
- "Let's try to think through what could happen if we can't come to an agreement ..."
- "Let me ask you to come around to our side of the table for a minute. How could we sell that idea to others on our side? ..."
- "We do have real interest in working toward a deal with you, but we also have some issues that very much concern us ..."
- "You say you'll have to consult with your client. I would propose that we all sit down and hash this out together. When could we get together as a group?"
- "One thing we definitely want is to be treated as well as you treat others that you're working with. And, my side is going to be unhappy if we learn that you gave a better deal on this to somebody else. Have you given more favorable terms before [in drafting this provision/supplying this material/selling this item ...]?"

4. Deflecting or Circumventing Phrases

Negotiators often find the need to deflect pressure from the other side or to sidestep certain matters that they are not prepared to reveal to their counterparts. One side demands to know something, but the other side would much prefer to keep that information private, and says, explicitly or in effect, "I don't want to get into that ..."

Once again, it can help to have a handful of phrases in mind used to circumvent statements or inquiries without causing unnecessary offense. Some typical phrases and counter-phrases follow.[1]

- *"Let's move next to x ..."*
  "Actually, I'm just not free to discuss that particular point with you. I'd suggest we move instead to talk about y."
- *"Your side needs to do better than that ..."*
  "We continue to believe that we've made a fair proposal ..."
- *"I have a registered check right here that we can use to settle this deal once and for all ..."*
  "I'm afraid you'll have to go get another check ..."
- *"It says right here that ..."*
  "At some point somebody or other sat down and wrote that out, but— knowing what we know—there's no reason we can't draft it better and differently ..."

5. Closing Phrases

Finally, in that culminating stage of a negotiation, when negotiators get very serious and either "cut the deal" or reject it, another set of common statements may be useful.

- "O.K., here's what we're prepared to do ..."
- "Can you help me with this final problem I'm facing ..."
- "Given all that's been said so far, I think the right number is ..."
- "I think we may be able to do x, but we'll then need you to do y ..."
- "We want to be clear, though, that our offer of x, y, and z is predicated on your w ..."
- "I'm sensing we're getting very close, but maybe not quite there yet. What would happen if ...?"
- "Can we think of any ways to expand the pie further, that is, to make this resolution better for all of us?"

- "How about a final compromise built on one last trade? I will commit to x, if you will commit to y."
- "I see the point you've made about x. So, what do you think we might do about it that would appeal to both of us?"
- "Is there a way to make this agreement better for anyone here at the table without also making it worse for someone else?"
- "To reach the best possible agreement for both sides, what concerns should we be having about this proposal, and how might we address them? ..."
- "My sense is that you are as serious as we are in bringing these talks to a final agreement. We'd like to see you take the next step and formulate a realistic [proposal/counterproposal]. This would be something that your side would like and stand behind, but that serves our interests well enough that we'd agree to it, too."

Notes

1. Various of these are drawn from Doug MacKay, *Outlining Negotiation Types and Processes*, in BASIC NEGOTIATION SKILLS 9–11 (Practising Law Institute, 2013).

Glossary of Negotiation Terms

Active listening involves posing open-ended inquiries and asking clarifying follow-up questions.

An *agenda* is a list of the items to be negotiated in the order the parties want them to be raised. See also *hidden agenda*.

An *agent* is a deputy authorized by a principal to act on his or her behalf by representing the principal's interests in negotiations with another. See also *fiduciary, principal*.

A negotiator's *alternatives* are the different routes that he or she might pursue if the negotiation does not produce an agreement. See also *Best Alternative to a Negotiated Agreement*.

To *anchor* a negotiation means to make a strong argument in favor of a particular number or point, usually early in the negotiations, in hopes that this opening position will influence other parties throughout the remainder of the discussions.

Ancillary issues. See *primary issues*.

In *arbitration* a dispute is referred to an impartial third person, chosen by the parties to the dispute, who agree in advance to abide by the arbitrator's award, issued after a hearing at which both sides have an opportunity to present arguments and evidence.

An *artificial deadline*, sometimes referred to an *exploding offer*, is a short time limit contrived by the person making an offer to another to pressure his or her counterpart into a response.

A negotiator's *authority* refers to the following items. What is the negotiation about, how freely can the negotiator pursue different aspects of the negotiation, what matters are open to discussion with the other side, and what are to be kept confidential, and what can the negotiator commit to do on behalf of his or her principal? *See also parameters*.

Back table negotiations are ongoing discussions between a client and his or her negotiator about what should happen and what is happening in the negotiation with the other side.

The *bait-and-switch technique* aims to interest a purchaser in something by alluding to an incredibly favorable sales price, but then "discover" that all have just been sold and try to substitute some alternative at a much higher price.

Bargaining is sometimes used as a narrower term than negotiation, consisting of "the presentation and exchange of more or less specific proposals for the terms of agreement on particular issues."[1]

A *bargaining chip* is an inducement to come to an agreement.

Bargaining room. See *room to negotiate.*

In *barter transactions* commodities are exchanged rather than money.

BATNA. See *Best Alternative to a Negotiated Agreement.*

Best Alternative to a Negotiated Agreement (BATNA), or walk-away option, is what a negotiator will do if no agreement is reached with the other side since it is the course of action most likely to serve his or her interests.[2]

A *blocking coalition* is a group of negotiators in a multi-party negotiation that comes together to thwart the efforts of another coalition. See also *coalition* and *cross-over player.*

Blue chip issue. See *primary issue.*

Bluffing signifies pretending something to be the case when it is not in order to see if the other side is foolish, inexperienced, or concerned enough to accept what is said at face value.

Body language means communicating via posture, gestures, or facial expressions. See also *gesture cluster.*

Bottom line. See *position.*

Brainstorming is an activity aimed at producing a number of ideas that might prove productive in the effort to come to a mutually agreeable resolution. See also *joint brainstorming.*

Brinkmanship is a term with its genesis in diplomatic maneuvering: an extreme variety of a bluff, in which one side or the other or both bring the parties to the edge of disaster—which could range from armed conflict to, simply, the termination of the negotiation—in hopes that the other side will back down.

Buyer's remorse refers to the last-minute doubts that may influence the thinking of negotiators, usually in the closing phase of a deal, as they consider the commitments their side is poised to make.

Casual commitment occurs when a negotiator, without considering the situation sufficiently carefully, vows to do something that his or her side does not want to carry through with.

In a *caucus* negotiators on one side of the problem meet to discuss what has occurred or in a group negotiation a small subset of negotiators, whether natural allies or negotiators contending with each other, meet to consider the problem for a time without the pressure of having to participate in the give-and-take of ongoing discussions among the whole group. See also *recess*.

The phrase *caves in* signifies that, often under the pressure of having to answer on the spot or under some duress, a negotiator accepts an outstanding proposal in full without requesting any changes.

In a *checklist negotiation* the parties negotiate a series of issues, individually, to resolutions. While certain of the issues may be temporarily set aside to be returned to later, the effort is to deal with each matter on its own merits, without linking one issue to another. See also *packaging negotiation*.

Claiming value refers to a situation where resources are in short supply and must be allocated between the parties, and each party tries to grasp as many of the assets at issue as possible. See also *creating value*.

Closer. See *ratifier*.

Closing a deal means coming to a final resolution.

A *coalition* is a group in a multi-party negotiation that joins to work as a unit to try to achieve some particular objective or objectives. See also *blocking coalition* and *cross-over player*.

Complementary schismogenesis is the idea that the culturally derived behavior of each negotiator drives his or her counterpart toward increasingly pronounced expressions of their own contrasting cultural approach in what has been characterized as a mutually aggravating spiral.

The term *complex negotiation* refers to negotiations that are complicated by multiple involved issues, numerous parties, scientific or technical intricacies, significant cross-cultural differences, or baggage-laden conflicts or disputes, whether personal, group, national, or international.

A *concession* is something yielded during a negotiation in a spirit of compromise. See also *negative concession*.

Conditions are options to get out of an agreement. They are statements "which, if not satisfied, 'relieve a party of its obligation to complete the transaction.'"[3]

With *conflicting interests* the underlying concerns or motivations of one side in a negotiation are at odds with those of the other side.

Consensus means that a decision "has the support of a large and representative majority and is not rejected by any members."[4]

In a *consistency trap* a negotiator first looks to persuade a counterpart to agree to the logic or fairness of an innocuous-sounding standard. He or she then tries to get the counterpart to concede that the standard also applies to the present situation.

Contingencies are things that might occur whether through chance, accident, or design.

Contingent agreement is a tentative resolution that depends upon some particular thing happening in order to become final. The particular thing could range from obtaining the approval of someone else to confirming that a particular fact is true.

A *covenant* is a promise that something shall be done or, occasionally, that a party will refrain from doing something.

Creating value refers to inventing something new, something the parties can do together that becomes a beneficial outcome for one or the other or both sides in a negotiation. See also *claiming value.*

Creative options are possible resolutions of a negotiating problem, or parts of such a resolution, that a negotiator formulates in a fresh or insightful way.

Cross-cultural noise means background distractions somehow tied to cultural differences that may obstruct effective negotiation by causing one side to feel disgust, tension, irritation, or awkwardness.

In a negotiation marked by contending coalitions, a *cross-over player* is a negotiator who might become a member of more than one coalition. See also *coalition* and *blocking coalition.*

Cultural hyper-correction refers to a situation when a negotiator, intent on demonstrating his or her cultural sensitivity, might go too far to be effective in trying to negotiate just the way someone from the culture of his or her counterpart might.

Culture refers to a distinctive set of values and attitudes, norms and beliefs, that usually evolve slowly with the experience and tradition of a particular group and that, to some extent, help to guide the actions and orient the behavior of many in that group.

A *deal-breaker* is a particular point of such importance to a party or parties that the entire negotiated agreement may hinge on whether it is resolved satisfactorily or not.

In a *deductive negotiation approach* one attempts at the beginning of the negotiation to agree on general principles that may then guide the resolution of specific issues. See also *inductive negotiation approach.*

Dickering. See *haggling.*

A *dispute-resolution provision* directs the parties as to how to handle any conflicts that might arise under the terms of the agreement. For instance, the parties might be directed to undertake mediation or arbitration should negotiations fail to produce a mutually agreeable resolution.

Distributional bargaining involves negotiations over those issues where any gain to one side will result in a loss to another. See also *face-to-face negotiating.*

Divisible commodities are things that can be counted, such as money.

Dovetailing interests refers to the situation when the interests of one negotiator mesh nicely with those of another.

The phrase *economies of scale* refers to the idea that when some business or government entity expands its various outputs, the cost per unit of each output often decreases.

The phrase *economies of scope* refers to the idea that costs of production can be lower when the same basic resources are devoted to producing a number of different goods or services rather than just one.

Exploding offer. See *artificial deadline.*

External negotiations are the negotiations between representatives of different parties as opposed to the internal negotiations that take place among colleagues on the same side of a negotiation. See also *internal negotiations.*

In an *extra-deal renegotiation* one party asks to renegotiate a deal without relying on any specific provision in the original agreement that gives them the right to do so. See also *renegotiation* and *intra-deal renegotiation.*

Face-to-face negotiating is sometimes used as a short-hand to refer to distributional bargaining. See also *distributional bargaining, side-by-side negotiating.*

The concept of *face-saving* refers to the idea that people have a psychological need not to look bad, weak, or foolish before themselves and others, especially those whose positive opinion of them they value.

A *fading opportunity* stands for the idea that the chances of reaching an agreement are going to dissipate over time.

A *fallback position* reflects a concession from the position you have taken toward your counterpart's current position. See also *concession, position.*

A *false demand* is a request that a negotiator makes not on its merits but in order to drop at the other side's insistence in exchange for a tradeoff, enabling the negotiator to achieve something he or she really does want.

A *fiduciary* acts not for his or her own benefit but for the benefit of another in a relationship of trust, confidence, and the utmost good faith, advancing the principal's best interests at all times. See also *agent, principal.*

A *force majeure clause* excuses a party for failing to perform its obligations for causes that are beyond its control and could not have been avoided even if the party had exercised due care.

Formulaic negotiation occurs when the parties come to an agreement on an equation, but they do not know the final outcome of the equation until certain missing information is gathered and inserted.

Fractionating refers to dividing up a complex problem into its component pieces to see if some resolution is possible even if it involves only a fraction of the larger problem.

To *frame* a negotiation is to define the negotiating problem or opportunity, identifying who are the parties and what are the issues.

A *game of chicken* is a reference to a game associated with teenaged drivers in the 1950s, where each driver hurtled forward in a car, trying not to be the one who swerved to avoid a collision.

Gesture-clusters are groups of related non-verbal body movements that together are likely to communicate some attitude. See also *body language*.

Goals for a negotiation are objectives that will please a party if attained. See also *interdiction goal*.

In a *good cop/bad cop routine* two colleagues negotiate as a team, and while one partner adopts a trusting, understanding, sympathetic persona, the other takes on a negative, difficult, uncompromising style. The hope is that manipulating these two psychological approaches will bring an advantageous resolution. (The name is derived from the fact that police departments have long used this approach to gain information from suspects.)

Grandstanding, or a *play to the gallery*, involves making a statement that is aimed not at one's counterpart but at some other party or parties who is likely to hear of the statement, directly or indirectly, and be pleased by it.

Ground rules are principles, agreed upon by the parties usually before substantive negotiations begin, aimed at governing the discussions in some orderly manner.

Group process refers to the manner in which the members of a group work with one another.

A *guarantee* is a formal, usually written, assurance about something of concern to one side in the negotiation, for instance, that a product will perform satisfactorily for some given period or that it is of specified quality.

Haggling or *dickering* involves the effort by each side in a negotiation to dislodge the other from its position and get it to adopt a new position nearer its own.

A *hard bargainer* is one who tries to coerce or compel his or her opponent into making concessions and ultimately giving in to the resolution the hard bargainer has in mind.

A *hidden agenda* refers to important matters that are purposefully kept off the agenda created with the other party, but that a negotiator expects to introduce at some moment that he or she finds particularly auspicious. See also *agenda*.

Horse-trading negotiation. See *packaging negotiation*.

A *hurting stalemate* is a conflict in which neither side is able achieve its goals at acceptable levels of costs.

With *inconsistent interests* pursuing or fulfilling one interest may make achieving another much more difficult to carry out, even perhaps impossible to achieve.

In an *inductive negotiation approach* the negotiators would concentrate on resolving a series of particular issues, which form the backbone for a general agreement. See also *deductive negotiation approach.*

Initialing items being negotiated involves representatives of each side formally agreeing to a resolution of those matters, an agreement that is signified by each negotiator placing his or her initials next to the agreed provision drafted for that item.

Instructions are detailed orders laying out objectives and strategy.

An *interdiction goal* is one party's objective of having its counterpart *not* gain or do something.

Interests refers to something that either objectively affects the welfare of a party to a negotiation or that subjectively affects that party, that is, something the party prefers, regardless of whether it actually serves the party's well-being or not. See also *dovetailing interests, objective interest, separate interests,* and *subjective interest.*

Interest-based negotiation is an approach that emphasizes using a handful of fundamental precepts to guide negotiators toward reaching an agreement by focusing on serving the interests of the different sides.

Internal negotiations, prior to and often during the external negotiation with the other side(s), aim to coordinate the team, especially to iron out the differing perceptions of interests, objectives, and strategies that the different team members bring to the negotiation. See also *external negotiations.*

An *intra-deal renegotiation* occurs when an agreement is re-negotiated midway through its term according to a provision permitting re-negotiation if certain specified circumstances occur. See also *renegotiation* and *post-deal renegotiation.*

Joint brainstorming refers to brainstorming alongside the other side or sides in a negotiation. See also *brainstorming.*

A *last best offer* is an ultimate proposal put forward in the closing stage of a negotiation to try to break an impasse.

A *last gap* refers to a final issue about which the parties fundamentally disagree and have become deadlocked.

To leave money on the table is a phrase that refers to concluding the negotiation for less money or other assets than the counterpart would actually have been willing to pay or transfer. Depending on the strategy and context, this can be a negative expression ("We should have kept bargaining, I think we left money on the table"), or it can be a positive one ("We granted a final concession, generously leaving something on the table for the other side, which we will be sure to remind them of in the next round of negotiations"). See also *to leave something on the table.*

To leave something on the table is a phrase that signifies granting your counterpart a final concession rather than trying to take that thing for your side of the negotiation. See also *to leave money on the table.*

Leverage refers to the ability a negotiator has to move the other side toward doing what he or she wants, ultimately increasing the negotiator's chances of attaining his or her goals. The reference is to the action of a lever, that is, a bar made of sufficiently strong material, placed in the correct position, then pushed, can move a large weight which might appear difficult or impossible to dislodge. See also *normative leverage.*

Logrolling refers to political tradeoffs. For instance, in a legislature a representative's vote on one issue might come in exchange for another's support on a different issue.

Loss of face refers to feelings of inadequacy that might arise when one is placed in an embarrassing situation.

A *low-ball offer or proposal* is one that is aimed at being barely sufficient to gain an agreement.

Material facts refers to information a negotiator would reasonably see as quite significant in determining how to proceed in a negotiation.

In *mediation* a dispute is referred to a neutral third party who attempts to assist the parties in resolving it by helping them to create a mutually agreeable resolution.

Minimum. See *reservation price.*

Moral hazard is a phrase negotiators use to denote that, rather than heeding the biblical injunction of doing unto others as you would have them do unto you, one party behaves in an underhanded manner that advantages itself and disadvantages its counterpart.

National negotiating characteristics refers to the way in which different nationalities might negotiate differently.

A *negative concession* is one that moves away from the other side, not toward it. See also *concession.*

A *negotiation* is a discussion that shares five defining characteristics. The parties identify a problem or opportunity and initiate communication about it. They set forth information about the situation they confront. After a conversation in which points are made and questions posed to one another, potential resolutions are formulated. The parties then decide what to do next, whether to confine themselves to an exchange of their views or move toward an actual agreement. If the latter, they work out details of a resolution which can be oral but is often laid out in written form. See also *preliminary negotiations, internal negotiations.*

A *negotiated rulemaking* is an effort to create a regulation via a negotiation among the principal stakeholders.

Neutral standards. See *objective criteria.*

A *non-negotiable* matter is one that a negotiator contends is beyond the scope of negotiation; the implication is that there is no sense in discussing a non-negotiable subject since no compromise is possible.

Normative leverage refers to a party's desire to act in accordance with its own norms, beliefs, and principles. See also *leverage.*

Objective criteria are factors or standards that a neutral and unbiased observer would see as a fair way to decide a contentious issue.

An *objective interest* is an interest that really does, in fact, promote the welfare of that side of the negotiation.

Optimistic overconfidence refers to a distorting of judgment in favor of your own side and against your counterparts.

Options are things the parties could agree to do, singly or together, as part of a negotiated resolution.

In a negotiation *over-commitment* refers to telling another party that you will do something, which you then end up not being able to do.

In a *packaging negotiation,* also sometimes called a *horse-trading negotiation,* the ultimate negotiated agreement takes the form of a package deal covering all of the different items or issues. See also *checklist negotiation.*

The *parameters* a negotiator faces signify the limits or constraints set by whomever he or she is negotiating on behalf of. This could be his or her agency, boss, client, department, corporation, etc. See also *authority.*

Pareto optimal frontier, named after Vilfredo Pareto, the economist who popularized the idea, describes the line on a graph representing negotiating efficiency in the sense that no joint gains are left and any improvement in the outcome for one side would entail a decrease in the benefits to another side.

The idea of *partisan perceptions* is that, when we like someone, we take what they do and say one way, placing positive connotations on their behavior whenever possible. If we fear, dislike them, or see them in competitive or adversarial terms, we hurry toward negative connotations and conclusions. and interpret their words and actions in the worst possible light.

Pattern bargaining refers to negotiations within an industry that follow a particular prototype or model. Agreements within the industry are quite similar, though not identical, since they are sometimes tailored to fit the particular needs of the parties.

A *perquisite,* or *sweetener,* is an incidental bonus, privilege, or fringe benefit aimed at making the agreement more attractive for one of the parties.

Personalism is a cultural trait that emphasizes close one-on-one relations in general and patron-client (*patrón/cliente*) relationships in particular. Various aspects of a personalistic society are so organized as to depend heavily on personal contact, including hierarchical relationships in which a superior gains the allegiance of a subordinate and then, in turn, looks after that person's interests.

Piggybacking is an exercise aimed at generating fresh new ideas in which a group focuses upon a promising idea with the members trying, each in turn, to suggest ways that it could be taken further.

A *play to the gallery.* See *grandstanding.*

A *position* is an effort by a negotiator to lay out, usually at the outset of a negotiation, a firm stance or demand in order to make clear what it will take to reach an agreement. A *fallback position,* or *bottom line,* would be the minimum resolution that a negotiator would need to have fulfilled in order to reach an agreement.

Positional bargaining refers to the tug of war between the positions of the different negotiators in which each tries to pull the other closer to its favored stance.

A *positive-sum game* is the opposite of a zero-sum game in which a side either comes out with all the gains or absorbs all the losses; instead, all the parties emerge with some benefits and, hence, are to some degree better off than they were before.

A *post-deal renegotiation* occurs when the period of the original agreement is drawing to a close and the parties come together to see if they can renew their agreement, though perhaps altering its terms with provisions that might spell out new rights, duties, responsibilities, or incentives. See also *renegotiation, intra-deal renegotiation,* and *extra-deal renegotiation.*

Posturing. See *grandstanding.*

Precedent refers to something that occurs that then has follow-up repercussions since people may view it as a justification for future actions of that sort or as an example of how something ought to be done.

Preliminary negotiations are the negotiations over logistics that often precede the negotiations regarding substantive issues.

The *primary issues* are those that are at the heart of the negotiation, while the *ancillary issues* are the auxiliary, supplementary, or subsidiary points designed to make the agreement more wide-ranging, durable, or optimal.

A *principal* is the party in a negotiation who has directed and authorized the agent to act subject to his or her ultimate control and direction. See also *agent.*

Principled negotiation. See also *interest-based negotiation.*

A *prisoner's dilemma* refers to a set of circumstances in which each side is tempted to pocket immediate benefits by breaking the trust of an associate or counterpart, even when more gains might flow over the long term from more cooperative behavior.

Problem-solving negotiation. See *principled negotiation.*

Professional negotiating characteristics refers to the ways in which the members of a particular profession—diplomats, lawyers, sports agents, etc.— may negotiate.

Parties to a negotiation advance a *proposal,* as opposed to suggesting a mere idea or a possible option, when they have formulated and then communicated to their counterparts a possible resolution that they stand behind in the sense that they would agree to it.

A *prototype* refers to typical qualities of a particular set of people, but focuses on "cultural averages on dimensions of behavior or values,"[5] and is often phrased in neutral rather than negative terms.

Puffing involves talking up or exaggerating points that benefit your side of the negotiation.

In a *quid pro quo exchange* a party gives one thing in order to get another.

A *ratifier* is the person who has the conclusive decision to approve or disapprove a negotiated deal.

Reactive devaluation refers to the psychological tendency of a negotiator to underrate or disparage an idea, concession, or proposal simply because another negotiator, about whom the negotiator harbors suspicions, jealousy, or dislike, first suggested it.

In a *recess* negotiators ask for a short period to take a break and clear their heads, usually by leaving the negotiating room. See also *caucus.*

A *remedy* spells out what a party will receive in redress if the agreement is not carried out.

A *renegotiation* is an effort by parties that have signed one agreement to determine if a new agreement is in order, usually with somewhat different terms. See also *post-deal renegotiation.*

A *representation* "is a detailed statement of fact about the subject of a transaction"; for instance, it "might describe the merchandise to be shipped."[6]

A *reservation price or value,* or *minimum,* refers to the minimum for which a negotiator would come to an agreement, a point just past the one at which a negotiator does not care whether he or she accepts an agreement or opts to pursue his or her BATNA. A reservation price is not necessarily identical to a BATNA, since a negotiator weighing whether to accept a proposal might take into account such factors as transaction costs, risk acceptance or aversion, and relative convenience or inconvenience of taking the deal as offered. See also *settlement price.*

Ripeness refers to whether the moment has arrived when parties are really ready to try to seriously negotiate the issues before them toward some resolution.

Role reversal refers to a practice in which, to gain a better understanding of the other side's perspective, one takes on the role of the other party, explains the perspectives of the other side, and in that way explores in detail their view of the situation.

Room to negotiate is a phrase used in positional bargaining that signifies staking out a position in such a way that one can move away from it and toward the other side's position, while still ending up with an attractive deal.

Salami tactics refers to an effort by one side to gain just a bit more in the way of concessions, blaming the state of affairs on the other side's ratifiers, who must be kept content.

With *separate interests* one negotiator has an underlying concern or motivation that does not impinge in any way on a different underlying concern or motivation of another.

A *settlement price* designates the point at which a party will decide to settle a legal claim, rather than pursue the case in court. See also *reservation price or value.*

With *shared interests* both sides in a negotiation have common underlying motivations or concerns.

A *side payment* is an offer by one side to do something for the other in exchange for getting something else in return. See also *trade-off.*

Side-by-side negotiating refers to times when negotiators are at work, together, on joint problem-solving, rather than distributional bargaining. See also *face-to-face negotiating.*

A *soft bargainer* emphasizes, above all else, creating and maintaining good terms with the other side, using a friendly, trusting, and cooperative approach to coax the kind of positive relationship with a counterpart that will help him or her to reach a beneficial negotiated resolution.

Splitting the difference involves resorting to an equal division to bridge a gap between two numbers.

A *spoiler* is a party that feels as though its interests will be better served by preventing a negotiated resolution than by joining one and, hence, tries to derail, subvert, or sabotage the negotiation.

Stakeholders are those who have an interest in the matter being negotiated since an agreement may help or harm them.

A *starting point* would be an initial statement about an issue being negotiated.

A *stereotype* is a simplified, standardized, and often pejorative generalization about how another is likely to behave based on how the speaker believes the people of a group that person belongs to often think or act. See also *prototype.*

To *stonewall* is to adamantly refuse to budge from a position or completely evade discussions about something in hopes that the party who wants to talk about it will give up or drop the subject.

A *strategy* is a detailed plan made up of various tactics and aimed at achieving particular objectives.

Strength of feeling refers to how intensely a party wants something. When parties have different strengths of feeling about a matter, they may trade across issues so that each gets more of what is most important to it.

A *subjective interest* is an interest that a party prefers, whether or not it actually serves his or her well-being.

A *suboptimal agreement* is one that could be better from the perspective of at least one party without being made worse from the perspective of another.

To *sugarcoat* matters in a negotiation involves a negotiator spinning points toward what the other side might like to hear at that moment, while obscuring what he or she truly thinks. The motivation is usually to nurture a positive working relationship, but sending inaccurate signals can create false expectations, bring on frustration, and elongate a negotiation.

Sweetener. See also *perquisite.*

Tabling an issue means to set it aside with the intent of coming back to it at a more propitious or advantageous moment.

A *take-it-or-leave-it offer* is a final proposal whose terms suggest that no more compromises are possible and a rejection will cause the negotiation to end.

The *time value of money* is the financial principle that gaining a sum of money today is more valuable than gaining the equivalent amount at some future date. The reason is that the sum at issue could be invested, with the recipient gaining the fruits of that investment with time.

To *trade across issues* involves one side sacrificing certain things that, relatively speaking, it does not feel so strongly about in order to gain other things that are really important to it.

In a *trade-off* one negotiator agrees to do *x*, in exchange for another agreeing to do *y*. See also *side payment.*

A *triangular negotiation* is one that occurs among three negotiators.

An *ultimatum* is a final proposal whose terms suggest that no more compromises are possible and a rejection will cause the negotiation to end.

Venting refers to a negotiator discharging tension by publicly expressing some point, often emotionally or passionately.

A *vested interest* is a personal stake or special attachment of some kind to an existing arrangement or institution.

Walking away from a negotiation means that one party ends the negotiation without an agreement.

Walk-away alternative. See also *Best Alternative to a Negotiated Agreement.*

A *warranty* is an assurance that some fact is correct or true. If the warranted fact proves not to be so, then the party who made the promise covers any losses that might accrue as a consequence.

A *working relationship* stands for relations between negotiators that are intellectual and professional in nature and are aimed at resolving problems, rather than relations aimed at developing or enhancing a friendship or other personal relationship.

A *yesable proposition* comes in the closing stage of a negotiation when a negotiator creates a proposal that is sufficiently comprehensive that the other side could simply say "yes," and the deal would be done.

Zero-sum game is a phrase borrowed from game theory to identify an all-or-nothing situation in which whatever one gains the other loses. Zero-sum thinking is also sometimes referred to as fixed-pie thinking, the reference is to a pie that cannot be enlarged to give each party a larger slice than it might otherwise have. See also *positive-sum game.*

Zone of Possible Agreement (ZOPA) signifies that field of potential resolutions to which the parties each would agree.

ZOPA. See also *Zone of Possible Agreement.*

Notes

1. Philip H. Gulliver, Disputes and Negotiations 71, n. 2 (1979).

2. Roger Fisher, William Ury and Bruce Patton, Getting to Yes 100 (2d ed. 1991).

3. Ronald Gilson, *Value Creation by Business Lawyers: Legal Skills and Asset Pricing*, 94 Yale L. J. 239, 261 (1984).

4. Ronald J. Fisher, *Prenegotiation Problem-solving Discussions, in* Getting to the Table 206, 227 (Janice Gross Stein ed., 1989).

5. Katie Shonk, *How to Resolve Cultural Conflict: Overcoming Cultural Barriers at the Negotiation Table,* Program on Negotiation, Harvard Law School, March 7, 2016, http://www.pon.harvard.edu/daily/conflict-resolution/a-cross-cultural-negotiation-example-how-to-overcome-cultural-barriers.

6. Robert H. Mnookin, Scott R. Peppet, & Andrew S. Tulumello, Beyond Winning: Negotiating to Create Value in Deals and Disputes 133 (2000).

Bibliography

AMERICAN BAR ASSOCIATION, MODEL RULES OF PROFESSIONAL CONDUCT, at http://www.americanbar.org/groups/professional_rules_of_professional_ conduct.html.

KEVIN AVRUCH, CULTURE AND CONFLICT RESOLUTION (1998).

ROGER E. AXTELL, GESTURES: THE DO'S AND TABOOS OF BODY LANGUAGE AROUND THE WORLD, rev. ed. (1998).

JAMES BAKER, WITH THOMAS M. DEFRANK, THE POLITICS OF DIPLOMACY: REVOLUTION, WAR AND PEACE 1989–1992 (1995).

Bruce Barry, Ingrid Smithey Fulmer, and Gerben A. Van Kleef, *I Laughed, I Cried, I Settled: The Role of Emotion in Negotiation*, in MICHELE J. GELFAND AND JEANNE M. BRETT, EDS., THE HANDBOOK OF NEGOTIATION AND CULTURE (2004).

James Bennett and Thomas Saaty, *Terrorism: Patterns for Negotiation*, in ROBERT KUPPERMAN AND DARRELL TRENT, EDS., TERRORISM: THREAT, REALITY, AND RESPONSE (1979).

Anita D. Bhappu, and Zoe I. Barsness, *Risks of E-Mail*, in ANDREA KUPFER SCHNEIDER AND CHRISTOPHER HONEYMAN, EDS., THE NEGOTIATOR'S FIELDBOOK: THE DESKBOOK FOR THE EXPERIENCED NEGOTIATOR (2006).

Lisa Blomgren Bingham, *Avoiding Negotiating*, in ANDREA KUPFER SCHNEIDER AND CHRISTOPHER HONEYMAN, EDS., THE NEGOTIATOR'S FIELDBOOK: THE DESKBOOK FOR THE EXPERIENCED NEGOTIATOR (2006).

Body Language in Negotiation Process and Beyond, Program on Negotiation, Harvard Law School, April 14, 2016, http://www.pon.harvard.edu/daily/ negotiation-skills-daily/negotiation-techniques-and-body-language-body-language-negotiation-examples-in-real-life.

SISSELA BOK, LYING: MORAL CHOICE IN PUBLIC AND PRIVATE LIFE (1978).

Jeanne M. Brett and Tetsushi Okumura, *Inter- and Intra-cultural Negotiation: U.S. and Japanese Negotiators*, 41 ACAD. OF MGMT. J. 495 (1998).

SUZANNE BROCK, IDIOM'S DELIGHT: FASCINATING PHRASES AND LINGUISTIC ECCENTRICITIES (1988).

Jennifer Gerarda Brown, *Creativity and Problem-Solving*, in ANDREA KUPFER SCHNEIDER AND CHRISTOPHER HONEYMAN, EDS., THE NEGOTIATOR'S FIELDBOOK: THE DESK REFERENCE FOR THE EXPERIENCED NEGOTIATOR (2006).

Jennifer Gerarda Brown and Jennifer K. Robbennolt, *Apology in Negotiation*, in ANDREA KUPFER SCHNEIDER AND CHRISTOPHER HONEYMAN, EDS., THE NEGOTIATOR'S FIELDBOOK: THE DESK REFERENCE FOR THE EXPERIENCED NEGOTIATOR (2006).

Julie M. Bunck, FIDEL CASTRO AND THE QUEST FOR A REVOLUTIONARY CULTURE IN CUBA (1994).

FRANÇOIS DE CALLIÈRES, ON THE MANNER OF NEGOTIATING WITH PRINCES, trans. A.F. Whyte (1919).

JIM CAMP, START WITH NO (2002).

Marcia Caton Campbell and Jayne Seminare Docherty, *What's in a Frame?*, in ANDREA KUPFER SCHNEIDER AND CHRISTOPHER HONEYMAN, EDS., THE NEGOTIATOR'S FIELDBOOK: THE DESK REFERENCE FOR THE EXPERIENCED NEGOTIATOR (2006).

DALE CARNEGIE, HOW TO WIN FRIENDS AND INFLUENCE PEOPLE, 2d ed. (1981).

WINSTON CHURCHILL, THE SECOND WORLD WAR: THE GATHERING STORM, vol. 1 (1948).

Inis L. Claude, Jr., *Valedictory, Mea Culpa, and Testament*, in KENNETH W. THOMPSON, ED., COMMUNITY, DIVERSITY, AND A NEW WORLD ORDER: ESSAYS IN HONOR OF INIS L. CLAUDE, JR. (1994).

_____, STATES AND THE GLOBAL SYSTEM: POLITICS, LAW, AND ORGANIZATION (1988).

PATRICK J. CLEARY, THE NEGOTIATION HANDBOOK (2001).

Jonathan R. Cohen, *Advising Clients to Apologize*, 72 S. CAL. L. REV. 1009 (1999).

_____, *The Ethics of Respect in Negotiation*, in CARRIE MENKEL-MEADOW AND MICHAEL WHEELER, EDS., WHAT'S FAIR: ETHICS FOR NEGOTIATORS (2004).

_____, *Legislating Apology: Pros and Cons*, 70 *Univ. of Cincinnati L. Rev.* 819 (2002).

RAYMOND COHEN, NEGOTIATING ACROSS CULTURES: COMMUNICATION OBSTACLES IN INTERNATIONAL DIPLOMACY (1991).

_____, *An Advocate's View*, in GUY OLIVIER FAURE AND JEFFREY Z. RUBIN, EDS., CULTURE AND NEGOTIATION (1993).

THOMAS R. COLOSI, ON AND OFF THE RECORD: COLOSI ON NEGOTIATION (1993).

Peter C. Cramton and J. Gregory Dees, *Promoting Honesty in Negotiation: An Exercise in Practical Ethics*, in CARRIE MENKEL-MEADOW AND MICHAEL WHEELER, EDS., WHAT'S FAIR: ETHICS FOR NEGOTIATORS (2004).

Joel Cutcher-Gershenfeld and Michael Watkins, *Toward a Theory of Representation in Negotiation*, in Lawrence Susskind and Robert H. Mnookin, eds., Negotiating on Behalf of Others: Advice to Lawyers, Business Executives, Sports Agents, Diplomats, Politicians, and Everybody Else (1999).

The Deal is Done—Now What?, Program on Negotiation, Harvard Law School, Oct. 8, 2013, http://www.pon.harvard.edu/daily/conflict-resolution/the-deal-is-done-now-what/.

Karl W. Deutsch, Analysis of International Relations (1978).

Christophe Dupont and Guy-Olivier Faure, *The Negotiation Process* in Victor A. Kremenyuk, ed., International Negotiation: Analysis, Approaches, Issues (1991).

Karen Elwood, *Facing Up to Face*, Daily Yomiuri [Japan], 30 November 2006, 17.

An Example of the Anchoring Effect—What to Share in Negotiation, Program on Negotiation, Harvard Law School, March 22, 2016, http://www.pon.harvard.edu/daily/negotiation-skills-daily/what-to-share-in-negotiation/?m.

Guy Olivier Faure, *International Negotiation: The Cultural Dimension*, in Victor A. Kremenyuk, ed., International Negotiation: Analysis, Approaches, Issues (2002).

Guy Olivier Faure and Gunnar Sjöstedt, *Culture and Negotiation: An Introduction*, in Guy Olivier Faure and Jeffrey Z. Rubin, eds., Culture and Negotiation: The Resolution of Water Disputes (1993).

Amy C. Finnegan & Susan G. Hackley, *Negotiation and Nonviolent Action: Interacting in the World of Conflict*, Program on Negotiation, Harvard Law School, Jan. 25, 2008, http://www.pon.harvard.edu/events/negotiation-and-nonviolent-action-interacting-in-a-world-of-conflict/.

Glen Fisher, International Negotiation: A Cross-Cultural Perspective (1980).

_____. Mindsets: The role of culture and perception in international relations, rev. ed. (1998).

Roger Fisher, *A Code of Negotiation Practices for Lawyers*, 1 Negotiation J. 105 (1985).

_____, *Beyond YES*, 1 Negotiation J. 67 (1985).

_____, *Fractionating Conflict*, in Roger Fisher, ed., International Conflict and Behavioral Science (1964).

_____, International Conflict for Beginners (1969).

_____, *An Interview with Roger Fisher and William Ury*, interview by Bert Spector, 18 Acad. of Mgmt. Executive 101 (2004).

_____, *Negotiating Inside Out: What Are the Best Ways to Relate Internal Negotiations with External Ones?*, 5 NEGOTIATION J. 33 (1989).

_____, *Negotiating Power: Getting and Using Influence*, 27 AM. BEHAVIORAL SCIENTIST 149 (1983).

_____, GETTING TOGETHER: BUILDING RELATIONSHIPS AS WE NEGOTIATE (1988).

Roger Fisher and Wayne H. Davis, *Authority of an Agent: When Is Less Better?*, in LAWRENCE SUSSKIND AND ROBERT H. MNOOKIN, EDS., NEGOTIATING ON BEHALF OF OTHERS: ADVICE TO LAWYERS, BUSINESS EXECUTIVES, SPORTS AGENTS, DIPLOMATS, POLITICIANS, AND EVERYBODY ELSE (1999).

ROGER FISHER AND DANNY ERTEL, GETTING READY TO NEGOTIATE: THE GETTING TO YES WORKBOOK (1995).

ROGER FISHER, ELIZABETH KOPPELMAN, AND ANDREA KUPFER SCHNEIDER, BEYOND MACHIAVELLI: TOOLS FOR COPING WITH CONFLICT (1994).

ROGER FISHER AND DANIEL SHAPIRO, BEYOND REASON: USING EMOTIONS AS YOU NEGOTIATE (2005).

ROGER FISHER, ALAN SHARP, AND JOHN RICHARDSON, GETTING IT DONE: HOW TO LEAD WHEN YOU'RE NOT IN CHARGE (1998).

ROGER FISHER, WILLIAM URY, AND BRUCE PATTON, GETTING TO YES: NEGOTIATING AGREEMENT WITHOUT GIVING IN, 2d ed. (1991).

Ronald J. Fisher, *Prenegotiation Problem-solving Discussions: Enhancing the Potential for Successful Negotiations*, in JANICE GROSS STEIN, ED., GETTING TO THE TABLE: THE PROCESSES OF INTERNATIONAL PRENEGOTIATION (1989).

MARY PARKER FOLLETT, DYNAMIC ADMINISTRATION: THE COLLECTED PAPERS OF MARY PARKER FOLLETT, HENRY C. METCALF AND L. URWICK, EDS. (1942).

Michael R. Fowler, *The Relevance of Principled Negotiation to Hostage Crises*, 12 HARV. NEGOTIATION L. R. 251 (2007).

_____, *Transplanting Active Learning Abroad: Creating a Stimulating Negotiation Pedagogy Across Cultural Divides*, 6 INT'L STUDIES PERSPECTIVES 155 (2005).

JAMES C. FREUND, SMART NEGOTIATING: HOW TO MAKE GOOD DEALS IN THE REAL WORLD (1992).

Raymond A. Friedman and Steven C. Currall, *Conflict Escalation: Dispute Exacerbating Elements of E-mail Communication*, 56 HUM. REL. 1325 (2003).

William R. Fry, Ira J. Firestone, and David L. Williams, *Negotiation Process and Outcome of Stranger Dyads and Dating Couples: Do Lovers Lose?*, 4 BASIC & APPLIED SOCIAL PSYCHOLOGY 1 (1983).

Howard Gadlin, Andrea Kupfer Schneider, and Christopher Honeyman, *The Road to Hell is Paved with Metaphors*, in ANDREA KUPFER SCHNEIDER AND CHRISTOPHER HONEYMAN, EDS., THE NEGOTIATOR'S FIELDBOOK: THE DESK REFERENCE FOR THE EXPERIENCED NEGOTIATOR (2006).

John Kenneth Galbraith, Economics, Peace, and Laughter (1971).
Johannes Galli, Intercultural Communication and Body Language (2000).
Kevin Gibson, *Ethics and Morality in Negotiation,* in Andrea Kupfer Schneider and Christopher Honeyman, eds., The Negotiator's Fieldbook: The Desk Reference for the Experienced Negotiator (2006).
Bee Chen Goh, *Typical Errors of Westerners,* in Andrea Kupfer Schneider and Christopher Honeyman, eds., The Negotiator's Fieldbook: The Desk Reference for the Experienced Negotiator (2006).
Alvin L. Goldman, Settling for More: Mastering Negotiation Strategies and Techniques (1991).
Gary Goodpaster, *A Primer on Competitive Bargaining,* 1996 J. of Dispute Resolution 325 (1996).
Philip H. Gulliver, Disputes and Negotiations: A Cross-cultural Perspective (1979).
Chris Guthrie and David F. Sally, *Miswanting,* in Andrea Kupfer Schneider and Christopher Honeyman, eds., The Negotiator's Fieldbook: The Desk Reference for the Experienced Negotiator (2006).
William M. Habeeb, Power and Tactics in International Negotiation: How Weak Nations Bargain with Strong Nations (1988).
W. Averell Harriman, *Observations on Negotiating: Informal Views of W. Averell Harriman,* interview by Edward W. Barrett, 9 J. of Int'l Aff. 1 (1975).
Geoffrey C. Hazard, Jr., *The Lawyer's Obligation to Be Trustworthy When Dealing with Opposing Parties,* in Carrie Menkel-Meadow and Michael Wheeler, eds., What's Fair: Ethics for Negotiators (2004).
William Hernández Requejo and John L. Graham, Global Negotiation: The New Rules (2008).
Art Hinshaw, Peter Reilly, and Andrea Kupfer Schneider, *Attorneys and Negotiation Ethics: A Material Misunderstanding?,* 29 Negotiation J. 265 (2013).
Christopher Honeyman, *Using Ambiguity,* in Andrea Kupfer Schneider and Christopher Honeyman, eds., The Negotiator's Fieldbook: The Desk Reference for the Experienced Negotiator (2006).
Townsend Hoopes, *A Critique of the Prime Mover John Foster Dulles,* in Thomas G. Paterson, ed., Major Problems in American Foreign Policy, 2d ed. (1984).
P. Terrence Hopmann and Daniel Druckman, *Arms Control and Arms Reduction: View I,* in Victor A. Kremenyuk, ed., International Negotiation: Analysis, Approaches, Issues (2002).
How to DEAL with Threats: 4 Negotiation Tips for Managing Conflict at the Bargaining Table, Program on Negotiation, Harvard Law School, March 10,

2016, http://www.pon.harvard.edu/daily/conflict-resolution/how-to-deal-with-threats/?mqsc=E38.

How to Negotiate with Friends and Family: When you add loved ones to your business negotiation, dealmaking can get complicated, Program on Negotiation, Harvard Law School, Feb. 2, 2016, http://www.pon.harvard.edu/daily/dispute-resolution/how-to-negotiate-with-friends-and-family/.

Daniel Kahneman and Amos Tversky, *Conflict Resolution: A Cognitive Perspective*, in KENNETH J. ARROW, ROBERT H. MNOOKIN, LEE ROSS, AMOS TVERSKY, AND ROBERT B. WILSON, EDS., BARRIERS TO CONFLICT RESOLUTION (1995).

Sanda Kaufman, *The Interpreter as Intervenor*, in ANDREA KUPFER SCHNEIDER AND CHRISTOPHER HONEYMAN, EDS., THE NEGOTIATOR'S FIELDBOOK: THE DESK REFERENCE FOR THE EXPERIENCED NEGOTIATOR (2004).

Karen N. King, *But I'm Not a Funny Person . . . : The Use of Humor in Dispute Resolution*, 4 NEGOTIATION J. 119 (1988).

HENRY KISSINGER, THE NECESSITY FOR CHOICE (1961).

KENJI KITAO AND S. KATHLEEN KITAO, INTERCULTURAL COMMUNICATION: BETWEEN JAPAN AND UNITED STATES (1989).

Clyde Kluckhorn, *The Study of Culture*, in DANIEL LERNER AND HAROLD D. LASSWELL, EDS., THE POLICY SCIENCES (1951).

Tommy Koh, *Great Negotiator Award Speech*, HARV. PROGRAM ON NEGOTIATION, HARV. UNIVERSITY, April 10, 2014.

Deborah M. Kolb, *Strategic Moves and Turns*, in THE NEGOTIATOR'S FIELDBOOK: THE DESK REFERENCE FOR THE EXPERIENCED NEGOTIATOR (2006).

DEBORAH M. KOLB AND JUDITH WILLIAMS, THE SHADOW NEGOTIATION: HOW WOMEN CAN MASTER THE HIDDEN AGENDAS THAT DETERMINE BARGAINING SUCCESS (2000).

Russell Korobkin, Michael L. Moffitt, and Nancy A. Welsh, *The Law of Bargaining*, in ANDREA KUPFER SCHNEIDER AND CHRISTOPHER HONEYMAN, EDS., THE NEGOTIATOR'S FIELDBOOK: THE DESK REFERENCE FOR THE EXPERIENCED NEGOTIATOR (2006).

JOHN KOTTER, POWER AND INFLUENCE (1985).

VICTOR A. KREMENYUK, INTERNATIONAL NEGOTIATION: ANALYSIS, APPROACHES, ISSUES (1991).

_____, INTERNATIONAL NEGOTIATION: ANALYSIS, APPROACHES, ISSUES, 2d ed. (2002).

_____, *A Pluralistic Viewpoint*, in GUY OLIVIER FAURE AND JEFFREY Z. RUBIN, EDS., CULTURE AND NEGOTIATION (1993).

WALTER LAFEBER, THE AMERICAN AGE: UNITED STATES FOREIGN POLICY AT HOME AND ABROAD SINCE 1750 (1989).

Donald C. Langevoort, *Half-Truths: Protecting Mistaken Influences by Investors and Others, in* CARRIE MENKEL-MEADOW AND MICHAEL WHEELER, EDS., WHAT'S FAIR: ETHICS FOR NEGOTIATORS (2004).
David A. Lax and James K. Sebenius, *Deal crafting: The Substance of Three-Dimensional Negotiations,* 18 NEGOTIATION J. 5 (2002).
_____, THE MANAGER AS NEGOTIATOR: BARGAINING FOR COOPERATION AND COMPETITIVE GAIN (1986).
_____, *Three Ethical Issues in Negotiation,* 2 NEGOTIATION J. 363 (1986).
Roy J. Lewicki, *Trust and Distrust, in* ANDREA KUPFER SCHNEIDER AND CHRISTOPHER HONEYMAN, EDS., THE NEGOTIATOR'S FIELDBOOK: THE DESK REFERENCE FOR THE EXPERIENCED NEGOTIATOR (2006).
ROY J. LEWICKI, ALEXANDER HIAM, AND KAREN WISE OLANDER, THINK BEFORE YOU SPEAK: THE COMPLETE GUIDE TO STRATEGIC NEGOTIATION (1996).
Roy J. Lewicki and Robert J. Robinson, *Ethical and Unethical Bargaining Tactics: An Empirical Study, in* CARRIE MENKEL-MEADOW AND MICHAEL WHEELER, EDS., WHAT'S FAIR: ETHICS FOR NEGOTIATORS (2004).
ROY J. LEWICKI, DAVID M. SAUNDERS, AND JOHN W. MINTON, ESSENTIALS OF NEGOTIATION, 2d ed. (2001).
SOL M. LINOWITZ WITH MARTIN MAYER, THE BETRAYED PROFESSION: LAWYERING AT THE END OF THE TWENTIETH CENTURY (1994).
Karl Llewellyn, *The Crafts of Law Re-Valued,* 28 ABA J. 801 (1942).
Keith Lutz, *Negotiation Examples in Business: Putting Your Negotiated Agreement into Action,* Program on Negotiation, Harvard Law School, Jan. 19, 2016, http://www.pon.harvard.edu/daily/negotiation-skills-daily/we-have-a-deal-now-what-do-we-do-three-negotiation-tips-on-implementing-your-negotiated-agreement.
NICCOLÒ MACHIAVELLI, THE PRINCE (1950).
Doug MacKay, *Outlining Negotiation Types and Processes, in* PRACTISING LAW INSTITUTE, BASIC NEGOTIATION SKILLS (2013).
Robert B. McKersie, *Agency in the Context of Labor Negotiations, in* ROBERT H. MNOOKIN AND LAWRENCE E. SUSSKIND, EDS., NEGOTIATING ON BEHALF OF OTHERS: ADVICE TO LAWYERS, BUSINESS EXECUTIVES, SPORTS AGENTS, DIPLOMATS, POLITICIANS, AND EVERYBODY ELSE (1999).
Brian S. Mandell, *Unnecessary Toughness: Hard Bargaining as an Extreme Sport,* in ROBERT H. MNOOKIN AND LAWRENCE E. SUSSKIND, EDS., NEGOTIATING ON BEHALF OF OTHERS: ADVICE TO LAWYERS, BUSINESS EXECUTIVES, SPORTS AGENTS, DIPLOMATS, POLITICIANS, AND EVERYBODY ELSE (1999).
ROBERT M. MARCH, THE JAPANESE NEGOTIATOR: SUBTLETY AND STRATEGY BEYOND WESTERN LOGIC (1990).

Willem F. G. Mastenbroek, *Development of Negotiating Skills*, in VICTOR A. KREMENYUK, ED., INTERNATIONAL NEGOTIATION: ANALYSIS, APPROACHES, ISSUES (1991).

Michael Meltsner and Philip Schrag, *Negotiating Tactics for Legal Services Lawyers*, in CARRIE MENKEL-MEADOW AND MICHAEL WHEELERS, EDS., WHAT'S FAIR: ETHICS FOR NEGOTIATORS (2004).

Carrie Menkel-Meadow, *The Ethics of Compromise*, in ANDREA KUPFER SCHNEIDER AND CHRISTOPHER HONEYMAN, EDS., THE NEGOTIATOR'S FIELDBOOK: THE DESK REFERENCE FOR THE EXPERIENCED NEGOTIATOR (2006).

_____, *Introduction: What's Fair in Negotiation? What is Ethics in Negotiation?*, in CARRIE MENKEL-MEADOW AND MICHAEL WHEELER, EDS., WHAT'S FAIR: ETHICS FOR NEGOTIATORS (2004).

Carrie J. Menkel-Meadow and Michael Wheeler, *Bargaining Tactics*, in CARRIE J. MENKEL-MEADOW AND MICHAEL WHEELER, EDS., WHAT'S FAIR: ETHICS FOR NEGOTIATORS (2004).

Robert H. Mnookin, *Why Negotiations Fail: An Exploration of Barriers to Conflict Resolution*, working paper no. 30, Stanford Center on Conflict and Negotiation (1995).

ROBERT H. MNOOKIN, SCOTT R. PEPPET AND ANDREW S. TULUMELLO, BEYOND WINNING: NEGOTIATING TO CREATE VALUE IN DEALS AND DISPUTES (2000).

_____, *The Tension Between Empathy and Assertiveness*, 12 NEGOTIATION J. 217 (1996).

Robert H. Mnookin and Lee Ross, *Introduction*, in KENNETH J. ARROW, ROBERT H. MNOOKIN, LEE ROSS, AMOS TVERSKY, AND ROBERT B. WILSON, EDS., BARRIERS TO CONFLICT RESOLUTION (1995).

Robert H. Mnookin and Lawrence Susskind, *Introduction*, in ROBERT H. MNOOKIN AND LAWRENCE E. SUSSKIND, EDS., NEGOTIATING ON BEHALF OF OTHERS: ADVICE TO LAWYERS, BUSINESS EXECUTIVES, SPORTS AGENTS, DIPLOMATS, POLITICIANS, AND EVERYBODY ELSE (1999).

Michael L. Moffit, *Contingent Agreements*, in ANDREA KUPFER SCHNEIDER AND CHRISTOPHER HONEYMAN, EDS., THE NEGOTIATOR'S FIELDBOOK: THE DESK REFERENCE FOR THE EXPERIENCED NEGOTIATOR (2006).

TERRI MORRISON, WAYNE A. CONAWAY, AND GEORGE A. BORDEN, KISS, BOW, OR SHAKE HANDS: HOW TO DO BUSINESS IN SIXTY COUNTRIES (1994).

WILLIAM F. MORRISON, THE PRENEGOTIATION PLANNING BOOK (1985).

Helmut Morsbach, *Aspects of Nonverbal Communication in Japan*, in INTERCULTURAL COMMUNICATION: A READER (Larry A. Samovar & Richard E. Porter eds., 1988).

Ramon Mullerat, *Foreword to the Third Edition*, in JAMES R. SILKENAT, JEFFREY M. ARESTI, AND JACQUELINE Klosek, EDS., THE ABA GUIDE TO INTERNATIONAL BUSINESS NEGOTIATIONS, 3d ed. (2009).

GERARD I. NIERENBERG AND HENRY H. CALERO, HOW TO READ A PERSON LIKE A BOOK (1971).

ALEXANDER G. NIKOLAEV, INTERNATIONAL NEGOTIATIONS: THEORY, PRACTICE, AND THE CONNECTION WITH DOMESTIC POLITICS (2007).

Eleanor Holmes Norton, *Bargaining and the Ethics of Process*, in CARRIE MENKEL-MEADOW AND MICHAEL WHEELER, EDS., WHAT'S FAIR: ETHICS FOR NEGOTIATORS (2004).

Dayle E. Powell, *Legal Perspective*, in VICTOR A. KREMENYUK, ED., INTERNATIONAL NEGOTIATION: ANALYSIS, APPROACHES, ISSUES (1991).

Chris Provis, *Interests vs. Positions: A Critique of the Distinction*, 12 NEGOTIATION J. 305 (1996).

Dean G. Pruitt, *Strategy in Negotiation*, in VICTOR A. KREMENYUK, ED., INTERNATIONAL NEGOTIATION: ANALYSIS, APPROACHES, ISSUES (1991).

DEAN G. PRUITT AND SUNG HEE KIM, SOCIAL CONFLICT: ESCALATION, STALEMATE, AND SETTLEMENT, 3d. ed. (2004).

Howard Raiffa, *Analytical Barriers*, in KENNETH J. ARROW, ROBERT H. MNOOKIN, LEE ROSS, AMOS TVERSKY, AND ROBERT B. WILSON, EDS., BARRIERS TO CONFLICT RESOLUTION (1995).

_____, THE ART AND SCIENCE OF NEGOTIATION (1982).

HOWARD RAIFFA, WITH JOHN RICHARDSON AND DAVID METCALFE, NEGOTIATION ANALYSIS: THE SCIENCE AND ART OF COLLABORATIVE DECISION MAKING (2002).

KATHLEEN KELLEY REARDON, THE SKILLED NEGOTIATOR: MASTERING THE LANGUAGE OF ENGAGEMENT (2004).

Rob Ricigliano, *A Three-Dimensional Analysis of Negotiation*, in ANDREA KUPFER SCHNEIDER AND CHRISTOPHER HONEYMAN, EDS., THE NEGOTIATOR'S FIELDBOOK: THE DESK REFERENCE FOR THE EXPERIENCED NEGOTIATOR (2006).

Robert Robinson, *Defusing the Exploding Offer: The Farpoint Gambit*, 11 NEGOTIATION J. 277 (1995).

Lee Ross, *Reactive Devaluation in Negotiation and Conflict Resolution*, in KENNETH J. ARROW, ROBERT H. MNOOKIN, LEE ROSS, AMOS TVERSKY, AND ROBERT B. WILSON, EDS., BARRIERS TO CONFLICT RESOLUTION (1995).

Nancy L. Roth, Todd Hunt, Maria Stavropoulos, and Karen Babik, *Can't We All Just Get Along: Cultural Variables in Codes of Ethics*, 22 PUB. REL. REV. 151 (1996).

Alvin B. Rubin, *A Causerie on Lawyers' Ethics in Negotiation,* in Carrie Menkel-Meadow and Michael Wheeler, eds., What's Fair: Ethics for Negotiators (2004).

Jeffrey Z. Rubin, *The Actors in Negotiation,* in Victor A. Kremenyuk, ed., International Negotiation: Analysis, Approaches, Issues (1991).

_____, *Psychological Approach,* in Victor A. Kremenyuk, ed., International Negotiation: Analysis, Approaches, Issues (1991).

_____, *Some Wise and Mistaken Assumptions About Negotiation,* 45 J. of Soc. Issues 195 (1989).

Jeffrey Z. Rubin and Bert R. Brown, The Social Psychology of Bargaining and Negotiation (1975).

Jeffrey Z. Rubin and Frank E. A. Sander, *Culture, Negotiation, and the Eye of the Beholder,* 7 Negotiation J. 249 (1991).

Jeswald W. Salacuse, *The Art of Advising Negotiators,* 11 Negotiation J. 391 (1995).

_____, *Law and Power in Agency Relationships,* in Robert H. Mnookin and Lawrence E. Susskind, eds., Negotiating on Behalf of Others: Advice to Lawyers, Business Executives, Sports Agents, Diplomats, Politicians, and Everybody Else (1999).

_____, *Making Deals in Strange Places: A Beginner's Guide to International Business Negotiations,* 4 Negotiation J. 5 (1988).

_____, *The Power of Standards,* Tufts Mag. (Winter 2007), http://emerald.tufts.edu/alumni/magazine/winter2007/columns/life.html.

_____, *Renegotiating Existing Agreements: How to Deal with "Life Struggling Against Form,"* 17 Negotiation J. 311 (2001).

_____, *Your Draft or Mine?,* 5 Negotiation J. 337 (1989).

David M. Sally and Kathleen M. O'Connor, *Negotiating in Teams,* in Andrea Kupfer Schneider and Christopher Honeyman, eds., The Negotiator's Fieldbook: The Desk Reference for the Experienced Negotiator (2006).

Thomas C. Schelling, *An Essay on Bargaining,* 46 Am. Econ. Rev. 281 (1956).

Andrea Kupfer Schneider, *Aspirations,* in Andrea Kupfer Schneider and Christopher Honeyman, eds., The Negotiator's Fieldbook: The Desk Reference for the Experienced Negotiator (2006).

_____, *Effective Responses to Offensive Comments,* 10 Negotiation J. 107 (1994).

Schumpeter: Executive Pay, The Economist, April 23, 2016, p. 60.

Maurice E. Schweitzer and Rachel Croson, *Curtailing Deception,* in Carrie Menkel-Meadow and Michael Wheeler, eds., What's Fair: Ethics for Negotiators (2004).

James K. Sebenius, *Dealing with Blocking Coalitions and Related Barriers to Agreement: Lessons from Negotiations on the Oceans, the Ozone, and the Climate*, in KENNETH J. ARROW, ROBERT H. MNOOKIN, LEE ROSS, AMOS TVERSKY, AND ROBERT B. WILSON, EDS., BARRIERS TO CONFLICT RESOLUTION (1995).

_____, *What Roger Fisher Got Profoundly Right: Five Enduring Lessons for Negotiators*, 29 NEGOTIATION J. 159 (2013).

_____, *Negotiation Analysis*, in VICTOR A. KREMENYUK, ED., INTERNATIONAL NEGOTIATION: ANALYSIS, APPROACHES, ISSUES (1991).

James K. Sebenius and Rebecca Hulse, Harvard Business School Case: Charlene Barshevsky (B) (2001).

Jeffrey R. Seul, *Religion and Conflict*, in ANDREA KUPFER SCHNEIDER AND CHRISTOPHER HONEYMAN, EDS., THE NEGOTIATOR'S FIELDBOOK: THE DESK REFERENCE FOR THE EXPERIENCED NEGOTIATOR (2006).

Daniel L. Shapiro, *Untapped Power: Emotions in Negotiation*, in ANDREA KUPFER SCHNEIDER AND CHRISTOPHER HONEYMAN, EDS., THE NEGOTIATOR'S FIELDBOOK: THE DESK REFERENCE FOR THE EXPERIENCED NEGOTIATOR (2006).

G. RICHARD SHELL, BARGAINING FOR ADVANTAGE: NEGOTIATION STRATEGIES FOR REASONABLE PEOPLE (1999).

Katie Shonk, *How to Resolve Cultural Conflict: Overcoming Cultural Barriers at the Negotiation Table*, Program on Negotiation, Harvard Law School, March 7, 2016, http://www.pon.harvard.edu/daily/conflict-resolution/a-cross-cultural-negotiation-example-how-to-overcome-cultural-barriers.

_____, *When to Make the First Offer in Negotiation*, Program on Negotiation, Harvard Law School, Oct. 8, 2015, http://www.pon.harvard.edu/daily/negotiation-skills-daily/when-to-make-the-first-offer-in-negotiation/.

JAMES R. SILKENAT, JEFFREY M. ARESTY, AND JACQUELINE KLOSEK, THE ABA GUIDE TO INTERNATIONAL BUSINESS NEGOTIATIONS: A COMPARISON OF CROSS-CULTURAL ISSUES AND SUCCESSFUL APPROACHES, 3d ed. (2009).

GUNNAR SJÖSTEDT, ED., PROFESSIONAL CULTURES IN INTERNATIONAL NEGOTIATION: BRIDGE OR RIFT? (2003).

ADAM SMITH, AN INQUIRY INTO THE NATURE AND CAUSE OF THE WEALTH OF NATIONS (1993).

BRIGID STARKEY, MARK A. BOYER, AND JONATHAN WILKENFELD, INTERNATIONAL NEGOTIATION IN A COMPLEX WORLD, 4th ed. (2015).

Janice Gross Stein, *Getting to the Table: The Triggers, Stages, Functions, and Consequences of Prenegotiation*, in JANICE GROSS STEIN, ED., GETTING TO THE TABLE: THE PROCESSES OF INTERNATIONAL PRENEGOTIATION (1989).

_____, Preface and Acknowledgments, in JANICE GROSS STEIN, ED., GETTING TO THE TABLE: THE PROCESSES OF INTERNATIONAL PRENEGOTIATION (1989).

Edward C. Stewart and Milton J. Bennett, American Cultural Patterns (1991).

Alan Strudler, *On the Ethics of Deception in Negotiation*, in Carrie Menkel-Meadow and Michael Wheeler, eds., What's Fair: Ethics for Negotiators (2004).

Lloyd Paul Stryker, The Art of Advocacy: A Plea for the Renaissance of the Trial Lawyer (1954).

Lawrence Susskind, *The Shifting Role of Agents in Interest-Based Negotiation*, in Robert H. Mnookin and Lawrence E. Susskind, eds., Negotiating on Behalf of Others: Advice to Lawyers, Business Executives, Sports Agents, Diplomats, Politicians, and Everybody Else (1999).

Lawrence Susskind and Robert H. Mnookin, *Major Themes and Prescriptive Implications*, in Robert H. Mnookin and Lawrence E. Susskind, eds., Negotiating on Behalf of Others: Advice to Lawyers, Business Executives, Sports Agents, Diplomats, Politicians, and Everybody Else (1999).

Deborah Tannen, Conversational Style: Analyzing Talk Among Friends (2005).

_____, *The Relativity of Linguistic Strategies: Rethinking Power and Solidarity in Gender and Dominance*, in Deborah Tannen, ed., Gender and Conversational Interaction (1993).

Kenneth W. Thompson, *New Reflections on Ethics and Foreign Policy*, 4 J. of Pol. 991 (1978).

Catherine H. Tinsley, *Culture and Conflict: Enlarging our Dispute Resolution Framework*, in Michele J. Gelfand and Jeanne M. Brett, eds., The Handbook of Negotiation and Culture (2004).

Catherine H. Tinsley, Jack J. Cambria, and Andrea Kupfer Schneider, *Reputations in Negotiation*, in Andrea Kupfer Schneider and Christopher Honeyman, eds., The Negotiator's Fieldbook: The Desk Reference for the Experienced Negotiator (2006).

Harry C. Triandis, Culture and Social Behavior (1994).

William L. Ury, Getting Past No: Negotiating Your Way from Confrontation to Cooperation (1993).

_____, *An Interview with Roger Fisher and William Ury*, interview by Bert Spector, 18 Acad. of Mgmt. Executive 101 (2004).

_____, The Power of a Postive No: How to Say No and Still Get to Yes (2007).

_____, The Third Side: Why We Fight and How We Can Stop (2000).

John H. Wade, *Crossing the Last Gap*, in ANDREA KUPFER SCHNEIDER AND CHRISTOPHER HONEYMAN, EDS., THE NEGOTIATOR'S FIELDBOOK: THE DESK REFERENCE FOR THE EXPERIENCED NEGOTIATOR (2006).

John H. Wade and Christopher Honeyman, *A Lasting Agreement*, in ANDREA KUPFER SCHNEIDER AND CHRISTOPHER HONEYMAN, EDS., THE NEGOTIATOR'S FIELDBOOK: THE DESK REFERENCE FOR THE EXPERIENCED NEGOTIATOR (2006).

J. E. Walsh, *Foreword*, in RAM PRAKASH ANAND, ED., CULTURAL FACTORS IN INTERNATIONAL RELATIONS (1981).

Gerald Wetlaufer, *The Limits of Integrative Bargaining*, in CARRIE MENKEL-MEADOW AND MICHAEL WHEELER, EDS., WHAT'S FAIR: ETHICS FOR NEGOTIATORS (2004).

Michael Wheeler, *First, Let's Kill All the Agents!*, in ROBERT H. MNOOKIN AND LAWRENCE E. SUSSKIND, EDS., NEGOTIATING ON BEHALF OF OTHERS: ADVICE TO LAWYERS, BUSINESS EXECUTIVES, SPORTS AGENTS, DIPLOMATS, POLITICIANS, AND EVERYBODY ELSE (1999).

James J. White, *The Pros and Cons of* "Getting to Yes," 34 J. OF LEGAL EDUC. 115 (1984).

————, *Machiavelli and the Bar: Ethical Limitations on Lying in Negotiation*, in CARRIE MENKEL-MEADOW AND MICHAEL WHEELER, EDS., WHAT'S FAIR: ETHICS FOR NEGOTIATORS (2004).

GERALD R. WILLIAMS, LEGAL NEGOTIATION AND SETTLEMENT (1983).

RAYMOND WILLIAMS, KEYWORDS: A VOCABULARY OF CULTURE AND SOCIETY (1983).

Anshar M. Wimmer, *The Jolly Mediator: Some Serious Thoughts About Humor*, 10 NEGOTIATION J. 193 (1994).

Gilbert R. Winham, *The Prenegotiation Phase of the Uruguay Round*, in JANICE GROSS STEIN, ED., GETTING TO THE TABLE: THE PROCESSES OF INTERNATIONAL PRENEGOTIATION (1989).

BOB WOOLF, FRIENDLY PERSUASION: HOW TO NEGOTIATE AND WIN (1990).

W. Howard Wriggins, *Up for Auction: Malta Bargains with Great Britain, 1971*, in I. WILLIAM ZARTMAN, ED., THE 50% SOLUTION: HOW TO BARGAIN SUCCESSFULLY WITH HIJACKERS, STRIKERS, BOSSES, OIL MAGNATES, ARABS, RUSSIANS, AND OTHER WORTHY OPPONENTS IN THIS MODERN WORLD (1987).

HARU YAMADA, AMERICAN AND JAPANESE BUSINESS DISCOURSE: A COMPARISON OF INTERACTIONAL STYLES (1992).

I. WILLIAM ZARTMAN, ED., THE 50% SOLUTION: HOW TO BARGAIN SUCCESSFULLY WITH HIJACKERS, STRIKERS, BOSSES, OIL MAGNATES, ARABS, RUSSIANS, AND OTHER WORTHY OPPONENTS IN THIS MODERN WORLD (1987).

I. William Zartman, *Introduction,* in I. William Zartman, ed., The 50% Solution: How to Bargain Successfully with Hijackers, Strikers, Bosses, Oil Magnates, Arabs, Russians, and Other Worthy Opponents in This Modern World (1976).

_____, *Prenegotiation: Phases and Functions,* in Janice Gross Stein, ed., Getting to the Table: The Processes of International Prenegotiation (1989).

_____, *Processes and Stages,* in Andrea Kupfer Schneider and Christopher Honeyman, eds., The Negotiator's Fieldbook: The Desk Reference for the Experienced Negotiator (2006).

_____, *Regional Conflict Resolution,* in Victor A. Kremenyuk, ed., International Negotiation: Analysis, Approaches, Issues (1991).

_____, *A Skeptic's View,* in Guy Olivier Faure and Jeffrey Z. Rubin, eds., Culture and Negotiation (1993).

_____, *Timing and Ripeness,* in Andrea Kupfer Schneider and Christopher Honeyman, eds., The Negotiator's Fieldbook: The Desk Reference for the Experienced Negotiator (2006).

I. William Zartman and Maureen R. Berman, The Practical Negotiator (1982).

Index

Note: Page numbers are placed in *italic* type to differentiate material found in the Appendix, the Boxes, the Checkpoints, the Glossary, the Master Checklist, and the Roadmaps from that found in the body of each Chapter.

nuclear, 52
dispute-settlement institution(s),
291
adjudication or litigation, 6–7,
19, 110, 134, 137, 141,
145, 173, 224, 269, 294,
318, 324
arbitration, 6, 79, 133, *165*,
183, 189, 254–56, 258,
395, 398
binational claims commis-
sion(s), 291
mediation, 133, *165*, 221,
255–56, 260, *398, 402*
distributional bargaining. *See* ,
bargaining, bargain, or bar-
gainer(s)
distrust. *See* trust, lack of, distrust, or mistrust
division of benefits or commodities. *See* bargaining, bargain,
or bargainer(s), distributional bargaining
Docherty, Jayne Seminare, 63 n. 5
Dulles, John Foster, 202
Dupont, Christophe, 300 n. 69
economics, or economies, 44,
268, 274
economies of scale or scope,
183–84, *399*
money, time value of, 182–83
either/or choices. *See* alterna-
tive(s), mutually exclusive
Elwood, Karen, 300 n. 81
emotion(s), anger, or offensive
comment(s), 22, *29*, 195,
202–7, 225, *228*, 289, *378*.
See also interpersonal relations, and conflict(s), diffi-

culty(ies), or problem(s);
tactic(s), emotional
emotion(s),
anger, causes of, 204–7, *378*
and circumstances, 202
and cultural differences, 202
empathy versus sympathy,
113, 213, 292, *379*
frustration, 275
indignation, 203
pent-up, 216
positive and negative or
problematic, 202–4
recognition, 162
revenge, 326
varieties of, *195*, 202
venting of, 72, *195*, 215–16,
224, *229*, *379*, *407*
intimidation, 45, 198, 206–8,
210
offensive or inflammatory
comment(s) or state-
ment(s), *195*–96, 225, *378*
accidental or purposeful,
195, 204–7, *228–29*, *378*
responses to, 220–22, *380*
Ertel, Danny, 28 n. 17, 64 n. 50,
190 n. 1, 191 n. 43, 192 n.
53, 262 n. 27
ethics, or ethical principle(s), 43,
85, 118, 138, 164, 213,
303–332, *384*. *See also* nego-
tiator(s), qualities or characteristics of, reputation of;
perception(s), partisan; tac-
tic(s), pressure, threat(s) or
warning(s)
bait-and-switch technique,
308, *396*

unilateral action(s) or
resolution(s), or self-help, 6,
133, 151
United Nations. *See* international
organization(s)
United States of America, 26, 52,
280, 283, 285–86, 289, 295,
308
Ury, William L., xxvi, 23, 28 n. 9,
28 n. 21, 28 n. 26, 44, 50, 63
n. 13, 63 n. 14, 63 n. 25, 64
n. 34, 64 n. 43, 64 n. 45, 93,
97 n. 58, 97 n. 61, 127 n. 7,
127 n. 10, 128 n. 24, 156 n.
2, 156 n. 3, 156 n. 16, 157 n.
45, 157 n. 47, 174, 179, 190
n. 8, 190 n. 9, 191 n. 19, 191
n. 27, 191 n. 29, 191 n. 31,
191 n. 33, 191 n. 36, 191 n.
41, 191 n. 42, 191 n. 46, 220,
225 n. 3, 225 n. 4, 225 n. 5,
226 n. 8, 226 n. 16, 226 n.
23, 226 n. 33, 227 n. 45, 227
n. 54, 227 n. 57, 262 n. 31,
263 n. 39, 300 n. 79, 300 n.
80, 300 n. 88, *408 n. 2*
value, 181, 200, 336. *See also* bargaining, bargain, or bar-
gainer(s), distributional
bargaining
claiming or creating, 20–21,
31, 54, 69, 82, 162–63,
177, *193*, *377*, *397–98*
depreciation of, 166
leaving, 339
taking away, 208, *229*, *379*
values, 102, 111–12, *129*, 135,
145, 168, 206, 232, 270, 277,
301, *370*. *See also* culture(s);

market rate(s) or values(s);
principles
Van Kleef, Gerben A., 226 n. 21
venting. *See* emotion(s), anger,
or offensive comment(s)
Vietnam, 285, 289
*Vulcan Metals Co. v. Simmons
Manufacturing Co.*, 331 n. 55
Wade, John H., 95 n. 2, 190, 192
n. 70, 192 n. 71, 262 n. 4,
262 n. 10, 262 n. 22, 262 n.
25, 263 n. 40
walking away. *See* negotiation(s),
process(es) of, terminating, or
walking away from; BATNA
Walsh, J.E., 299 n. 35
warning(s). See tactic(s), pressure
Watkins, Michael, 64 n. 41, 127
n. 4, 331 n. 70
Welsh, Nancy A., 329 n. 5, 331 n.
54, 331 n. 56, 331 n. 71
West Germany, 111
Wetlaufer, Gerald, 192 n. 59
Wheeler, Michael, 156 n. 6, 156
n. 12, 167, 190 n. 11, 300 n.
67, 330 n. 22
White, James J., 226 n. 35, 329 n.
1, 330 n. 31, 330 n. 34
Wilkenfeld, Jonathan, 28 n. 6
Williams, David L., 95 n. 6
Williams, Gerald R., 329 n. 6
Williams, Judith, 28 n. 32, 63 n.
8, 84, 95 n. 7, 96 n. 48, 96 n.
52, 96 n. 54, 96 n. 56, 111,
127 n. 13, 128 n. 15, 128 n.
28, 154–55, 157 n. 48, 192 n.
67, 221–22, 225 n. 1, 226 n.
20, 226 n. 26, 227 n. 59
Williams, Raymond, 298 n. 3